Introduction to Human Services

Through the Eyes of Practice Settings

Michelle E. Martin

Judson College

PEARSON

Boston ▪ New York ▪ San Francisco
Mexico City ▪ Montreal ▪ Toronto ▪ London ▪ Madrid ▪ Munich ▪ Paris
Hong Kong ▪ Singapore ▪ Tokyo ▪ Cape Town ▪ Sydney

Senior Series Editor: *Patricia Quinlin*
Editorial Assistant: *Nakeesha Warner*
Marketing Manager: *Laura Lee Manley*
Production Editor: *Roberta Sherman*
Editorial-Production and Electronic Composition
  Services: *Pine Tree Composition, Inc.*
Composition Buyer: *Linda Cox*
Manufacturing Buyer: *JoAnne Sweeney*
Interior Design: *Denise Hoffman*
Photo Researcher: *Annie Pickert*
Cover Administrator: *Linda Knowles*

For related titles and support materials, visit our online catalog at www.ablongman.com.

Between the time website information is gathered and then published, it is not unusual for some sites to have closed. Also, the transcription of URLs can result in typographical errors. The publisher would appreciate notification where these errors occur so that they may be corrected in subsequent editions.

Library of Congress Cataloging-in Publication Data

Martin, Michelle E.
  Introduction to human services : through the eyes of practice settings / Michelle E. Martin.
    p. cm.
  ISBN 0-205-43961-6
  1. Human services—Vocational guidance—United States. I. Title.
  HV10.5.M37 2007
  362.023'73--dc22

                                                          2006017167

Printed in the United States of America

10 9 8 7 6 5 4 3 2 1   RRD-VA   10 09 08 07 06

Photo Credits: p. 2, Robert Warren/Taxi/Getty Images; p. 20, Courtesy of L.W. Hine/Library of Congress; p. 29, Courtesy of L.W. Hine/Library of Congress; p. 36, Bill Aron/PhotoEdit; p. 60, Courtesy of Library of Congress; p. 66, Childrens Aid Society; p. 67, Kansas State Historical Society; p. 93 (top), Courtesy of U.S. Army Military History Institute; p. 93 (bottom), Courtesy of Frances Benjamin Johnston/Library of Congress; p. 108, Charles Gupton/Corbis; p. 122, SuperStock; p. 132, Ariel Skelley/Corbis; p. 144, Joseph Sohm/ChromoSohm/Bettmann/Corbis; p. 162, Jana Leon/Stone/Getty Images; p. 165, Peter Turnley/Corbis; p. 196, Bushnell/Soifer/Stone/Getty Images; p. 202, Courtesy of Samuel H. Gottscho/Library of Congress; p. 203, Courtesy of Dorothea Lange/ Library of Congress; p. 224, Geri Engberg/The Image Works; p. 236, Joanne O'Brien/Alamy Images; p. 254, Andy Sotiriou/Photodisc/Getty Images; p. 288, Mary Kate Denny/PhotoEdit; p. 298, Will Hart/PhotoEdit; p. 316, Robin Nelson/PhotoEdit; p. 323, AP Wide World Photos; p. 350, A. Lichtenstein/Corbis/Sygma; p. 364, AP Wide World Photos; p. 380, Michael S. Yamashita/Corbis; p. 395, Ulrike Kotermann/EPA/Corbis; p. 408, Images.com

To my son, Xander Martin

contents

p a r t two

Clinical Issues and the Role of the Human Service Professional   35

c h a p t e r 3

Skills and Intervention Strategies for Generalist Practice   36

c h a p t e r **4**

Child and Family Services   60

Adolescent Services   108

chapter **6**

Aging and Services for the Elderly   132

chapter **7**

Mental Health and Mental Illness   162

chapter 8

Homelessness   196

chapter 9

Health Care and Hospice   224

chapter 10

Substance Abuse and Treatment   254

chapter **11**

Human Services in the Schools   288

chapter **12**

Faith-Based Agencies   316

chapter 13

Violence, Victim Advocacy, and Corrections   350

part **three**

Macro Practice, Ethics, and Future Considerations   379

chapter **14**

Macro Practice and International Social Justice   380

chapter 15

Professional Ethics and Values in Human Services   408

The human services profession is a broad one encompassing many different professions under its "umbrella," including human service generalists, social workers, counselors, marriage and family therapists, psychologists, and psychiatrists. What is it that these professionals have in common? They all work in the human services field focusing on helping people meet their basic needs that they cannot meet themselves, often because of various social conditions such as social and economic injustice, oppression, institutionalized racism, and intergenerational poverty. Thus someone may be a licensed practitioner but if she works for a battered women's shelter, she is a human service professional. Someone may be a licensed social worker and if he works with victims of violent crime, he is a human service professional. And finally, if someone is a licensed psychologist for an adolescent residential facility, she is a human service professional.

I have worked in the human services field for over 20 years, and during that time I have worked in a number of different practice settings including adolescent residential treatment, adoptions, victim services, outpatient mental health, schools, hospice, and private practice. When I began teaching human services courses I designed my class curriculum based on my experience in practice where the role of the human service professional is determined by the setting where the practitioner is working. However, I was surprised to learn that I had difficulty finding a textbook written in this manner.

The book I have written is in many respects similar to other excellent textbooks on the market, but it is different in that the various roles and functions of the human service professional are explored through the lens (or "eyes") of the most common practice settings where human service professionals work. For instance, a human service professional who works with children in a school setting will have a significantly different role and function than a human service professional who works with children in a hospice setting, or children who were victims of a crime.

Another reason to approach an introductory human services textbook from a perspective of the practice setting is because the human services profession grew out of a concern for social problems that created barriers to many people getting their needs met, rather than individual psychopathology like so many other professions within the mental health field. The social problem (poverty, domestic violence, child abuse) or target population (crime victims, prisoners, immigrants) is the starting point, then, in understanding and exploring what it means to work as a human service professional.

Acknowledgments

There are many people I would like to thank who were very instrumental in providing support and assistance in the writing of this book. First and foremost I must thank my son Xander for his enduring love and patience. He was only eight years old when I began this project—he will be 11 at the time of publishing. It is my hope that as a single parent I have modeled for my son an example of hard work, perseverance, and a commitment to endure to create a better life. It is also my hope that he will eventually forgive me for bringing my laptop to every one of his baseball games.

To my friends the Santizos and Tonnes, I express my appreciation for all the support—for bringing dinners, doing laundry, and taking care of my son during the writing of this book; and for reading chapters and giving me honest feedback. I also want to thank my entire family, including my brother Glenn and his wife, and my good friend, Julie, my sister Sheri and her family, and my mother, Joline. A special thanks to my aunt Jeri Serpico and my cousin Patricia Serfas, both of whom provided me with never-ending support and encouragement, sometimes very late into the night.

I would like to thank Beth White at Lowell Elementary School for her assistance in providing information on school social workers, and Imran Baig and Ahmed Qadeer for their very valuable information on the Muslim faith and social services in the Islamic community.

Thanks to my colleagues, clients, and students, who provided honest feedback and support, I thank you for all of your help. Finally, I would like to thank my editors, Pat Quinlin, Sara Holliday, and David Estrin—Pat for giving me a chance and for believing in me, Sara for providing me with assistance the moment I asked, and David for your tireless and constant encouragement and a wonderful sense of humor that kept me laughing, even at 3:00 AM.

I would also like to thank everyone at the National Labor Committee, especially Amanda Teckman, who graciously provided me with information on human rights violations of workers in the global economy, including young girls who work in deplorable conditions in sweatshops around the globe. Thank you for your quick responses to my many email questions and for providing me with the dramatic testimonies of exploited workers.

I want to thank the numerous reviewers of this first edition for their kind remarks and helpful suggestions: Stephany Briggs, Central Piedmont Community College; Diane L. Brown, Binghamton University, SUNY; Susan Claxton, Floyd College; Joyce Clohessy, Westmoreland County Community College; Jean Granger, California State University, Long Beach; Jill Keogh, University of Missouri, Columbia; Susan Kinsella, Brewton-Parker College; Pamela M. Kiser, Elon University; Peter Konwerski, George Washington University; John D. Matthews, Eastern Washington University; Wm. Lynn McKinney, University of Rhode Island; Jackie McReynolds, Washington State University; and Rhonda A. Richardson, Kent State University.

Finally, to all single mothers everywhere. Dare to dream—the hard work will pay off in the end (and yes, sleep is very much overrated).

Michelle Martin, MSW, LSW, is program director of the human services program at Judson College in Elgin, Illinois. She has taught across a variety of disciplines, including social work, psychology, and human services. She has been a practicing social worker for over 20 years, having worked in a variety of practice settings throughout her career. She earned her Bachelors degree at San Diego State University and her MSW at the University of Illinois at Chicago, Jane Addams College of Social Work. She is currently enrolled in a doctoral program at the University of Bristol in England, in the School for Policy Studies. Michelle lives in Wheaton, Illinois with her 11-year old son Xander.

part one

Human Services as a Profession

chapter 1

Introduction to the Human Services Profession

Purpose, Preparation, Practice, and Theoretical Orientations

 The Many Types of Human Service Professionals

Sara works for a hospice agency and spends one hour twice a week with Steven, who has received a diagnosis of terminal cancer of the liver. He has been told he has approximately six months to live. He has been estranged from his adult daughter for four years, and Sara is helping him develop a plan for reunification. Sara helps Steve deal with his terminal diagnosis by helping him talk through his feelings about being sick and dying. Steve talks a lot about his fear of being in pain and his overwhelming feeling of regret for many of the choices he has made in his life. Sara listens and also helps Steve develop a plan for saying all the things he needs to say before he dies. During their last meeting, Sara helped Steve write a list of what he would like to say to his daughter, his ex-wife, and other family members. Sara is also helping Steve make important end-of-life decisions, including planning his own funeral. Sara and Steve will continue to meet until his death, and if possible, she will be with him and his family when he passes away.

■ ■ ■

Gary works for a public middle school and meets with six seventh-graders every Monday to talk about their feelings. Gary helps them learn better ways to explore feelings of anger and frustration. During their meetings, they sometimes do fun things like play basketball, and sometimes they play a board game where they each take turns picking a "self-disclosure" card and answering a personal question. Gary uses the game to enter into discussions about healthy ways of coping with feelings, particularly anger. He also uses the game to get to know the students in a more personal manner, so that they will open up to him more. Gary spends one session per month to discuss their progress in their classes. The goal for the group is to help the students learn how to better control their anger and to develop more prosocial behavior, such as empathy and respect for others.

■ ■ ■

Cynthia works for her county's district attorney's office and has spent every day this past week in criminal court with Kelly, a victim of felony home invasion, aggravated kidnapping, and aggravated battery. Cynthia provides Kelly with both counseling and advocacy. Kelly was in her kitchen one morning feeding her baby when a man charged through her back door. The offender was recently released from state prison, had just robbed a gas station, and was running from the police in a stolen car. He ran from home to home until he found an unlocked door and entered it, surprising Kelly. Kelly immediately started screaming but stopped when he pulled a gun out and held it to her baby's head. During the next hour the defendant threatened both Kelly and her infant son's life and at one point even threatened to sexually assault Kelly. The offender became enraged and hit Kelly several times when she couldn't find any cash in her home. The police arrested him when he was attempting to force Kelly to drive him to a cash machine to obtain money. Cynthia keeps Kelly apprised of all court proceedings and accompanies her to court, if Kelly chooses to assert her right to attend the proceedings. She also accompanies Kelly during all police interviews and helps her prepare for testifying. During these hearings, as well as during numerous telephone conversations, Cynthia helps Kelly understand and deal with her feelings, including her recent experience of imagining the violent incident again and again, her intense fear of being alone, and her guilt that she had not locked her door. Lately, Kelly has experienced an increasing amount of crying and unrelenting sadness, so Cynthia has referred her to a licensed counselor, as well as to a support group for Kelly and her husband.

■ ■ ■

Frank works for county social services, child welfare division, and is working with Lisa, who recently had her three young children removed from her home for physical and emotional neglect. Frank has arranged for Lisa to have parenting classes and individual counseling so that she can learn how to better manage her frustrations with her children. He has also arranged to have her admitted to a drug rehabilitation program to help her with her addictions to alcohol and cocaine. Frank and Lisa meet once a week to talk about her progress. He also monitors her weekly visitation with her children. Frank is required to attend court once per month to inform the judge of Lisa's progress on her parenting plan. Successful completion of this plan will enable Lisa to regain custody of her children. Frank will continue to monitor her progress, as well as the progress of the children, who are in foster care placement.

■ ■ ■

Allison is currently lobbying several legislators in support of a bill that would increase funding for child abuse prevention and treatment. As the social policy advocate for a local grassroots organization, Allison is responsible for writing position statements and contacting local lawmakers to educate them on the importance of legislation aimed at reducing child abuse. Allison also writes grants for federal and private funding of the agencies' various child advocacy programs.

What do all these professionals have in common? They are all human service professionals working within the interdisciplinary field of human or social services, each possessing a broad range of skills and having a wide range of responsibilities related to their roles in helping people overcome a variety of social problems. The National Organization for Human Services (NOHS) defines the human services profession in this way: "The Human Services profession is one which promotes improved service delivery systems by addressing not only the quality of direct services, but by also seeking to improve accessibility, accountability, and coordination among professionals and agencies in service delivery." Human services is a broad term covering a number of careers, but all have one thing in common—the helping of people meet their basic physical and emotional needs that for whatever reason cannot be met without outside assistance. The human services field can include a variety of job titles, including social worker, caseworker, program coordinator, outreach counselor, crisis counselor, and victim advocate, to name just a few.

Why Is Human Services Needed?

All human beings have basic needs, such as the need for food, health, shelter, and safety. People also have social needs, such as the need for interpersonal connectedness and love, and psychological needs, such as the need to deal with the trauma of past abuse, or even the psychological ramifications of disasters such as a hurricane or house fire. People who are fortunate have several ways to get their needs met. Social and psychological needs can be met by family, friends, and places of worship. Needs related to food, shelter, and other more complicated needs such as health care can be met through employment, education, and family.

But some people in society are unable to meet even their most basic needs either because they do not have a supportive family, or they have no family at all. They may have no friends or have friends who are either unsupportive or are unable to provide help. They may have no social support network of any kind, having no faith community, no supportive neighbors, perhaps due to apartment living or the fact that many communities within the United States tend to be far more transient now than in prior generations. They may lack the skills or education to gain sufficient employment, thus they may not have health insurance or earn a good wage. Perhaps they've spent the majority of their lives dealing with an abusive and chaotic childhood and are now suffering from the manifestation of that experience in the form of psychological problems and substance abuse and thus cannot focus on meeting their basic needs until they are able to deal with the trauma they've been forced to endure.

Some people, particularly those who have good support systems, may falsely believe that anyone who cannot meet their most basic needs of shelter, food, health care, and emotional needs must be doing something wrong. This belief is incorrect because numerous barriers exist that keep people from meeting their own needs, some of which might be related to their own behavior, but more often, the reasons why someone cannot meet their needs are quite complicated and often lie in dynamics beyond their control. Thus although someone who is fortunate enough to have a great family, wonderfully supportive friends, the benefit of a good education, and no significant history of abuse or loss may be self-sufficient in meeting their own needs, this does not mean that others who find themselves in situations where they cannot meet their own needs are doing anything wrong. Human service agencies come into the picture then when people find themselves confronting barriers to getting their needs met and they do not have anyone or anything in their lives that can assist them in overcoming these obstacles. Some of these barriers include

- ▶ Lack of family (or supportive family)
- ▶ Lack of friends
- ▶ Mental illness
- ▶ Poverty
- ▶ Racism
- ▶ Oppression
- ▶ Trauma
- ▶ Natural disasters
- ▶ Lack of education
- ▶ Lack of employment skills
- ▶ Unemployment
- ▶ Physical and/or intellectual disability

A tremendous amount of controversy surrounds how best to help people meet their basic needs, as well as various philosophies regarding what types of services truly help and which services may seem to help initially but actually create more problems down the road. For instance, most people have heard the very old saying, "Give a man a fish and you feed him for a day, but teach him to fish and you feed him for a lifetime." One goal of the human services profession is to teach people to fish. This means that human service professionals are committed to helping people develop the necessary skills to become self-sufficient and function at their optimal level within society. Thus although an agency might pay a family's rent for a few months when they are in a crisis, human service professionals will then work with the family to remove any barriers that keep them from meeting their housing needs in the future, such as substance abuse disorders, a lack of education or vocational skills, health problems, or mental illness.

In addition to a commitment to working with high-need, **marginalized populations** and providing them with necessary resources to get their basic needs met, human service professionals are also committed to working on a *macro* or societal level to remove barriers that affect large groups of people. By advocating for changes in laws and various policies, human service professionals have helped make great strides in reducing prejudice and discrimination related to one's race, gender, sexual orientation, socioeconomic level (SES), or any one of a number of characterizations that might marginalize someone within society.

Human service professionals continue to work on all social fronts so that every member of society has an equivalent opportunity for happiness and self-sufficiency. The chief goal of the human service professional is to support individuals as well as communities function at their maximum potential, overcoming personal and social barriers as effectively as possible in the major domains of living.

Human Service Professionals: Educational Requirements and Professional Standards

Each year numerous caring individuals will decide to enter the field of human services and will embark on the confusing journey of trying to determine what level of education is required for specific employment positions, when and where a license is required, and even what degree is required. There is no easy answer to these questions, because the human services profession is a broad one encompassing many different professions such as social workers, human service generalists, psychologists, and psychiatrists, all of whom are considered human service professionals because they work in a human services agency working in some manner with marginalized, displaced, or other individuals who are in some way experiencing problems related to various social or systemic issues.

Another area of confusion relates to the educational and licensing requirements needed to work in the human services field. Determining what educational degree to earn, the level of education required, and what professional license is needed depends in large part on variables such as state and federal legislation (for highly regulated fields), industry standards, and even agency preference or need. To make matters even more confusing, these variables can vary dramatically from state to state, thus a job that someone can do in one state with an Associate of Arts degree (AA) requires a Masters in Social Work (MSW) and a clinical license in another state. In addition, many individuals may work in the same capacity at a human service agency with two different degrees.

According to the National Organization for Human Services (NOHS) Web site a "human service professional" is

> A generic term for people who hold professional and paraprofessional jobs in such diverse settings as group homes and halfway houses; correctional, mental retardation, and community mental health centers; family, child, and youth service agencies, and programs concerned with alcoholism, drug abuse, family violence, and aging. Depending on the employment setting and the kinds of clients served there, job titles and duties vary a great deal. (www.nohse.org)

Within this text, I use the term *human service agency,* but this term is often used synonymously in other literature with *social service agency.* I also use the title *human service professional* to refer to all professionals working within the human services field, but if I use the term *social worker,* then I am referring to the legal definition and professional distinction of a licensed social worker, indicating either an earned Bachelor's of Social Worker (BSW) or a Master's of Social Worker (MSW) level of education.

One reason for the dramatic variation in educational and licensing requirements is that the human services field is a growing profession, and with the evolution of professionalization, comes increasing practice regulations. Yet, issues such as the stance of legislators in a particular state regarding practice requirements, the need for human service professionals within the community, or even whether the community is rural or urban, can affect the level of educational and licensing requirements for a particular position within the human services profession (Gumpert & Saltman, 1998).

Some human service agencies are subject to federal or state governmental licensing requirements, such as the health-care industry (hospitals, hospices, home health care), government child welfare agencies, and public school districts, and as such may be required to hire a professional with an advanced degree in any of the social science fields, or a particular professional education requirement might be specified. For instance, in many states school social workers must have an M.S.W. and credentials in social work.

There is still considerable variability among state licensing bodies in terms of how professional terms such as *counselor, social worker,* and *related field* are defined. For instance, most states require hospice social workers to be licensed social workers (thus requiring either a BSW or an MSW, but in Illinois, for instance, the *Hospice Pro-*

gram Licensing Act provides that a hospice agency can also employ bereavement counselors who have a bachelor's degree in counseling, psychology, or social work with one year of counseling experience. Some states require child welfare workers to be licensed social workers or have an MSW, whereas other states require child welfare workers to have a master's degree in any related field (i.e., psychology, human services, social work, sociology). But in states where there is a significant need for bilingual social workers, such as California, educational requirements are lessened if the individual is bilingual and has commensurate counseling experience.

Keeping such variability within specific human services fields in mind, as well as differences among state licensing requirements, Table 1.1 shows a very general breakdown of degrees in the mental health field, their possible corresponding licenses, as well as what careers these professionals might be able to pursue, depending on individual state licensing requirements.

Human Service Education and Licensure

The Council for Standards on Human Service Education (CSHSE) was established in 1979 for the purposes of guiding and directing human service education and training programs. They have developed national standards for the curriculum and competencies in human service degree programs and serve as the accreditation body for approximately 70 colleges offering degrees in the human services or mental health discipline at the associate's, bachelor's, and master's level.

The CSHSE requires that curriculum in a human services program cover the following standard content areas: *knowledge* of the human services field through the understanding of relevant *theory, skills, and values* of the profession; *history* of the profession; *human systems; scope* of the human service profession; standard clinical *interventions;* common *planning and evaluation* methods; and information on *self-development.* The curriculum must also meet the minimum requirements for *field experience* in a human service agency, as well as appropriate *supervision.*

The term *human services* is new compared to the title *social work* and grew in popularity partly in response to the narrowing of definition and increasing professionalization of the social work profession. For instance, in the early 1900s those who worked in the social work field were called social workers. But as the social work field continued to grow, the professional title of social work eventually became reserved for those professionals who had either an undergraduate or graduate degree in social work from a program accredited by the Counsel on Social Work Education (CWSE), the accrediting body responsible for the accreditation of social work education programs in the United States.

In the 1960s through the 1980s the majority of social workers had a BSW and could become licensed as a social worker. Currently most states require that social workers have at least a BSW, but the professional standard is an MSW. Most states also require that practicing social workers be licensed, certified, or credentialed by

■ Table 1.1   Multiple Discipline Degree Requirements

Degree	Academic Area/Major	State License	Possible Careers
BA/BS	Psychology, Sociology	N/A	Group home counselor, hospice bereavement counselor, residential counselor, job coach
BSW	Social Work (program accredited by CSWE)	Basic Licensing (LSW) depends on state	Same as above, depends on state requirements.
MA/MS 45 to 60 units	Counseling Psychology	LCP (on graduation) LCPC (Licensed Clinical Professional Counselor—~3000 postgrad supervised hours)	Private practice, some governmental and social service agencies
MSW 60 units	Social Work (Program accredited by CSWE)	LSW (on graduation) LCSW (Licensed Clinical Social Worker—~3200 postgrad supervised hours)	Private practice, all governmental and social service agencies (some requiring licensure)
PsyD 120 units	Doctor of Psychology	PSY# (Licensed Clinical Psychologist—~3500 postgrad supervised hours)	Private practice, many governmental and social service agencies, teaching in some higher education institutions.
PhD 120 units	Doctor of Philosophy in Psychology	PSY# (Licensed Clinical Psychologist—~3500 postgrad supervised hours)	Private practice, many governmental and social service agencies, teaching in higher education institutions.

taking a national examination. The Association of Social Work Boards (ASWB) is legally responsible for regulating the social work profession, developing and maintaining licensing exams for all states, as well as serving as a central clearinghouse of information on the legal regulation of social work. The ASWB has identified professional standards for the practice of social work and defines by law the requirements for each level of licensure as a social worker. There are four levels of practice that states can legally regulate, each with increasingly difficult written examinations (see Table 1.1), but as you'll note from Table 1.2, not all states recognize each level of practice.

■ **Table 1.2** ASWB Levels of License Examinations

ASWB License Level	Description
Bachelor's Exam (formerly called Basic Exam):	Baccalaureate degree in social work from a school accredited by the Council on Social Work Education (CSWE)
Master's Examination (formerly called Intermediate Exam):	Master's degree in social work (MSW) from CSWE accredited school, with no postdegree experience
Advanced Generalist Organization (formerly called Advanced):	MSW with two years postmaster's supervised experience
Clinical Exam:	MSW with two years postmaster's direct clinical social work experience

The wide variation between states in licensing and education levels, as well as the variation in titles used to identify social workers and human service professionals, is included in the comparative table entitled *ASWB License Examination Requirements by State* contained in the Appendix. As the table indicates, in some states the level of practice is correlated with the human service professional's level of education, but in other states the level of education does not necessarily correlate with higher level exams (see California), but issues such as insurance reimbursement and entry into management positions serve as worthwhile incentives to take the higher level exams. In many states the human services profession is still largely unregulated, but this is quickly changing for several reasons, including the fact that many third-payer insurance companies will not reimburse for services unless rendered by a licensed social worker (Beaucar, 1999).

Duties and Functions of a Human Service Professional

Despite the broad range of skills and responsibilities involved in human services, most human services positions have certain work-related activities in common. The NOHS describes the general functions and competencies of the human service professional on its Web site located at www.nohse.org.

1. Understanding the nature of human systems: individual, group, organization, community and society, and their major interactions. All workers will have preparation

which helps them to understand human development, group dynamics, organizational structure, how communities are organized, how national policy is set, and how social systems interact in producing human problems.

2. Understanding the conditions which promote or limit optimal functioning and classes of deviations from desired functioning in the major human systems. Workers will have understanding of the major models of causation that are concerned with both the promotion of healthy functioning and with treatment-rehabilitation. This includes medically oriented, socially oriented, psychologically-behavioral oriented, and educationally oriented models.

3. Skill in identifying and selecting interventions which promote growth and goal attainment. The worker will be able to conduct a competent problem analysis and to select those strategies, services or interventions that are appropriate to helping clients attain a desired outcome. Interventions may include assistance, referral, advocacy, or direct counseling.

4. Skill in planning, implementing and evaluating interventions. The worker will be able to design a plan of action for an identified problem and implement the plan in a systematic way. This requires an understanding of problems analysis, decision-analysis, and design of work plans. This generic skill can be used with all social systems and adapted for use with individual clients or organizations. Skill in evaluating the interventions is essential.

5. Consistent behavior in selecting interventions which are congruent with the values of one's self, clients, the employing organization and the human service profession. This cluster requires awareness of one's own value orientation, an understanding of organizational values as expressed in the mandate or goal statement of the organization, human service ethics and an appreciation of the client's values, life style and goals.

6. Process skills which are required to plan and implement services. This cluster is based on the assumption that the worker uses himself as the main tool for responding to service needs. The worker must be skillful in verbal and oral communication, interpersonal relationships and other related personal skills, such as self-discipline and time management. It requires that the worker be interested in and motivated to conduct the role that he has agreed to fulfill and to apply himself to all aspects of the work that the role requires.

National Association of Social Worker (NASW) website includes a list of work activities common to most social workers. These include:

1. Determining people's social, emotional, and economic problems and needs. Providing services to address the needs of people, or referring clients for appropriate professional or community services

2. Developing resources, programs and social policies to address unmet community needs

3. Assessing, diagnosing and/or treating mental health and emotional problems (Clinical Social Work: psychotherapy and counseling)

4. Working to improve social programs and health services through research and by encouraging communities and organizations to be responsive to identified needs

5. Helping people improve personal and/or social functioning by providing or referring for education, training, employment and personal growth services

6. Coordinating and working with governmental, private, civic, religious, business, and/or trade organizations to combat social problems through community awareness and response programs

How Do Human Service Professionals Practice?

Since human beings have walked this planet, people have been trying to figure out what makes them "tick." If one were to construct a historical time line, one would see that each era tends to embrace a particular philosophy regarding the psychological nature of man. Were we created in the image of God? Are we inherently sinful? Are we inherently good? Are personal problems a product of social oppression, or are individuals responsible for their lot in life? Do we have various levels of consciousness, with feelings outside our awareness motivating us to behave in certain ways? What will make us happy? What leads to our emotional demise? These questions are often left to philosophers and more recently to psychologists, but they also relate very much to human services practice because the view of humankind held by human service professionals will undoubtedly influence how they both view and help their clients.

One of the most common questions human service professionals are asked in a job interview is what their theoretical orientation is. I recall having a professor in my Masters of Social Work program who cautioned that when we were asked that question to make sure we never said we were **eclectic** in our theoretical orientation because this was a clear indication to any employer that we had no idea what theoretical orientation we embraced. Essentially what this question is addressing is what theoretical orientation the human service professional operates from. In any mental health clinic, one practitioner might counsel from a psychoanalytic perspective, another from a humanistic perspective, and yet another from a cognitive-behavioral perspective. The theoretical orientation of mental health professionals will serve as a sort of lens through which they view their clients. Depending on the theory, it may include an *underlying assumption* of human behavior (what motivates humans to behave in certain ways), it may include *descriptive aspects* (i.e., common experiences of women in middle adulthood), it may include *prescriptive aspects,* defining adaptive versus maladaptive behaviors (for example, is it normal for children to experience separation anxiety in the toddler years? Is adolescent rebellion a normal developmental stage?).

Most theoretical orientations will also extend into the clinical realm by outlining ways to help people become emotionally healthy based on the presumption of what caused them to become unhealthy in the first place. For instance, if a practitioner embraces a psychoanalytic perspective that holds to the assumption that early childhood experiences influence adult motivation to behave in certain manners, then the counseling will likely focus on the client's childhood. If the practitioner embraces a cognitive-behavioral perspective, the focus of counseling will likely be on how the client frames and interprets the various occurrences in his or her life.

Theoretical Frameworks Used in Human Services

When considering all the various theories of human behavior, it is essential to remember that culture and history affect what is considered healthy thinking and behavior. Common criticism of many major psychological theories is that they are often based on **mores** common in Western cultures and are not necessarily representative of individuals living in lesser industrialized or Eastern societies. In other words, is it appropriate to apply **Freud's psychoanalytic theory of human behavior,** which was developed from his work with society women in the Victorian era, to individuals who live in a Massai tribe in Africa? Or, is it appropriate to use a theory of human behavior developed during peacetime when working those who grow up in a time of war? Any theory of human behavior one considers using in relation to understanding the behavior of clients should include a framework addressing many systems such as culture, historical era, ethnicity, and gender, as well as other systems within which the individual operates. In other words, it is imperative that the human service professional consider environmental elements that may be a part of the client's life as a part of any evaluation and assessment.

Consider this example:

> A middle-aged woman is feeling rather depressed. She spends her first counseling session describing her fears of her children being killed. She explains how she is so afraid of bullets coming through her walls that she doesn't allow her children to watch television in the living room. She never allows her children to play outside and worries incessantly when they are at school. She admits that she has not slept well in weeks, and she has difficulty feeling anything other than sadness and despair.

Would you consider this person paranoid? Correctly diagnosing her does not depend solely on her thinking and behavior, but on the *context* of her thinking and behavior, including the various elements of her environment. If this woman lived in an extremely safe gate-guarded community where no crimes had been reported in 20 years, then a diagnosis of some form of paranoia might be appropriate. But what if she lived in a high-crime neighborhood, where "drive-by" shootings were a daily event? What if you learned that her neighbor's children were recently shot and killed while watching television in the living room? Her thinking and behavior do not seem as bizarre when considered within the context or systems in which she is operating.

Human service professionals are often referred to as **"generalists,"** implying that their knowledge base is broad and varied. This does not mean that they do not have areas of specialization, in fact, in the last 100 years human service professionals have increasingly ventured into practice areas previously reserved for psychologists and clinical counselors (Rullo, 2001). But many believe that to be most effective, human service professionals must be competent working with a broad range of individuals and a broad range of issues, using a wide range of interventions. A conceptual framework that is most commonly associated with human services generalist practice is one that views *clients* in the context of their *environment,* specifically focusing on the transaction or relationship between the two.

Several theories capture this conceptual framework, and virtually all are derived from general systems theory, which is based on the premise that various elements in an environment interact with each other, and this interaction (or transaction) has an impact on all elements involved. This has certain implications for the hard sciences such as ecology and physics, but when applied to the social environment its implications involve the dynamic and interactive relationship between environmental elements such as one's family, friends, neighborhood, culture, and church on the thoughts, attitudes, and behavior of the individual. Thus, if someone asked you who you were, you might describe yourself as a female, who is a college student, married, with two school-aged children, who attends church on a regular basis. You might further describe yourself as having come from an Italian family with nine brothers and sisters, and a Catholic.

On further questioning you might explain that your parents are elderly and you have been attempting to help them find alternate housing that can help them with their extensive medical needs. You might describe the current problems you're having with your teenage daughter, who was recently caught "ditching" school by the truancy officer. Whether you realize it or not, you have shared that you are interacting with the following environments (often called ecosystems): gender, friendships, neighborhood, Italian-American culture, church, marriage covenant, adolescence, the medical community, the school system, and the criminal justice system.

Your interaction with each of these systems is influenced both by your expectations of these systems as well as their expectations of you. For instance, what is expected of you as a college student? What is expected of you as a woman? Of a wife? Of a Catholic? What about the expectations of a married woman who is Catholic? What about the expectations of your family? As you attempt to focus on your academic studies, do these various systems offer stress or support? If you went to counseling, would it be helpful for the practitioner to understand what it means to be one of nine children from a Catholic, Italian-American family?

This focus on **transactional exchange** is what distinguishes the field of human services from other fields such as psychology and psychiatry, although recently systems theory has gained increasing attention in these latter disciplines as well. Several theories have been developed to describe the reciprocal relationship between individuals and their environment. The most common are *Ecological Systems Theory,* *Person-in-Environment* (PIE), and *Eco-Systems Theory.*

Bronfenbrenner's Ecological Systems Theory

Urie Bronfenbrenner (1986) developed the Ecological Systems Theory. In his theory, Bronfenbrenner categorized an individual's environment into four expanding spheres, all with increasing levels of intimate interaction with the individual. The Microsystem includes the individual and his or her family, the Mesosystem (or Mezzosystem) includes entities such as one's neighborhood and school, the Exosystem includes entities such as the state government, and the Macrosystem would include the culture at large. Figure 1.1 illustrates the various systems and describes the nature of interaction with the individual. Again, it is important to remember that the primary principle of Bronfenbrenner's theory is that individuals can best be understood when seen in the context of their relationship with the various systems in their lives. Understanding the nature of these reciprocal relationships will aid in understanding the individual.

PIE—Person in Environment

Another theory that is similar in nature to Ecological Systems Theory is referred to as "Person-In-Environment," or PIE. The premise of this theory is quite similar to Bronfenbrenner's theory, as it encourages seeing individuals within the context of their environment, both on a micro level (i.e., interpersonal relationships, family dynamics), as well as a macro level (i.e., the individual is an African American, who lives in an urban community with significant cultural oppression).

Eco-Systems Theory

Similar to Bronfenbrenner's theory, in Eco-Systems Theory the various environmental systems are represented by overlapping concentric circles indicating the reciprocal exchange between person and environmental system. Although there is no official recognition of varying levels of systems (from micro to macro), the basic concept is very similar, and most who embrace this theory understand that there are varying levels of systems, all interacting and thus impacting the person in various ways. It is up to the human service professional to strive to understand the transactional and reciprocal nature of these various systems (Meyer, 1988).

It is important to note that these theories do not presume that an individual is necessarily aware of the various systems they operate within, even if they are actively in-

■ **Figure 1.1** Example of Common Eco-Systems
with the Person in the Middle

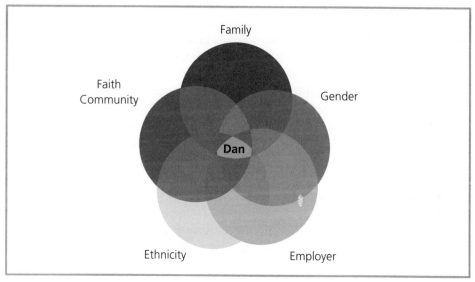

teracting with them. In fact, effective human service professionals will help their clients
increase their personal awareness of the existence of these systems and how they are
currently operating within them (i.e., nature of reciprocity). It is through this awareness that clients increase their level of empowerment within their environment and
consequently in all aspects of their life.

Understanding Human Services through a Look at Practice Settings

It is important to remember that the nature of intervention is completely dependent
on the specific practice setting where the human service professional is providing direct service. Thus, how clients are helped to improve their personal and social functioning will look very differently depending on whether services are provided in a
school setting, hospice, or a county social service agency. Human service professionals practice in numerous settings, some of which include schools, hospitals, advocacy
organizations, faith-based agencies, government agencies, hospices, prisons, and police departments, as well as in private practice.

It would be difficult to present an exhaustive list of categories of practice settings
due to the broad and often very general nature of this career. Practice settings could

be categorized based on the social issue (i.e., domestic violence), target population (i.e., the elderly, the chronically mentally ill), or the area of specialty (i.e., grief and loss, marriage and family). Regardless of how we choose to categorize the various fields within human services, it is imperative that the nature of this career be examined and explored through the lens of practice settings in some respect to truly understand both the career opportunities available to human service professionals, as well as the functions they perform within these various settings.

Some of these practice settings include (but are not necessarily limited to), medical facilities, including hospitals and hospices; schools; geriatric facilities, including assisted-living facilities; victim advocacy agencies, including domestic violence, sexual assault, and victim–witness assistance departments; child and family service agencies, including adoption agencies and child protective service agencies; services for the homeless, including shelters, and the government housing authority; mental health centers; faith-based agencies; and social advocacy organizations such human rights agencies and policy groups.

Regardless of the manner in which practice settings are categorized, there is bound to be some overlap because one area of practice could conceivably be included within another field, and some practice settings could also be considered an area of specialization. For instance, there are Christian hospices (medical social work and faith-based practice), some human service professionals work with both victims of domestic violence (victim advocacy) and batterers (forensic human services), and adoption is sometimes considered a practice setting unto itself and sometimes included under the umbrella of child and family services.

For the purposes of this text, the skills and functions of human service professionals will be explored in the context of particular practice settings, as well as areas of specialization within the human services field—general enough to cover as many functions and settings as possible within the field of human services, but narrow enough to be descriptively meaningful. The role of the human service professional will be examined by exploring the history of the practice setting, the range of clients, the clinical issues most commonly encountered, mode of service delivery, case management, and most common intervention strategies within the following practice settings and areas of specializations: child and family, adolescents, elderly and aging, mental health and illness, homelessness, health care and hospice, substance abuse, schools, faith-based agencies, violence, victim advocacy and corrections, and macro practice.

references

Beaucar, K. O. (2000). Licensing a mixed bag in '99. *NASW News, 45(2)*, 9.

Bureau of Labor Statistics, United States Department of Labor, *Occupational outlook handbook, 2004–05 edition*, Social and Human Service Assistants. Retrieved May 5, 2004, from http://www.bls.gov/oco/ocos059.htm

Gumpert, J. & Saltman, J. E. (1998). Social group work practice in rural areas: The practitioners speak. *Social Work with Groups, 21(3),* 19–34.

Hospice Program Licensing Act, Illinois Public Acts, 210 ILCS 60/1.

Kendall, K. A. (2000). *Social Work Education: Its Origins in Europe, Council on Social Work Education.* Alexandria, VA: Council on Social Work Education

Meyer, C. H. (1988). The eco-systems perspective. In R. A. Dorfman, (Ed), *Paradigms of clinical social work* (pp. 275–294). Philadelphia Brunner/Mazel, Inc.

National Association of Social Workers. (n.d.). *Social work profession: overview.* Retrieved March 12, 2003, from   http://www.socialworkers.org/profession/overview.asp#who

Rullo, D. (2001). The profession of social work. *Research on Social Work Practice, 11(2),* 210–216.

Rittner, B. & Wodarski, J. S. (1999). Differential uses for BSW and MSW educated social workers in child welfare services. *Children & Youth Services Review, 21(3),* 217–238.

suggested   reading

Collison, B. B. & Garfield, N. J. (1996). *Careers in counseling and human services.* Washington, DC: Taylor & Francis.

Doelling, C. N. (2005). *Social work career development: A handbook for job hunting and career planning* (2nd ed.). Washington, DC: NASW Press.

Edwards, R. L. (Ed.). (2002). *Encyclopedia of social work (with 2003 Supp).* Washington, DC: NASW Press.

Gibelman, M. (1995). *What social workers do.* Washington, DC: NASW Press.

Grobman, L. M. (2004). *Days in the lives of social workers: 50 professionals tell "real-life" stories from social work practice* (3rd ed.). Harrisburg, PA: White Hat Communications.

National Organization for Human Services. (n.d.). *The human service worker: A generic job description* (a joint publication of NOHS and CSHSE). Retrieved on October 23, 2005, from http://www.nohse.com/hsworker.html#competencies

Reamer, F. G. (2005). *Pocket guide to essential human services.* Washington, DC: NASW Press.

internet   web   sites   related
to   human   services   careers

Council for Standards for Human Service Education: **http://www.cshse.org/**
Counsel on Social Work Education: **http://www.cswe.org**
Human Services Career Network: **http://www.hscareers.com/**
National Association of Black Social Workers: **http://ssw.unc.edu/professional/NABSW.html**
National Association of Social Workers: **http://www.nasw.org**
National Organization for Human Services: **http://www.nohse.org**
The New Social Worker Online: **http://www.socialworker.com**
Social Worker Salary Information: **http://www.naswdc.org/naswprn/surveyOne/income2.pdf**

chapter 2

History and Evolution of the Human Services Profession

The practice of helping others in need has existed since the beginning of time and can certainly be traced back to Biblical times, but the human services profession in its current context has historic roots dating back to at least the late 1800s. The development of the social welfare system in the United States was very much influenced by England's social welfare system, therefore it is important to understand the evolution of how the poor were treated in England to truly understand how the social welfare policy has developed within this country.

The Feudal System of the Middle Ages

A good place to begin this examination would be in England's Middle Ages (the eleventh century), where a system called feudalism prevailed as England's primary manner of caring for the poor. Under this elitist system, privileged and wealthy landowners would parcel off small sections of their land, which would then be farmed by peasants or "serfs." Many policy experts frame the feudal system as an effective method for controlling poverty, but also as a governmentally imposed form of slavery or servitude because individuals became serfs through both racial and economic discrimination and were commonly born into serfdom with little hope of ever escaping. Serfs were considered the legal property of their landowner, or "lord," thus although the lords were required to provide for their care and support in exchange for farming their land, the lords had complete control over the serfs and could sell them or give them away as they deemed fit (Trattner, 1998).

Despite the seeming harshness of this system, it did provide insurance against many of the social hazards associated with being poor, and it was complemented by the prevailing attitude toward the poor during this time period, which was based on the notion that there was no shame in poverty. In fact, the commonly held societal more during medieval times was that poverty within society was unavoidable, and the poor were a necessary component of society, in that it gave an opportunity for the rich to show their grace and goodwill through the giving of alms to those less fortunate than themselves.

This attitude was certainly influenced by religious teachings, particularly teachings within the Judeo-Christian tradition, and was reinforced by church authorities, who shouldered the primarily responsibility, from a governmental capacity, of administering relief to those unable to support themselves. Thus, caring for the poor was perceived as a noble duty that rested on the shoulders of all those who were able-bodied, and almost in the same way that evil was required to highlight good, poverty was likewise necessary to highlight charity and goodwill as required by God. In Matthew 25, Jesus admonished everyone to feed the hungry, give drink to the thirsty, give shelter to the homeless, give clothes to the shivering, tend to the sick, and visit those in prison (Matthew 25: 32–46, NLT).

A policy of charity is not limited to Judeo-Christian faiths, though; in fact, most religions include charity as requirements of faith, including Islam, which requires that a fifth of all income go to the poor (Qur'an 8:41), that believers practice regular charity (Qur'an 2:43), and care for the orphans (Qur'an 2:177). Buddhism (more correctly referred to as a philosophy than a religion because of the lack of deity) professes the belief that suffering and giving are foundational to understanding the meaning of life.

The Middle Ages was a time when there was no separation of church and state, therefore the church and government were one and the same. Poor relief was handled on a local level, with bishops administering aid through the town parish, supported by mandatory taxes or tithing (which was compulsory). Much of the reason for the relative success of this system was due to the absence of many of the issues with which contemporary society must contend. Populations were not nearly as transient as they are now; in fact, residency requirements were strictly enforced, thus many of the poor were known within the community and had perhaps been former contributing members who had fallen on difficult times. The concept of community as family is easier to envision when communities were small and completely governed by the church (Trattner, 1998).

Poor Laws of England

Many economic and environmental conditions led to the eventual phasing out of the traditional feudal system in the middle of the fourteenth century to the mid-sixteenth century (1350 through 1550), including several natural disasters such as massive crop failures, the bubonic plague, mass urbanization spawned by the wool industry, as well as the Industrial Revolution in general. The increased demand for factory wage labor in the cities ultimately led to droves of individuals moving to the city to work in factories, and this trend, coupled with the decline of the feudal system as well as the diminishing influence of the church with its complex and effective framework of charitable provision, led to the need for a complete overhaul of the social welfare policy in England. Thus, although this vast wave of urbanization led to freedom of serfdom for the poorest in England, it also created a vacuum in how poverty was managed, creating the necessity for the development of England's earliest poor laws (Trattner, 1998).

Although these social changes were gradual, they led not only to a dramatic shifting of how poverty was managed, but also how poverty was perceived. It is always easier to extend a gracious attitude and a helping hand to someone we know, but such graciousness becomes more challenging when the poor are no longer extended family and longtime neighbors, whose personal circumstances are well known, but rather are nameless, faceless strangers living en masse, often from different countries, speaking different languages, and behaving in very different manners. In addition to the decreased personal nature of poor relief was the influence of the Protestant Reformation, which among other things resulted in the fading away of traditional ways of perceiving the poor as blessed (Trattner, 1998).

Calvin's concept of **predestination** espoused the notion that some people were preselected for heaven and some were not, and it wasn't long before Calvinists and other Puritans began to see financial worth as the premiere and perhaps even the primary sign that one's salvation was secure. The other side of this coin, of course, was that those who were poor were clearly not chosen by God. Poverty then became one of the most obvious signs of spiritual condemnation.

The concept of predestination not only removed much of the incentive for providing for the poor in the hopes of being blessed (because such good works no longer held the incentive of salvation), but it also led to a shift in the general attitude toward the poor. **Social Darwinism,** the theory that espoused that people evolved socially and psychologically as a means for adapting to the challenges of life, led to a belief that charity was actually working against God's grand design to weed out those who were ill equipped to manage life's complexities (Trattner, 1998).

All these forces combined, including the increasing complexity of life in the city, led to the belief that the incorporation of punitive measures into relief policy was needed to control what was becoming a true social ill: begging, vagrancy, and increased crime in the cities. In response, England passed several relief laws during the mid-1500s through early 1600s, which set forth guidelines for dealing with the poor. England's relief act of 1536 placed responsibility for dealing with the poor at the local level and reflected a complete intolerance of idleness. Local law enforcement scoured the cities in search of beggars and vagrants, and once found, a determination was made as to whether they were true victims of poverty (the worthy poor) or legally defined vagrants (the unworthy poor). Legislative guidelines typically stipulated that only pregnant women, individuals who were extremely ill and unable to work, or any person over the age of sixty were considered justifiably poor, and thus they were treated more leniently, including given governmental authorization to beg (typically in the form of a letter of authorization), or they were given other forms of sustenance. If a man or a woman was found to be able-bodied and unemployed, he or she was determined to be vagrants, punishable by whippings, naked parading through the streets, being returned to the town of their birth, or incarceration. Repeat offenders were often subject to having an ear cut off or even death (Beier, 1974).

Clearly, there was no sympathy to be had for any individual, male or female, who was deemed capable of working but found themselves without a job or any means to support themselves, and little consideration was given to economic difficulties or what is now termed the "cycle of poverty." There was also little sympathy extended to children, particularly adolescents who were found begging, and district officials often took these children into custody, placing them into an apprenticeship program, which was later considered to be little different from child slavery. Thus, **vagrancy** was handled as a criminal matter, and the local authorities provided sustenance only for those truly unable to work (Trattner, 1998).

The Elizabethan Poor Laws

The earlier English poor laws laid the foundation for The Elizabethan Poor Laws of 1601, which in turn acted as a foundation for American social welfare policy. Thus rather than viewing the Poor Laws of 1601 as a single act, it is more appropriate to view it as an evolution, and the more final in a series of previous acts. The Elizabethan Poor Laws of 1601 served to set the stage for poor relief for several centuries and is still considered foundational in contemporary social welfare policy in both England and America. This act established three driving principles as the foundation for social legislation, including the belief that (1) the primary responsibility for provision lay with one's family, (2) that poor relief should be handled at the local level, and finally, that (3) no individual should be allowed to move to a new community if they were unable to provide for themselves financially.

Charity included both *indoor* and *outdoor* relief, with the former referring to assistance provided in almshouses and other institutionalized settings, and the latter referring to services provided in the home environment of the person in need, and might involve the delivery of food baskets or medicine.

It was quite common for community members to bring charges against another if it could be proved that they had moved into the district within the last 40 days and had no means to support themselves. Local officials would then take this vagrant into custody and return them to their home district. The underlying notion was that local parishes didn't mind supporting those individuals who had fallen on hard times after years of paying taxes, but they didn't want to be forced to support strangers who came to their district for the sole purpose of receiving aid. Elements of these residency requirements can be found among current U.S. welfare policy; in fact, most welfare reform bills today contain residency requirement language.

The Elizabethan Poor Laws of 1601 were then an organized merging of England's earlier, sometimes conflicting and erratic, social welfare legislation, which not only brought order and organization to England's poor laws, but also served as the foundation for such legislation in colonial America. Life in colonial America offered tremendous opportunity, but also presented significant hardship related to life on the frontier. Many immigrants were quite poor to begin with, and the long and difficult ocean voyage to the New World often left them unprepared for the rigors of life in America. Thus, even though colonial America offered many opportunities not available in the Old World, such as land ownership and numerous employment opportunities, many of the social ills plaguing new immigrants in their homeland followed them to America.

English colonization of North America began around the sixteenth century and continued throughout the seventeenth century. Because there was no existing infrastructure in the original 13 colonies (such as religious monasteries or other social welfare programs) poor relief consisted primarily of mutual kindness, family support, and distant help from the motherland. Self-sufficiency was a must, and life was not easy on the frontier. But as the population increased within the colonies, the need arose for a more organized form of relief, and it makes sense that the colonies would rely on the English Poor Laws of 1601.

Although the prevailing assumption among many is that the United States was founded based on a desire to be completely different than England, in reality, the overriding reasons for the American Revolution, although certainly complex, were based more on the desire for independence, rather than solely on the desire for a completely different governmental structure. This presumption is evident in the development of many of the social customs, governmental infrastructures, and legislation, including the social welfare policy of the American colonies. Thus the colonies not only adopted the social welfare legislation of England, but much of the perceptions of and attitudes about the poor and indigent as well.

The practice of human services is wholly influenced by social welfare policy in the United States, and to be truly effective in helping the poor and indigent, it is essential that all human service providers gain a level of social and cultural objectivity so that they can more fully understand both how social welfare policy and legislation has evolved over the years, as well as understanding the complex relationship between such legislation and the current prevailing attitudes toward the poor. It would be naïve to assume that any current trends in how the poor are perceived and treated developed in a vacuum, thus a general understanding of the roots of current social welfare legislation, policy, and attitudinal trends is essential to any practicing human service professional.

Charity Organization Societies

The Charity Organization Societies (COS) movement started in about 1870 in response to frustration with the current welfare system that was less of a system and more of a disorganized and often chaotic practice of almsgiving. The movement itself was started by a pastor, Rev. S. Humphreys Gurteen, who believed that it was the duty of good Christians everywhere to provide an organized and systematic way of addressing the plight of poverty. Gurteen and his colleagues strongly believed that the indiscriminate giving of many of the relief agencies of that time encouraged fraud and abuse, which in turn encouraged laziness on the part of those who were beneficiaries of relief.

Gurteen had many goals in mind. His first was to organize or make rational the current system of giving. This he believed would eliminate duplicative giving, thus reducing welfare fraud, but his other goal was to develop a system in which each case of aid was thoroughly investigated so that the root cause of poverty could be determined. In this way the whole person could be treated, dependency and abuse would be avoided, and self-sufficiency eventually gained, if at all possible.

The COS philosophy was built on the spirit of cooperation in which various charities worked within a larger network coordinating services delivered to the local community. The first COS was created in New York in 1877, and the concept quickly spread to large cities across the nation. Soon, most large cities had at least one COS serving the community acting as an umbrella organization for smaller agencies and churches offering human services to the community.

The COSs did not initially provide direct relief to clients, primarily because they believed that too many agencies were already providing material relief and doing it quite poorly. Instead, they organized charities by keeping a registry of philanthropic organizations, separating large cities into smaller districts to ensure charitable coverage. They also kept very detailed records of individuals seeking aid to avoid possible welfare abuse. Thus, one of the primary goals of the COSs was to maximize the best use of material relief (Schlabach, 1969).

An overriding fear of COS leaders was that providing nothing more than material relief encouraged a general lack of respect and lack of motivation on the part of recipients. This fear that giving money directly to the poor would lead to dependence, particularly for the unworthy poor, led most COS organizations to caution volunteers to use material aid as wisely as possible and to always explore other means for helping those in need (Schlabach, 1969). In this respect, the COS movement embraced the concepts of the unworthy and worthy poor, and it was their goal to determine which category aid recipients fell into, and then prescribe what each recipient actually needed—material aid for those who would not abuse it and other services for those who would. To accomplish this goal, the COSs employed "friendly visitors," an early version of caseworkers, who visited the homes of aid applicants and attempted to diagnose the reason for their poverty and, if possible, develop a "case plan" to authentically alleviate their suffering (Trattner, 1998).

Mary Richmond, General Secretary of the Baltimore COS, is often associated with the COS movement because of her passion for social advocacy and social reform. Richmond believed that charities could employ both good economics and compassionate giving. Richmond became well known for increasing pubic awareness of the COS movement and for her fund-raising efforts. Richmond's compassion for the poor was the likely result of her own sufferings from poverty. Orphaned at the age of two and later left by an aunt to fend for herself in New York when she was only 17 years old, Richmond no doubt understood the social components of poverty.

Richmond was responsible for the early conception of casework, having written several books and articles on the subject. As a result the concept of the friendly visitor grew, and the debate about material relief continued, with many arguing that the best opportunity to truly effect change in those suffering from poverty was the relationship with the friendly visitor who could help identify and address the barriers to self-sufficiency (Kusmer, 1973).

Despite the general success of the COS movement and the difficult task of basically cleaning up the social welfare system in the post–Civil War climate, the COS philosophy was somewhat tinged by the Reformation ethic that anyone who worked hard enough could rise from the depths of poverty. This sentiment added to the general sense of rugged individualism often worn as a badge of strength by U.S. citizens. But it was naïve to presume that poverty was primarily caused by individual failure and that material relief would lead to moral decline. The country was about to learn a very hard lesson during the Depression era, one that immigrants and minorities had known for years, which is that sometimes conditions exist that are beyond an individual's control and that create immovable barriers to self-sufficiency, leading to poverty and complete destitution.

Jane Addams and the Settlement House Movement

If you are taking a class in the human services discipline, then you are most likely a caring person who is interested in helping your "fellow man." Have you ever felt as though you are somewhat helpless in your desire to help? Have you ever wondered what impact you could possibly have as just one person? Jane Addams was such a woman, but she managed to leave an indelible mark on the human services and social work landscape, regardless of the severe limitations placed on her, not only by society, but by chronic illness as well.

Addams was born in Cedarville, Illinois, in 1860. She was raised in an upper-class home where higher education and philanthropy were highly valued. Addams greatly admired her father, who encouraged her to pursue an education at a time when women were primarily encouraged to pursue only marriage and motherhood. She graduated from Rockford Female Seminary in 1881, the same year her father died. After her father's death, Addams entered Woman's Medical College in Pennsylvania, but dropped out because of chronic illness. Addams had become quite passionate about the plight of immigrants in the United States, but due to her poor health and the societal limits placed on women during this era, she did not believe that she had a role in social advocacy.

The United States experienced another significant wave of immigration in the nineteenth and early twentieth centuries, with 23 million people emigrating from Europe, including Eastern Europe, between 1860 and 1910. Many of these immigrants were from non-English-speaking countries such as Italy, Poland, Russia, and Serbia, thus did not speak English, and were very poor. Unable to obtain work in the skilled labor force, many immigrants were forced to live in subhuman conditions, crammed together with several other families in deplorable tenements in large urban areas. New York's Lower East Side had 330,000 inhabitants per square mile (Trattner, 1998). With no labor laws for protection, racial discrimination and a variety of employment abuses were common, including extremely low wages, unsafe working conditions, and child labor. Poor families, particularly non-English-speaking families had little recourse, and their mere survival depended on their coerced cooperation.

Addams was aware of these conditions because of her father's political involvement, but she was not sure how to respond. Despondent after her father's death and her failure in medical school, as well as over her chronic medical problems, Addams took an extended trip with friends to Europe, where among other activities she visited Toynbee Hall, England's response to poverty and other social problems. Toynbee Hall was a settlement house, which was essentially a neighborhood welfare institution in an urban slum area, where trained workers endeavored to improve social conditions, particularly by providing community services and promoting neighborly cooperation.

This concept was revolutionary in that in its attempt to improve conditions through the promotion of social and economic reform, it actually called for the settlement house workers to reside in the home alongside the immigrant families they helped. In addition to providing a safe, clean home, settlement houses also provided comprehensive care, such as assistance with food, health care, English language lessons, child care, and general advocacy. Addams returned home convinced that it was her Christian duty to do something similar in the States, and with the donation of a building in Chicago, Illinois, the Hull House became America's first settlement house in 1889.

The settlement house movement was different from the traditional charity organizations, in that it had as its goal the mission of no longer distinguishing between the worthy and unworthy poor. Addams and her counterparts were committed to viewing all individuals equally, to be treated with respect and dignity. Addams clearly saw societal conditions and the hardship of immigration as the primary cause of poverty, not necessarily one's own moral failing. Another important distinction between the settlement houses and the traditional charity organizations is that the latter were primarily concerned with the indigent, whereas the settlement house workers focused on what would now be considered the "working-class poor."

The settlement house movement not only radically transformed how the poor were cared for, but how they were *perceived* by the majority population as well. Now, immigrants had a safe place to live, a voice to advocate for them, and a way to better integrate into American society, so that their dream to obtain a better life for themselves and their children, could actually be realized. Addams also lobbied tirelessly for the passage of child labor laws and other legislation that would protect the working-class poor, who were often exploited in factories with sweatshop conditions.

Yet, as effective as they were in meeting the complex needs of their immigrant residents, this movement was not without its critics. Contemporary critics, for instance, argue that these houses were nothing more than institutions for American assimilation, where in the name of Christianity, immigrants were encouraged to abandon their traditional culture to adapt to the cultural mores of the majority population, primarily those from English ancestry (Lissak, 1989).

Although there are no working settlement houses today, the prevailing concept espoused by this model remains, with the recognition of the need for comprehensive care for individuals who suffer from poverty and social displacement. Elements of

■ Jane Addams advocated tirelessly for families such as this one where children were often forced to work long hours in plume factories alongside their parents.

this concept of comprehensive care can be seen in the current U.S. social welfare system, as well as our current mental health system (see chapter 5), and although the settlement house movement cannot claim sole credit for this model of delivery service, its authors certainly contributed to the notion that individuals have the greatest likelihood of achieving social and economic freedom when all their needs are met in a comprehensive fashion.

The settlement house movement also had a significant impact on the evolution of the social work profession. Because the leaders in this movement, as well as many volunteers, were from the upper echelon of Christian society, many social welfare experts believe that the human services profession gained a level of social acceptance and professionalism not previously enjoyed.

Influences of African-American Social Workers

A review of the historical elements influencing the development of the human services field would be remiss if the influences of African-Americans reformers, particularly women in the last part of the nineteenth century, weren't at least briefly explored. Black activists had a significant influence on the development of social justice and human services, particularly in the South, filling the vacuum left by a racist society that often created barriers to service in the black community in earlier eras.

In this absence of mainstream human services, African-American social welfare reformers operated in a tight community, developing close relationships with each other, even though many of these women were spread across the United States. Because racism excluded African-Americans from receiving many services, including educational opportunities and health services, many early social welfare reformers focused on these two areas, developing "Negro" schools and health-care facilities. One such reformer was Modjeska Simkins, who developed health-care programs for the black community focusing on everything from infant mortality to tuberculosis. Another creative example of human services in the face of extreme opposition was the work of the black sorority Alpha Kappa Alpha, whose members were determined to provide health-care services to sharecroppers in Mississippi. When the white community refused to rent them office space, they offered the health services from cars (Gordon, 1991).

Other black women who significantly influenced social welfare reform include Ida Wells, who spoke out against the lynching of African Americans; Anna Cooper, who pushed for increased educational opportunities for blacks; and Jane Hunter, who formed the first black YWCA (Gordon, 1991). Although often unreported and undervalued, African-American social welfare reformers not only assisted their own communities but helped the broader community as well by modeling the power of networking and relentlessly pursuing social justice for all, particularly for those who are the subject of social oppression and discrimination.

The New Deal and the Social Security Act of 1935

In 1929 the stock market crashed, leading to a series of economic crises such as the United States had never before experienced. For the first time in modern history large segments of the middle-class population were unemployed, and within a very short time thousands of people who had once enjoyed secure lives were without jobs and soon without homes and food as well. This served as a wake-up call for social workers, many of whom had abandoned their earlier commitment to social reform, and many within the human services field started pushing President Hoover to develop the country's first federal system of social welfare.

Hoover was resistant, though, fearing that federal social welfare would create dependency and displace private and local charities. He wanted to allow time for democracy and capitalism to self-correct before intervening with broad entitlement programs. But much of the country, many of whom were literally starving, apparently did not agree, and in 1933 Hoover lost his bid for reelection, and Franklin D. Roosevelt was elected as president. Roosevelt immediately set about to create dramatic changes in federal policy with regard to social welfare, promising a *New Deal* to the country where a minimum standard of living was seen as a right, not a privilege.

Within his first 100 days in office, Roosevelt passed 13 acts including the Civilian Works Administration (CWA), which provided over a million temporary jobs to the unemployed; the Federal Emergency Relief Act (FERA), which provided direct aid and food to the unemployed; and the Civilian Conservation Core (CCC), which put thousands of young men ages 18 to 25 to work in reforestation and other conservation programs. Yet as progressive as Roosevelt was, and as compassionate as the country had become due to the realization that poverty could strike anyone, racism was still rampant, as illustrated by Roosevelt placing a 10 percent limit on the enrollment of black men in the CCC program (Trattner, 1998).

By far the most famous of all programs in the New Deal were those created in response to the Social Security Act of 1935, which among other things created old age assistance, unemployment compensation, aid to dependent mothers and children, and aid to the blind and disabled. In total Roosevelt created 15 federal programs as a part of the New Deal, some of which remain and some of which were dismantled once the crisis of the Depression subsided. Although some claim that the New Deal was not good for the country in the long run, it did pull the country out of the Depression, and it provided relief for millions of Americans who may have literally starved had the federal government not stepped in when it did. Programs such as the Federal Deposit Insurance Corporation (FDIC), which provided insurance for deposits, helped to instill a sense of confidence in the banking system once again, and the development of the Securities and Exchange Committee (SEC), which regulated the stock market, helped to ensure that a crash similar to the one in 1929 would be unlikely to occur again.

Concluding Thoughts on the History of Human Services

It is clear that society fluctuates in its attitude toward its most financially vulnerable members. A review of this evolution reveals that the roots of social welfare policy and attitudes about the poor lie in the monasteries' professing the blessedness of poverty and the reformation Puritans espousing the blessedness of wealth. The poor have typically been categorized as either worthy or unworthy, but the definition of these terms has changed significantly over the past several hundred years. Thus, a woman who experienced poverty due to having a child out of wedlock in the seventeenth century would most assuredly be considered the unworthy poor and as a result would experience difficulty mustering any sympathy, understanding, and support from society. Yet a woman experiencing these same circumstances today would likely face no such stigma, particularly if residing in an urban community. There have also been significant changes in policy with regard to the best way of solving the problem of societal poverty and social displacement, including focusing on the individual problems resulting in poverty or focusing on the social problems causing barriers to self-sufficiency.

The practice of human services is wholly influenced by social welfare policy in the United States, and to be truly effective in helping the poor, indigent, and hurting members of our society, it is essential that all human services providers gain a level of social and cultural objectivity so that they can more fully understand how social welfare policy and legislation has evolved over the years and how the complex relationship between social welfare policy and the prevailing attitudes toward the poor influence one another.

references

Beier, A. L. (1974). Vagrants and the social order in Elizabethan England. *The New England Quarterly, 43(1),* 59–78.

Birtles, S. (1999). Common land, poor relief and enclosure. *Past & Present [Great Britain] (165),* 74–106.

Gordon, L. (1991). Black and white visions of welfare: women's welfare activism, 1890–1945. *The Journal of American History, 78(2),* 559–590.

King, S. (1997). Poor relief and English economic development reappraised. *Economic History Review [Great Britain], 50(2),* 360–368.

Kusmer, K. (1973). The functions of organized charities in the progressive era: Chicago as a case study. *Journal of American History, 60(3),* 657–678.

Lissak, R. S. (1989). *Pluralism and progressives: Hull House and the new immigrants, 1890–1919.* Chicago: University of Chicago Press.

National Organization for Human Services. (n.d.). *Human service worker: A generic job description.* Retrieved February 2, 2004, from http://www.nohse.com/hsworker.html

Schlabach, T. (1969). *Rationality & welfare: Public discussion of poverty and social insurance in the U.S. 1875–1935.* Social Security Commission, Research Notes and Special Studies. Retrieved September 18, 2005, from http://www.ssa.gov/history/reports/schlabachpreface.html

Stephenson, C. (1943). Feudalism and its antecedents in England. *The American Historical Review, 48(2),* 245–265.

Trattner, W. (1998). *From poor law to welfare state* (6th ed.). New York: Free Press.

suggested   reading

Carlton-LaNey, I. B. (2001). *African American leadership an empowerment tradition in social welfare history.* Washington, DC: NASW Press.

Katz, M. B. (1996). *In the shadow of the poorhouse: A social history of welfare in America.* New York: Basic Books.

Katz, M. B. *Undeserving poor.* (1990). New York: Pantheon.

Linn, J. W. & Scott, A. F. (2000). *Jane Addams: A biography.* Chicago: University of Illinois Press.

Martin, J. M. & Martin, E. P. (1985). *The helping tradition in the black family and community.* Washington, DC: NASW Press.

Reisch, M. & Andrews, J. (2002). *The road not taken: A history of radical social work in the U.S.* Washington, DC: Taylor & Francis.

internet   web   sites   related
to   the   history   of   human   services

Jane Addams Hull House: **http://www.hullhouse.org/**
Jane Addams Hull House Museum: **http://wall.aa.uic.edu:62730/artifact/HullHouse.asp**
The Social Work History Online Timeline: **http://www.gnofn.org/~jill/swhistory/**

part two

Clinical Issues and the Role of the Human Service Professional

chapter 3

Skills and Intervention Strategies for Generalist Practice

All professionals use tools to accomplish their job duties. A professional baseball player uses a bat, a ball, and a mitt. An accountant uses a calculator; an airline pilot uses an airplane. What is unique about the human services field is that the professional is the tool. Most people who enter this field do so because they possess some basic inclination toward counseling, advocacy, and caregiving. One might question, then, why someone who is a natural counselor needs a professional education to become a human service professional. Even the most naturally talented counselor needs training and refinement, needs to be taught useful techniques, and will be able to benefit from the results of broad-based research, the knowledge of others concerning professional issues, such as multicultural considerations, and collaboration with other professionals with years of practice experience.

I mentioned earlier how human service professionals are generalists in that they have a wide range of skills that they use with a diverse population. Therefore, the skills and intervention strategies referenced in this chapter will be general enough to be applied to a variety of situations and clients. More specific skills and intervention strategies will be discussed in successive chapters as they apply to clients seeking services in particular practice settings.

Because the human service professional is the primary tool for intervention, many of the skills listed here could almost be considered personality characteristics. *Empathy* and *compassion* are powerful and necessary skills and often appear naturally engrained in someone's personality or character. Nevertheless, even if someone is naturally empathetic and a naturally good listener, it is imperative that these skills be sharpened and more fully developed to be truly useful in the human services field. Other skills are less natural and must be taught. For instance, although some people might be a good judge of character, they need to be taught various clinical assessment skills and techniques.

Informed Consent and Confidentiality

Prior to any discussion on counseling competencies and generalist skills, the important topics of informed consent, confidentiality, and the limits of confidentiality must first be discussed. Informed consent refers to disclosing to clients the nature and risks of the counseling relationship prior to their engaging in these services. According to the NASW Ethical Code, clients should be provided a written document that fully informs them (in clear and understandable language) the nature, extent, and risks of services, including whether the client can terminate services voluntarily or, in the case of mandated clients, what the consequences are for terminating services (NASW, 2002).

Confidentiality is an important aspect of the counselor–client relationship, where clients are assured that whatever they share with their counselor will not be shared with others. This commitment to keep whatever clients share within the counseling relationship private is not merely a clinical issue practiced by most in the mental health field—it is considered so vital to mental health treatment that confidentiality is a legal mandate in every state in the nation. Thus, any professional offering counseling services must by law maintain confidentiality or face losing their professional license or other sanction.

The importance of confidentiality is based on the belief that for trust to develop in the counseling relationship, clients must be assured that they have a safe place to discuss their most private thoughts, fears, and experiences. Without such a guarantee, clients might not be willing to discuss their fears that they are not good parents, their intermittent desire to abandon their families because they are so overwhelmed in life, or their histories of child sexual abuse. Knowing that they have a safe place to talk about their most private thoughts with someone who is not personally affected by their feelings, experiences, or choices makes this exploration possible for thousands of individuals enabling clients to become better parents, becoming less overwhelmed in their lives, and learning how to turn childhood victimization into a survivor mentality.

The Limits of Confidentiality

There are *limits to confidentiality,* though, designed to ensure the safety of the client and the general public. Although there are no national standards for the limits of confidentiality in mental health services, each state has laws that establish exceptions of confidentiality related to both voluntary and involuntary disclosures. These laws determine how and when client information can be disclosed to other treatment providers, insurance companies, and caregivers, which typically require the client signing an *authorization to release information,* a legal document signed by the client that provides all relevant information about what information will be released and for what purpose.

There are also occasions when a mental health practitioner is permitted and/or required by law to violate confidentiality without the permission of the client. In general, these limits involve the counselor's duty-to-warn and duty-to-protect and relate to situations where through direct disclosure clients share that they are a threat to themselves (suicidal) or others (homicidal). For instance, if a client shares with a human service professional that he plans on leaving the office and committing suicide, the practitioner has the legal obligation to disclose this information to the client's family or even the police to ensure the client's safety. If a minor child client discloses during the counseling session that she is being sexually abused by her uncle, the practitioner is legally obligated to report this information to child protective services to ensure the child's safety.

Disclosures are not always so clear-cut or direct, though, and there are many occasions where human service professionals find themselves needing to use their clinical skills to determine whether violating confidentiality is the appropriate course of action. For instance, consider the client who *may* be suicidal and who discloses a level of despair that *may* indicate suicidal ideation. Couple this with a disclosure that he attempted suicide four months before and told no one; that he uses alcohol to "make the pain go away"; and that although he won't admit to a suicide plan, he doesn't always feel safe. A client who shares this type of disclosure—denying any outright plan to commit suicide, but appearing to manifest many signs of suicidal behavior—may very well be at real risk for committing suicide, but might be resistant to sharing this clearly either because he is confused about how he feels (wants to end his life one moment and wants to live the next), or he may have already planned to commit suicide and does not want anything or anyone to get in his way.

This scenario requires the practitioner to take a clinical risk—if the practitioner takes no action the client may indeed commit suicide, but if the practitioner violates confidentiality and the client was not really at risk for suicide then the counselor–client relationship might be seriously damaged. Because confidentiality does not bar professional discussions among practitioners within the same agency, clinical dilemmas are most appropriately explored in clinical supervision where a team of counselors discusses the risks involved and as a group attempts to make the best decision possible.

Another challenging clinical scenario involves a minor child client who discloses possible abuse—a spanking that seems to the practitioner to go beyond mere discipline, verbal abuse that might meet the criteria of child maltreatment, or a some other indication that the child *may* be experiencing abuse in the home. Determining when that line has been crossed is a clinical issue, best explored within clinical supervision, but it is important to note that legally, it is the practitioner who is responsible for complying with disclosure laws, and it is the practitioner's professional license that will be at risk if the appropriate actions are not taken. In some states a failure to report suspected child abuse can result in criminal misdemeanor charges, thus although clinical supervision can be of significant assistance in making these types of clinical decisions, the practitioner must make the final decision on whether to violate confidentiality to protect the client's welfare.

Another limit to confidentiality involves a client who discloses during the counseling relationship that he or she has a plan to cause serious and immediate harm to another person. Laws in most states dictate specifically how, when, and to whom this information is to be disclosed. Duty-to-warn laws have been influenced greatly by a tragic incident that occurred on the University of California, Berkeley campus when a student disclosed to a campus psychologist his intent to kill his girlfriend. Although the psychologist informed various individuals, including his supervisor and campus police, he did not inform the intended victim or her family. The girlfriend was later killed by the client. The family of the victim sued the university for the psychologist's failure to warn the victim. The case, *Tarasoff v. The Regents of University of California*, resulted in two decisions by the California Supreme Court in 1974 and 1976 (*Tarisoff I and II*, respectively). *Tarasoff I* (1974) found that a therapist has a duty to use reasonable care to give threatened persons a warning to prevent foreseeable danger. *Tarasoff II* (1976) was more specific referencing the therapists' duty and obligation to warn intended victims if necessary to protect them from serious danger of violence. Virtually every state in the nation now uses the *Tarasoff* decisions as a foundation for the development of duty-to-warn laws (Fulero, 1988).

Although clients are told about the limits of confidentiality by the written informed consent, they may forget or be confused about what would warrant violation of the confidentiality privilege. Clients who share deeply personal information with their counselors may feel betrayed by the counselor who informs them that a disclosure is going to be shared with someone to protect the client or others. It is vital that this topic be fully discussed during the first counseling session so the client knows what disclosures do and do not limit confidentiality. For instance, disclosures of shoplifting, cheating on one's taxes, lying to an employer, having an affair, or *feeling* like attacking a coworker do not limit confidentiality, but admissions of plans to kill oneself or someone else, to set someone's house on fire or admissions of child maltreatment (as defined in chapter 4) do limit confidentiality requiring disclosure. Child and adolescent clients can be particularly taken by surprise when their confidentiality is violated, thus it is often a good idea for the counselor to remind clients of these limits intermittently throughout the counseling relationship.

Skills and Competencies

Sympathy and Empathy

Escalas and Stern (2003) discussed the traditional definition of both sympathy and empathy (commonly confused responses). They define sympathy as sorrow or concern for another's welfare, whereas empathy is defined as a person's absorption in the feelings of another. The difference between these two responses, although seemingly subtle, is significant when one considers that the response of empathy goes one step further, allowing oneself to actually feel what another feels.

In a counseling setting empathy involves the willingness and ability to truly understand a client's beliefs, thoughts, feelings, and experiences from the client's own perspective. Sympathy is not a difficult emotional response to muster for the true victims of this world. Imagine watching the news and hearing about the plight of a young couple whose five-year-old child was recently abducted. Your immediate response would likely be to express feelings of sorrow for them, and you might express concern for their welfare, wondering what will become of the little girl and to the family as they search for her. You might stop short, though, of allowing yourself to feel the actual feelings of grief and fear that this couple is no doubt feeling. Allowing yourself to immerse so deeply in what you imagine their feelings to be might hit too close to home, particularly if you have children. You might feel compelled to distance yourself emotionally—to resist putting yourself in their place. You shiver as you watch your own five-year-old playing on the swing set in your backyard and will yourself not to give this situation another thought, lest you find it impossible to sleep tonight.

Effective practitioners cannot limit their emotional responses to sympathy alone, and to be effective counselors and advocates they must be willing to go on the emotional roller coaster ride with the client. This requires emotional maturity, the ability to be honest with oneself, the capacity for immersing oneself in another's emotional crisis without getting lost in the experience, and being able to keep the focus on the client, not on themselves. I have often referred to the empathetic response in counseling as having the emotional capacity to not only see the client's world through the client's eyes, but to also be willing to walk alongside the client through a difficult time. This can be emotionally exhausting, but if I am working with a victim of rape, and if I want to be truly effective in helping my client navigate through this crisis, then I need to be willing to understand what it feels like to be sexually violated as best I can without having gone through this experience myself, what it feels like to be humiliated, and what it feels like to be filled with shame and embarrassment. Thus although the concept of empathy might seem appealing, many practitioners resist truly empathizing with their clients because it requires them to search their own minds and hearts, to reflect on past hurts, and in this case, past times in their lives where they have been humiliated, shamed, and embarrassed—experiences many are not particularly inclined to revisit.

Another challenge in responding empathetically to clients is when one is working with clients who do not appear to deserve sympathy or empathy. How do counselors empathize with pedophiles, with parents who abuse their children, or with the drunk driver who drove her car into a family of five, killing a child? Unlike therapists in private practice who typically have complete control over their caseloads, human service professionals rarely have such control and are often given a caseload, depending on the practice setting, with clients who the general public might deem undeserving of anything other than a prison sentence.

Looking at the world through the eyes of a serial rapist, a domestic batterer, or a raging drunk might be the last thing any sane human being would want to do, but the willingness to do so is a requirement for human service professionals, who will likely find themselves working with *mandated clients,* individuals who are required by some governmental agency (the courts, department of probation, child welfare, etc.) to seek treatment.

So how does one accomplish this feat, when the behavior of such a client is often morally incomprehensible, or at the least abusive? The first step is in understanding that to empathize does not mean to condone. Consider the last motion picture that you watched. It is the director's job to help the viewer see the world through each of the characters' eyes. Considering the role of the director, although not a direct parallel, illustrates the concept of the human service professional essentially sitting alongside those in counseling and seeing the world through their eyes. You do not have to agree with their perspective, and you certainly do not have to agree with their actions, but to be a truly effective human service professional you must be willing and able to understand what it feels like to be them.

Although it might not make sense that a victim of abuse goes on to become the batterer, this dynamic is quite common. The boy who was sexually abused *may* grow up to be a pedophile, the child who was beaten may grow up to beat her own children, and the boy who witnessed his father beat his mother may grow up to beat his own wife. The nature of this dynamic will be discussed in later chapters, but understanding that most abusive behavior is borne out of pain might help to see mandated clients not as monsters, but as broken human beings who have suffered greatly themselves, yet rather than remaining vulnerable so healing could occur, their hearts were hardened and sometimes they become like those who hurt them.

Boundary Setting

Any discussion of empathy and the need for emotional immersion in another's problems must be considered in the context of boundary setting. Although human services certainly is not the sort of career one can leave at the office, it would be imprudent to become so immersed in a client's problems that practitioners cannot distinguish the difference between their problems and the problems of their clients. It is probably easier to discuss good boundary setting by giving examples of poor boundary setting. The practitioner who counsels a victim of domestic violence and spends the majority of the session talking about her own abusive relationships has poor boundaries. The practitioner who becomes so upset about a parent abusing her child that he takes the child home with him is not setting good boundaries. The practitioner who becomes so upset at a client who projects anger in the counseling session that she cries and tells the client how she is having a horrible day and that he just made it worse is not setting good boundaries. Finally, the practitioner who gets so immersed in his clients' problems that he becomes convinced his clients cannot survive without him is not setting good boundaries.

Personal boundaries are sometimes compared to physical boundaries such as the property line around one's house, porous enough that someone can enter the property, but solid enough that a neighbor knows not to set a shed up in another neighbor's yard (Cloud & Townsend, 1992). So too must human service professionals establish boundaries in our mental, physical, and emotional lives to determine what falls within our domain and responsibility and what does not.

In the human services field some boundaries are determined by the ethical standards of the field. For instance, having a sexual relationship with a client violates an ethical boundary because this type of intimacy can exploit the practitioner–client relationship that grants the practitioner a significant measure of control—even authority—over the client. Violating the prohibition against having sexual relations with a client is so serious that it can result in the suspension of one's professional license. Violating this ethical boundary might seem like an obviously bad idea to most people, but it occurs more often than many suspect. Counseling someone of the opposite sex creates a sense of intimacy that can sometimes foster romantic feelings, particularly on the part of the client.

Much like the child who develops a crush on a teacher, a client who is depressed and lonely may experience the practitioner's comfort, nurturing, and guidance as intimate love. But a sexual relationship when one party possesses power and control and the other is vulnerable and broken will always result in emotional and physical exploitation. A practitioner who respects this boundary will recognize the clinical nature of the client's feelings and will help the client see that experiencing intimacy can be a very positive experience, but developing a romantic relationship should only occur when it can be truly reciprocal. This is an example of a clearly marked boundary, and it is difficult to step over this boundary line without knowing one is in dangerous territory. However, other boundaries are not so clear and are frequently violated by human service professionals.

My first job in human services was as an adolescent counselor at a locked residential facility. I was 23 years old, fresh out of college, and excited to finally be making a difference in people's lives. I became too involved in my clients' lives, though, and quickly began to overidentify with the teens on my caseload. I was so flattered by my clients' expressed need for me that I was willing to work any hours necessary to make sure they knew how much I cared. If I worked a 3:00 PM to midnight shift, and one of the girls on my caseload told me that she needed me there in the morning, I would make sure I was there at 8:00 AM, even if it meant getting little sleep. If another counselor called me at home because a teen on my caseload was insisting that she would only talk to me, I dropped whatever I was doing and rushed down to the facility, feeling good that I was so needed.

This sort of behavior on my part indicated several problems. First, it led to a situation where I almost left the field of human services all together because after three years I was so burned out that I was no longer sure I wanted to be a human service professional in any respect. It also encouraged a sense of dependency among the girls on my caseload. Because it felt good to be needed, I neglected one of the fundamental values of human service professionals: **empowering** clients to be more self-sufficient. Setting boundaries would have encouraged my clients to develop relationships with other counselors and to rely on themselves and newly developed skills to cope with their struggles.

Since that point in my career I have developed some "rules for the road" for determining necessary boundaries and for making sure that I consistently enforce them. One rule is that I never work harder than my client. This does not mean that I do not advocate for clients, or that I do not assist clients in performing various tasks, but what it does mean is that I recognize that I am not truly helping clients who are not motivated to change because a counselor who overfunctions in a counseling relationship helps no one. Thus, when I begin to feel exhausted in my work with a client, I recognize this as a potential sign that I'm doing too much work, perhaps out of impatience and a need to see progress, and recognize that it is time to step back a bit and give my clients room to decide the best course of action for themselves.

I have also come to see my clients' lives as *their* journey, not mine. This conceptualization allows me to view myself as one of many individuals who will come alongside a client and help them at some point along their journey, just as various people have helped and influenced me along my own life journey. This conceptual framework helps to remind me that my clients have free will to make whatever choices they deem fit. This self-determination means that they can accept my help and suggestions, or they can reject them.

A final conceptualization that can help establish and maintain healthy boundaries in a counseling relationship is to recognize that people grow and change at varying rates and in their own unique way. Thus, when I am working with someone and it appears as though nothing I am doing or saying is making a difference, I remember that I might be the *seed planter*. Seed planters do just as it sounds—they plant the seeds of future growth, but oftentimes they do not have the benefit of seeing these changes come to fruition. It is often this way when working with adolescents. I rarely witnessed the results of my work with my teen clients, but I had to trust that in five or ten years, something I said, some kindness I had shown, some **reframing** I did would result in healthy personal growth.

The Hallmarks of Personal Growth

It is equally important to recognize the role of the *fertilizer* and the *harvester* in counseling relationships. These are the counselors who come into the lives of clients after the seeds have already been planted. The fertilizer is the practitioner who helps the client do productive work—this is no easy task, but the counselor has the benefit of seeing the results of the counseling and intervention strategies. The harvester is probably the most gratifying role a human service professional can have. This practitioner comes along when everything seems to align for the client. She is ready to make the necessary changes for a healthy life, she recognizes past negative patterns in relationships and choices, and she has the necessary insight and motivation to effect true change.

I recently had a client who was at this point in her life. Fortunately, I was able to recognize that I could not take full credit for helping her to make the significant realizations and changes she was making in counseling. She'd had several prior counseling experiences, and my role was to help her to merge all that she had previously learned so that she could finally make the necessary, permanent changes in her attitude and approach to life, so that she could be a healthy and happy productive individual, recognizing her own right to self-determination and dignity and her responsibilities to herself, her family, and her community. If you are working productively with a client but see little to no progress, you may very well be the seed planter. If you are working productively with a client but it seems as though change is still a long way off, then you are probably the fertilizer, and if you are reaping changes left and right with a client, then you may very well be the harvester.

Seeing yourself operating as a part of a team, even though you will likely never meet the practitioners who came before you or those who may come after, helps to ease the burden of feeling so responsible for a client's growth, as well as helping to resist the temptation to take full credit for the client's progress.

The Clinical Assessment

The process of assessing the clinical issues of a client utilizes a combination of numerous skills, such as *patience, active listening skills,* and *good observation skills,* as well as more tangible skills, such as being familiar with how to administer various psychological tests and assessments. The tools for conducting an effective assessment are numerous. The first session is often spent conducting an intake interview, which includes collecting basic demographic information about the client (age, marital status, number of children, ethnicity, etc.). Other pertinent information includes the nature of the identified problem(s), employment status, housing situation, physical health status, medications taken, history of substance abuse, criminal history, history of trauma, any history of mental health problems (including depression, suicidal thoughts, or other mental illness, and any history of mental health services).

When I was in graduate school I recall being taught that the first five sessions with a client should be focused almost exclusively on assessment, but I quickly realized that if some intervention does not occur during those first few sessions, clients are not likely to return. Unlike many clients who come to see a clinical psychologist in private practice, many human service clients are in crisis, and they often need immediate intervention. Thus, human service professionals often find themselves jumping in with both feet, sizing up the client and the situation rather quickly so that some intervention strategies can be employed.

This by no means indicates that the assessment process should be shortchanged due to the frequent crisis nature of many human services agencies. Quite the opposite in fact—although it is true that the practitioner will be focusing more on assessment the first few sessions, the process of assessing the mental health functioning, as well as the client's situation, is ongoing and should continue throughout the counseling process. This is important for two reasons. First, before effective **intervention strategies** can be identified and used, the practitioner needs to know what the client's issues are. In addition, more often than not, new information will continue to emerge long after the formal assessment period is over, and if practitioners assume the assessment is complete, they might overlook important information about the client that emerges later in the counseling relationship.

Patience

Patience, therefore, is imperative in conducting an effective assessment. One reason why people enter the field of human services is because they love to figure other people out, but a seasoned professional will not allow this passion to result in a rush to judgment. It is important to hold at bay the intense desire to exclaim "Ah ha!" too quickly. I used to work with victims of domestic violence—a practice setting that I am passionate about because I am an advocate for those who are vulnerable. I recall one female client who shared stories of her controlling and abusive husband. Her stories seemed valid, and there was not anything in particular that would cause me to believe that she was not telling me the truth. In fact, what she shared about her husband's behavior met many of the hallmark signs of domestic violence relationships—her husband controlled the finances, and she had little or no access to the bank accounts; her husband appeared jealous and possessive, consistently demanding to know her constant whereabouts; and many of the arguments she reiterated to me reflected what appeared to be her husband's critical response to her in all respects, ranging from her housekeeping ability to the way she managed their children.

I quickly began to view her low **self-esteem** and depression as being the *result* of his abusive behavior and counseled her accordingly. Yet several sessions into our counseling relationship she retold a story, which she apparently did not recall telling me before. This version, though, was considerably different. I knew she was reciting the same story, but this time the events illustrating her husband's abusive behavior were different. I was not sure whether she was simply merging stories accidentally, or whether this was an indication that she was not being completely honest with me. I made a note to explore this area further and to be more diligent in determining the veracity of her stories.

After interviewing her husband and children and spending more time assessing my client, I discovered that she was actually the abusive member of the family! She feared her husband leaving her and seeking custody, thus she hoped to enter into a counseling relationship and manipulate the counselor, so that she was perceived as the victim, and the counselor would therefore support her version of events in court. If practitioners are not diligent in thoroughly assessing their clients, they will be far likelier to be manipulated by some of their clients, thus doing more harm than good.

Human service professionals should always approach clients with the understanding that the client's perspective is just that—the client's perspective. Moreover, I was once told that truth comes in three parts: what you said happened, what the other person said happened, and what really happened. Understanding this does not detract from the counselor's advocacy role of his or her client, but rather supports the counselor's ability to help clients reframe various incidences and situations in their lives to help clients gain a healthier and more balanced perspective.

Thus, although a clinical assessment is a broad and ongoing process, it is also specific: the human service professional is assessing both the mental health of the client as well as conducting a needs assessment to determine the quality and level of functioning in the various domains of their lives (interpersonal, work, family, social, spiritual, community). An affective clinical assessment depends on many skills, some of which have already been discussed earlier in this chapter. But two of the most important skills necessary for a effective clinical assessment relate to the practitioner's ability to listen well and be sufficiently observant.

Active Listening Skills

Active listening skills involve the ability to attend to the speaker fully, without distraction, without preconceived notions of what the speaker is saying, and without being distracted by thoughts of what one wants to say in response. Active listening in the counseling relationship also includes such behaviors as maintaining direct eye contact and observing the client's body language. It also involves considering virtually everything that the client says as relevant. It is often the subtle, offhand comment that yields the most information about the client's interpersonal dynamics.

I recall working with one client for depression and parenting issues who in response to my questions regarding her perception of the origin of her problems spent a considerable amount of time discussing her troubled marriage and her difficulty making friends. In the midst of sharing a particularly painful story about her difficult college years, she made a casual comment about how one of her college roommates said something to her once that reminded her of something her mother always said. If I had not been actively listening I could have missed the significance of that seemingly unimportant comment. It was stated as a joking aside, but I also noticed her brief pause and a quick, almost imperceptible, sadness in her eyes. The entire exchange lasted no more than a few seconds, but it completely turned the course of my assessment. I made a mental note to revisit the issue of her mother during a later session when we knew each other better and she knew she could trust me. Eventually it became clear that her core emotional issues resided in her tumultuous relationship with her mother, but she had previously been so protective of this relationship that it felt far too unsafe for her to recognize that her primary issues revolved around her relationship with a controlling, shaming mother. Over the course of the next several months I continued to revisit the issue, slowly at first and then more boldly once we were on solid ground in our own relationship, and she was finally able to recognize the hold her mother had on her all these years. Had I not been as attentive, responding instead to only what the client wanted to focus on, we would have spent our time together focusing on residual issues.

Observation Skills

Good *observation skills* are also an important part of the assessment process because individuals communicate as much through their bodies as they do through their words. Practitioners should watch their clients' eye contact, whether they are shifting uncomfortably in their seats when talking about certain subjects, crossing their arms self-protectively, or tapping their feet anxiously. All these behaviors can be clues or indicators of deeper dynamics. Employing good observation skills can also yield information about whether a client is being direct or evasive, genuine or masked, sincere or manipulative, open or guarded.

Family Genograms

A more comprehensive assessment tool involves constructing a *genogram* of the client's family. Murray Bowen (1978) developed Family Systems Theory, which is based on the premise that inter- and intrarelational patterns are transmitted from one generation to the next. Thus, one way to grasp the "big picture" of the client's life is to study this intergenerational transmission as it relates to issues such as communication style, emotional regulation, and various other "rules for living" (for example, it is good to express emotions, it is bad to express emotions). Bowen believes that the goal for achieving positive well-being is to find the balance between achieving personal autonomy and individuation while maintaining appropriate closeness with one's family system. Those who are so close to their family system that they cannot make decisions without family approval without the fear of being considered betrayers of the family are considered **enmeshed,** and those who find it necessary to emotionally distance themselves to the point of estrangement to achieve independence are considered *cut off.*

Most people have some information about their parents, limited information about their grandparents, and oftentimes no information whatsoever about their great-grandparents. They may have grown up hearing one-sided (and unquestioned) versions of family feuds or odd distant relatives, but to gain accurate and valuable information about one's family system information seeking must be intentional. This can be uncomfortable and may ruffle some feathers because it is often the family members who have been cut off, or are considered the "black sheep," who hold the family secrets that will unlock the true underlying dynamics of a family system. Poking around the skeleton closet can often threaten families, particularly in **closed family systems,** but this information may also hold the key to truly unlocking hidden dynamics that have been in place sometimes for numerous generations.

Genograms use a variety of symbols designed to indicate gender, the type of relationship (married, divorced, etc.), the nature of the relationships (cut off or enmeshed). Traumatic events, such as deaths, divorces, and miscarriages are noted as are the responses to them (for example, "never discussed"). Typically, shameful events are also relevant, such as out-of-wedlock births (particularly relevant in earlier generations), abortions, extramarital affairs, domestic violence, alcohol abuse, sexual abuse and assault, and job losses. Such events are often kept secret but can affect family members for generations to come. The shame of an extramarital affair and an out-of-wedlock birth that was hushed up several generations back can have a profound affect on how emotions are handled and how feelings are communicated.

I once worked with a woman who struggled to understand why her mother never seemed to accept or approve of her. She had spent years in counseling attempting to understand her mother's and her own intense perfectionism and refusal to accept even the smallest of mistakes. My client was convinced that her mother was ashamed of her and this belief affected every area of her functioning. A genogram revealed that my client's grandmother was raped, and my client's mother was the product of that rape. Both the grandmother and my client's mother lived their lives in constant shame, and their high expectations of my client were really a reflection of their desire to protect her from the shame they were forced to endure, not some statement of their disapproval of her. It was through the development of a genogram that enabled my client to take a few emotional steps back and see her family system with more clarity.

A family genogram provides a structured way to obtain a comprehensive family history so that the practitioner and client can develop a more complete understanding of the family dynamics that are affecting the client in ways perhaps never before recognized or acknowledged. It also provides for an objective and nonshaming way to gain a level of objective understanding of various issues within one's family system that can potentially pave the way for the client to view relationships and various events without personalizing hurtful experiences, including gaining an objective understanding of the nature of conflict-filled family relationships. No longer is the client blaming himself for his father's seeming disapproval or feeling hurt because his mother seemed emotionally distant and rejecting. Instead clients can develop a greater understanding of the broader picture and can see their family members as individual people who are as much a victim of circumstances as the client. Thus, a family genogram is not merely an effective assessment tool, but is also a very effective intervention tool that can be used to address long-standing issues that have potentially kept clients in emotional bondage for years.

Psychological Testing

Counselors have numerous other tools at their disposal as well, including various objective assessments tools, such as inventories designed to assess levels of depression, anxiety, social functioning, and personality style. Less objective measures, such as interpretive drawing exercises, free choice drawing, clay manipulation, and structured play therapy, can also be useful. These assessments work particularly well when working with clients who are either less verbal or who are dealing with particularly painful emotional issues.

When working with traumatized children I would often ask them to draw a picture of their families. Although the results always need to be considered cautiously, and in the context of all other information gleaned during sessions, it is always interesting to see how children conceptualize themselves and their various family members. For instance, drawing a picture where the father is significantly larger than the rest of the family might indicate a perception that the father is overbearing. A child who draws himself floating away or standing separately from the rest of the family might indicate a feeling of being disconnected from the rest of the family members. Again, it is essential that practitioners use great caution when interpreting subjective techniques, and all assessment material should be considered as a whole, rather than giving too much weight to any one particular measure.

Clinical Diagnoses

Most human service professionals use the Diagnostic Statistical Manual, Fourth Edition, Text Revision (DSM-IV-TR) (American Psychiatric Association [APA], 2000) to diagnose the mental and emotional disorders of their clients. The DSM-IV-TR is a classification system developed by the American Psychiatric Association. It includes criteria for mental and emotional disorders such as schizophrenia, depressive disorders, anxiety disorders, and personality disorders such as narcissistic personality disorder and antisocial personality disorder (sociopathy). The DSM-IV-TR is a multiaxial diagnostic system, which means that individuals are diagnosed on five axes, or five different areas of functioning.

Clinical disorders requiring clinical attention, such as schizophrenia or depression, are diagnosed on Axis I. **Personality disorders,** such as Borderline Personality Disorder and mental retardation, are diagnosed on Axis II. General medical conditions that might have an impact on one's mental health are diagnosed on Axis III. Psychosocial and environmental problems, such as problems with housing and employment, are diagnosed on Axis IV; Axis V is reserved for the client's global assessment of functioning (GAF). The GAF scale ranges from 0 to 100, with 0 indicating someone at a homicidal or suicidal level and 100 indicating a functioning level far higher than any of us will likely ever achieve. Although the assessment of one's GAF is somewhat subjective and arbitrary, the DSM-IV-TR contains a guide that assists practitioners in determining where their clients might fall in their overall functioning level. In general, individuals who are struggling in most areas of their lives and are in need of clinical intervention will be functioning somewhere in the range of 0 to 50.

Criticisms of the DSM-IV-TR

Although the diagnostic criteria of the DSM-IV-TR relies significantly on professional peer consensus and review and is backed by a large body of research, many professionals in the human services field have concerns about the DSM-IV-TR because it applies the medical model to emotional disorders. This paradigm in many respects pathologizes what might just be a broader range of human thoughts and behaviors, which in turn tends to create a stigma for those who are suffering from emotional problems. Consider someone who has recently been the victim of a violent crime. If he experiences mental flashbacks of the traumatic event, is he exhibiting behaviors that are adaptive and expected? Or, in the alternative, is he suffering from Post Traumatic Stress Disorder? Is the angry adolescent whose parents were just divorced exhibiting a normal grief response to this loss? Or is does he have Oppositional Defiance Disorder? Even if a human service professional does not naturally view human behavior from a disease perspective, using the DSM-IV-TR can influence a practitioner to view their clients from a pathological perspective (Duffy, Gillig, Tureen, & Ybarra, 2002).

Yet even if one believes that the medical or disease model is appropriate to use when evaluating psychological disorders, an important distinction between the diagnostic system used to diagnose medical conditions and the system used to diagnose mental disorders is that the DSM-IV-TR uses criteria based on symptoms, whereas medical conditions are diagnosed based on the etiology (cause or origin) of the disorder. Thus rather than diagnosing a patient with a stomachache, which could potentially have many causes, the medical diagnosis would be a virus, an ulcer, or cancer. Yet when considering mental disorders one is not diagnosed with a neurotransmitter disorder, negative thinking, or an abusive childhood, but is diagnosed with Major Depressive Disorder based on the symptoms the client is experiencing, not on etiology.

Other criticisms of the DSM-IV-TR include questioning the process that determines what behaviors are deemed abnormal enough to be included in the DSM-IV-TR, and which behaviors are not, and whether it is appropriate to categorize human behavior, pathologizing alternative understandings of human behavior (Duffy et al., 2002).

Many practitioners have also expressed concerns about health insurance companies' reliance on the DSM-IV-TR for the diagnoses of mental disorders required for reimbursement, which can put both practitioner and client in a precarious position—the practitioner who might feel compelled to diagnose a client to get paid, and the client who may have difficulty obtaining insurance coverage in the future if diagnosed with a serious mental health disorder. Yet despite the criticism of the DSM-IV-TR, it remains the most well-researched, collaborative classification system for mental pathology currently in existence and does provide a means for organizing various emotional problems and mental disorders.

Many human service professionals use the DSM-IV-TR but in general rely on it less than other mental health disciplines because the human services profession is based on empowerment theory, where clients are encouraged to recognize that they have more control over their lives than they may have previously thought. Self-determination is a related concept and refers to the rights of all individuals to make choices that they believe are in their own best interest. Self-determination can be empowering as clients realize that they have learned to have good judgment, which increases their sense of competency and self-reliance.

Continuum of Mental Health

Another important consideration when evaluating someone's level of functioning and mental health status is to recognize that virtually all behaviors occur on a continuum. It is only when a particular behavior occurs frequently enough, and at an intensity level high enough to interfere with normal daily functioning for a significant amount of time, that this behavior becomes the subject of clinical attention. All of us feel sad at times, but if we are so intensely sad that we stop eating and want to stay in bed all day, then we may be suffering from clinical depression. Similarly, many of us become concerned from time to time that our friends might be talking behind our backs, or that one of our coworkers is trying to get us fired, but if we're convinced that everyone is out to get us, even people we've never met, then we may be suffering from some form of paranoia.

The DSM-IV-TR accounts for this continuum by including criteria relating to frequency and intensity of psychological experiences. For instance, to meet the criteria for Major Depressive Disorder, an individual does not just have to be depressed, but he must have a depressed mood nearly every day for at least a two-week period. An individual who meets the criteria for Generalized Anxiety Disorder isn't someone who worries from time to time, but is someone who worries *excessively,* more days than not, for at least six months.

In summary, the value of services provided depends on the effectiveness of the assessment. A good assessment defines the problem or problems the client is experiencing, develops a needs assessment to determine where the client's strengths and deficits lie, ascertains the client's social support system, and develops an appropriate treatment plan. It is also important to reassess the client at various points in the counseling process, to monitor new or previously masked issues, and to make sure that treatment goals are consistent with the assessment.

Case Management and Counseling

It is important to understand the qualitative differences between case management and counseling services. Although both encompass a broad range of activities, they are distinctly different. Counseling is focused more on an individual's psychological growth and the development of emotional insight and personal growth, whereas case management involves coordinating services with other systems impacting the life of the client. A case manager might coordinate services with a client's school social worker, the housing authority, the local rape crisis center, or even a court liaison, all in an attempt to meet the needs of the client who is interacting in some manner with each of these systems. The goal of the case manager is to assist the client in plugging in to necessary and supportive social services within the community and to learn how to improve the reciprocal relationship or transaction with each of these social systems. These efforts have many purposes and goals, but chief among them is the caseworker's proactive attempt to strengthen and broaden the client's social support network. The NASW provides the following definition of case management:

> Social work case management is a method of providing services whereby a professional social worker assesses the needs of the client and the client's family, when appropriate, and arranges, coordinates, monitors, evaluates, and advocates for a package of multiple services to meet the specific client's complex needs. A professional social worker is the primary provider of social work case management. Distinct from other forms of case management, social work case management addresses both the individual client's biopsychosocial status as well as the state of the social system in which case management operates. Social work case management is both micro and macro in nature: intervention occurs at both the client and system levels. It requires the social worker to develop and maintain a therapeutic relationship with the client, which may include linking the client with systems that provide him or her with needed services, resources, and opportunities. Services provided under the rubric of social work case management practice may be located in a single agency or may be spread across numerous agencies or organizations. (NASW, 2002)

Basic Counseling Techniques for Generalist Practice

Although the assessment process is ongoing, once the initial assessment is complete a treatment plan is developed that is designed to address the client's identified issues. I will cover counseling techniques appropriate for clients served in particular practice settings in more detail in subsequent chapters, but there are basic techniques involved in generalist practice that apply in a broad way to most counseling and intervention situations.

Many individuals seeking services at a human services agency will need assistance with developing better coping skills. Regardless of whether the problems experienced by the client are pervasive or more limited, most clients can benefit from learning to manage high levels of stress, learning to prioritize the various problems in their lives, and learning how to manage the current crisis in a way that diminishes the possibility of a domino effect of crises. A crisis with one's child requiring a significant amount of time and attention can quickly result in a job loss, which can in turn result in the loss of housing. Confronting crises effectively, though, can have a positive impact on one's life, including an increase in self-esteem, the development of new and more effective coping skills, the gaining of wisdom and the development of new social skills, and the development of a better overall support system.

Most mental health experts recognize that one of the best opportunities for personal growth is a crisis, due to the possibility of shaking up long-standing and entrenched maladaptive patterns of behavior. Park and Fenster (2004) studied stress-related growth in a group of college students who experienced a stressful event and found that the struggle involved in a life crisis produced personal growth. This is only true, though, for those who expend the necessary energy to work through their struggles in a positive way. Those in the study who remain negative and avoided dealing with the problems borne out of the crisis did not take advantage of the growth-producing opportunities and thus did not experience any significant personal growth. Those who worked hard to manage the stress resulting from their crisis and were able to see the crisis as an opportunity for growth often developed better personal mastery skills and developed a changed and healthier perspective. Recognizing this potential for personal growth provides the practitioner with a framework for assisting clients in developing better coping skills that can better assist them in the management of concrete problems, but can also help them to shift their entire perspective of life struggles in general. For instance, clients who once saw themselves as powerless victims can begin to see themselves as empowered survivors.

Task-Centered Casework

When most individuals are confronted with a crisis, panic sets in, and it becomes difficult to address the problem in a healthy or meaningful way. Most of us can relate to feeling completely overwhelmed when facing a life crisis. We know there are things we need to do to manage the crisis, but all we see is a gigantic mountain looming before us. For some, this has a motivating effect, and they attack the mountain until every issue is resolved. But for some, particularly those with a long history of crises, those with poor coping skills, or those suffering from emotional or psychological problems with diminished personal management skills, the mountain can seem virtually insurmountable, and their response is to shrink away with a feeling of despair and defeat.

A counseling technique called the *Task-Centered Approach,* an intervention strategy developed by the School of Social Services at the University of Illinois (Reid, 1975), works well with clients who feel paralyzed in response to the challenges of various psychosocial problems. Treatment is typically short, lasting anywhere between two to four months, and is focused on problem solving. The client and counselor or caseworker define the problems together and develop mutually agreed-upon goals. Each problem is broken down into smaller and more easily manageable tasks. Goals can be as tangible as finding a new job or as intangible as more effectively managing frustration and anger. Rather than having one broad goal of obtaining a job, a client might have a week-one goal of doing nothing more than looking at the want ads in the local newspaper, a week-two goal of making one phone call to a prospective employer. Dividing large goals into smaller, specific, "stepping-stone" goals diminishes the possibility that clients will allow their anxiety to overwhelm them. By focusing on specific problems and breaking them into "bite-sized," manageable pieces, clients not only learn effective problem-solving skills, but also gain insight into the nature of their problems, develop increased self-esteem as they experience success rather than failure in response to meeting goal expectations, and learn to manage their emotions such as anxiety and depression, without allowing such states to overtake and overwhelm them.

The counselor or caseworker assists clients in meeting goal expectations through a variety of intervention strategies specific to the actual problem, but can include planning for obstacles, role-playing (where the client can actually act out difficult situations in the safety of the counselor's office as a way of practicing communication, etc.), and mental rehearsal (similar to role-playing but involves the client thinking or fantasizing about some specific situation—such as an upcoming job interview or a difficult confrontation) (Reid, 1975). Revisiting original goals and evaluating client progress are also powerful tools in helping clients experience a sense of personal mastery and empowerment as they are helped to recognize their progress.

Consider the following case study below.

---

case study 3.1

Case Example of Task-Centered Approach

Mary is the 34-year-old single parent of a 5-year-old boy. She has been living with her mother since her own divorce three years ago. This is a negative situation because her mother is verbally abusive of Mary and her son, abuses alcohol, and smokes inside the home. In addition, their living space is small, and Mary and her son share a bedroom. Mary's original goal was to live with her mother for only six months, but whenever she considers moving out she becomes overwhelmed with the prospect of not only finding an appropriate apartment, but of finding child care as well, because despite her mother's abusive behavior, Mary has been relying on her mother for before- and after-school child care while she works. Mary feels trapped but completely powerless to do anything about her situation. During Mary's intake interview she described her prior counseling experiences, sharing that she quit counseling because whenever she was faced with the prospect of finding an apartment her fears would snowball into so many fears that she simply couldn't even bring herself to make the first phone call in search of housing. She ended up feeling embarrassed, as if she were letting the counselor down, and just decided she could not deal with any more failures, so she stopped going to counseling. Mary explained that throughout the past several years her mother has consistently reminded her that she would never make it out on her own, that she would surely fail, and that she would end up destroying her life and the life of her son. Her mother also told Mary that if she moved and ran out of money she would not bail her out again and would instead force Mary and her son to go to a shelter. Opening the newspaper to look for a rental advertisement resulted in a flood of worries and concerns—some specific and some she could not even put into words. She worried about everything from whether she would know what to say when calling on an apartment, to whether she be able to support herself and her son. What if she was laid off from her job and could no longer afford her apartment and had to live in a shelter? What if she couldn't find a babysitter she could afford? What if she found an apartment and got a babysitter, but the babysitter ended up abusing her son worse than her mother did? She read about such things all the time in the newspaper, she reasoned. Or what if she found an apartment, but she had a financial emergency such as her car breaking down, and she started falling behind in her rent and was evicted? She couldn't fathom the thought of moving out and then having to move back in with her mother again, or worse what if her mother made good on her threat and refused to allow them to move back in with her? Once confronted with this slippery slope of catastrophizing, she would resist even taking the first step toward independence and could not bring herself to even look at rental ads. Mary's mood became increasingly melancholy over the years, and after years of verbal abuse from her mother, her ex-husband, and now her mother again, she had no confidence in her ability to financially support her own son or even to manage her own life without her mother's assistance. Mary's caseworker reassured her that there was absolutely no rush in finding an apartment. In fact, she reminded Mary that she was in charge of her own life and could make the choices she thought were best for her and her son. During the first two sessions, Mary and her caseworker developed realistic goals for her, including securing an apartment when Mary had the funds to ensure financial security. Mary and her caseworker developed a detailed budget and determined that she would need three months salary put away in a savings account to ensure against any realistic financial emergencies. By identifying possible obstacles to Mary achieving independence, decisions were made based on facts and realistic risks, not on undefined and generalized fear. Once goals were developed and obstacles identified, Mary and her caseworker agreed on tasks to be accomplished by the following week. Mary's task for the first week was to look through the newspaper and circle rental advertisements within her price range. She was not to call any of them though, even if she found one that seemed ideal. Mary came in the second week with the newspaper filled with circled apartment ads. Mary and her caseworker spent the first portion of the session discussing how Mary felt while circling these ads. Mary explained that her initial excitement was quickly followed by intense anxiety, but that when she realized she could not call the apartments even if she had wanted to, she calmed down almost immediately. The next portion of the session was spent on determining tasks for the following week. The first task included circling all appropriate ads and calling on two apartments for informational purposes only. Because Mary had a significant amount of anxiety about calling and talking to a stranger, Mary and her caseworker wrote a script and rehearsed it by doing a role-play with her caseworker playing the part of the potential landlord. Mary's additional task for the week was to talk to her boss seeking reassurance that her employment was secure. Mary returned the following week excited. She called on two apartments and followed the script on the first one, but the second call went so well she did not even need the script. Her discussion with her boss also went well, and he reassured her that her job was secure. Mary shared excitedly that her boss was pleased that Mary showed assertiveness in approaching him and offered her an opportunity to attend some training courses so that she could be promoted. For the next three months Mary's counseling proceeded in a similar fashion with weekly tasks that inched her along slowly enough that she did not become overwhelmed by unreasonable fears, but quickly enough that she gained confidence and courage with each successive step. Mary rented an apartment during her fourth month of counseling with three months income safely tucked away in a savings account, a promotion with a raise, and reputable and affordable day care.

Perceptual Reframing, Emotional Regulation, Networking, and Advocacy

Another general counseling method includes the **reframing** of a client's perception of a situation emphasizing the importance of viewing various events, relationships, and occurrences from a variety of possible perspectives. For some reason it seems easier for human beings to assume the negative in many situations. Whether considering the intentions of a boyfriend or the prospects of getting a better job, most of us seem to gravitate toward negative assumptions. Many people in the midst of a physical or emotional crisis of any proportion will often resort to taking a somewhat polarized negative stance on an issue and would benefit from assistance in seeing situations and relationships from a different perspective. A client's perception that life is unfair and nothing good ever happens to her can be encouraged to see life struggles as normal and even good because they promote positive personal growth. A client who feels shame because he was recently fired from a job he despised can be encouraged to see this incident as a disguised blessing opening the door for him to find a career for which he is far better suited.

Additional intervention goals include assisting clients with *emotional regulation* teaching them how to sit with their emotions rather than immediately acting on them, developing a better *social support network* so that they can become emotionally independent and self-reliant, and *advocating for clients* who are being oppressed, either within their family systems or in society in general.

Concluding Thoughts on Generalist Practice

Although human service professionals work with a very wide range of clients presenting with an equally diverse range of psychosocial problems, these skills and intervention techniques can be broadly applied in generalist practice. Understanding that people are not pathological by nature, but often are responding to real traumas, tragedies, and crises in a natural way (for example, it is normal to become depressed after experiencing a loss) helps the human service professional look for a client's strengths, rather than solely assessing a client's perceived deficits.

The unique nature of the human services profession encourages practitioners to view the individual as a part of a greater whole, thus a client's social world is assessed and evaluated, which enables human service professionals to help their clients better navigate their world. Essentially, it is the human service professional's commitment to working with displaced populations, assessing not only clients but the worlds they live in, and applying various intervention techniques designed to encourage, empower, and integrate some of society's most broken and marginalized members helping them to become whole and functional, perhaps for the first time in their lives.

r e f e r e n c e s

American Psychiatric Association. (2000). *Diagnostic and statistical manual of mental disorders* (4th ed., Text Revision) (DSM-IV-TR). Washington, DC: American Psychiatric Association.

Bowen, M. (1978). *Family therapy in clinical practice.* New York: Jason Aronson.

Cloud, H. C. & Townsend, J. (1992). *Boundaries.* Grand Rapids, MI: Zondervan.

Duffy, M., Gillig, S. E., Tureen, R. M. & Ybarra, M. A. (2002). A critical look at the DSM-IV-TR. *The Journal of Individual Psychology, 58(4),* 362–373.

Escalas, J. E. & Stern, B. B. (2003). Sympathy and empathy: Emotional responses to advertising dramas. *Journal of Consumer Research, 29,* 566–578.

Greenberg, L. S., Elliot, R., Watson, J. C. & Bohart, A. C. (2001). Empathy. *Psychotherapy: Theory, Research, Practice, Training, 38(4),* 380–384.

National Association of Social Workers. (2000). *Code of ethics of the National Association of Social Workers.* Retrieved March 28, 2006, from http://www.naswdc.org/pubs/code/default.asp.

National Association of Social Workers. (2002). *NASW standards for social work case management.* Retrieved on May 25, 2004, from http://www.naswdc.org/practice/standards/sw_case_mgmt.asp#intro

Park, C. L. & Fenster, J. R. (2004). Stress-related growth: Predictors of occurrence and correlates with psychological adjustment. *Journal of Social and Clinical Psychology, 23(2),* 195–215.

Prest, L. A. & Protinsky, H. (1993). Family systems theory: A unifying framework for codependency. *The American Journal of Family Therapy, 21(4),* 352–360.

Reid, W. J. (1975). A test of a task-centered approach. *Social Work,* 20(1), 3–9.

suggested reading

Bowen, M. (1985). *Family therapy in clinical practice.* New York: Jason Aronson.

Epstein, L. & Brown, L. B. (2001). *Brief treatment and a new look at the task-centered approach.* Boston: Allyn & Bacon.

Fulero, S. M. (1988). Tarasoff: Ten years later. *Professional Psychology,* 19, 84–90.

Nash, K. A. & Velazquez, J. (2003). *Cultural competence: A guide for human service agencies.* Atlanta, GA: CWLA Press.

Reamer, F. G. (2005). *Pocket guide to essential human services.* Washington, DC: NASW Press.

Russo, J. R. (2000). *Serving and surviving as a human-service worker.* Long Grove, IL: Waveland Press.

Tarasoff v. Regents of the University of California, 118 Cal. Rptr. 129, 529 P.2d.533 (Cal. 1974).

Tarasoff v. Regents of the University of California, 113 Cal. Rptr. 14, 551 P.2d.334 (Cal. 1976).

Wodarksi, J. S., Rapp-Paglicci, L. A., Dulmus, C. N. & Jongsma, A. E. *The social work and human services treatment planner.* Hoboken, NJ: John Wiley & Sons.

internet web sites related to generalist practice

American Counseling Association: **http://www.counseling.org**

Genograms: **http://www.genopro.com/genogram/**

chapter 4

Child and Family Services

Overview and Purpose of Child and Family Services Agencies

The field of child and family services generally involves the care and provision of children who cannot be appropriately cared for by their biological parents, as well as providing assistance for those who need support and assistance in the management and provision of their families. This practice setting is primarily concerned with children in foster care placement, but may also involve family preservation services and adoption services as well. A human service professional working in a child and family services setting may be involved in the following activities:

- ▶ Child abuse investigations
- ▶ Child abuse assessments
- ▶ Case management and counseling of the child in placement, foster families and biological parents
- ▶ Case management and counseling of families in crisis
- ▶ Case management and counseling of potential adoptive parents, adult adoptees, and birth parents

The clinical issues involved in this field are quite broad but involve issues related to abandonment and loss, posttraumatic stress disorder (PTSD), cultural sensitivity, child development, parenting issues, substance abuse, anger management, and the ability to work with a broad range of life stressors and maladaptive responses that might lead to breakdowns within the family.

In addition to the wide range of activities in which a human service professional might engage within a child and family services agency, there is also a wide range of practice settings where one might work, the largest being a state's child protective services agency (CPS). Human service professionals also work at not-for-profit agencies, some of which are contracted by the state to provide mandated services to children in substitute care, and some of which provide voluntary services to any family in crisis. Within these agencies a human service professional may be involved in a number of activities, including counseling, case management, and writing grants for increased funding. Many human service professionals working in the field of child welfare may do so on a volunteer basis, and although these individuals are not paid professionals, the work they do is so vital, their role in the welfare of children must be mentioned. For instance, CASA (court appointed special advocates) volunteers are court-appointed advocates for children who are placed into state care, working to protect the best interest of the child by being their voice in all court proceedings.

The History of the Foster Care System in the United States

The child welfare system in the United States has undergone significant changes in the last several hundred years due to numerous factors such as urbanization, industrialization, immigration, mass life-threatening illness, changes within the family system, changing social mores (including the reduction of shame associated with divorce, out-of-wedlock births, and single parenting by choice), and the eventual availability of government financial assistance for those in need. Thus, to truly understand the current child welfare system it is vital to understand its past.

In 2001 ABC's news show *Nightline* aired a documentary featuring the horrible plight of the street children of Romania (Belzberg, 2001). After the show, U.S. citizens flooded the network with telephone calls, expressing outrage and horror at the images that flashed across their television screens for almost two hours. The documentary revealed children as young as six living on the streets, with no food to eat, with only slightly older children and liquid glue to keep them warm at night. The reporter explained how political events in Romania created a situation where impoverished families could no longer care for their offspring, thus the streets became flooded with marauding children, in desperate search of money and food. These children, who often resorted to pickpocketing and other petty crimes were considered by most mainstream Romanians to be the scourge of society, pests to be avoided.

The U.S. response was one of literal horror, not only at the conditions in which the children were forced to live but also at the apparent apathy of most Romanians, particularly those in government, including the Romanian police force. The documentary showed numerous incidences of police mistreatment, including one young boy whose leg was broken in a scuffle with a police officer. This seeming indifference shocked viewers, who expressed outrage at the heartlessness necessary to not only accept orphans living on the street, but to actually perceive these orphans as social pariahs. These concerned and outraged Americans are apparently unaware that our own recent past includes alarmingly similar conditions and attitudes toward orphans, with only 150 to 200 years separating the United States from Romania in this regard.

The U.S. Orphan Problem

The United States also experienced several waves of political, economic, and environmental tragedies that resulted in strikingly similar conditions as those experienced in Romania today. During the 1700s and 1800s in particular attitudes toward children were harsh, and many orphaned or uncared for children roamed the streets, particularly in growing urban areas such as New York. These street children were often treated harshly and punitively. If children were on the streets because their parents were destitute, they were often sent to almshouses, regardless of their harsh conditions, to work alongside their homeless parents. Many homeless and orphaned children were forced into a form of indentured servitude called "apprenticeships," which taught them a trade and provided cheap labor during an era that saw many economic depressions and a shortage of available workers (Katz, 1996).

The plight of the orphan did not appear to tug at the heartstrings of the average U.S. citizen during that era, both because of the vast amount of abandoned and orphaned children (which appears to have a desensitizing affect on the human psyche), but also because during the seventeenth through the middle of the nineteenth century, children were not perceived to be in need of special nurturing, because childhood was not considered a distinct stage of development until years later. The influence of Puritanical religious thought as well as the general mores of the times led to the common belief that children needed to be treated with harsh discipline or they would fall victim to sinful behaviors such as laziness and vice (Trattner, 1998).

A significant shift in child welfare policy occurred in the mid-1800s, though, when the Civil War left thousands of children orphaned, making tragedy a visitor in some respect to virtually every U.S. family. Coinciding with this increase in concern over the plight of the disadvantaged child was a dramatic shift in the way children on the whole were viewed. The development of the field of psychology in the first quarter of the twentieth century, as well as a transition in religious thought toward a more compassionate and loving God, led to the emerging belief that children were essentially good by nature and needed to be treated with kindness, love, and nurturing to enhance their development and ultimate potential as adults (Trattner, 1998).

In addition to these changes, the **Industrial Revolution** reduced the need for apprenticeship, and at the same time stories of abhorrent conditions and mass abuse in almshouses (particularly involving abuses against children) were being widely reported. Settlement house workers, COSs, and government officials alike were eager to address the problem of orphaned and abused children in the latter part of the nineteenth century, and the most commonly suggested solution was the creation of institutions designed solely for the care of orphaned and needy children.

The Orphan Asylum

Although some orphanages existed in the 1700s, they did not become the primary means for handling needy and orphaned children until the middle to late 1800s, and by the 1890s there were more than 600 orphanages in existence in the United States (Trattner, 1998). Orphanages, or orphan asylums as they were often called, did not house just children who lost both parents to death, but also became the solution for many of the economic and environmental conditions of the time. Even though mortality rates were down in both the United States and Europe during the Industrial age (Condran & Cheney, 1982) several factors existed that resulted in the increasing need for orphanages.

Poor safety conditions in factories resulted in a relatively high prevalence of work-related injuries and death among the poorest members of society, leaving many children orphaned or fatherless. Coupled with this was a significant influx of poor immigrants in the late 1800s and early 1900s resulting in a vulnerable segment of society often not having an extended family on which to rely in cases of parental death or disability. This was often true of recently emigrated families, who left their extended families behind in their venture to the New World.

Families who were for whatever reason suddenly unable to support their children could leave them in the temporary care of an orphanage for a small fee, but if they missed some monthly payments, the children would become wards of the state, and the parents would lose all legal rights to them (Trattner, 1998). In addition, although infectious disease was nothing new to colonial America, several infectious disease epidemics spread through urban United States between the mid-1800s and the early part of the 1900s, including smallpox, influenza, yellow fever, cholera, typhoid, and scarlet fever, leaving many children orphaned (Condran & Cheney, 1982).

Although the orphanage system was originally perceived as a significant improvement over placing children in almshouses or forcing them into indentured servitude, these institutions were not without their share of trouble, and in time reports of harsh treatment and abuses were common in orphanages as well. Although some orphanages were government run, most were privately run with governmental funding, but had little if any oversight or accountability. Because the government paid on a per child basis, there was a financial incentive to run large operations, with some orphanages housing as many as 2,000 children under one roof. Obedience was highly valued in these institutions out of sheer necessity, whereas individuality, play, and creativity were discouraged through strict discipline and harsh punishment (Trattner, 1998).

The next wave of child welfare reform involved the gradual shift from institutionalized care to the substitute family foster care system, or the placing-out of children into private homes prompted by the development of compulsory public education, which meant that the education of an orphan was no longer linked with the provision of housing.

The Seeds of Foster Care: The Orphan Trains

Have you ever wondered where the expression "farming kids out" came from? The origin of this term is rooted in what is called the Orphan Train movement, a program developed by the first agency to utilize in-home placement rather than institutionalized care. The New York Children's Aid Society was founded by Rev. Charles Loring Brace, who recognized the serious problem of children growing up on the streets of New York due to several tragic events from the middle of the nineteenth century. Brace estimated that as many as 5,000 children were homeless and forced to roam the streets in search of money, food, and shelter. Brace was shocked at the cruel indifference of most New Yorkers, who called these children "Street Arabs" with "bad blood." He was also appalled at reports of children as young as five years old being arrested for vagrancy (Bellingham, 1984; Brace, 1967).

Many factors contributed to the serious orphan problem in New York. Historians estimate that approximately 1,000 immigrants flooded New York on a daily basis in the mid-1800s (Von Hartz, 1978). Mass urbanization remained the trend with poor rural families flocking to the cities looking for factory work. Industry safety standards were essentially nonexistent, thus factory-related deaths were at an all-time high. An outbreak of typhoid fever also left many children orphaned or half-orphaned with new widows who had virtually no way to support their children because government aid was not yet available. These harsh social conditions, coupled with the absence of any organized governmental subsidy, left many children to fend for themselves on the streets of New York, resorting to any means for survival.

Brace feared that the temptations of street life would preclude any possibility that these children would grow up to be God-fearing, responsible adults, and he reasoned that children who had no parents, or whose parents could no longer care for them, would be far better off living in the clean open spaces of the farming communities out west, where fresh air and the need for workers were plentiful. Because the rail lines were rapidly opening up the West, Brace developed an innovative program where children would be loaded onto trains and taken west to good Christian farming families. Notices were sent in advance of train arrivals, and communities along the train line would come out and meet the train, so that families who had expressed an interest in taking one or more children could examine the children and take them right then, if they desired. Brace convened committees who would interview families to ensure that they met the standards for qualified adoptive or foster families.

Survivors of these orphan trains have talked about how they felt like cattle, being paraded across a stage. Interested foster parents would often feel the children's muscles and check their teeth before deciding what child they would take. Few parents would take more than one child, thus siblings were most often split up, sometimes without even a passing comment made by the child care agents or the new parents (Patrick, Sheets, & Trickel, 1990). It was almost as if the breaking of lifelong family

■ Typical wanted advertisement posted throughout the Midwest by the Children's Home and Aid Society between 1854 and 1929.

bonds were considered trivial compared to the gift these children were receiving by being rescued from their hopeless existence on the streets.

Most children were not legally adopted, but were placed with a family under an indentured contract, which served two purposes. First, this type of contract allowed the placement agency to take the children back if something went wrong with the placement. Second, children placed under an indentured contract could not inherit property, thus farming families could adopt boys to work on the farm or girls to assist with the housework, but didn't have to worry about them inheriting the family assets (Trattner, 1998; Warren, 1995).

■ Children on the Orphan Train

The orphan trains ran from 1854 to 1929, delivering approximately 150,000 children to new homes across the west, from the midwestern states to Texas, and even as far west as California. Whether this social experiment was a glowing success or a miserable failure (or somewhere in between) depends on who one asks. Some children were placed in wonderful, loving homes and grew up to be happy and responsible adults, who feel strongly that the Orphan Trains were a true blessing. But other survivors of the Orphan Trains shared stories of heartache and abuse. Some tell stories of lives no better than that of slaves, where they were taken in by families for no other reason than to provide hard labor for the cost of bed and board. Others tell stories of having siblings torn from their sides as families chose one child, leaving brothers and sisters on the train. And still others tell stories of failed adoptions, where farming families exercised their one-year return option, sending the children back to the orphanage, or allowing the children to drift from farm to farm to earn their keep (Holt, 1992).

Eventually new child welfare practices caught up with new child development theories leading to a general focus shifting from one of work virtue to one of valuing childhood play. By the early twentieth century the practice of "farming out" children received increasing criticism, and the last trainload of children was delivered to its many destinations in 1929. Despite the controversy surrounding the Orphan Train movement and the many similar outplacement programs that followed across the country, even its harshest critics agreed that it was a far better alternative than allowing children to fend for themselves on the streets of New York. Also, despite the program's many shortcoming including poor oversight and insufficient screening of the families, it is considered the forerunner of the current foster care system in the United States, where children are placed in available private homes, rather than in institutions (Trattner, 1998).

Overview of the Current U.S. Child Welfare System

Caring for orphaned and abused children has slowly transitioned from institutionalized care, to primarily substitute family care, or foster care over the past 100 years. By 1980, virtually no children remained in institutionalized care in the United States, excluding group homes, treatment centers, and homes for developmentally disabled children (Shughart & Chappell, 1998). Government public assistance programs, which developed in the 1960s, reduced the necessity for the removal of children from their homes due to poverty, because single mothers now had someplace to go for financial help in raising their children (Trattner, 1998).

The demographic makeup of children currently in the foster care system differs considerably from the children institutionalized in orphanages in the 1800s, as well as the children of the Orphan Train era. Thus, gone are the days where the majority of children being placed into substitute care were orphaned due to industrial accidents, war, or illness. Instead, the majority of children currently in child protective custody have been removed from their homes due to serious maltreatment. Also, unlike earlier eras when orphanage placements were most often permanent, almost half of all children currently in foster care have the goal of reunifying with their biological parents (U.S. Department of Health and Human Services, 2005).

In 2003 (the most recent statistics available) there were approximately 523,000 children in the U.S. foster care system. Table 4.1 shows the demographic breakdown of children in foster care placement as of 2003, revealing that the greatest number of children in foster care placement are between the ages of 11 and 15 years, followed by children ages 1 through 5. The majority of children are in nonrelative foster care placement. The median length of stay in foster care is about 18 months, but it appears that if children aren't placed in the first 18 months of placement, chances increase that children will remain in placement for several years (U.S. Department of Health and Human Services, 2005).

The U.S. child welfare system exists to provide a safety net for children and families in crisis. A primary goal of the foster care system is to reunite foster care children

■ **Table 4.1** The AFCARS Reports Children in Foster Care

Preliminary FY 2003 Estimates as of April 2005 (10)
How many children were in foster care on September 30, 2003? 523,000

Ages of the children in foster care

Mean Years	10.2	
Median Years	10.9	
Under 1 Year	5%	25,070
1 thru 5 Years	25%	129,470
6 thru 10 Years	21%	108,500
11 thru 15 Years	30%	154,970
16 thru 18 Years	18%	93,810
19 Years or More	2%	9,690

Placement settings of children in foster care

Preadoptive Home	5%	24,650
Foster Family Home (Relative)	23%	121,030
Foster Family Home (Nonrelative)	46%	239,810
Group Home	9%	45,700
Institution	10%	51,370
Supervised Independent Living	1%	5,570
Runaway	2%	10,560
Trial Home Visit	4%	19,700

Lengths of stay in foster care

Mean Months	31	
Median Months	18	
Less than 1 Month	5%	23,950
1 to 5 Months	18%	93,900

Case goals of the children in foster care

Reunify with Parent(s) or Principal Caretaker(s)	48%	246,650
Live with Other Relative(s)	5%	24,090
Adoption	20%	103,460
Long-Term Foster Care	8%	43,250
Emancipation	6%	31,370
Guardianship	3%	15,470
Case Plan Goal Not Yet Established	10%	48,530

(continued)

■ **Table 4.1**   *(continued)*

Race/ethnicity of the children in foster care		
AI/AN Non-Hispanic	2%	10,260
Asian—Non-Hispanic	1%	3,280
Black—Non-Hispanic	35%	184,480
Hawaiian/PI—Non-Hispanic	0%	1,540
Hispanic	17%	91,040
White—Non-Hispanic	39%	203,920
Unknown/Unable to Determine	3%	13,360
Two or More—Non-Hispanic	3%	14,310
Gender of the children in foster care		
Male	53%	274,820
Female	48%	248,150

Source: U.S. Department of Health and Human Services, Administration for Children and Families, Administration on Children, Youth and Families, Children's Bureau, www.acf.hhs.gov/programs/cb

with their biological parents whenever possible (Sanchirico & Jablonka, 2000). Federal and state laws have established three basic goals for children in its child welfare system:

▶ *Safety* from abuse and neglect
▶ *Permanency* in a stable, loving home (preferably with the biological parents)
▶ *Well-being* of the child with regard to his physical health, mental health, and developmental and educational needs

How these goals are met depends on the specific issues involved in each case, but before these various alternatives are considered, it is important to understand how a child enters the child welfare system in the first place.

Getting into the System

So, how does a child end up in foster care? Made-for-television movies might have the public thinking that child welfare workers have the power to remove children from homes with minimal evidence of abuse. Yet in reality several criteria must be met to place a child into protective custody, and a child cannot be removed from a family home without a judge's approval. The U.S. Constitution guarantees certain liberties to parents by giving them the right to parent their child in the manner they see fit. But such liberties are balanced by the parents' duty to protect their child's safety and ensure their well-being. If parents cannot or will not protect their children from *significant* harm, the state has the legal obligation to intervene (Goldman & Salus, 2003).

The U.S. Congress has passed several pieces of legislation that support the state's obligation to protect its youngest residents, including *The Child Abuse Prevention and Treatment Act (CAPTA) of 1974,* which was established to ensure that children of maltreatment are reported to the appropriate authorities. This act (which was most recently amended in 2003 with the *Keeping Children and Families Safe Act*) also provides minimum standards for definitions of the different types of child maltreatment. The *Adoption Assistance and Child Welfare Act of 1980* requires that states develop supportive programs and procedures enabling maltreated children to remain in their own homes and to assist family reunification following out-of-home placements.

Other legislation is aimed at (1) improving court efficiency so that child abuse cases will not languish in the court system for years, (2) providing assistance to foster care children approaching their 18th birthday, and (3) bolstering family preservation programs designed as an early intervention program in the hopes of circumventing out-of-home placement (Goldman & Salus, 2003).

In 1997 the president signed into law the *Adoption and Safe Families Act,* which amended and made improvements to the *Adoption Assistance and Child Welfare Act of 1980.* Among the amendments the act provides are incentives for families adopting children in the foster care system and mandates that states provide evidence of adoption efforts. Amendments also set a new accelerated time line for terminating the rights of parents whose children are in foster care placement. As we will see in subsequent sections of this chapter, there are both positive and negative aspects of this legislation. Certainly no one wants abused and neglected children to languish in temporary placement, but expediting the finding of permanent homes should not be at the expense of biological parents' rights to have an appropriate amount of time to meet the state's criteria for regaining the custody of their children. Balancing the rights of the biological parents with the best interest of their child is challenging, particularly in light of the complexity involved in many foster care cases.

Child Abuse Investigations

Mandated Reporters

There are several ways that a child abuse investigation may be initiated, but all have their origin in a concern that a child is being mistreated in some manner. Many professionals, such as counselors, teachers, physicians, and even Sunday school teachers are required by law to call their state's child abuse hotline immediately if they suspect that a child is being abused or neglected. *Mandated reporters* typically fall into one of several categories and include professionals who work with children as a part of their normal work duties. Mandated reporters include personnel in the following fields: medical, schools, social service, mental health, law enforcement, child care, and members of the clergy.

Most states have strict laws that define the parameters of child abuse reporting, including delineating what constitutes a reportable concern, the time frame in which a mandated reporter must report the suspected abuse, and the consequences of failing to report suspected abuse, such as the suspension of one's professional license. In fact, in most states, the failure to comply with mandated reporting requirements is a crime (a misdemeanor or even a felony for repeated failures). In many states, the majority of calls made to the child abuse hotline are from mandated reporters, but this does not preclude anyone from calling the child abuse hotline if they suspect that a child is being abused or neglected by a parent or caregiver. Thus, it is not uncommon for neighbors, friends, or even relatives to report suspected child abuse, and those who are not mandated reporters are allowed to call anonymously.

Sequence of Events in the Reporting and Investigation of Child Abuse

A child abuse investigation is initiated when someone, either a concerned individual or a mandated reporter, places a call to the state child abuse hotline. Due to the intrusive nature of an abuse investigation, federal and state laws exist to protect the privacy of family life. Thus hotline workers must adhere to strict guidelines regarding what reports can and cannot be accepted. If the report of alleged abuse meets the stated criteria, then the report will be accepted and investigated in a timely manner.

For state CPS agencies to receive federal funding, the federal law mandates that all child abuse reports be screened immediately and investigated in a timely manner (Child Abuse Prevention and Treatment Act, 2003). Although federal law does not specify a particular time frame, most states have compliance laws stipulating specific guidelines mandating that reports of abuse be investigated anywhere from immediately after receiving a report for cases involving imminent risk, to 10 days in some states for reports with moderate to minimal risk to the child (Kopel, Charlton, & Well, 2003).

Once a hotline worker makes the decision to accept a child abuse report, the case is sent to the appropriate regional agency and assigned to an abuse investigator, who is a licensed social worker or other licensed human service professional. The actual investigation will vary depending on the specific circumstances of the allegations, but most investigations will involve interviewing the child, the nonoffending parent(s), and the alleged perpetrator. Although the sequence of the interviews might alter depending on the specific circumstances of the case, most investigators prefer to interview the child before the parents or caregivers to avoid the potential for influencing or intimidating the child.

Types of Child Maltreatment

Child maltreatment is a crime regardless of who the perpetrator is and should always be reported to authorities, but a state's CPS agency becomes involved when the abuse is perpetrated by someone who is acting in a caregiving role to the child. This includes a parent, a relative, a parent's boyfriend or girlfriend, a teacher, or even a babysitter.

Although each state is charged with the responsibility for defining child abuse and neglect according to state statute, the federal government has developed a definition of what constitutes the minimum standard for child abuse and neglect and has created four general categories of child maltreatment, including neglect, physical abuse, sexual abuse, and emotional abuse. The following is the U.S. Health and Human Services' definition of each type of abuse, but again it is important to remember that each state, although bound to this minimum standard, will likely have additional criteria and scenarios that qualify as abuse (National Clearinghouse on Child Abuse and Neglect Information, 2005).

Neglect is failure to provide for a child's basic needs. Neglect may be

▶ Physical (e.g., failure to provide necessary food or shelter, or lack of appropriate supervision)

▶ Medical (e.g., failure to provide necessary medical or mental health treatment)

▶ Educational (e.g., failure to educate a child or attend to special education needs)

▶ Emotional (e.g., inattention to a child's emotional needs, failure to provide psychological care, or permitting the child to use alcohol or other drugs)

Because cultural values, standards of care in the community, and poverty may be contributing factors related to caregiving challenges, the existence of some of these problems does not necessarily indicate that the legal abuse of a child is occurring. Rather, the manifestation of certain problems within a family system, such as not sending a child to school, may indicate an overwhelmed family's need for information and general assistance. Yet, if a family fails to utilize the information, assistance, and resources provided and the child's health or safety is determined to be at risk, then CPS intervention may be required.

Physical abuse includes physical injury (ranging from minor bruises to severe fractures or death) as a result of punching, beating, kicking, biting, shaking, throwing, stabbing, choking, hitting (with a hand, stick, strap, or other object), burning, or otherwise harming a child. An injury is considered abuse regardless of whether the caretaker intended to hurt the child.

Sexual abuse includes activities by a parent or caretaker that includes fondling a child's genitals, penetration, incest, rape, sodomy, indecent exposure, and exploitation through prostitution or the production of pornographic materials.

Emotional abuse involves a pattern of behavior that impairs a child's emotional development or sense of self-worth. This may include constant criticism, threats, or rejection, as well as withholding love, support, or guidance. Emotional abuse is often difficult to prove, and therefore, CPS may not be able to intervene without evidence of significant harm to the child. Emotional abuse is almost always present when other forms of abuse are identified.

The Forensic Interview

In the past 25 years, allegations of child abuse, particularly child sexual abuse, have sky-rocketed. Reasons for this include increased public awareness, mandatory reporting requirements, and a significant change in attitudes regarding child abuse, with an increasing sentiment that abuse is no longer a private family matter. Yet, as the pendulum swung, the 1970s witnessed a sort of frenzy in child sexual abuse reporting, and a popular contention among mental health experts was that children were incapable of making false allegations. This belief fostered a sense of overeagerness on the part of some therapists, who sometimes used inappropriate interviewing techniques, with leading ("Did he touch you on your privates?"), forced choice ("Did he touch you under your clothing, or over your clothing?"), option posing ("I heard that your uncle has been bothering you."), or suggestive questions ("Many kids at your school have said that your teacher has touched them, did he touch you too?").

Eventually this method of questioning was met with overwhelming criticism, particularly by members of the legal community, who were charged with defending those individuals falsely accused of sexually abusing children in their charge. These types of questions significantly increased the likelihood of erroneous disclosures, particularly with preschool-aged children (Hewitt, 1999; Peterson & Biggs, 1997; Poole & Lindsay, 1998).

In response to such criticism, CPS agencies across the country developed pilot programs that combined the resources from several investigative branches, including CPS agencies, police departments, and district attorneys offices. This coordinated approach not only prevents the trauma of duplicative interviews by separate enforcement agencies, but it also allows for the highly specialized training of investigators on forensic interviewing techniques that avoid any type of suggestive or leading questions.

Although there is a general understanding among investigators of what constitutes a forensic interview, there was still concern that many interviewers used types of questions that were somewhat leading in nature, including an interviewer's inadvertent reaction to a child's response that either encouraged or discouraged an honest disclosure. For instance, an investigator who strongly believes that a child has been abused may inadvertently respond with frustration if a child denies the abuse, which may influence the child, who wants to please the investigator, to give a false disclosure of abuse. Even an expression of sympathy on the part of the interviewer, in response to disclosures of abuse, can inadvertently encourage a child to embellish somewhat to receive more of the interviewer's compassion.

The National Institute of Child Health and Human Development (NICHD) developed a forensic interviewing protocol that teaches interviewers how to ask open-ended questions, using retrieval cues that rely on free recall. "Tell me everything you can remember," is an example of an open-ended question. "Tell me more about the room you were in," is an example of a retrieval cue (Bourg, Broderick, & Flagor, 1999; Sternberg, Lamb, & Orbach, 2001).

To Intervene, or Not Intervene: Models for Decision Making

Many variables influence the outcome of an investigation, including the criteria with which a CPS agency uses to determine (1) whether abuse is occurring, and (2) whether the abuse rises to the level of warranting intervention. In other words, it is possible for some abuse reports to be determined as *unfounded,* even though the investigator may strongly suspect that an unhealthy home environment does exist. But another reason for not substantiating an incident of child abuse relates more to poor or inconsistent decision-making policies within a CPS agency as they attempt to balance the dual roles of protecting children at risk and preserving the biological family. DePanfilis and Scannapieco (1994) discussed the vital importance of CPS agencies developing and adhering to a consistent and realistic decision-making model when determining whether family intervention is warranted. Child abuse investigators are responsible for:

1. Assessing the safety of children who are at risk of maltreatment,
2. Deciding what types and levels of services may be immediately needed to keep children safe, and
3. Determining under what conditions children must be placed in out-of-home care for their protection. (p. 229)

The *Child at Risk Field System,* a decision-making model that has been tested in the field, provides the following guidelines for abuse investigators making a determination about abuse:

Where children were determined to be maltreated and unsafe, the offending parents were

1. out of control,
2. frequently violent,
3. showed no remorse,
4. may actually request placement,
5. did not respond to previous attempts to intervene,
6. whereabouts were unknown.

7. the caseworker believed the parents were a flight risk,
8. the child had special needs the parents could not meet,
9. the conditions in the home are life-threatening, and/or,
10. the nonoffending parent could not protect the children.

Where children were determined to be maltreated and *safe*, the parents:

1. possessed a sufficient amount of impulse control,
2. accepted responsibility for the situation in their home,
3. had appropriate understanding of the child, showed concern for the child and remorse for the maltreatment,
4. had a history of accessing help and services, and
5. exhibited knowledge of good parenting skills.

Thus, although definitions of child maltreatment are statutorily defined, there is a tremendous amount of latitude that an investigator has in determining whether child maltreatment is occurring and whether the extent of the abuse warrants intervention. Primarily, it is through the use of an effective and well-tested decision-making model that an abuse investigator will have the greatest likelihood of making an appropriate determination in a child abuse investigation.

Working with Children in Placement

Permanency Plans

When an abuse investigator determines that a child must be placed into protective custody the child is removed from the home and placed in one of many environments, including relative foster care, nonrelative foster care, or an emergency shelter pending more permanent placement. The case is then transferred to a family caseworker, who evaluates all the relevant dynamics of the case (i.e., reason for placement, nature of abuse, attitude of the parents), as well as assessing the strengths and weaknesses of the biological parents and the family structure. A permanency goal for the child must then be determined and can include

1. Reunification with the biological parents
2. Living with relatives
3. Guardianship with close friends
4. Short-term or long-term foster care
5. Emancipation (with older adolescents)
6. Adoption with termination of parental rights

Although reunification with the biological parents remains the most common permanency plan, recent changes in many state and federal laws have shifted the focus from protecting the biological family unit to considering the "best interest of the child." The reason for this shift can be traced to several high-profile cases in the mid-1990s where children were either seriously abused or killed after being reunified with their biological parents. Well-meaning child advocates launched campaigns in Washington, D.C., appealing to Congress to do something about the horrible plight of children who were returned to their biological families only to face further abuse and sometimes their deaths in a failed effort to save troubled families.

Although there was no documented increase of child maltreatment during this time period, newspaper and magazine articles highlighting tragic (but rare) cases of continued abuse or deaths when children were reunited with their families were passed around Congress, and articles such as "The Little Boy Who Didn't Have to Die" were utilized in an effort to make an emotional appeal to legislators to shift priorities from family reunification to parental termination and subsequent adoption (Spake, 1994). The result of this campaign was the passage of the *American Adoption and Safe Family Act of 1997,* which marked a clear departure away from abuse prevention and family preservation and toward paving the way for the termination of the biological parents' rights, clearing the way for the adoption of children in foster care placement.

The *best interest of the child* standard may sound great on the surface, but it has been the subject of significant scrutiny, with critics questioning just how this standard is being applied. In other words, best interest of the child according to whom? According to the foster parents? The courts? The caseworker? It doesn't take much analysis to see how easily this standard can be abused. For instance, what if the caseworker determines that it is in the best interest of the child to be placed permanently with a two-parent financially secure home rather than be returned to the child's poor single mother, regardless of how diligently this parent works to regain custody? The potential to make permanency plans that discriminate against biological parents who are marginalized members of society, such as parents who are poor, single, of a minority race, homosexual, and perhaps even undocumented immigrants is significant.

Dorothy Roberts, author of *Shattered Bonds: The Color of Child Welfare* (2002) cautions that the new federal law creates many problems, including a conflict created when caseworkers are required to pursue two permanency plans at the same time to comply with the new permanency plan time frames—reunification with the family and possible adoption. What many caseworkers do to accomplish this task is to place foster children in *preadoptive* homes while at the same time planning for reunification with the biological parents. This creates a situation where the biological parents' rights are often in conflict with the child's rights, and where foster care families, who are by definition charged with the responsibility of fostering a relationship between the child and his biological parents, are now competing for the child.

Another possible conflict according to Roberts includes the act's adoption incentive program, where states are given financial incentives of $4,000 for each child placed for adoption (above a baseline) and $6,000 for a special-needs adoption. The potential for agency abuse is evident as states scramble to replace lost revenue due to the poor economy. Roberts warns that this new legislation was not directed at effecting faster termination of parental rights in cases with severe abuse because these cases were always relatively "open-and-shut." Rather, it is the cases involving poverty-related maltreatment, most often in African-American and Native American homes, that have been most affected by this new federal law, which Roberts fears has led to increased social injustice in many CPS agencies.

For this reason as well as many others, the caseworker must be careful in determining what criteria to use in making permanency determination recommendations. For instance, some experts have suggested using attachment ties as a guide in deciding a permanent placement plan (Gauthier, Fortin, & Jeliu, 2004). These researchers suggest that a child should remain with the family who they appear to have the greatest attachment with to avoid further emotional ruptures. Yet the potential for foster parent bias is great, particularly in light of the fact that the foster parents will have a greater advantage over the biological parents because children will, of course, have a greater likelihood of developing a stronger attachment to the family they are living with, particularly if biological parents are restricted from participating regularly in their children's lives through regular visitation. U.S. history is filled with reports of abuses of this sort, where parents considered unworthy have experienced unfair treatment by CPS agencies (see discussion on Native Americans), and this legislation risks escorting in a new dawn of similar abuses.

Working with Biological Families

A caseworker works with the biological parents most closely when it is determined that the most appropriate permanency plan is parent reunification. Once a child has been placed into foster care, the caseworker must prepare a detailed service plan, typically within 30 days, outlining goals that the biological parents must accomplish before regaining custody of their child. The specific goals must be related to the identified parenting deficits, but can include such goals as:

1. Counseling
2. Parenting classes
3. Treatment for substance abuse
4. Anger management
5. Securing employment
6. Securing housing
7. Maintaining regular contact with children

It is then the responsibility of the caseworker to facilitate the biological parents achieving these goals. This might involve giving referrals to the parents or securing the services for them, as well as monitoring their ongoing progress.

It is also important for caseworkers to be aware that biological parents who have had their children removed may be enduring emotional trauma in response to this loss, which may result in them behaving in ways that could be uncharacteristic for them. The strain of having to be accountable to external forces exerting control over their lives makes many biological parents vulnerable to feeling overwhelming shame, which may manifest in defensiveness that could be misinterpreted as indifference or a lack of remorse. An effective caseworker will understand this possible dynamic and will create an environment where biological parents will be able to overcome the barrier of defensiveness and shame and work on the issues identified in their service plan.

The intergenerational nature of child abuse has been well documented in research (Bentovim, 2002, 2004; Erensaft, Cohen, & Brown, 2003; Newcomb, Locke, & Thomas, 2001; Pears & Capaldi, 2001), and although the majority of individuals who have been abused in childhood do not go on to abuse their own children, parents who are abusive to their children have likely been abused in their childhoods. Homes marked by violence, drug abuse, neglect, and sexual abuse create patterns that can be passed down to the next generation. Although it might not initially make sense that someone who endured the pain of abuse would inflict this same abuse on their own child, the complex nature of child abuse often times renders abuse patterns beyond the control of the batterer without some form of intervention. For instance, consider the adjacent case study about Rick.

c a s e   s t u d y   4.1

Case Example of the Intergenerational Cycle of Child Abuse

Rick grew up in a home marked with domestic violence, which oftentimes extended to the children. Rick's mother was chronically depressed and often resorted to using alcohol to avoid dealing with her feelings. Rick recalls days and sometimes weeks where she refused to get out of bed, and he was responsible for caring for his younger siblings. His father also had an alcohol problem and would fly into nightly rages where he would physically abuse his mother. When Rick got older, he attempted to intervene and protect his mother, which only resulted in his father physically abusing him. In addition to physical abuse, Rick was also the victim of emotional abuse and neglect. Rick's father would often call him derogatory names and humiliate him by telling him that he would amount to nothing in life. It seemed as though Rick could do nothing right, and when he was about 12 years old, he promised himself that he would never allow anyone to hurt or humiliate him again. Rick married when he was 21 and was hopeful that his life of being victimized was over. He loved his wife very much and was determined to be the best husband and father he could possibly be. He vowed not to repeat the mistakes of his parents. But deep inside he was plagued with fears that he wasn't good enough for his wife, and that she would eventually leave him. He became increasingly jealous and accused his wife of wanting to leave him. If she tried to convince him otherwise, he accused her of lying. When she became pregnant he was thrilled, but after the baby was born he became upset because his wife seemed to want to spend all her time with the baby, leaving him to fend for himself. One day Rick's boss called him into his office and pointed out a mistake that Rick made. All Rick could think of was the promise he had made to himself years ago to never allow anyone to hurt or ridicule him again. Even though his boss's comments would have seemed reasonable to most people, to Rick it was a re-creation of the abuse he endured as a child. He lost control of his temper, slammed his fist into the wall, and quit his job. When he got home he told his wife and fully expected her to sympathize with him and support his decision to not tolerate such abuse, but instead she complained that his act was selfish, particularly in light of his responsibilities as a father. Rick completely lost his temper and in a blinding rage accused his wife of betraying him. In the blur that followed, Rick accused her of cheating on him, of caring about the baby more than him, and of even getting pregnant by another man. In the midst of his angry outburst he shoved his wife against the wall. All he could think of was how this woman who he thought was his savior was really his enemy, and at that moment he hated her for allowing him to lower his guard and trust her. All the pain of his childhood, with all the hurt and humiliation, came rushing back, and he began to choke her. When his baby interrupted his rage, he screamed at his son to shut up. When his baby's crying got louder, he picked him up and shook him violently. ■

The case study about Rick illustrates some of the dynamics at play with the intergenerational transmission of abuse, and why it is so important for caseworkers to understand what may occur in the mind of someone who has endured physical, emotional, and sexual abuse at the hands of parents and other caregivers. Individuals who have suffered significant childhood abuse often suffer from low frustration tolerance, displaced anger, inability to delay gratification, **impulse control** problems, problems with **emotional regulation,** difficulty attaching to others, and an unstable self-identity (Bentovin, 2002, 2004). Issues such as poor parental modeling, lack of understanding about normal child development, and an individual's level of residual anger and frustration tolerance affect a person's ability to positively parent their children.

Biological Parents and Their Children: Maintaining the Connection

A part of any good reunification plan will involve a visitation schedule that supports and encourages the child's relationship with the biological parents and provides them with applying new parenting techniques that they've learned in parenting classes and counseling (Sanchirico & Jablonka, 2000).

An effective caseworker will give consistent feedback to the biological parents about their progress toward meeting service plan goals, will balance constructive feedback with encouragement, will protect the parent–child relationship, and will do whatever possible to remove barriers to complying with their service plan, such as finding alternate mental health providers when waiting lists would cause unreasonable delays and resolving conflicts between goals, such as not scheduling visitation during the parents' working hours when maintaining stable employment is a service plan goal.

Working with Foster Children: Common Clinical Issues

Foster children obviously come in all "shapes and sizes," so it is difficult to summarize the issues and experiences of the majority of children in foster care in a page or two. But certain generalizations can be made, particularly with regard to the types of experiences that bring a child into substitute care, as well as the range of short-term and long-term emotional and psychological manifestations many children in foster care may experience. The clinical issues that a caseworker may deal with will vary depending on such variables as the age of the child, the length of time in placement, the reasons for placement, and the plan for permanency (i.e., adoption or family reunification). Younger children are typically easier to place and may display less oppositional behavior than adolescents, who are often placed in group homes.

Children who have been sexually abused often manifest emotional problems that require sophisticated handling on the part of the caseworkers, therapists, and foster parents. Sexually abused children may act out sexually with their foster parents as well as other children, which can create an uncomfortable situation, particularly for those who are unfamiliar with such acting out behavior. In addition, most children who have been mistreated in some manner may behave well during the honeymoon period of placement, but then act out once they begin to feel more secure. This phenomenon can lead to disrupted placements if the foster parents are unaware of the dynamics behind this shift in behavior.

A recent national survey of approximately 4,000 foster care children, ages 2 through 14, who had been removed from their homes due to maltreatment revealed that nearly half of these children had clinically significant psychological and/or behavioral problems. Alarmingly though, only about half of these children had received any counseling in the past year. The children who were the most likely to receive mental health services were younger children who had been victims of sexual abuse. African-American children were the least likely to receive mental health services, as were children who remained living in their biological homes (Burns, Phillips, & Wagner, 2004). Sui and Hogan (1989) identified five clinical themes experienced by most children in foster care and made recommendations for how child welfare caseworkers should respond. These include issues related to (1) *Separation;* (2) *Loss, Grief, and Mourning;* (3) *Identity Issues;* (4) *Continuity of Family Ties;* and (5) *Crisis.*

Separation

Children involved in the child welfare system are either contending with issues related to their separation from their biological family members or the threat of separation. Sui and Hogan (1989) recommended that caseworkers be familiar with the psychological dynamics involved in such separations as they relate to each developmental stage. It is important for caseworkers to acknowledge that these children are not just being separated from their biological parents, but are experiencing multiple separations, such as separation from their extended family, perhaps their siblings, their familiar surroundings, including their bedroom, house, neighborhood, and even their family pets. Caseworkers need to confront these separation issues head on with the children, resisting the temptation to avoid them in response to their own separation anxiety.

Children often go through different stages when confronted with significant separation, beginning with the *preprotest* stage, where children accept removal from their home with little protest. But this stage is ultimately followed by the *protest* stage, where children can respond with outright combative and oppositional behavior or with a more subtle uncooperative attitude. The third stage is marked by *despair,* where the child often submits to the placement with a sense of brokenness and hopelessness. The final stage involves *adjustment* to the placement, but involves a sense of detachment to that which the child had been attached—namely, their biological families (Rutter, 1978).

Caseworkers can respond to a child dealing with separation issues by being honest with the child (in an age-appropriate manner) regarding what is happening with his or her family and by helping to prepare the child for the upcoming changes to reduce the anxiety associated with anticipating the unknown. Younger children are far more likely to be operating in the "here and now," thus it is important for the caseworker to reassure the child that the separation is only temporary (if the goal is family reunification), and that the feelings of sadness and discomfort experienced after being separated will not last forever.

Children who have been removed from their homes also need to be reassured that they are not the cause of the family disruption. It is quite common for foster care children to feel responsible for their parents "getting into trouble," and they may even be tempted to recant their disclosures of abuse in the hope that they can return home. Such children often reason that enduring the abuse is better than having their family torn apart and their parents in trouble. In fact, many abused children have been told for years that if they ever did disclose the abuse that the parents would go to jail and the children would be taken away. Thus, it is important that the caseworker anticipate the possibility of such prior conversations between child and parent and address this by encouraging the child and reassuring him or her that the current course of action will actually benefit and strengthen the entire family.

Loss, Grief, and Mourning

Coming alongside a child who has experienced a loss and permitting them to grieve involves having a high tolerance for a wide range of emotions. Siu and Hogan (1989) cited the importance of caseworkers understanding the nature of grieving and thereby assisting foster care children to grieve the loss of their families. It is vital for caseworkers to be familiar with the possible expressions of depression among grieving children, which often manifest as irritability and can easily be mistaken for misbehavior. It is also quite common for children to express heartfelt grief for parents who have horribly abused them. Even children who have been sexually abused often express missing their abusive parent. Caseworkers must be careful to allow these children to grieve their parents, despite the fact that the parents have hurt them.

Identity Issues

Identity is a multifaceted concept referring primarily to one's self-knowledge, self-appraisal, and self-assessment. Developmental theorist Erik Erikson (1963, 1968, 1975), believed that identity formation involves the integration of numerous and sometimes conflicting childhood identities. Erikson believed this convergence of identities took place during the adolescent stage of development, when the adolescent developed an internal continuity and consistency that integrated all different aspects of the self allowing one's real identity to emerge. Our individual identities are based on several factors, some involving internal traits and some involving external traits. As an individual matures, his basis for identity becomes more internally based. But a child, particularly a younger child, will typically base his identity on more external attributes, rather than internal. For instance, if someone were to ask you to describe yourself, you might begin by saying that you are a college student (external). You might then share that you are a soccer player (external) and on student counsel (external). But, you might then describe yourself as an extrovert (internal), who is courageous (internal), loyal (internal), and kind (internal). The more internally based one's identity is, the more resilient a person will be in times of crisis and transition.

Children tend to be far more external in their self-identity, and their self-appraisal can be quite fragile varying dramatically if their external structure is removed. Siu and Hogan (1989) suggested that caseworkers become familiar with the process of identity development, and how the removal of children from their family of origin can significantly affect their sense of personal identity. The nature of this impact will depend, of course, on the age of the child and their stage of development, but can also be affected by several other variables as well. Some of the factors involved in identity formation include one's gender, ethnic and cultural identity, extracurricular activities, talents, socioeconomic status, and relationships with others. Children are often unaware of how they are affected by such things as their socioeconomic status, but it affects them nonetheless.

One's positive identity is dependent on an affirming reciprocal exchange between the various aspects of identity and one's environment. Consider this reciprocity as a mirror reflecting back either a positive or negative image of how one is perceived and valued by others. Essentially the positive or negative nature of one's identity is based at least in part on how these various aspects of one's self is valued by others. An individual who is extremely talented musically may only perceive this talent as a positive part of her identity if her family and community perceive musical talent as valuable. A child who is an intellect but is raised in a family that values athletic prowess may not perceive his intellectual ability as a positive and valuable trait. A child who is removed from her home for maltreatment and is placed in a new environment will struggle with identity issues because despite being in a more positive environment, she is no longer the youngest sibling, no longer the owner of a small dog, no longer the funniest girl in her class, and no longer the best bike rider in her neighborhood. Now she is a foster child, different and set apart, perhaps living in a home much nicer than her own, leaving her feeling somewhat deficient and "less than"; she is no longer funny because she knows no one in her class, and she is not a kid sister because she is the only foster child in her new home.

Because so much of a child's identity resides outside the self and is dependent on external validation and encouragement, an effective caseworker must understand the various dynamics of identity development, understanding how removing children from their homes, even an abusive home, can undermine a child's identity development. Any acting out behavior on the part of the child should be viewed through this lens of identity disruption, and the caseworker can then respond by providing comfort and encouragement to the child during this transition. A child who has only received praise for his ability to play good basketball is going to struggle immensely with his identity if placed in a home that values academic performance or musical ability. A caseworker can assist this child in recognizing that his worth is internal and should not be based solely on the approval and affirmation of others.

Continuity of Family Ties

Picture yourself in a boat moored to a dock on the shore of a large lake. Being anchored here provides you with a connection to the mainland and a sense of security, without fearing becoming adrift at sea. But what if you need to get to the other side of the lake? You would have to pull up your anchor and drift across the water, and it wouldn't be until you reached the other side and safely anchored yourself against that shore that you would feel secure and stable again. Many significant life transitions are like this time adrift in the sea—caught between two shores, where continuity and stability are temporarily lost. Children who have been removed from their biological homes will undoubtedly lose their sense of continuity with their biological families and will feel adrift at sea during the time period when they have not yet established new bonds with their foster family.

Siu and Hogan (1989) strongly recommended that caseworkers consider the importance of continuity and stability when considering where to place a child. Ready access to the biological family and even close friends should always be a priority in placement decisions, and although this can become challenging, particularly in low-income areas where there may be a limited number of available foster families, consideration should still be given to a placement that will facilitate ongoing parental involvement.

At times siblings must be placed in separate foster homes, and consideration to continuity issues needs to be extended to this situation as well. Far too often siblings in foster families do not visit with each other regularly because of the geographic constraints placed on foster families, who are often responsible for providing transportation.

Caseworkers may find themselves in double-bind situations, though, where they must make difficult choices regarding keeping siblings together by placing them in a foster home that is a significant distance away from a parent who does not have transportation or placing the children in different foster homes that are closer to their biological parents, but precludes family visitation due to the difficulty in coordinating visits among various foster families. Caseworkers must rely on their clinical skills in deciding on the right course of action and should then recognize and acknowledge how this interruption of family continuity and stability will affect the children, particularly early in the placement.

Far too often the foster care system, with all its complications, does not do an effective job of *fostering* a relationship between children in placement and their biological families, because if children do not have ready access to their biological families, they will most likely search for continuity and connectedness with their foster families, which although necessary and important, can pose a risk to the continuing bond with their biological parents.

Research has clearly shown that children who visit their biological parents more frequently have a stronger bond with them and have fewer behavioral problems, were less apt to take psychiatric medication, such as antidepressant medication, and were less likely to be developmentally delayed, which underscores the importance of strengthening the attachment between foster children and their biological parents through regular and consistent visitation (McWey & Mullis 2004). Restricting visitation for any reason other than the safety of the child will have a negative affect on this attachment and might even be subsequently used against the biological parents when it comes time to make reunification plans.

Crisis

Removing children from their biological homes and placing them into foster care constitutes a crisis. Sui and Hogan (1989) referred to this crisis as a critical transition, which throws an already fragile family into complete disequilibrium. In fact, most child welfare experts put foster care placement in the category of a *catastrophic crisis.* Crises are not always bad though, and a popular contention among mental health experts discussed in chapter 3 is that a crisis provides the best opportunity for personal growth and authentic change.

Ordinary coping skills are typically not going to be enough to help a child deal with the trauma associated with being placed in foster care. But an effective and seasoned caseworker can help a child develop more effective coping skills that can help them respond to the multiple crises of being removed from their home and placed with strangers.

Working with Foster Parents

Foster care can refer to many placement settings, including kinship care, an emergency shelter, a residential treatment center, a group home, or even an independent living situation (with older adolescents), but most frequently foster care involves placing a child with a licensed foster family (two-parent or single-parent). Every state has certain guidelines and standards that prospective foster parents must meet to qualify to become licensed (Barth, 2001). Licensure typically requires that families participate in up to 10 training sessions focusing on topics such as the developmental needs of at-risk children, issues related to child sexual abuse, appropriate disciplining techniques for at-risk children, ways that foster parents can support the relationship between the foster children and their biological parents, and ways to manage the stress of adding new members to their family. In addition, individuals who will be foster parenting children of a different ethnicity will undergo training focusing on transcultural parenting issues.

Foster parents provide an invaluable service by accepting troubled children into their homes and providing love, nurturing, and security, even though they know the children may only be in their homes for a short time. In addition to good training, foster parents benefit from caseworkers who are consistently supportive and available to them, particularly during high stress times when foster children are acting out. Foster placement will be far less likely to fail if the foster parents feel sufficiently well prepared and supported by their caseworker.

Because the majority of foster children return to their biological parents, foster parents must be supported in their role in the reunification process. The success of a reunification plan depends largely on the cooperation of the foster parents. A foster parent who eagerly facilitates visitation and the sharing of vital information with the biological parents will help protect and maintain the continuity between the foster children and their biological parents. The caseworker plays a pivotal role in providing support and assistance to foster parents. A foster parent who feels unsupported will be far more likely to either purposely or inadvertently undermine the relationship between the foster child and the biological parents. Much of the time this action comes in the form of advocacy for the child. Unfortunately, though, this advocacy, as well meaning as it may be, has the potential of disrupting the necessary process of reunification. Thus although it is certainly understandable that the process of emotional bonding with the foster child makes a foster parent vulnerable to advocating for the best interest of their foster children, foster parents who take it upon themselves to protect their foster child by discouraging the relationship with the biological parents in any way are violating their designated roles, and their effectiveness as foster parents will most likely be seriously compromised.

The PBS documentary entitled *Failure to Protect: The Taking of Logan Marr* documents the removal of five-year-old Logan and her baby sister, Baily, from their young biological mother, Christie Marr. The documentary reveals how Maine's child welfare system, the Department of Human Services (DHS) removed Logan from her mother's care on the presumption that the child might be abused at some *future* time based on some dynamics in the home. After years of jumping through hoops and getting Logan back, Christie had another child, but ultimately lost both of her girls after marrying someone who DHS did not approve. Regardless of Christie's compliance with her parenting plan, the caseworker placed her girls with another DHS worker who was also a licensed foster parent. The foster mother wanted to adopt the Marr girls and actively hindered the relationship between the girls and their mother. In this situation, as well as many others, the foster mother was responsible for providing transportation for visitation, as well as for keeping Christie comprised of major events in the girls' lives. Thus, she had tremendous power to limit visitation if she so desired or to be begrudging with vital information about the girls.

Logan ultimately died in this foster mother's care, and her death led to an uproar over the treatment of Christie, the apparent "cozy" relationship between the foster mother and the DHS caseworker, as well as the caseworker's refusal to investigate Logan's earlier complaints that her foster mother had abused her. This tragic case illustrates how vital it is for foster parents to be well trained and sufficiently supported by their caseworker. An effective caseworker will be able to sense when a foster parent is either burning out or is overstepping appropriate boundaries and will respond with support and limit setting as necessary.

Reunification

The decision of whether or when to reunify foster children with their biological parents is based on many factors, including the biological parents' success in meeting their service plan goals. Even if these goals are sufficiently met, the timing of reunification may depend on minimizing disruptions in the child's life, such as switching schools in the middle of the school year. If reunification is the plan from the beginning of placement, then the caseworker should be planning for this event from the initial stages of the case. Problems arise when issues such as court postponements, additional service plan goals, changes in caseworker assignments, and other factors lead to delays in reunification. A judge may deem it perfectly reasonable to postpone a reunification hearing so that a child can complete the final four months of school without disruption, but such a decision can be devastating for the biological parents who have worked diligently to reach all service plan goals and go to court expecting to leave with their biological child, only to be told they must wait an additional four months to avoid their child changing schools in the middle of the school year. The potential for a biological parent to give up attempting to regain custody, to relapse into unhealthy behaviors out of discouragement and frustration is great, and caseworkers must be sensitive to the possibility of such frustrations leading to despair or relapse.

Therefore, even though reunification with biological parents is associated with several changes in the child's life, many of which may be negative in nature (Lau, Litrownik, Newton, & Landsverk, 2003), an effective caseworker will begin preparing the child for these transitions from the beginning of placement in foster care. Simply verbalizing what is going to happen, telling the child what to expect in the future, and giving such children a voice in expressing their fears and frustrations, even if they do not have decision-making power, will go a long way in minimizing the negative effect of reunification, particularly for children who have been in placement for a significant amount of time.

Reunification is not just stressful for the child, though, it is stressful for the biological parents as well, and many biological parents are the most vulnerable to stress-related relapse in the weeks following reunification. The combination of increased stress and the acting out of the child due to yet another transition can create a potentially volatile situation where negative behavior patterns resurface. Any good reunification plan involves ongoing monitoring and provision of in-home services to prevent any such problems during the reunification transition. These services can be provided by the county child welfare office directly or by a contracted agency-based practice that specializes in providing such services as in-home case management and support. With good support services, many reunifications go quite smoothly, and in time the children and parents settle in to a regular routine where healthier communication patterns and positive parenting styles will lead to a positive response from the children.

 ## Family Preservation

Because the number of children placed in substitute care rose consistently since the 1980s, particularly in most urban communities, there has been an increasing focus on early intervention and prevention programs since the early 1990s. Family preservation programs are designed to reduce the need for out-of-home placement by intervening in a family process before the dynamics deteriorate to the point of requiring the removal of the children. These programs are comprised of a variety of short-term, intensive services designed to immediately reduce stress and teach important skills that will reduce the likelihood of out-of-home placement. Services can include family counseling, parenting training, assistance with household budgeting, stress management, child development, respite care for caregivers, and in some cases cash assistance (Child Welfare League of America, n.d.).

Although there has been some controversy surrounding the success of these programs in reducing foster care placements, the federal government remains committed to early intervention programs, and many counties report that approximately 80 percent of families who have participated in family preservation programs remained intact in the year following the suspension of services (Child Welfare League of America, n.d.).

Family preservation programs are strictly voluntary, and a family can opt out of services at any time. But caseworkers can often create an incentive for participation by offering the family preservation program in lieu of eventual removal of the children. Thus an important clinical assessment is whether a family is appropriate for family preservation, or whether the problems in the home have progressed beyond what these services are designed to address.

Minority Populations and Multicultural Considerations

Children of color are overrepresented in the foster care system, comprising nearly 60 percent of all placements in the year 2003 (Table 4.2). This is nearly twice their representation in the general population. Children of color are not just disproportionately represented in the foster care system in the United States, but far fewer of these children are reunited with their families. In fact, of the 22 percent of children whose permanency plan was adoption in 2003, 61 percent were children of color (Child Welfare League of America, 2002). This overrepresentation is fueled by other long-standing factors such as social oppression, negative social conditions, racial discrimination, and **economic injustice.** For instance, African-American children were initially excluded from the child welfare system, but are now the most overrepresented of all racial groups (Smith & Devore, 2004).

Some reasons for this overrepresentation relate to complex social issues such as institutionalized racism, intergenerational poverty, and culturally based drug abuse. But other possible causes include racism within the child welfare system.

Types of racial discrimination include:

1. *Racial bias in referring families for family preservation programs versus out-of-home placement.* Certain special populations, including African-American families, are

■ **Table 4.2**   Race/Ethnicity Foster Care Rates 2002

For every 1,000 **African American/Black** children in the U.S. population, there were **17** in foster care on September 30, 2002. While African American/Black children represented 16% of the total population under the age of 18, they were 38% of the foster care population. African American/Black children experience longer stays in care.

For every 1,000 **American Indian/Alaska Native** children in the U.S. population, there were more than **12** in foster care on September 30, 2002. While American Indian/Alaska Native children represented 2% of the total population under the age of 18, they were 2% of the foster care population.

For every 1,000 **Hispanic** children in the U.S. population, there were **6** in foster care on September 30, 2002. While Hispanic children represented 18% of the total population under the age of 18, they were 15% of the foster care population.

For every 1,000 **White** children in the U.S. population, there were **5** in foster care. While White children represented 61% of the total population under the age of 18, they were 38% of the foster care population.

For every 1,000 children of **2 or more races** in the U.S. population, there were **8** in foster care. While they represented 3% of the total population under the age of 18, they were 3% of the foster care population.

For every 1,000 **Asian or Pacific Islander** children in the U.S. population, there were **2** in foster care. While Asian/Pacific Islander children represented 4% of the total population under the age of 18, they were 1% of the foster care population.

On average for **all races,** for every 1,000 children, **7** were in foster care.

Sources: AFCARS FY 2002 & Census Data (2002) & Child Maltreatment 2002 (NCANDS). Calculations by CWLA. http://ndas.cwla.org/research_info/specialtopic1a.asp?printview=yes&

not consistently targeted for family preservation programs. Reasons for this include caseworker bias based on the belief that the needs of the African-American community may be too great to be appropriately handled by this program (Denby & Curtis, 2003).

2. *Racial partiality in assessing parent–child attachment leading to delays in returning children to their biological parents.* A 2003 study of approximately 250 black and white children in foster care placement found that racial partiality existed in assessing the parent–child attachment when the caseworker was of a different race than the biological parent. Although this result was reciprocal (i.e., black caseworkers showed partiality to black families, and white caseworkers show partiality to white families), the affect of this trend has particular relevance to the African-American community because the majority of caseworkers are Caucasian, and African-American children are disproportionately represented among

children in foster care. The results of this study revealed that Caucasian case-workers might have erred when they concluded that African-American mothers were poorly attached to their children because of the caseworker's lack of understanding of cultural differences between Caucasian and African-American customs (Surbeck, 2003).

3. *Caseworkers who are poorly trained in cultural competencies.* For a caseworker to accurately assess many of the factors necessary in determining whether out-of-home placement is warranted, such as the level of violence in the home, the ability of parents to protect their children, or the level of parental remorse, a caseworker must be aware of commonly held negative stereotypes of various racial groups. It is unacceptable for a member of the majority culture to claim not to hold any negative stereotypes, and it is only through the honest admission of overt and subtle negative biases toward other cultures that a caseworker can begin to work effectively with a variety of ethnic groups.

Placing Children of Color in Caucasian Homes

Considerable controversy exists surrounding the placement of children of color in Caucasian homes. Many advocacy organizations do not support this practice, whereas others claim that it is not in the best interest of children to experience placement delays simply because there are no foster families available that are the same race as the child. From a "micro" perspective, this latter argument makes sense. If an African-American child is in desperate need of a long-term foster home, how much sense would it make to have a policy in place that prevents placement in a suitable home only because the foster family is Caucasian? After all, all children deserve loving homes, and the color of their skin should not keep them from being placed in one. Right?

Yet from a "macro" perspective a different viewpoint is revealed. Consider the equity of a majority culture systematically destroying an entire race, as the United States has done to the African-American population during the slavery and post–Civil War era, or to the Native American population during colonial times and the era of early occupation of the United States. How do you think these racial groups would perceive this same majority culture then rushing in to "rescue" the children who were maltreated in great part because of this cultural genocide and the resultant social breakdown?

Advocates of placing children of color in homes of the same race cite such cultural genocide in their arguments. Alternatives to transracial placement include the development of kinship care programs, where members of a child's extended family act as foster parents, often made possible through financial assistance. The National Association of Black Social Workers (NABSW) cite the long-standing tradition of informal kinship care within the African-American community extending back to the Middle Ages and solidified during the slavery era, when many African Americans acted in the informal capacity of parents for children whose biological parents were sold and sent away. Such cultural traditions can serve as a precursor for federally funded programs that promote kinship care foster programs, which respect cultural identity and tradition (NABSW, 2003).

Native Americans and the U.S. Child Welfare System

The British colonization of North America involved an organized and methodical campaign to decimate the Native American population through invasion, trickery (such as trading land for alcohol), and ultimately the forced relocation of all Native Americans onto government-designated reservations, where the assimilation into the majority culture became a primary goal of the U.S. government (Brown, 2001). The few Native Americans who survived this genocide were broken physically, emotionally, and spiritually, suffering from alcoholism, rampant unemployment, and debilitating depression.

In the early part of the nineteenth century the U.S. government assumed full responsibility for educating Native American children. It is estimated that from the early 1800s through the early part of the twentieth century virtually all Native American children were forcibly removed from their homes and reservations and placed in Indian boarding schools, where they were not allowed to speak in their native tongues, practice their cultural religion, or wear traditional dress. During school breaks many of these children were placed as servants in Caucasian homes rather than being allowed to return home for visits. The result of this forced assimilation amounted to cultural genocide where an entire generation of Native Americans was institutionalized, deprived of a relationship with their biological families, and robbed of their cultural heritage.

This ongoing campaign to assimilate the Native Americans into European American culture became even more aggressive between 1950 and 1970, when social workers with governmental backing removed thousands of Native American children from their homes on reservations for alleged maltreatment, placing them in adoptive Caucasian homes. In reality, many of the problems on the reservations were the product of years of governmental oppression resulting in extreme poverty and other commonly associated social ills, and the U.S. government response to this was to tear Native American families apart rather than intervene with mental health services.

Between 1941 and 1978, approximately 70 percent of all Native America children were removed from their homes and placed either in orphanages or with Caucasian families, many of whom later adopted them (First Nations Orphan Association, n.d.). In truth, few of these children were removed from their homes due to maltreatment as it is currently defined. Rather, approximately 99 percent of these children were removed because social workers believed that the children were victims of social deprivation due to the extreme poverty common on most Indian reservations (U.S. Senate, 1974). The result of this government action has been nothing short of devastating. Native Americans have one of the highest suicide rates in the nation, with Native American youth, particularly those who have spent time in U.S. boarding schools,

■ Student body assembled on the Carlisle Indian School Grounds

■ Native Americans during mathematics class at Indian School

having on average five to six times the rate of suicide compared to the non–Native American population. When these children graduated from high school they were adults without a culture—no longer feeling comfortable on the reservation after years of being negatively indoctrinated against their cultural heritage, yet not being accepted by the white population either. The response of many of these individuals was to turn to alcohol in an attempt to drown out the pain.

In 1978, the *Indian Child Welfare Act* (PL 95-608) was passed, which prevented the unjustified removal of Native American children from their homes. The act specifies that if removal is necessary then the child must be placed in a home that reflects his or her culture and preserves tribal tradition. Tribal approval must be obtained prior to placement, even when the placement is a result of a voluntary adoption proceeding (Kreisher, 2002). This act has for the most part successfully stemmed the tide of mass removal of thousands of Native American children from their homes on the reservations, but unfortunately many caseworkers still do not understand the reason why such a bill was passed in the first place, or why it is necessary, and mistakenly believe that this act hampers placing needy children in loving homes.

Gaining a fuller understanding of the history between people of color and the U.S. child welfare system will make it easier to understand why some minority groups may not trust human service professionals in issues regarding allegations of abuse. The social worker might not be aware of the long-standing negative history between government child welfare agencies and a particular racial group, but members of that particular group are most likely aware of this history. It is vital that human service professionals develop cultural competencies, regardless of whether they are actively working with minority populations. It is only through a comprehensive understanding of the history of child welfare policies and abuses of power of the U.S. child welfare system will truly achieve its goal of respecting the autonomy and dignity of all people, regardless of race, gender, age, nationality, and sexual orientation.

Concluding Thoughts on Child Protective Services

Human service professionals who work with troubled families have the opportunity to effect change that positively affects not only the present families, but all future generations within that family system as well. CPS caseworkers often experience high caseloads and can feel overwhelmed and burned out in the face of such immensely complicated dynamics commonly involved in child welfare cases.

An increased focus on family preservation programs and other early intervention programs offer the best opportunity for reducing out-of-home placements, but these programs must be offered to all potentially appropriate families without bias. This can occur through sufficient federal and state funding of child welfare programs and the effective recruitment and training of human service professionals willing to work with a variety of families, from various cultures dealing with a wide range of life challenges.

Adoption Services

Child and family service agencies frequently offer adoption services, including domestic adoption (adoption of U.S.-born infants), international adoption, and special-needs adoption (adoption of foster care children or other children who have emotional or medical special needs).

Domestic Adoption

Domestic adoption involves the placement of children under the age of five (typically infants) with a licensed adoptive parent or parents. The practices and policies associated with domestic adoptions have changed significantly in the past 50 to 60 years. Domestic adoptions were open and informal during the eighteenth, nineteenth, and early twentieth centuries, but laws passed in the 1940s began a trend of anonymity in the adoption process, requiring the sealing of adoption records. These laws were based in part on the belief that out-of-wedlock births were shameful and needed to be kept secret. The majority of adoptions between 1940 and 1970 were closed, meaning that information identifying the birth parents and adoptive families was not disclosed (Baumann, 1999).

In fact, it was a common practice for caseworkers to be authoritarian in directing unwed mothers to "give up" their children for adoption, based on the widely held belief that young single women who became pregnant out of wedlock were incapable of making good decisions, let alone parenting a child (Biestek, 1957). Newborns were often whisked away from the birth mother quickly after birth to avoid the unnecessary bonding of mother and child, believed to only cause further pain and confusion on the part of the birth mother.

Adoptive families were encouraged to take their newly adopted infant home and act as though they were like any other biological family. In this way, they avoided the burden of feeling different from biological families. Adopted children were often not told of their adoptive status, or parents waited until the last possible moment to share their histories with their adopted children (sometimes waiting well into an adoptee's adolescent or adult years). Closed adoptions also allowed adoptive parents psychological and physical protection from birth parents, who many adoptive parents feared might resurface in their children's lives (Baumann, 1999).

Research in the 1960s began to explore the possibility that such practices might create problems with the identity and emotional stability in the adoptee population.

Marshall Schechter (1960) conducted a study that found that adoptive children were 100 times more likely to seek psychological services than children raised in their biological family. Some of the reasons for this increase included identity issues relating to feeling different than children who were raised in their biological families who could see a physical resemblance between themselves and their other family members, and who knew their family history.

David Kirk (1964) wrote a groundbreaking book on adoption discussing two ways of addressing how adoptive families managed the differences they encountered because they were a family developed through adoption. Kirk noted that some families simply rejected any real differences by pretending that they were a biological family (including never telling their children they were adopted), whereas other adoptive families openly acknowledged their differences from biological families by addressing the reality of adoption, including fears on the part of the adoptive family that the biological parents might return and intrude on their lives and fears that their adoptive child might never consider them real parents. Kirk suggested that openly addressing the differences involved in an adoptive family might lend to a trend of embracing diversity within families.

Schechter's and Kirk's books began a movement toward perceiving domestic adoption as a social institution that had broad social implications, as well as contributing toward the recognition that adoptees had valid identity issues that needed to be addressed. These acknowledgements moved the country toward a trend of openness in adoptions where the birth mother was viewed as an important member of the **adoption triad** and the secrecy of the adoption process was replaced with varying degrees of openness, including the sharing of identifying information and ongoing contact between birth parents and the adoptive child after placement.

Another trend in domestic adoption includes the significant decrease of adoptive placements, particularly of Caucasian infants, over the last 50 years. Overall, the number of domestic adoptions has declined since peaking at 175,000 in 1970 (Maza, 1984; Flango & Flango, 1994). Likely reasons for this decline include the reduction of the stigma associated with single parenting, the legalization of abortion, and the increase in contraception use. Currently there are approximately 25,000 to 30,000 domestic adoptions finalized each year in the United States, but this number includes foster care and relative adoptions, thus the number of adoptions of Caucasian newborns into nonrelative families is even smaller.

The issue of same-sex couple adoption remains controversial, but is increasingly common, both in private independent adoptions and in agency adoptions. Historically, many same-sex couples would adopt as individuals, which meant that only one parent in the partnership was the legal parent of the child, creating problems with custody in the event of a relationship breakup or the death of the legal adoptive parent. Several states have now passed laws that allow same-sex parents to openly adopt a child, giving both parents legal status. The states that allow same-sex adoption are California, Massachusetts, New Jersey, New Mexico, New York, Ohio, Vermont, Washington, Wisconsin, and Washington, D.C. These laws do not mandate agencies to place infants with same-sex couples though, and many agencies continue to bar same-sex couple adoptions based on religious or other grounds.

The domestic adoption of newborns can be facilitated in two primary ways: independent adoption and private agency adoptions.

Independent Adoption

An *independent adoption* typically involves a private adoption that is arranged between the preadoptive family and the birth parent(s) by a facilitator or attorney. A human service professional is often retained to counsel the birth parent(s). Approximately 50 percent of all domestic adoptions are independent adoptions.

One advantage of an independent adoption is that it provides adoptive parents with more control over the selection of a birth mother, but there are also risks for both birth parents and adoptive families. Birth parents who do not receive adequate option counseling in preparation for placement of their infants may feel pressured to place their baby during a vulnerable time in their lives. Prospective adoptive parents who do not receive adequate counseling and preparation may become too involved in the birth parents' lives because they are so eager to have a child in their lives. This overinvolvement might put them at risk of financial exploitation out of fear that saying "no" to a request might encourage the birth parents to find another adoptive family more willing to provide assistance. It is for these reasons that Delaware, Connecticut, and Massachusetts have passed laws making independent adoptions illegal because of the risk of the exploitation of either birth parents or preadoptive parents.

Private Agency Adoptions

Preadoption Services. Approximately 50 percent of all domestic Caucasian newborn adoptions are facilitated by a private human services agency. Agencies that offer domestic adoption programs hire human service professionals to work as adoption caseworkers who work with both the birth parents and preadoptive parent(s). In many agencies preadoptive parent(s) and birth parents have different adoption workers due to the importance of neutrality and objectivity in the counseling relationship. For instance, an adoption worker might become so invested in a preadoptive couple's desire to have a child that he or she inadvertently pressures a birth mother to place her newborn, even if that is not what the birth mother desires.

The human service professional working with women experiencing the crisis of an unplanned pregnancy often engage in "option counseling," where the options of parenting, pregnancy termination, and adoption are explored. If the birth parent(s) chooses the adoption option, the adoption worker will assist the birth parent(s) in selecting an adoptive family. Most adoption agencies maintain portfolios of their licensed adoptive families, which consist of photograph albums and letters to the prospective birth parent(s) sharing the personal stories, values (including thoughts in child raising), faith perspective, and reasons for wanting to adopt a child.

Once the birth parent(s) have selected the preadoptive parents, the caseworker may suggest a meeting to begin the process of getting to know each other. But when and if this meeting occurs depends in large part on the wishes of the birth parent(s). During the course of the pregnancy the adoption worker will continue to help the birth mother process her decision to place her unborn infant for adoption. These issues include anticipating the grieving process after placement.

Some birth parent(s) may have the luxury of months of option counseling, adoption preparation, and preparation for grief recovery (see following), or they may have only a few weeks, depending on when they began the counseling process. Regardless of the time involved, it is vital for the birth parent(s) and preadoptive family to remember that the decision to place a baby for adoption cannot be legally made until after the infant is born. Thus, although the adoptive family and birth parents may have met and begun a relationship, the adoption worker and preadoptive family should continue to consider the possibility that the birth parent(s) may change their minds once their baby is born. The adoption worker should also encourage the birth parent(s) to continue the process of considering the parenting option so that they are not unprepared in the event they do change their minds after giving birth.

The adoption caseworker working with the preadoptive family typically begins the counseling relationship by addressing the various clinical aspects of infertility (if this is the reason for pursuing adoption). Although some agencies do permit adopting couples to continue with infertility treatments, most adoption agencies require preadoptive couples to stop fertility treatments and begin the process of grieving the loss of their anticipated biological child before they begin the adoption process.

Unresolved grief relating to infertility may create problems in bonding with and parenting of the adopted child. Research has consistently shown that infertility can have an impact on the attachment of parents and children, specifically in how adoptive parents parent young children. A 1999 study found that adoptive parents, particularly mothers, spent less time holding and feeding their adopted infants than biological parents (Holditch-Davis, Sandelowski, Harris, & Glenn, 1999). The reasons for this difference is unknown but presumed to be related to many factors, including unresolved feelings about their infertility and a feeling on the part of many adoptive mothers that the adoptive child is not really theirs and may be taken away from them. Adoption workers will assist the preadoptive couples in facing their feelings about their infertility, which will allow them to openly grieve this loss and prepare them to accept adoption not as "plan B" but as an effective means for bringing a child into their family.

The adoption worker also works with preadoptive parent(s) in the adoption licensing process. Most states require that preadoptive parent(s) participate in several weeks of adoption training, have a comprehensive criminal background check, and have numerous sessions with the adoption worker (including several home visits) to determine their appropriateness as adoptive parents. The licensing process is not only used as an assessment tool, but also prepares the preadoptive families for the adoption experience.

In addition to licensing requirements, many agencies offer a series of workshops designed to assist preadoptive parent(s) prepare for adoption. Workshops typically cover such issues as infertility, parenting an adopted child, issues related to attachment, the nature of open adoption, and the importance of the birth parents in the adoption triad. Because the majority of domestic adoptions are open (to varying degrees), it is important that preadoptive parent(s) understand the value of an open adoption so they do not feel threatened in any way by the nature of an open adoption.

Open adoptions can include anything from intermittent exchanging of letters and videos to periodic meetings. When openness first began to be practiced in some adoption agencies, some expressed the fear that giving adoptees information about their birth parents at an early age might create confusion, both about their parentage as well as their true identity. Yet research does not support this contention. A large-scale study on adoptees found that the majority of adoptees felt better about their adoption if they had some contact with their birth parents compared to adoptees who did not have contact with their birth families (Mendenhall, Berge, Wrobel, Grotevant, & McRoy, 2004).

Many agencies have birth mothers present their adoption stories at adoptive parent training workshops as a way of "demystifying" birth parents, helping preadoptive parents see them as allies, not adversaries who have the potential to take their adoptive children away.

One challenge in counseling preadoptive parent(s) relates to the anxiety many feel in response to the undefined waiting period. Although it might have been possible to adopt an infant within a few months in the 1950s, that scenario is rarely the case now. It is impossible for an agency to predict how long preadoptive parent(s) might have to wait, with some adoptive families having a relatively short wait (perhaps a year) and some couples waiting several years. Assisting families manage their anxiety and frustration is a critical component of counseling preadoptive couples. Being chosen by birth parents who have later changed their minds about placing significantly adds to the frustration and anxiety experienced by many preadoptive parent(s). Adoption workers can assist such couples by encouraging their involvement in support groups with other adoptive parents who are also waiting for a placement. Such groups offer an effective means for reducing frustration by allowing waiting couples to gain support and strength from each other, such as sharing strategies for maintaining hope.

Postadoption Services. Adoption agencies frequently offer postadoption services to the birth parents, adoptive family, and adoptee in the form of counseling, education, and informational updates. Postadoption services are often offered throughout the life of the adoptee.

Birth parents are offered grief counseling after the placement of their child, and most agencies also facilitate grief support groups for birth mothers or birth parents at various stages in the grieving process. Birth parents who recently placed a child for adoption often gain reassurance from seeing the emotional progress of a birth parent who placed one or two years ago.

Postadoption counselors also facilitate the ongoing contact between birth parents and the adoptive parents, including making arrangements for visits. Some open adoptions are structured with adoptive families providing letters, photographs, and videos on a set schedule, whereas others are more flexible, with adoptive families and birth parents meeting periodically throughout the year. Many birth parents are comforted by the knowledge that they will be receiving information about their child throughout the year, which can help with the grieving process.

When I worked as an adoption worker counseling biological parents, I recall working with a 17-year-old birth mother who placed her infant son for adoption in an open adoption arrangement. During the first year she received letters, photographs, and an occasional video. She explained that this ongoing contact helped her to grieve because it reassured her that she had made the right decision. She also shared that if she had no information about her son, she would become afraid for him every time she heard about a child his age being hurt, kidnapped, or abused. By seeing him grow throughout the years, seeing him smiling in photographs, playing in videos, and by seeing him once a year in an agency facilitated visit, she received reassurance that he was happy and well cared for. The infant she cradled in her arms for three days would always be her child, but as her biological son grew she recognized that the boy in the photographs and videos was their child. Several years later my client married, and her adopted son, now in his early teen years, and his family sat in the church with the rest of the bride's family and friends, celebrating her new life and the healing that it reflected.

Postadoption services for birth parents are also offered years after a birth parent places a child for adoption. When open adoption became the trend in the 1980s and 1990s many birth parents began contacting their placement agencies searching for information about their biological child. If the adoptee is under the age of 18, most agencies may make contact with the adoptive family to determine if they want contact. Agencies might also encourage birth parents to write a letter, which is then kept in the adoptee's adoption file in the event that the adoptive family and/or adoptee ever requests updated information.

Postadoption services for the adoptive family are available as well. Immediately following the adoption, the adoption worker assists the adoptive family with the transition into parenthood, as well as assisting the parents with any adjustment issues related to feeling comfortable parenting a child that they did not give birth to. Legal assistance is also provided, which includes postplacement home visits needed to legally finalize the adoption.

Adoptive families face many of the same struggles as biological families, but the adoptee may experience certain developmental milestones differently. For instance, as adoptees develop abstract reasoning ability, they often begin to understand their adoption story in a more profound way, which can lead to questions about the circumstances of their placement, expressed concern about their birth mother, or fears that they may have been abandoned. The postplacement counselor can work with adoptive families years after placement to assist the adoptee and adoptive family navigate these difficult transitions.

An adoption can also place additional stress, or put a different spin on normal childhood behavior. For instance, a biological child who cries in the midst of a tantrum "I wish you weren't my mom! I wish I had a new mom!" may elicit frustration in a biological parent, but is often easily disregarded as a classic childhood statement. But this normally innocuous statement can elicit deep pain and perhaps insecurity in adoptive parents, who may wonder if such a statement is an indication that their child wants to return to his or her birth mother. Postplacement counseling can assist adoptive parents in putting such childhood behavior in the proper context, discerning what behaviors are related to the adoption and which are likely unrelated.

Postplacement services can also assist adult adoptees who choose to search for their birth parents. The trend toward increasing openness in adoptions also created an awareness among many adoptees that their birth parents might not be rejecting if they attempted contact (a common fear among both adoptees and birth parents). When I worked in postplacement adoptions, I organized many postplacement reunions. Prior to searching for the birth parents, though, I made sure to counsel the adoptee in preparation for the meeting because years of fantasizing about their birth parents can sometimes contribute to unrealistic expectations, which can later result in disappointment. A well-prepared adoptee is encouraged to approach a reunion slowly, allowing the relationship to grow naturally. Adoptees must also be prepared for having a mix of emotions, including feeling as though they are betraying their adoptive parents if they express a desire to search for their biological parents. Yet postplacement counselors can work with the adoptee, adoptive parents, and birth parents so that everyone in the adoption triad feels comfortable with the adoptee's decision to search for his or her biological roots.

International Adoption

An increasing number of preadoptive parent(s) are pursuing international adoption because of the decline in domestic adoptions and significantly shorter waiting periods, with some countries having waiting periods as short as one year. International adoption programs also offer far less stringent agency criteria, both with regard to age restrictions as well as family type. Because many countries allow single-parent adoptions, many singles enter international adoption programs. Adoption workers working with single clients assist them in preparing emotionally for the rigors of raising a child alone. Many human service agencies, churches, and advocacy organizations offer single-parent support groups, and adoption workers often assist single clients in finding a network of social support.

The licensing and preparation process of preadoptive parent(s) is similar in many respects to couples adopting domestically, except that rather than focusing on openness and birth parent identification, international adoption focuses on issues related to cultural identification.

Countries with active international adoption programs include Russia, Eastern European countries, the Philippines, Korea, Viet Nam, China, and many countries in Central and South America. Adoption agencies that offer international adoption must be approved and registered with the placement country, thus not every agency will offer adoption with every available country. Most countries require that adoptive families travel to the child's country to complete the adoption legally and to escort their new child home. This can be a wonderful cultural experience for adoptive families who often travel as groups, sometimes with the adoption worker who works with the agency in the foreign country and assists the families with travel and legal arrangements. Adoptive families often take photographs of the foster family or orphanage that served as their adopted child's first home for their adopted child's "baby book" and to help with the cultural identification process that will occur later in the child's life.

Postadoption services for international adoptive parents includes helping parents manage ongoing cultural issues, including helping adopted children address questions and concerns they may have related to coming from a different country and culture than their adoptive family. Questions about birth parents are also common and must be addressed even though information might be limited.

Families in urban communities frequently find it easier to embrace their adopted child's original culture, but families from rural areas may find it more challenging to make these cultural connections. Adoption workers can assist these families to remain tied to their child's original culture by organizing intermittent agency cultural events with other adoptive families in the region.

International adoption has grown tremendously in recent years and is expected to continue to grow as domestic adoption continues to decline. International adoption not only helps preadoptive individuals who want to parent a child, but it also helps children in impoverished countries who might otherwise languish in an orphanage for years facing an uncertain future.

Special-Needs Adoption

Special-needs adoption involves the adoption of any child that may present adoptive parents with special parenting challenges. Special-needs adoptions fall into several categories including older children; children with mental, physical, or emotional disabilities; children over the age of five; sibling groups; and at-risk children (those who are at risk for developing problems later in life such as genetic problems, fetal alcohol syndrome, and learning disabilities). Some agencies consider transracial children in the category of special-needs adoptions because agencies often have not recruited a sufficient number of families to adopt children of color, particularly boys. Transracial adoptions also call for cultural competence on the part of adoption workers as well as adoptive families if they are of a different race than the adoptive child, with a focus on how individuals of color have been oppressed within the U.S. culture (McRoy & Grape, 1999).

Many special-needs adoptions involve the placement of foster care children in either a relative's or nonrelative's home, but private adoptions of special-needs children are also quite common. Human service professionals who work in special-needs adoptions may work for a county child protective services agency or a private human services agency offering special needs adoptions services.

Preadoptive parent(s) in a special-needs program can be married, single, same-sex couples (depending on state laws and agency policy), younger, or older. Clinical issues typically involve attachment issues, particularly with children who have experienced significant abuse and loss in their lives, and behavioral problems due to earlier life disruption. Managing children with medical or behavioral difficulties can be challenging, and preadoptive parent(s) need preparation, training, support, and assistance in learning how to manage the practical and emotional rigors of special-needs children. It is vital that preadoptive parent(s) understand the challenges they are about to face so that the adoption doesn't fail, requiring the removal of the child.

Children who have a history of abuse can be significantly challenging to parents. Behaviorally disordered children often experience a honeymoon period when first placed in an adoptive home leading adoptive parents to believe that the transition will be smooth and the parenting "normal." But in many special-needs placements once the honeymoon period is over behaviorally disordered children often act out, sometimes out of fear and sometimes because they finally have a safe place to express their years of pent-up anger and emotional pain. Adoption workers assist special-needs adoptive families in the initial transition making sure that all members in the family are aware of what to expect during each stage of the acclimation process, as well as assisting special-needs adoptive families with each successive stage, including managing expectations, conflict, and even disappointment as the reality of raising a special-needs child becomes apparent to the adoptive parents.

A 1999 study found that special-needs adoptive families most appreciated the coordination of services provided by their placement agency, which enabled them to link up with other community services (Kramer & Houston, 1999). Many agencies offer ongoing counseling to special-needs adoptive families, who sometimes remain in counseling for years. Many special needs adoptions proceed with relative ease with all parties adapting well, and thus do not require postadoption services, and others still seem to adjust well in the child's early years, but require counseling assistance once the adopted child reaches adolescence. For this reason, human service professionals may enter an adoptive family at any point in the child's life ensuring that earlier trauma can be addressed at any point in the child's development.

Concluding Thoughts on Child and Family Services

Child and family services include a broad range of issues and services designed to address many problems and challenges currently facing families in contemporary society. Changes in our national economic structure that are contributing to an increase in poverty, changes within the family system such as divorce and single parenting, and welfare reform that limits long-term public assistance all contribute to the complexity of maintaining a positive and healthy atmosphere in many families within the United States. Human service agencies assist all types of families facing all types of challenges including poverty, parenting (including child maltreatment), and infertility. Human service professionals working in child welfare agencies work as CPS investigators, caseworkers, and adoption workers. This is a practice setting that will continue to grow because the need will continue to grow, and although increasing professionalization will contribute to the ongoing trend of requiring higher levels of education, the high need for human service professionals in all areas of child and family services will likely mean that bachelor's-level human service professionals will consistently be able to find employment in both county and private agencies in need of committed professionals willing to work with parents and children from diverse backgrounds with diverse needs.

r e f e r e n c e s

Barth, R. P. (2001). Policy implications of foster family characteristics. *Family Relations, 50(1)*, 16–19.

Baumann, C. M. (1999). Examining where we were and where we are: Clinical issues in adoption 1985–1995. *Child & Adolescent Social Work Journal, 14(5)*, 313–334.

Bellingham, B. (1984). *Little wanderers: A socio-historical study of the nineteenth century origins of child fostering and adoption reform, based on early records of the New York Children's Aid Society.* Unpublished Ph.D. thesis, University of Pennsylvania. Available from University Microfilm Incorporated (UMI), Ann Arbor Michigan.

Belzberg, E. (Director). (2001). *The forgotten children underground* [Docudrama].

Bentovim, A. (2002). Preventing sexually abused young people from becoming batterers, and treating the victimization experiences of young people who offend sexually. *Child Abuse & Neglect, 26(6–7)*, 661–678.

Bentovim, A. (2004). Working with abusing families: General issues and a systemic perspective. *Journal of Family Psychotherapy, 15(1–2)*, 119–135.

Biestek, F. P. (1957). *The Casework Relationship.* Chicago, IL: Loyola University Press.

Bourg, W., Broderick, R. & Flagor, R. (1999). *A Child Interviewer's Guidebook.* Thousand Oaks, CA: Sage Publications.

Brace, C. L. (1967). *The dangerous classes of New York and twenty years work among them.* Montclair, NJ: Patterson Smith.

Brown, D. (2001). *Bury My Heart at Wounded Knee: An Indian History of the American West.* New York, NY: Henry Holt and Company.

Burns, B. J., Phillips, S. D., Wagner, H. R., Barth, R. P., Kolko, D. J., Campbell, Y. & Landsverk, J. (2004). Mental health need and access to mental health services by youths involved with child welfare: A national survey. *Journal of the American Academy of Child & Adolescent Psychiatry, 43(8)*, 960–970.

Child Abuse Prevention and Treatment Act. (2003). 42 U.S.C. § 5106 *et seq.* Retrieved October 22, 2005, from http://frwebgate.access.gpo.gov/cgi-bin/multidb.cgi

Child Welfare League of America. (n.d.). *Family preservation and permanency planning: About the program.* Retrieved on March 2, 2004, from http://www.cwla.org/programs/familypractice/fampractabout.htm

Child Welfare League of America. (2002). Minorities as majority: Disproportionality in child welfare and juvenile justice. *Children's Voice.* Retrieved on March 4, 2005, from http://www.cwla.org/articles/cv0211minorities.htm

Condran, G. A. & Cheney, R. A. (1982). Mortality trends in Philadelphia: Age and cause-specific death rates 1870–1930. *Demography, 19(1)*, 97–123.

Denby, R. W. & Curtis, C. M. (2003). Why special populations are not the target of family preservation services: A case for program reform. *Journal of Sociology & Social Welfare, 30(2)*, 149–173.

DePanfilis, D. & Scannapieco, M. (1994). Assessing the safety of children at risk of maltreatment: Decision-making models. *Child Welfare, 73(3)*, 229–246.

Ehrensaft, M. K., Cohen, P. & Brown, J. (2003). Intergenerational transmission of partner violence: A 20-year prospective study. *Journal of Consulting & Clinical Psychology, 71(4)*, 741–753.

Erikson, E. H. (1963). *Childhood and Society* (2nd ed.). New York: W. W. Norton & Co.

Erikson, E. H. (1968). *Identity: Youth and crisis.* London: Faber & Faber.

Erikson, E. H. (1975). *Life history and the historical moment.* New York: Norton.

Escalas, J. E. & Stern, B. B. (2003). Sympathy and empathy: Emotional responses to First Nations Orphan Association. (n.d.). Retrieved March 28, 2006, from http://geocities.com/fnoac/ advertising dramas. *Journal of Consumer Research, 29(4)*, 566–578.

Flango, V., & Flango, C. (1994). *The flow of adoption information from the States.* Williamsburg, VA: National Center for State Courts.

Gauthier, Y., Fortin, G. & Jéliu, G. (2004). Clinical application of attachment theory in permanency planning for children in foster care: The importance of continuity of care. *Infant Mental Health Journal, 25(4)*, 379–396.

Goldman, J. & Salus, M. (2003). *A coordinated response to child abuse and neglect: The Foundation for Practice.* Washington, DC: U.S. Department of Health and Human Services, National Center on Child Abuse and Neglect.

Hewitt, S. K. (1999). *Assessing allegations of sexual abuse in preschool children: Understanding small voices.* Thousand Oaks, CA: Sage Publications.

Holditch-Davis, D., Sandelowski, M. & Harris, B. G. (1999). Effect of infertility on mothers' and fathers' interactions with young infants. *Journal of Reproductive and Infant Psychology, 17(2)*, 159–173.

Holt, M. (1992). *The orphan trains: Placing out in America.* Lincoln: University of Nebraska Press.

Katz, M. B. (1996). *In the Shadow of the Poorhouse: A social history of welfare in America.* New York: Basic Books.

Kirk, D. H. (1964). *Shared fate: A theory of adoption and mental health.* New York: The Free Press of Glencoe.

Kopel, S., Charlton, T. & Well, S. J. (2003). Investigation laws and practices in child protective services. *Child Welfare, 82(6)*, 661–684.

Kramer, L. & Houston, D. (1999). Hope for the children: A community-based approach to supporting families who adopt children with special needs. Special issue: Achieving excellence in special needs adoption. *Child Welfare, 78(5)*, 611–635.

Kreisher, K. (2002, March). Coming home: The lingering effects of the Indian adoption project. *Children's Voice* Article. Child Welfare League of America. Retrieved July 10, 2004, from http://www.cwla.org/articles/cv0203indianadopt.htm

Lau, A. S., Litrownik, A. J. Newton, R. R. & Landsverk, J. (2003). Going home: The complex effects of reunification on internalizing problems among children in foster care. *Journal of Abnormal Child Psychology, 31(4)*, 345–358.

Maza, P. (1984). Adoption trends: 1944–1975, at Table 1, *Child Welfare Research Notes*, No. 9. Washington, D.C.: Administration on Children, Youth, and Families.

McRoy, R. & Grape, H. (1999). Skin color in transracial and inracial adoptive placements: Implications for special needs adoptions. *Child Welfare, 78(5)*, 673–693.

McWey, L. & Mullis, A. K. (2004). Improving the lives of children in foster care: The impact of supervised visitation. *Family Relations: Interdisciplinary Journal of Applied Family Studies, 53(3)*, 293–300.

Mendenhall, T. J., Berge, J. M., Wrobel, G. M, Grotevant, H. D. & McRoy, R. M. (2004). Adolescents' satisfaction with contact in adoption. *Child & Adolescent Social Work Journal, 21(2)*, 175–190.

National Association of Black Social Workers. (2003). *Kinship care position paper.* Retrieved on October 23, 2005, from http://www.nabsw.org/mserver/KimshipCare.aspx?menuContext=760

National Association of Black Social Workers. (2003). *Kinship Care.* Retrieved March 28, 2006, from http://nasbw.org/mserver/Kinshipcare.aspx

National Clearinghouse on Child Abuse and Neglect. (2005). *Definition of child abuse and neglect state statutes* Series 2005. U.S. Department of Health and Human Services, Administration for Children & Families. Retrieved May 30, 2004, from http://nccanch.acf.hhs.gov/general/legal/statutes/define.cfm

Newcomb, M., Locke, D. & Thomas F. (2001). Intergenerational cycle of maltreatment: A popular concept obscured by methodological limitations. *Child Abuse & Neglect, 25(9)*, 1219–1240.

Patrick, M., Sheets, E. & Trickel, E. (1990). *We are a part of history: The Orphan trains.* Virginia Beach, VA: The Donning Co.

Pears, K. C. & Capaldi, D. M. (2001). Intergenerational transmission of abuse: A two-generational prospective study of an at-risk sample. *Child Abuse & Neglect, 25(11)*, 1439–1461.

Peterson, C. & Biggs, M. (1997). Interviewing children about trauma: Problems with "specific" questions. *Journal of Traumatic Stress, 10(2)*, 279–290.

Poole, D. A. & Lindsay, D. S. (1998). Assessing the accuracy of young children's reports: Lessons from the investigation of child sexual abuse. *Applied & Preventive Psychology, 7(1)*, 1–26.

Roberts, D. (2002). *Shattered bonds: The color of child welfare.* New York: Basic Civitas Books.

Rutter, B. (1978). *The parents' guide to foster family care.* New York: Child Family League of America.

Sanchirico, A. & Jablonka, K. (2000). Keeping foster children connected to their biological parents: the impact of foster parent training and support. *Child and Adolescent Social Work Journal, 17(3)*, 185–203.

Schechter, M. D. (1960). Observations on adopted children. *Archives of General Psychiatry 3(21)*, 29, 31.

Shughart, W. F. & Chappell, W. F. (1999). Fostering the demand for adoptions: An empirical analysis of the impact of orphanages and foster care on adoptions in the U.S. In R. D. McKenzie (Ed.), *Rethinking orphanages for the 21st century* (151–171). Thousand Oaks, CA: Sage Publishers.

Siu, S. & Hogan, P. T. (1989). Common clinical themes in child welfare. *Social Work, 34(4)*, 229–345.

Smith, C. J. & Devore, W. (2004). African American children in the child welfare and kinship system: From exclusion to over inclusion. *Children & Youth Services Review, 26(5)*, 427–446.

Spake, A. (1994, November). The little boy who didn't have to die. *McCall's*, p. 142.

Sternberg, K. J., Lamb, M. E. & Orbach, Y. (2001). Use of a structured investigative protocol enhances young children's responses to free-recall prompts in the course of forensic interviews. *Journal of Applied Psychology, 86(5)*, 997–1005.

Surbeck, B.C. (2003). An investigation of racial partiality in child welfare assessments of attachment. *American Journal of Orthopsychiatry, 73(1)*, 13–23.

Trattner, W. (1998). *From poor law to welfare state* (6th ed.). New York: Free Press.

U.S. Department of Health and Human Services, Administration for Children and Families, Administration on Children, Youth and Families, Children's Bureau. (2005). *The AFCARS Report*. Retrieved October 22, 2005, from http://www.acf.hhs.gov/programs/cb/publications/afcars/report10.htm

U.S. Senate. (1974). *Hearings before the Subcommittee on Indian Affairs of the Committee on Interior and Insular Affairs*, 99th Cong., 2d Sess. (testimony of William Byler). Washington, DC: U.S. Government Printing Office.

Von Hartz, J. (1978). *New York street kids.* New York: Dover.

Warren, A. (1995). *Orphan train rider: One boy's true story.* Boston: Houghton Mifflin Co.

suggested reading

Holt, M. I. (1994). *The orphan trains: The placing out in America.* Lincoln: University of Nebraska Press.

Lavin, P. & Park, C. (1999). *Despair turned to rage: Understanding and helping abused, neglected, and abandoned youth.* Atlanta, GA: CWLA Press.

Mars, B. (1998). *Bobbie's story: A guide for foster families.* Atlanta, GA: CWLA Press.

O'Malley, B. (2005). *My foster care journey: A foster/adoption lifebook.* Winthrop, MA: Adoption-Works.

Patrick, M., Sheets, E. & Trickel, E. (1990). *We are a part of history: The story of the orphan trains.* Santa Fe, NM: The Lightening Tree.

Richards, K. N. (1998). *Tender mercies: Inside the world of a child abuse investigator.* Atlanta, GA: CWLA Press.

internet web sites related to child and family services

Black Administrators in Child Welfare (BACW): **http://www.blackadministrators.org**
Carlisle Indian Industrial School: **http://www.historicalsociety.com/ciiswelcome.html**
Child Welfare League of America: **http://www.cwla.org/**
National Center on Substance Abuse and Child Welfare: **http://www.ncsacw.samhsa.gov/**
National Indian Child Welfare Association: **http://www.nicwa.org/**
The Orphan Train Collection: **http://www.orphantrainriders.com/**

chapter 5

Adolescent Services

One second she's curled up in my lap asking me to stroke her hair as she cries about a fight she had with one of her girlfriends, and the next second she's screaming at me, telling me she doesn't need a mother, and that her father and I are ruining her life. She is so dramatic and her moods shift from moment to moment. She's driving us crazy, and I'm wondering where my sweet little girl went." So complains one of my neighbors about her 15-year-old daughter. The stage of adolescence is as confusing for adults as it is for the adolescents. This stage of development serves as the bridge from childhood to adulthood, and crossing this bridge often involves several circuitous routes that sometimes appears to parents as though no progress toward maturity is being made.

My neighbor's teenaged daughter Chelsea describes adolescence this way:

> Being a teenager is full of drama and mixed emotions. I have the pressure of my friends who expect me to be cool, but I also have the pressure of my boyfriend who doesn't want me to be cooler than he is. School is always a pressure, and I feel like I always have to worry about keeping my parents happy. I want to be the same person at school as I am at church. I don't want to be two-faced, but this can be hard because everybody expects something different from me, and sometimes those things are completely opposite of each other. Sometimes I just wish I could go back to being little again where my parents made all my decisions for me, but at the same time I fight to make my own decisions because I want to be more independent. Either way, it's not easy!

Adolescence is an interesting stage of development for many reasons. The concept of this stage is rather new as there was little acknowledgment or understanding of adolescence as a separate stage of development until the latter part of the nineteenth century. But even now, when adolescence is accepted as a distinct stage of development, there are significant differences in how the stage of adolescence is perceived among various cultures, both within the United States as well as internationally. In addition, many societal changes have occurred in the last 150 years that have had a dramatic impact on adolescents themselves, creating new dynamics and issues reflected in developmental theories.

Adolescence: A New Stage of Development?

It has been widely reported among psychologists, sociologists, and historians that the stage of adolescence is relatively new, not having been formally acknowledged until psychologist G. Stanley Hall began his study of adolescence in 1882, culminating in his groundbreaking book on adolescence published in 1904. Yet it would be misleading to assume that because society did not formally acknowledge the stage of adolescence that it did not exist. There was little acknowledgment of childhood being a distinct stage of development prior to the late 1800s, but that does not mean that children did not tantrum, play, and essentially act and feel like children. Hall's earliest writing on the study of adolescence sounds strikingly similar to contemporary descriptions of adolescent behavior. Hall described adolescents as possessing a "lack of emotional steadiness, violent impulses, unreasonable conduct, lack of enthusiasm and sympathy" (p. 635).

But even if adolescents have always behaved as adolescents, there have been significant shifts in child and adolescent developmental theories, influenced by the societal changes that have occurred over the past few hundred years. These changes have influenced not only how the stages of childhood and adolescence are perceived, but also the course of development itself. Lifestyles were quite different two hundred years ago when the United States was a new country. The U.S. economy was different, livelihoods were different, neighborhoods were different, and families were different. An important question to consider is what kind of impact these changes have had on adolescent development and whether adolescent behavior has changed, or whether society's expectations and perception of adolescents have changed.

There is no question that the mass urbanization of the past two-hundred years has had an impact on individual and family lives, including the lives of adolescents, who at one point in history worked alongside family members on the family farm, but who in contemporary times have far less vocational responsibility, as an increasing amount of focus is placed on the academic education of adolescents. Even the way in which many adolescents are educated has changed, likely influencing adolescent development, as teens spend significantly more time with their peers in large school environments, with increasing exposure to violence (Larsen, 2003; Raywid, 1996; National Center for Education Statistics, 1999).

Thus, although adolescents of the past acted in ways that are strikingly similar to the ways in which they act today, the many profound changes within U.S. society, including changes in family structure, the public educational system, and expectations of adolescents within these systems, have influenced the ways in which many contemporary adolescents both develop and behave.

Developmental Perspectives

To understand the behavior of adolescents, it is important to understand the developmental stages that children and adolescents progress through on their way to adulthood. Development occurs within various domains including the intellectual, emotional, psychosocial, moral, and even the spiritual spheres. Many theories of development propose that individuals progress through distinct stages of growth with earlier stages acting as foundations for successive stages. Because the course of development is influenced by many factors, both on an individual as well as a broader societal level, thus it is important to consider both developmental theories and the course of developmental growth and maturity of children and adolescents within various contexts. For instance, in the previous section we discussed changes that have occurred in families in the United States since the mid-nineteenth century. It is likely that what was considered "normal" behavior for adolescents in 1900 would not necessarily be considered "normal" in contemporary society.

In other words, it is important to consider the normative aspects of adolescent development within a *historical context*. What is expected of an adolescent, and what is considered adaptive and healthy behavior, depends on what is occurring in the world during the time in which the adolescent lives. A world war with a mandatory draft forces adolescents to grow up quickly, just as the Great Depression shortened childhoods across the country as adolescents were looked upon to help support their families. Yet in contemporary society childhoods are often considered lengthened by a good economy, which reduces the need for adolescent employment, an increase in educational requirements required for professional employment, and the cessation of a mandatory draft, all of which have led to many believing that society has lower expectations of adolescents than in past eras. Adolescents who did not work during the Great Depression would likely have been considered irresponsible for not being willing to assist in the support of their families, but adolescents who do not work in contemporary society are likely presumed to be focused solely on their academic studies in preparation for college.

It is also important to consider developmental issues within a *cultural context*. What is considered normative and emotionally healthy within one culture may be considered maladaptive in another, and what is considered respectful and honorable behavior in one culture may be a sign of an emotional disorder in another. For instance, in many cultures, remaining in the family home until marriage is considered the norm. It is common in collectivist cultures, such as Asian, Latino, and even some European cultures, for single adult children as old as 30 years of age to live at home with their parents. In many of these cultures it would be considered a sign of disrespect for a single adult to move from the family home to gain independence prior to getting married. The United States is, for the most part, an individualistic society that values independence and autonomy, thus many within the U.S. culture may perceive the

30-year-old male still living with his parents as a sign of unhealthy emotional enmeshment, where the boundaries between parent and adult child are blurred.

Finally, it is important to consider development within a *regional context*. Although urbanization over the last two hundred years within the United States has resulted in the majority of people living in urban or suburban communities, rural life still exists in this country and some research suggests that there are significant differences between adolescent life in rural communities compared to life in urban communities. Although there is not a wide body of research comparing urban and rural adolescents, a study conducted in 2001 found that rural adolescents felt less pressure to become involved in gang activities, were confronted with less violence both on campus as well as off, and felt less academic pressure, both from their school as well as their parents, compared with adolescents residing in urban areas (Gandara, Gutierrez, & O'Hara, 2001).

Understanding the natural course of development will assist the human service professional to correctly evaluate an adolescent's behavior, framing it as either adaptive or maladaptive, depending on the context within which the behavior is exhibited. For instance, understanding that it is normal for an adolescent to act in a self-centered and dramatic manner will aid the human service professional in framing behavior that, in an adult, would be indicative of a personality disorder.

Keeping historical, cultural, and regional contexts in mind will assist the human service practitioner in not mischaracterizing certain behaviors because their origin is either misunderstood or not valued by the majority culture. Adolescents in contemporary culture may act in a different manner than adolescents in past generations, yet this does not necessarily mean that adolescents today are any less respectful than those of the past. It is also important for those in human services to understand that an adolescent who immigrated to this country from a Latin American country might act in a different manner than adolescents who have lived in the United States their entire lives, or that an adolescent who recently moved from a farming community to a large city school might act differently than adolescents who grew up in an urban community. Having a competent grasp of normative development can be a guide for human service professionals who work with adolescents and must evaluate and assess their behavior before determining the appropriate level of intervention, or whether intervention is warranted at all.

Most of the developmental theorists agree that adolescence is a time of searching for one's own identity and developing a sense of autonomy. Trying on different "selves" is a common mental and behavioral activity of adolescents who are in the process of developing an internally anchored sense of who they are, rather than defining themselves by what others think or expect of them (including their parents) (Erikson, 1968; Kerpelman & Pittman, 2001). Many normal and healthy adolescents can be quite dramatic and egocentric in their behavior, and although this might give many parents cause for concern, most adolescents grow out of this stage to become giving and compassionate adults.

Common Clinical Issues and the Role of the Human Service Professional

My first job in human services was working for an adolescent residential facility in Colorado. I still remember my first day, which was filled with anxious anticipation. I was one of those individuals who always knew I was going to be a counselor, and it seemed as though I had waited far too long to be able to counsel professionally. I was assigned to the high-risk unit, which housed newly admitted girls, as well as girls who were at risk of suicide or self-injury. I couldn't wait to jump in and start rescuing these girls! Thus, you can imagine my surprise when the unit supervisor strapped on my own body alarm and explained that if I was physically attacked, my natural body movements would trigger the alarm and all available staff would come running to my aid. Attacked? Why would these girls attack me when all I was doing was trying to help them? I had spent four years as an undergraduate preparing to help my fellow human being, and the thought that my efforts would not only go unappreciated, but would be perceived as threatening was shocking. Such was my professional introduction into the world of working with adolescents. I learned on my first day of work that the adolescent population could be a challenging one to work with and that my adolescent clients might not always express their appreciation for the work I was doing with them.

The common stereotype of adolescents being generally rebellious and out of control is both true and untrue. Many adolescents are quite responsible and do not have mental health problems. But adolescence is a time of stress, of trying on different "selves," and of exploring undiscovered issues, attitudes, and behaviors. There are many reasons for these dynamics. Most developmental theorists consider this time in one's life to be transitional, and typically all transitions can be stormy. But there are other relevant issues that make adolescence unique among the various developmental stages of life, which has an impact on providing counseling services to those adolescents who are troubled.

Abstract Reasoning: A Dangerous Weapon in the Hands of an Adolescent

Jean Piaget, a Swiss-born biologist turned psychologist, developed a theory of cognitive development that is still the dominant theory of intellectual development today (Piaget, 1950). Among Piaget's many findings, he discovered that children, adolescents, and adults each think differently. Most notably, Piaget discovered that younger children think concretely, meaning that they lack the ability to understand many adult concepts such as parables and analogies, as well as other abstract concepts. If a group of adults were asked what it meant to "let the chips fall where they may," they will most likely explain that this is an idiom meaning to let things happen naturally. But if a group of children were asked what this statement meant, they will most likely reply that it means that if chips fall on the ground, one should not pick them up.

Piaget believed that as children approached adolescence they began to develop the ability for logical reasoning involved in abstract thought (Piaget, 1950). Abstract thought or reasoning enables us to have empathy by "putting ourselves in someone else's shoes." It allows us to think metaphorically, to understand sarcasm, to deduce, analyze, synthesize, and to rationalize. It also allows us to understand, and thus internalize, moral standards: to not just know that something is wrong, but to understand *why* it is wrong. If children of the age of five are asked why it is wrong to hit another child on the playground, they might state that it is wrong because they will get in trouble. Yet most adults would be able to explain that this act is wrong because it violates another person's personal rights, that violence does not resolve conflict, and that they would not want to be hit, even if someone else was angry with them. This type of reasoning requires empathy, the ability to see situations from multiple perspectives, the ability to draw on other experiences, and the ability to connect the immediacy of hitting someone to the generalized concept of violence—all of which require abstract reasoning ability.

It is through the development of abstract reasoning ability that an adolescent discovers that their parents might not always be right, that lying can be rationalized, that breaking the rules can sometimes be fun, and that authority can be questioned. When a child asks, "Why?" the question usually relates to why the sky is blue and the grass green. But when an adolescent asks, "Why?" it often relates to asking why sex before marriage is wrong, why education must occur in a 20' × 20' classroom, why drinking alcohol is bad, and perhaps even such existential questions as whether God is real, or why they were put on this earth.

Abstract reasoning is a useful and powerful intellectual tool and can be a lethal weapon in the hands of an unstable and angry adolescent. Existential questions about the meaning of life can quickly spiral into questioning why one should exist at all, and questions about the concept of authority can quickly evolve into abandoning the concept of obeying authority all together. The necessary skill of logical or abstract reasoning often enables a troubled adolescent to rationalize away reasons not to rebel.

Adolescent Rebellion

As long as there have been adolescents, one can be assured that there has been adolescent rebellion. Casually defined, adolescent rebellion can include any behavior on the part of an adolescent that is in marked opposition to standard rules, either within the family or within society in general. Determining what specifically constitutes rebellious behavior, though, can be a bit more challenging and often depends on current social mores, as well as one's own personal value system. Behaviors that involve outright destruction and the breaking of laws are easily characterized as "rebellious." But whether the more subtle challenging of rules is considered rebellious is certainly in the eye of the beholder, where one person's rebellion is another person's sign of autonomy and individuation. For instance, most would agree that behaviors such taking illegal drugs, habitual lying, and engaging in chronic truancy are rebellious behaviors, but what about the occasional drinking of alcohol, or the intermittent breaking of a curfew? Many mental health experts and even some parents might normalize this behavior as being typical of the majority of adolescents who are striving for increased independence and testing limits along the way.

In general, though, any behavior in adolescents should be considered maladaptive if it is interfering with normal functioning and causing problems in the adolescent's everyday life. For instance, an adolescent who skips one day of school in an entire year would not be considered "rebellious," but adolescents who are truant several times per week, thereby affecting their ability to pass their classes, would likely be characterized as rebellious.

Externalizing Behaviors

Conduct disorder (CD) and oppositional defiant disorder (ODD) are disorders included in the DSM-IV-TR that are diagnosed during adolescence to describe behavioral problems in children and adolescents. CD the more serious of these two disorders involves a consistent pattern of behaviors in which social mores and rules are habitually broken, and the rights of others are consistently violated without regard to the other person's feelings. To avoid a child being diagnosed with CD in response to uncharacteristic or minor rebellion, children cannot receive this diagnosis unless they meet at least three of the following four criteria in the preceding 12-month period:

1. Exhibiting aggression to people and animals, such as bullying, threatening or intimidating others, initiating fights, using weapons, exhibiting physical cruelness toward people or animals, stealing from a victim (for example, armed robbery), or forced sexual activity.

2. Destroying property, such as destructively setting a fire, or deliberately destroying another person's property, fire setting with the intention of causing serious damage.

3. Deceitfulness or theft, such as breaking into someone's home or car, lying to obtain something desired, nonviolent stealing such as shoplifting.

4. Serious violations of rules, such as frequently staying out at night despite parental curfew, running away from home, and frequent truancies from school. (American Psychiatric Association, 2000)

Again, what most often determines the difference between the adolescents who are harmlessly spreading their wings and CD is the *frequency, persistence,* and *seriousness* of the maladaptive behavior. A 12-year-old who "runs away" to the next-door neighbor's house or a 16-year-old who breaks curfew by 30 minutes on only a few occasions would certainly not be diagnosed with this disorder. But the 12-year-old who runs away for weeks at a time or a 16-year-old who comes home whenever she or he pleases certainly might.

ODD is another emotional disorder commonly diagnosed in adolescence and is characterized by a milder set of behavioral problems including negative, hostile, and defiant behavior such as losing one's temper, arguing with adults, and consistently refusing to obey rules. Other criteria include blaming others for personal mistakes, being easily annoyed, frequent feelings of anger and resentment, spite, and vindictiveness.

Because human service professionals always evaluate the mental health of individuals *within the context of their environment,* it is vital to examine any potential environmental causes or influences of an adolescent's maladaptive behavior. For instance, socioeconomic status, gender, parenting styles, environment, genetic influences, cognitive deficits, and temperament have all been associated with juvenile delinquency (Lahey, Moffit, & Caspi, 2003). It is important to note, though, that although such research indicates some type of a relationship between conduct disorders and these various influences, they do not specify whether any of these variables actually *cause* conduct disorders in adolescents. Thus it would be incorrect to assume that because a child is from a lower socioeconomic status family that he or she will engage in juvenile delinquency. More likely, families that are chaotic, perhaps even abusive, are likely to be from a lower socioeconomic level because such behaviors are often not amenable to the skill sets required to be a high wage earner.

I have worked with adolescents for years—first in a residential setting, then in a school setting, and now in my private practice, and I have found that adolescents typically act out for specific reasons. Clinically evaluating the entire picture is extremely important as many children and adolescents who meet the criteria for CD or ODD come from homes where maladaptive behavior abounds (Frick, 2004). Such behaviors are often a manifestation of earlier abuse, neglect, and general chaos in the home environment. In general, if children and adolescents cannot talk out their feelings, they will likely act them out, often in a negative manner. Thus, if adolescents have neither the opportunity nor the maturity to connect behaviors with feelings, they will be at greater risk of expressing negative feelings in a destructive way. I have never worked with an adolescent with normal cognitive abilities who rebelled without reason— granted that reason might be buried under layers of the family's good impression management, but the reasons for any serious rebellion virtually always surface at some point during the counseling relationship.

Internalizing Behaviors

Adolescents, like children and adults, do not always manifest their emotional problems in outward ways. In fact, some of the most emotionally disturbed adolescents turn their anxiety, anger, and sadness inward with behaviors that reflect forms of depression. These adolescent are often overlooked, particularly within a school system, because they are not disruptive, often sitting in the back of the class quietly, disturbing no one. Yet emotional disturbances turned inward can often be the most serious of all, putting these adolescents at higher risk of depression, self-abuse, and suicide.

Depression and Anxiety. Everyone experiences depression from time to time, but when feelings of sadness become so pronounced and long-standing that these emotions become barriers to normal functioning, then the individual may be suffering from clinical depression, also referred to as major depressive disorder. The *Diagnostic and Statistical Manual of Mental Disorders* (DSM-IV-TR) lists several criteria for major depressive disorder, including abnormally depressed mood, loss of interest and pleasure, inappropriate guilt, and disturbances in sleep, appetite, energy level, memory, and concentration, and, in serious cases, frequent thoughts of suicide. In children and adolescents the melancholy can often appears as irritability, which can lead to confusion in diagnosing the appropriate disorder because an irritable teenager can look far more oppositional than a sad or melancholy one.

The term used to indicate the existence of two emotional disorders simultaneously is *comorbidity,* and the comorbidity of depression and anxiety is quite high, with approximately 80 percent of those with depression also suffering from anxiety of some type (Gorwood, 2004). Although anxiety has a completely different set of diagnostic criteria (see the DSM-IV-TR), if one examines the possible origin of mood disorders then it makes sense that the emotional issues that can make someone feel depressed could likely lead to feelings of anxiety as well.

There are many treatments for depression and anxiety, ranging from counseling to drug therapy, including antidepressants and antianxiety medication. However, working with adolescents is a special challenge because adolescents can be impulsive, dramatic, and narcissistic as a normal part of development, but a depressed adolescent who is impulsive, dramatic, and narcissistic can be dangerous.

I discussed earlier how some adolescents express their negative, uncomfortable emotions by acting *out* in aggressive and destructive ways toward others, but another way that adolescents deal with their problems is by turning all their emotions inward. Adolescents suffering from depression and anxiety often manifest many self-destructive behaviors, the most serious being suicide. But there are many other self-abusive behaviors that emotionally disturbed adolescents may engage in that, although certainly not as serious as suicide, still warrant serious clinical intervention.

Self-Injury. Self-injury, also called *self-mutilation,* is defined as any deliberate, repetitive attempt to harm one's own bodily tissue without a conscious desire to commit suicide (Nock & Prinstein, 2005). Self-injury most often includes cutting the arms and legs with a razor blade or any sharp object (such as a paper clip), but can also include burning, picking at wounds, and even head-banging. People who self-mutilate using a sharp object are commonly called "cutters."

Although self-injury occurs in the adult population (occurring in about 4 percent of the general population), adolescents are at increased risk for self-injury, with 39 percent of the adolescent population admitting to having self-injured at some point in their lives, and 61 percent of adolescents in a psychiatric in-patient setting having self-injured (Nock & Prinstein, 2005). Self-injury can be a difficult issue to treat because so little is known about its causes. In addition, this type of behavior tends to be resistant to treatment. What is known is that females tend to self-injure far more than males, with some studies indicating that of all those who self-abuse, 97 percent are women (Nock & Prinstein, 2005). One reason for this may be due at least in part to how females are socialized to internalize their negative feelings, whereas males are socialized to externalize their feelings.

The precise reasons why adolescents self-mutilate is unknown, but self-injury has been associated with a host of emotional and psychological problems, including suicidal thoughts, eating disorders, chronic feelings of hopelessness and despair, depression and anxiety, sexual abuse, physical abuse, severe emotional abuse, perfectionism, and a pervasive sense of loneliness (Nock & Prinstein, 2005). The National Institutes of Mental Health estimate that approximately 50 to 60 percent of cutters were sexually abused as children (Crowe & Bunclark, 2000).

Many adolescents who self-injure cite many reasons for physically harming themselves, including the belief that the cutting or burning allows them to feel something in the midst of emotional numbness. Yet some adolescents claim that self-injury actually numbs them in a manner similar to alcohol or drugs, and there is some evidence that such self-injury causes the release of naturally occurring opiates (known as endorphins). Other reasons for self-injury relate to the internal expression of rage and relieving intolerable tension resulting from deep feelings of anger, frustration, despair, and loneliness. Adolescents who are survivors of sexual molestation often claim that they cut in response to the shame they felt, thus this behavior may also act as a form of self-punishment.

The majority of these adolescents had few coping mechanisms to deal with extremely intense emotions, and some claimed to have started cutting because a friend did it or to get attention, but the more serious "cutters" were deeply ashamed of their behavior and did their best to hide the evidence, such as wearing long sleeves, even during warm weather. I noted common elements among my adolescent clients who were serious and habitual self-mutilators, including the chronic tendency to suppress or outright deny their anger, the tendency to be extremely impulsive, high levels of depression, a pervasive sense of hopelessness, a tendency to be self-deprecating, a chronic sense of emptiness, and an inability to regulate their emotions.

A human service professional will likely encounter adolescent clients who self-injure in a variety of practice settings, including adolescent residential facilities, group homes, foster homes, schools, and any other setting where adolescents are served. It is important that clinicians always be on the lookout for common warning signs of self-injury, even if the adolescent or the parents deny the behavior. Adolescents who self-mutilate for attention will often flaunt their "work" by showing off what frequently amounts to superficial cuts on the forearm or thighs. But as mentioned earlier, serious self-mutilators will often hide their wounds, thus a human service professional would be wise to note suspicious behaviors, such as consistently wearing long sleeves and pants, even on warm days. More obvious signs of self-injury may include parallel scars on the forearm or thighs, burn marks in these same places or even on the fingertips, or any unexplained or suspicious wound, particularly wounds that tend not to heal (due to chronic reinjury).

As with many habitual behaviors, self-mutilation can quickly become compulsive, outliving its usefulness, which is one of the primary reasons why this behavior is so challenging to treat. But there is hope because many former self-mutilators go on to live lives free of self-injury. The most successful treatment programs include a combination of individual, group, and family therapy with the goal of increasing the adolescent's personal insight and awareness of the dynamics underlying the compulsion to self-injure. Issues such as *impulse control* and *emotional regulation* are paramount in any successful treatment plan, as is assisting the adolescent client in learning how to understand and effectively manage intense or uncomfortable emotions in a direct manner. This approach will allow self-abusive adolescents to own their emotions, rather than deny or suppress them.

Suicide. The ultimate internalizing behavior is, of course, the killing of oneself, and although people have been committing suicide for centuries, understanding the dynamics of suicidal behavior, or **suicidal ideation,** remains a relatively new area of study. Of particular interest to social scientists and mental health practitioners is discovering how to most effectively prevent suicide attempts. As with self-injury, adolescents are at particularly high risk of suicide and suicidal ideation for several reasons, including their propensity for **impulsivity,** as well as their frequent feelings of **omnipotence.**

In 2001 (the most recent data available) suicide was the third leading cause of death among individuals between the ages of 15 through 24 years of age (Anderson & Smith, 2003). Adolescent suicidal behavior can include **suicidal gestures,** suicide attempts, and serious suicide attempts and suicide completions. Each of these behaviors can result in a completed suicide, even if that is not the intention of the adolescent, but it is important to distinguish between each of these types of suicidal behavior for the purposes of intervention, as well as developing an understanding of what goes on in the mind of an adolescent who engages in any type of suicidal behavior.

Suicidal Gestures. A suicidal gesture typically involves behavior on the part of an adolescent that is unlikely to result in a completed suicide, but is more often a cry for help or attention. Even if a practitioner does not believe that their adolescent clients truly wish to kill themselves, these gestures should not be taken lightly, because it is always possible that the adolescent will kill himself even if this wasn't the intended outcome.

Suicide Attempts and Complete Suicide. Certainly the most serious of all suicidal behavior involves actions that are intended to end one's life. As with the adult population, it is not necessarily the adolescents who scream their suicidal intentions from the rooftop who clinicians need to be the most concerned about, but the sad, hopeless, and depressed adolescents who quietly slink away, without drawing any attention, determined to kill themselves in a manner that precludes intervention. Fortunately, not all serious attempts are successful. Some adolescents experience a last-minute change of heart and call a family member or friend, reach out to a suicide hotline, or call 9-1-1.

The types of adolescents who attempt suicide are different than those who complete suicides. For instance, research indicates that about 85 percent of "attempters" are female (Andrus, Fleming, Heumann, Wassell, Hopkins, & Gordon, 1991), whereas about 80 percent of suicide completers are typically male (Arias, Anderson, Kung, Murphy, & Kochanek, 2003). Reasons for this might be related to the social acceptance of males completing suicide rather than making an attempt (Moskos, Achilles, & Gray, 2004).

Assessment, Intervention, and Treatment of Suicidal Behavior. Recognizing whether an adolescent is at real risk of attempting suicide is an important clinical skill that develops with education and experience. One of the most intimidating issues facing any human service professional is knowing how to predict suicidal behavior. The answer to that question is that it is virtually impossible to definitively predict when anyone will make an attempt to end his or her life, but there are indicators and precursors that practitioners can look for, such as the psychosocial risk factors discussed in the previous section.

Although any human service professional should have a "safety first" approach to treatment, there are valid concerns for not calling 9-1-1 each time an adolescent client sounds hopeless or immersed in despair, including not wanting to destroy the counseling relationship by overreacting. When adolescent clients share that they sometimes wonder what it might feel like to die, and an anxious practitioner responds by having the adolescent involuntarily hospitalized, trust can certainly be destroyed. But in light of the alarming increase in adolescent suicides since the mid-1990s, particularly within the adolescent male population, safety is of paramount importance. Thus, some sort of balance must be struck between honoring the privacy and safety of the counseling relationship and making sure that the adolescent remains safe.

Before any successful intervention strategy can be developed, the questions of why so many teenagers are killing themselves and who is most at risk must be addressed. Suicide rates of African-American males is increasing dramatically, particularly among those in higher socioeconomic status, and suicide rates in the adolescent Native American population are exceedingly high (Moskos, Achilles, & Gray, 2004).

Rutter and Behrendt (2004) conducted a study of 100 at-risk adolescents, focusing on psychosocial risk factors. Their research revealed that those adolescents who were plagued by feelings of *hopelessness,* had little to no *social support,* had feelings of *hostility,* and had a *negative self-concept* were at the greatest risk for committing suicide. This research is consistent with the research on self-injury, which revealed that self-mutilation was often the manifestation of rage and hostility turned inward, and as previously mentioned, suicide is the most injurious of all self-abusive behaviors.

Other risk factors for suicide include having a friend commit suicide (Hazell & Lewin, 1999), and for males having a gun available was a significant risk factor, and for girls low self-esteem. Research also showed that deep involvement in school activities markedly decreased the potential for suicidal behavior (Bearman & Moody, 2004). Treatment will then emanate directly from any deficits found in these areas of functioning and will include the development of emotional insight and better coping skills to deal with all these emotions and insights.

If an adolescent is assessed to be a suicide risk, a safety plan must be developed with the parents or primary caregivers, because the desire to commit suicide can only come to fruition if there is opportunity. Thus it is important for the adolescent's environment to be as free of risk as possible. For instance, a good home safety plan will include the removal of all pharmaceutical drugs, guns, kitchen knives, and loose razor blades. A depressed and socially isolated adolescent who is not actively suicidal but who thinks about dying from time to time may not need to be hospitalized, but should be monitored at all times so that any escalation in depressive symptoms can be addressed immediately. At any time that adolescent clients acknowledge suicidal intent, admit to feeling frightened of their desire to harm themselves, or disclose having a suicide plan, the human service professional may decide hospitalization is warranted, and in that case, the family will be directed to either call 9-1-1 or to take their teen to their local emergency room.

Spirito and his colleagues found that the single most powerful predictors of continued suicidal behavior are the existence of depression and family dysfunction. Therefore any treatment plan designed to address suicidal behavior must seriously address what is most likely the interplay between negative family relations and the adolescent's feelings of depression (Spirito, Valeri, Boergers, & Donaldson, 2003).

Current treatment intervention focuses on school-based suicide prevention education programs, crisis centers including teen suicide hotlines, screening programs aimed at identifying high-risk adolescents within their community, peer support programs, and public awareness campaigns, including pleas to remove guns from homes with at-risk adolescents. Suggestions for future programs include recommendations that the juvenile justice system coordinate efforts with the school-based programs and other youth outreach agencies, because over 60 percent of adolescents who committed suicide also had a history of involvement with the justice system (Moskos, Achilles, & Gray, 2004).

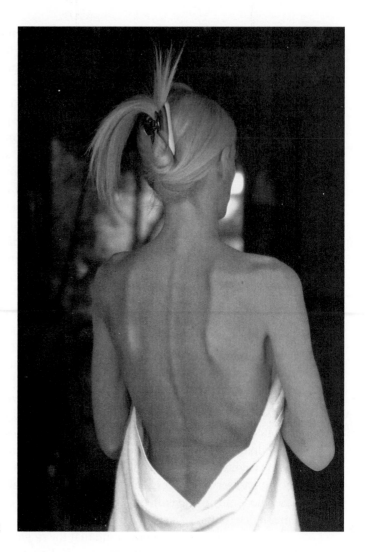

■ A sufferer of
Anorexia Nervosa
who is clearly below
her ideal body weight

Human service professionals must be prepared to deal with the growing trend of suicidal behaviors in the adolescent population. Through education, prevention, and intervention strategies, including a multidisciplinary approach that addresses depression from an emotional and social, as well as a medical, perspective, mental health experts are optimistic that adolescent suicide can be successfully addressed.

Eating Disorders in the Adolescent Population

Another set of disorders common to adolescents is eating disorders, including anorexia nervosa and bulimia nervosa. Although individuals of all ages suffer from eating disorders, the primary onset of eating disorders occurs during adolescence (Ray, 2004).

Females tend to suffer from eating disorders far more often than males, comprising approximately 85 to 90 percent of all documented cases of eating disorders, but the incidence of eating disorders in males is increasing, particularly among male athletes (Walcott, Pratt, & Patel, 2003).

Anorexia involves the intentional starving of oneself and the refusal to maintain expected body weight. The DSM-IV-TR criteria for anorexia includes a body weight of less than 85 percent of normal body weight, an intense fear of gaining weight, distortion of how one's body is perceived, and the absence of a menstrual cycle for at least three months (APA, 2000).

Among the various theories of the causes of anorexia, the most popular tend to focus on maladaptive family patterns where the adolescent's anorexia is presumed to help protect unhealthy family dynamics. These maladaptive patterns can include conflict avoidance, rigidity, and family enmeshment (Lock & le Grange, 2005). It is for this reason that family counseling is the most common recommended treatment for adolescents suffering from anorexia, in addition to in-patient treatment for adolescents who are at risk of serious health complications (Fairburn, 2005).

Bulimia involves a pattern of binge eating indicating a lack of control followed by purging in the form of self-induced vomiting, use of laxatives, or excessive exercise in an attempt to rid oneself of the abundance of food (APA, 2000). Bulimia is far more prevalent in the adolescent population than anorexia (van Hoeken, Seidell, & Hoek, 2003).

Common risk factors of adolescents suffering from bulimia include perfectionism, body dissatisfaction, and low self-esteem (Vohs et al., 2001). Adolescents who engage in binging behavior often experience significant shame once the binging phase is over. These feelings of shame are often dealt with by purging to rid the body of the excess food. This binging-purging cycle often becomes a compulsion robbing the adolescent of the ability to stop the behavior.

Treatment for bulimia often includes insight therapy, family therapy, and cognitive behavioral therapy (CBT), which focuses on the negative self-statements the adolescent thinks in response to life events, as well as negative self-appraisals (Gowers & Bryant-Waugh, 2004). Depression and anxiety are often associated with both anorexia and bulimia, thus a course of antidepressant or antianxiety medication is often considered appropriate.

Schizophrenia in the Adolescent Population

Schizophrenia is a psychotic (or thought) disorder that is a concern to human service professionals working with the adolescent population because this disease is most often diagnosed in late adolescence and early adulthood, with men typically developing the first symptoms of schizophrenia in their late teens and women in their early to midtwenties (National Institutes of Mental Health, 2005).

Symptoms of schizophrenia include delusions (unclear or illogical thinking); hallucinations, which may include hearing, seeing, feeling, or smelling something that is not there (with the most frequent hallucination being auditory); cognitive impairment; disorganized behavior; and an inability to express emotions or respond emotionally to typically pleasurable activities (American Psychological Association [APA], 2000; National Institutes of Mental Health, 2005). Schizophrenia has several subtypes, including paranoid, catatonic, and disorganized types. The most common subtype of schizophrenia is paranoid, where the affected individuals have delusions that others are conspiring against them (Fenton, McGlashan, Victor, & Blyler, 1997).

Schizophrenia is a serious and debilitating brain disease that affects approximately 1 in 100 adults, causing dysfunction in virtually every area of life. Human service professionals working with the adolescent population, particularly older adolescents, must be aware of the early signs and symptoms of schizophrenia because early intervention may have a positive impact on the course of treatment. Early signs of schizophrenia onset during adolescence often include increasing social isolation, particularly from peers (Mackrell & Lavender, 2004), intellectual decline in all areas of cognitive functioning, indications of confused thought, and hallucinations (Fitzgerald, Lucas, & Redoblado, 2004).

Adolescents who are in the early stages of schizophrenia are about 30 times more likely to commit suicide than adolescents in the general population, with approximately 10 percent of all those with schizophrenia ending their lives by suicide at some point (Jarbin & Von Knorring, 2004). This increased risk may be due to unclear thinking and hallucinations (particularly with those suffering from paranoid schizophrenia), but researchers found that subjects who were addicted to smoking cigarettes had a substance abuse problem, or were depressed were at the highest risk of attempting or committing suicide (Jarbin & Von Knorring, 2004). Those with paranoid schizophrenia had three times the rate of suicide than those with other subtypes of schizophrenia (Fenton, McGlashan, Victor, & Blyler, 1997). A strong religious belief system is one of the few variables that seemed to protect schizophrenic teens from suicidal behavior (Jarbin & Von Knorring, 2004).

Treatment of schizophrenia consists primarily of antipsychotic medication, such as Risperdol, which controls the hallucinations and often helps clear up delusional thinking. Human service professionals working with adolescents diagnosed with schizophrenia, or who are in the early stages of this psychotic disorder, can benefit from basic skill-building such as self-care and management (i.e., hygiene, medication compliance), social skills, and interventions that target the reduction of risk factors such as nicotine use, substance abuse, and social isolation.

Other Clinical Issues Affecting the Adolescent Population

Other issues that are commonly diagnosed in adolescents include substance abuse, discussed in detail in Chapters 10 ("Substance Abuse and Treatment") and 11 ("Human Services in the Schools"). Attention deficit issues, such as attention deficit disorder (ADD) and attention deficient hyperactivity disorder (ADHD), are also a growing concern in the adolescent population, particularly in school settings, and thus are discussed in detail in chapter 11 ("Human Services in the Schools").

Adolescence is a time of sexual discovery and experimentation and thus is an issue that must be acknowledged and addressed in a counseling setting Issues related to sexual behavior and teen pregnancy are explored in chapter 11 ("Human Services in the Schools"). Adolescents are also at increased risk for homelessness and for academic failure and sexual exploitation once homeless. The problem of homelessness among the adolescent population is explored in chapter 8 ("Homelessness").

Practice Settings Specific to Adolescent Treatment

There are many practice settings where adolescents receive clinical services, as well as many ways in which these services are provided. Some adolescents may receive individual counseling from therapists who are in private practice. These counseling services can be provided by anyone who has a license to provide independent counseling services such as *psychiatrists, psychologists, marriage and family therapists* (MFTs), *licensed clinical professional counselors* (LCPCs), and *licensed clinical social workers* (LCSWs). Counseling typically occurs in the counselor's office as often as the practitioner and parents deem necessary, but once a week is the most common schedule.

Counseling also occurs in many other settings, such as in schools by school social workers, counselors, and psychologists (see chapter 11); human service agencies that specialize in adolescent issues; outreach organizations such as after-school programs; religious organizations such as Jewish Community Centers (see chapter 12); therapeutic foster care; and counseling provided through the juvenile justice system.

Residential care is a practice setting often utilized for adolescents who are severely behaviorally disordered and at high risk of self-harm and destructive behaviors. Although institutionalized care has steadily decreased for most segments of the population, this institutionalized care for the adolescent population has literally skyrocketed since the 1980s (Wells, 1991). These institutions can be locked or open, private or governmental, short- or long-term, therapeutic or more punitive in nature, but all provide some level of mental health services in relatively large, dormitorylike settings, where the adolescent residents sleep and attend school.

Residential treatment programs vary widely in type and nature, with some residential programs offering services making them sound more like a boarding school than a treatment facility, boasting equine programs, river rafting, and "therapeutic" skiing programs, whereas others are far more sterile offering few extracurricular activities. One reason for this difference can be directly related to the range of populations served. For instance, behavior on the part of an adolescent that results in court intervention and juvenile detention in a residential facility would not necessarily be conducive to a therapeutic ski trip to Vail, Colorado.

Placement times can also vary, with some adolescents being placed in a residential facility for a few months to some who require several years, again depending on the severity of their problems. One popular short-term residential program is Outward Bound, a wilderness therapy program that uses physical challenges to help adolescents deal more effectively with their emotional problems. These programs are offered in various locations within the United States and range from 21 to 28 days in length.

Group homes (or therapeutic foster homes) offer less structured residential care, where various community services are often accessed and where adolescents attend the local public high school and are not isolated from the general community.

More structured residential treatment programs are a bit more sterile in nature, offering services to adolescents whose conduct problems or self-destructive behaviors require a more long-term, in-depth, and controlled environment. Adolescents in these programs are isolated from the general population and even attend school within the facility where they are housed. Treatment modalities in these facilities often include a combination of behavior modification where desirable behaviors are rewarded and undesirable behaviors are punished, individual therapy, group therapy, and family therapy. Referrals to such programs can be made by parents, public schools, or the juvenile court system.

The most structured and most serious of all residential treatment programs include correctional institutions for adolescents, most commonly referred to as juvenile hall or juvenile detention centers. These facilities are reserved for adolescents who have been convicted of breaking some law, and although there is far more of an emphasis on rehabilitation than in adult correctional facilities, there is a far greater emphasis on corrections and punishment than in a therapeutic treatment center.

A creative version of the juvenile correctional institution that has received mixed reviews are "boot camp" programs, which offer rehabilitation (as well as restraint) in the form of a militarylike, highly structured environment. The philosophy behind these boot camps is that adolescents or young adults who suffer from poor impulse control, low self-esteem, and high acting out can benefit from a militarylike structured setting that pushes them to their limit (both physical and emotional). The high emphasis on structure and self-discipline, coupled with the push to achieve, is believed to have a positive impact on both self-esteem and self-respect, which is hoped to generalize into more respectful behavior in society. Many parents and participants commonly claim dramatic changes in the behavior of participants after a boot camp experience, but research appears to indicate that boot camps do not necessarily reduce recidivism rates in young offenders (Peters, Thomas, & Zamberlan, 1997).

Another type of treatment facility for adolescents experiencing mental health problems is in-patient psychiatric hospitals. These programs tend to be acute (short term), focusing on stabilizing the adolescent's high-risk behaviors, such as suicidal behavior, self-abuse, substance abuse, and eating disorders. Some in-patient programs specialize in one or more of these disorders or are more general in nature offering short-term acute services to any adolescent who cannot be maintained safely outside a hospital setting. Many of the same type of therapies are available in an in-patient setting as in a residential treatment center, with the exception that drug therapies may be more prevalent in a psychiatric hospital. In-patient hospitals also rely heavily on discharge planning, a task that typically falls to a hospital social worker or other human service professional who works with the family and community resources to ensure that the adolescent will transition back to home and school with enough outpatient support to minimize the need for rehospitalization.

Multicultural Considerations

It would be naïve to assume that race and ethnicity did not have a significant affect on adolescent development, including the types of problems adolescents of various races experience as well as the various responses to those problems, both within the family as well as within the community. Human service professionals must be aware of the way in which race and ethnicity affect adolescent development and behavior, as well as any negative stereotypes that might affect the types of diagnoses adolescents receive.

A 2001 study found that African-American adolescents were more commonly diagnosed with conduct disorders, whereas Caucasian adolescents more often received a diagnosis of depression (DelBello, Lopez-Larson, & Soutullo, 2001). But is this because more African-American adolescents actually have conduct disorders? Or is it because the negative stereotype that African-American males are typically more violent influenced the practitioner rendering the diagnosis? DelBello, Lopez-Larson, and Soutullo (2001) doubted that the difference in diagnosing reflected any real variation in disorders among adolescents of different races, but was more likely attributable to such variables as misdiagnosing based on cultural differences and misperceptions.

Other research indicates that Latino adolescents, specifically Mexican Americans, are at higher risk of delinquency, depression, and suicide than Caucasians (Roberts, 2000). African-American youth tend to show the greatest need for mental health services, yet were severely underserved, and although most mentally ill African-American adolescents had a long history of diagnosable mental health problems, often their first exposure to treatment was within the juvenile justice system. One reason for this might be that there is a negative stigma associated with mental health disorders in certain ethnic minority groups. But another equally significant reason is likely the lack of affordable mental health services in ethnically diverse neighborhoods, as well as issues such as poor or no insurance coverage for mental health services in ethnically diverse populations. It is interesting to note that Latino adolescents were rated as the most underserved of all racial groups, despite the fact that they had significant needs, and Caucasians were reported to have the highest rate of mental health utilization, although they have less serious mental health diagnoses compared to other racially diverse groups (Rawal, Romansky, & Jenuwine, 2004).

Certainly not all differences in adolescent diagnoses can be attributed to cultural misperceptions, misdiagnoses, and underutilization of services. Social conditions, such as poverty, high crime neighborhoods, and unemployment likely contribute to a significant proportion of mental health problems in racially ethnic youth. Rawal, Romansky, and Jenuwine (2004) noted that African-American adolescents are far more likely to be raised in single-parent households, be placed in foster care, and experience significantly higher rates of familial abuse and neglect, all of which can be expected to have a negative impact on their mental health. Latino adolescents also exhibited higher incidences of acting out and antisocial behaviors, such as juvenile delinquency, compared to Caucasians, yet they also had greater familial support with their caregivers exhibiting greater understanding and involvement in their mental health issues, which might act as an intervention negating the necessity of more serious intervention.

Regardless of the reasons for the differences in mental health issues among adolescents of different races, it is imperative that human service professionals be trained to deliver culturally competent counseling. Education that addresses all these issues, including institutionalized racism, both within the community, as well as within the juvenile justice system, culturally based stigmas associated with mental health issues, social conditions affecting adolescents of all races, and the relevant histories of various racially ethic minority groups within the United States (for example, the history of slavery among African Americans or the history of forced institutionalized care among Native American youth), will assist the human service professional render a bias-free mental health evaluation and provide the most appropriate treatment for the adolescent client.

Concluding Thoughts on Adolescents

Clearly, our society will continue to change and evolve, affecting all its members, including adolescents. As our society becomes more technologically based, it will become more complex as well, which will no doubt mandate increasing levels of education—a trend that this country has seen steadily increase in the last 50 years at least. This does not mean that juvenile violence will continue to rise. Most mental health experts refuse to adopt such a fatalistic attitude. History reveals that adolescence has always been a difficult stage to navigate, long before it was even recognized as an official stage of development. The greatest hope one can offer parents and educators alike is that adolescents who often seem destined for a lifetime of narcissistic obsession most often evolve into loving, caring, and responsible adults. Human service professionals can help families ensure that this is the path for as many adolescents as possible through effective program development and supportive services on all levels.

references

American Psychiatric Association. (2000). *Diagnostic and statistical manual of mental disorders* (4th ed., Text Revision) (DSM-IV-TR). Washington, DC: American Psychiatric Association.

Anderson, R. N., & Smith, B. L. (2003). *Deaths: leading causes for 2001. National Vital Statistics Report 2003,* 52(9), 1–86.

Andrus, J. K., Fleming, D. W., Heumann, M. A. Wassell, J. T., Hopkins, D. D. Y., Gordan S. (1991). Surveillance of attempted suicide among adolescents in Oregon, 1988. *American Journal of Public Health,* 81, 1067–1069.

Arias, E., Anderson, R. N., Kung, H. C., Murphy, S., & Kochanek, K. D., (2003). Deaths: Final Data for 2001. National Vital Statistics Reports; 52(3). Hyattsville, Maryland: National Center for Health Statistics.

Bearman, P. S. & Moody, J. (2004). Suicide and friends among American adolescents. *American Journal of Public Health, 94(1),* 89–95.

Crowe, M. & Bunclark, J. (2000). Repeated self-injury and its management. *International Review of Psychiatry, 12(1),* 48–53.

DelBello, M., Lopez-Larson, M. P., & Soutullo, C. A. (2001). Effects of race on psychiatric diagnosis of hospitalized adolescents: A retrospective chart review. *Journal of Child and Adolescent Psychopharmacology, 11(1),* 95–103.

Erikson, E. H. (1968). Identity: Youth and crisis. New York: Norton.

Fairburn, C. G. (2005). Evidence-based treatment of anorexia nervosa. *International Journal of Eating Disorders, 37(Suppl),* S26–S30.

Fenton, W. S., McGlashan, T. H., Victor, B. J., & Blyer, C. R. (1997). Symptoms, subtypes, and suicidality in patients with schizophrenia spectrum disorder. *American Journal of Psychiatry,* 154(2), 199–204.

Fitzgerald, D., Lucas, S. & Redoblado, M. (2004). Cognitive functioning in young people with first episode psychosis: Relationship to diagnosis and clinical characteristics. *Australian and New Zealand Journal of Psychiatry, 38(7),* 501–510.

Frick, P. (2004). Developmental pathways to conduct disorder: Implications for serving youth who show severe aggressive and antisocial behavior. *Psychology in the Schools, 41(8),* 823–834.

Gandara, P., Gutierrez, D., & O'Hara, S. (2001). Planning for the future in rural and urban high schools. *Journal of Education for Students Placed at Risk,* 6(1–2), 73–93. ERIC Document Reproduction Service No. UD 522844.

Gorwood, P. (2004). Generalized anxiety disorder and major depressive disorder comorbidity: An example of genetic pleiotrophy? *European Psychiatry, 19(1),* 27–33.

Gowers, S. & Bryant-Waugh, R. (2004). Management of child and adolescent eating disorders: The current evidence base and future directions. *Journal of Child Psychology & Psychiatry, 45(1),* 63–83.

Hall, G. S. (1882, January). The moral and religious training of children. *Princeton Review,* 26–48, as cited in Demos, J. & Demos, V. (1969). Adolescence in a historical perspective. *Journal of Marriage and the Family, 31(4),* 632–638.

Hazell, P. & Lewin, T. (1999). Friends of adolescent suicide attempters and completers. *Journal of American Academy of Child & Adolescent Psychiatry, 32 (11),* 76–81.

Jarbin, H. & von Knorring, A. (2004). Suicide and suicide attempts in adolescent-onset psychotic disorders. *Nordic Journal of Psychiatry, 58(2),* 115–123.

Jewell, J. D. & Stark, K. D. (2003). Comparing the family environments of adolescents with conduct disorder or depression. *Journal of Child & Family Studies, 12(1),* 77–89.

Kerpelman, J. L. & Pittman, J. F. (2001). The instability of possible selves: Identity processes within late adolescents' close peer relationships. *Journal of Adolescence, 24(4),* 491–512.

Lahey, B. B., Moffitt, T. E. & Caspi, A. (Eds.). (2003). *Causes of conduct disorder and juvenile delinquency.* New York: Guilford Press.

Larsen, M. (2003). *Violence in U.S. public schools: A summary of findings.* New York: ERIC Document Reproduction Service No. ED482921.

Lock, J. & le Grange, D. (2005). Family-based treatment of eating disorders. *International Journal of Eating Disorders, 37(Suppl),* S64–S67.

Mackrell, L. & Lavender, T. (2004). Peer relationships in adolescents experiencing a first episode of psychosis. *Journal of Mental Health (UK), 13(5),* 467–479.

Moskos, M. A., Achilles, J. & Gray, D. (2004). Adolescent suicide myths in the U.S. *Journal of Crisis Intervention & Suicide Prevention, 25(4),* 176–182.

National Center for Education Statistics. (1999). *Digest of education statistics.* Washington, DC: National Research Council Panel on High Risk Youth, National Academy of Sciences.

National Institutes of Mental Health. (2005). *Schizophrenia.* Bethesda, MD: National Institute of Health. Retrieved on November 15, 2005, from http://www.nimh.nih.gov/publicat/schizoph .cfm#definition

Nock, M. K. & Prinstein, M. J. (2005). Contextual features and behavioral functions of self-mutilation among adolescents. *Journal of Abnormal Psychology, 114(1),* 140–146.

Peters, M., Thomas, D., & Zamberlan, C. (1997). *Boot camps for juvenile offenders.* Office of Juvenile Justice and Delinquency Prevention, U.S. Department of Justice. Washington, DC: U.S. Government Printing Office.

Piaget, J. (1950). *The psychology of intelligence.* London: Routledge & Kegan Paul.

Rawal, P., Romansky, J., & Jenuwine, M. (2004). Racial differences in the mental health needs and service utilization of youth in the juvenile justice system. *Journal of Behavioral Health Services & Research, 31(3),* 242–254.

Ray, S. L. (2004). Eating disorders in adolescent males. *Professional School Counseling,* 8(1), 98–102.

Raywid, M. (1996). *Downsizing schools in big cities, ERIC digest no. 112.* New York, NY: ERIC Clearinghouse on Urban Education. (ERIC No. ED393958).

Roberts, R. E. (2000). Depression and suicidal behaviors among adolescents: The role of ethnicity. In I. Cuéllar & F. A. Paniagua (Eds.), *Handbook of multicultural mental health* (pp. 360–389). San Diego, CA: Academic Press.

Rutter, P. A., & Behrendt, A. E. (2004). Adolescent suicide risk: Four psychosocial factors. *Adolescence, 39(154),* 295–302.

Spirito, A., Valeri, S., Boergers, J., & Donaldson, D. (2003). Predictors of Continued suicidal behavior in adolesents following a suicide attempt. *Journal of Clinical Child and Adolescent Psychology, 32(2),* 284–289.

van Hoeken, D., Seidell, J., & Hoek, H. (2003). Epidemiology. In J. Treasure, U. Schmidt, & E. van Furth (Eds.), *Handbook of eating disorders* (2d ed., pp. 11–34). Chichester, England: Wiley.

Vohs, K. D., Voelz, Z. R., Pettit, J. W., Bardone, A. M., Katz, J., Abramson, L. Y., Heatherton, T. F., & Joiner, T. E. (2001). Perfectionism, body dissatisfaction, and self-esteem: An interactive model of bulimic symptom development. *Journal of Social & Clinical Psychology, 20,* 476–497.

Walcott, D. D., Pratt, H. D. & Patel, D. R. (2003). Adolescents and eating disorders: Gender, racial, ethnic, sociocultural, and socioeconomic issues. *Journal of Adolescent Research, 18,* 223–243.

Wells, K. (1991). Long-term residential treatment for children: Introduction. *American Journal of Orthopsychiatry, 61,* 324–326.

suggested reading

Cloud, H. & Townsend, J. (2001). *Boundaries with kids.* Grand Rapids, MI: Zondervan.

Mattaini, M. A. (2001). *Peace power for adolescents strategies for a culture of nonviolence.* Washington, DC: NASW Press.

Roles, P. (2005). *Facing teenage pregnancy: A handbook for the pregnant teen.* Atlanta, GA: CWLA Press.

Ungar, M. (2002). *Playing at being bad: The hidden resilience of troubled teens.* Washington, DC: NASW Press.

Ungar, M. (2003). *Nurturing hidden resilience in troubled youth.* Washington, DC: NASW Press.

internet web sites related to adolescence

Adolescence and Peer Pressure: **http://ianrpubs.unl.edu/family/nf211.htm**

Child and Adolescent Mental Health: **http://www.nimh.nih.gov/healthinformation/childmenu.cfm**

Mental Health Risk Factors for Adolescents: **http://education.indiana.edu/cas/adol/mental.html**

Outward Bound: **http://www.outwardbound.org**

WHO Adolescent Health: **http://www.who.int/child-adolescent-health/OVERVIEW/AHD/adh_over.htm**

chapter 6

Aging and Services for the Elderly

Carrie looked on the sea of faces before her. They looked empty—almost as if they had no souls. The only sounds in the camp were the incessant, never ceasing buzzing of hungry flies. Even the children were quiet. Carrie reasoned that the calm was due to hunger—people were often subdued when they hadn't eaten well in days, but she knew this calm was related to something far removed from hunger.

Just three days ago the people in this camp were victims of an Arab militia known as the Janjaweed. These bands of marauding fighters combed the countryside indiscriminately killing black Africans. As the villagers looked on in horror, Janjaweed militia began to systematically slaughter the innocent villagers one-by-one. Not even infants were spared as some militia tossed babies and toddlers into the air, calling them future enemies, as they shot them with machine guns. The few villagers that managed to escape joined other escaping villagers running through the desert and were eventually picked up by the American Red Cross.

Carrie is a missionary with an organization that specializes in sending retirees abroad. When Carrie became a widow at the age of 71 she thought her life was over. However, the pastor at her church approached her, and after months of talking, he finally convinced her that her years of nursing experience need not go to waste. Carrie was initially skeptical when her pastor shared the stories of other retirees, many of whom were widows, who served in clinics and refugee camps overseas in countries like Guatemala, Burma, and Sudan, but it wasn't until she met some elderly missionaries at home on sabbatical that she finally realized that this was something she could do.

Of course, Carrie's adult children thought she'd lost her mind, they even questioned whether her decision to become a missionary was a sign of early Alzheimer's, but they eventually grew to understand her decision and even respect it, although she was certain that they never felt truly comfortable with the thought of their elderly mother living in a refugee camp in the middle of a war-torn country. Carrie's contemplative thoughts were interrupted with the announcement of the most recent influx of shell-shocked and injured refugees, and she ventured out of the makeshift hospital to meet the new arrivals.

Dan was shocked as he walked down La Salle Avenue, in the heart of the business district in Chicago, Illinois. He was used to seeing homeless people, either standing or sitting along the side of the road with signs asking for money, but he had never seen an elderly couple begging for money before. What was unique about this couple was that they looked as though they could be his own mother and father.

He began to walk by them, avoiding their stare as he usually did when people begged for money, but this time was different, and he could not resist approaching this couple. "Hi, my name is Dan, and I'd love to give you some money." The couple looked at him sheepishly, and he noticed the shame in their eyes. "Thank you," the woman said quietly, diverting her glace downward. Dan handed them a $10 bill and started to walk away, but curiosity got the better of him. He turned around and asked them if he could talk to them about their situation. The husband and wife looked at each other, and Dan did not know if it was with suspicion or simple caution, but they eventually agreed once Dan offered to buy them lunch.

Over their meals of hot soup and sandwiches, Rosemary and Donald shared about their all-American lives. They raised two children in a suburb of Chicago, owned a home, and even had a family dog. They were like anyone else in the neighborhood or their church, until Donald was laid off two years before his scheduled retirement when the company he had worked for 40 years downsized. Donald was unable to find a job due to his age, and eventually they had to let their health insurance lapse because they could no longer financially handle the extremely high monthly premiums.

Unfortunately, Rosemary became ill the following month with a bout of influenza that ultimately developed into pneumonia. The hospital bill for her two-week stay was almost $10,000. With no retirement and only Social Security benefits to count on, and with their two adult children serving overseas in the military, Donald and Rosemary began a downhill financial descent that didn't stop until they depleted their life savings and ultimately lost their house. Thus, although most couples like Donald and Rosemary spend their "Golden Years" playing golf in Florida, Donald and Rosemary spend their days sitting outside the train station, begging for money.

These two vignettes highlight the vast range of experiences Americans living in the United States can have in the last decades of their lives—what is normally called old age. And although there are some similarities between the elderly of today and the elderly of 100 years ago, there are also significant differences brought on by many of the societal changes referenced in earlier chapters, including ongoing urbanization, changes in the family structure, and the dawning of the technological era. However, there have also been transitions in culture and society that have affected the elderly community in a unique way. These include such issues such as increasing longevity, the global community and economy, as well as other economic shifts, the advent of long-distance travel enabling family members to move further and further away from one another, the health-care "crisis," significant demographic shifts, as well as the increasing complexity of society in general. Each of these issues and their impact on the elderly population affects the human services field as it attempts to meet the complex needs of this growing population.

The Aging of America: Changing Demographics

The opening vignette illustrates the vast range of experiences of those considered elderly in the United States. Today's elderly in the United States experience a broader range of lifestyles than ever before, but they experience a greater range of challenges as well. There are several reasons for this vast array of lifestyle choices and options, including the increase in the human life span, changes in the perception of old age in general, changes in the economy, and finally changes in the nature and definition of the U.S. American family, including a dramatic increase in divorce and a dramatic increase in the two-parent working families.

Read just about any article relating to the elderly population, and you will likely read about the "Graying of America." This term relates to the increase in the elderly population in the United States This dramatic increase, as well as the continued projected increase in the United States elderly population between now and 2025 at least, is directly related to the aging of a **cohort** of individuals referred to as the *baby boomers*. The baby boomers are popularly defined as those having been born between 1946 and 1964. The name refers to the *boom* of births after World War II, which caused an unusual spike in the U.S. population. Approximately 76 million individuals (roughly 29 percent of the U.S. population) fall into the cohort of baby boomers. It is obvious why this cohort has been the focus of particular interest to social scientists, the media, politicians, and others. For one thing, despite the somewhat broad range of ages within this cohort, similarities between members are numerous, including their socioeconomic status, which tends to be higher than earlier cohorts, consumer habits, and political concerns. As the boomers age, their tastes and concerns transition, and in recent years their collective focus has included discussions regarding the consequences of this large cohort heading into their retirement years. The "Graying of America," then, refers to the projected increase in the elderly population because of the aging boomers.

The aging of the baby boomers is not the only variable leading to the increase in the elderly population. Other factors include the 50 percent increase in the human life span our country has experienced during the twentieth century. In 1900 the average human life span in the United States was about 47 years. But by 1999 it had increased to about 77 years, which is where it stands today, although it is expected to increase at least another 15 years by the year 2100 (Arias, 2004).

This life expectancy increase is due to many variables including improved medical technology, medical discoveries such as antibiotics and immunizations for various life-threatening diseases, and generally safer lifestyles. In fact, some sociologists and public policy analysts predict that the U.S. population ages 65 and over will increase from 35 million in the year 2000 to an amazing 78 million in 2050 (U.S. Census Bureau, 2002). When one considers that in the year 1900 the over-65 population in the United States was only 3.1 million (4.1 percent of the population), it is not difficult to understand why the field of gerontology has received so much attention in recent years!

So far this all sounds pretty good—we're living longer, and in the next 10 or 20 years a third of the population will be classified as elderly, which will no doubt increase the attention paid to social and political issues important to those in their retirement years. However, the landscape for the elderly in the United States is not completely rosy; quite the opposite, in fact. Some will no doubt enjoy their longer life span, but for many, their extra years on this earth may be spent in a long-term care facility with chronic health problems far too complex to make remaining in their home a possibility. Increases in rates of dementia, depression, and alcohol abuse are also valid concerns for the elderly as they face a multitude of challenges in a rapidly changing world.

Changes in the U.S. economy also risks leaving many approaching retirement in economically vulnerable positions as companies shift away from offering employees lifelong careers with permanent and secure retirement plans. In addition, sharp increases in the cost of medical care and possible changes in Social Security benefits put seniors at risk of financial vulnerability. Thus, an increasingly older population will no doubt have an impact on the financial, housing, medical, mental health, and even transportation needs of the elderly population. Add to that, changes in the U.S. family, such as the significant increase in divorce rates, have put some seniors in the position of having to provide day care for their grandchildren and in some cases even parenting their grandchildren. Thus, although some elderly will be able to take advantage of the many medical advances, healthier lifestyles, and increased opportunities for enjoying life, many others will not.

This chapter will explore the wide range of issues confronting the elderly population in the United States, as well as exploring some issues projected to be relevant in the future. The role of the human service professional will be explored as well, with a special focus on how the field of social gerontology has changed in recent years, expanding the role of the human service professional in various practice settings.

Old and Old-Old: A Developmental Perspective

Before beginning any real discussion about clinical issues affecting the elderly or the role of the human service professional, it is important to understand the various aspects of physical, social, and emotional development common to individuals in the last quarter or so of their lives. Although there is no specific age limit marking the end of middle age and the beginning of the elderly years, most contemporary developmental theorists consider old age to begin at around the age of retirement.

Many theorists have argued that adults do not go through systematic and uniform developmental stages in the same way that children do, thus earlier developmental theories typically stop at early adulthood or lump all adult development into one category stretching from adolescence and beyond. One reason for this approach is that if development consists of the combined impact of physical, cognitive, and emotional maturity, then certainly one can see that children who are spurred on to extend their social boundaries will be motivated to push themselves from a crawl to a walk. Yet once one has reached physical and cognitive maturity, this interplay between physical ability and emotional desire (where one spurs on the other) subsides, and the motivation to pursue a particular life course becomes more based on personal choice and internal motivation, making adult maturity anything but systematic or universal.

Nevertheless, should we assume that adults do not continue to develop in any sort of consistent or predictable way? Would it be correct to assume that once individuals have reached all physical developmental milestones (somewhere after puberty) that emotional development occurs in a completely unique and individualistic manner? Most of us have heard about the infamous "midlife crisis" marking the entry into middle age, and regardless of the validity of the universality of such a stage, it does seem reasonable to assume that individuals within a culture will respond and adapt to both internal and external demands and expectations placed on them by cultural mores and norms, and that there would be some interplay between their physical development (or physical decline) and their emotional and cognitive development.

Cultural expectations in the United States such as marriage, child rearing, employment, and home ownership certainly have an impact on those in early and middle adulthood, just as retirement, increased physical problems, and widowhood will have an impact on those in later adulthood. Yet because the options and choices available to adults are so broad, any developmental theory must be considered in somewhat broad and descriptive terms, rather than the narrower and more prescriptive terms often used to evaluate and consider child developmental theories.

Erik Erikson (1959, 1966), a psychodynamic theorist who studied under Sigmund Freud (the father of psychoanalysis), developed a theory of psychosocial development, beginning with birth and ending with death. According to Erikson each stage of development presented a unique challenge or crisis brought about by the combining forces of both physiological changes and psychosocial need. Successfully resolving the developmental crisis resulted in being better prepared for the next stage. The eighth stage of Erikson's model is *Integrity versus Despair* and spans from age 65 to death. Erikson believed that individuals in this age range needed to reflect back on their lives, taking stock of their choices and the value of their various achievements. If this reflection resulted in a sense of contentment with one's choices and life experiences, then the individual will be able to accept death with a sense of integrity, but if he or she does not like the choices made, the relationships developed, and the wisdom gained then he or she will face death with a sense of despair.

Because the successful navigation of each stage is dependent on the successful navigation of the preceding stages, Erikson believed that individuals who did not develop a sense of basic trust in others or in the world (Stage One), struggled developing a sense of personal autonomy (Stage Two), had difficulty developing any personal initiative (Stage Three), or a sense of accomplishment (Stage Four), faced challenges in adolescence when attempting to discover a personal identity (Stage Five), making it difficult to develop truly intimate relationships with others (Stage Six), leaving him incapable of offering true guidance and generativity to the younger generations (Stage Seven), which would likely mean that he would not reflect back on his life with any sense of contentment and satisfaction, and would then likely face impending death with a true and deep sense of despair.

Daniel Levinson (1978, 1984) is probably one of the most well-known adult developmental theorists, having developed a life span theory extending from birth through death. Levinson wrote two books explaining his theory, *The Seasons of a Man's Life* (1978) and *The Seasons of a Woman* (1984), where he focused on middle adulthood, but what was revolutionary about his theory was his argument that adults do continue to grow and develop on an age-related timetable. Levinson noticed that adults in the latter half of their lives are more reflective, and as they approached a point in their lives where they had more time behind them than ahead of them, this reflection intensified. Levinson also believed that individuals progress through periods of stability that are followed by shorter stages of transition. The themes in his theory most relevant to human service professionals include this notion of life reflection—the taking stock of one's life choices and accomplishments, the need to be able to give back to society, which encompasses an acknowledgment that at some point the goal in life is not solely to focus on one's own driving needs, but to give back to others and community through the sharing of gained wisdom and mentoring.

Finally, Levinson's belief that as people age they need to become more intrinsically focused rather than externally based is equally relevant. Consider the man who in his thirties gains self-esteem and a sense of identity through working 80 hours per week and running marathons. How will this same man define himself when he is 70 and no longer has the physical stamina or agility to perform these activities? Levinson believed that a developmental task for aging adults was to become more internally anchored, more intrinsic in their self-identify, lest they develop a sense of despair and depression later in life when they are no longer able to live up to their own youthful expectations.

Successful Aging

A recent concept that has become popular in relation to the study of geriatrics is the concept of *successful aging,* which is used to describe the process of getting the most out of one's life in later years. Successful aging literally means to add years to one's life and to get the most out of living (Havighurst, 1961). Researchers have examined individuals who age better than others to determine what differences might account for their "success," and some of the variables at play include maintaining a moderately high physical and social activity level, including keeping active in hobbies, social events, and regular exercise (Warr, Butcher & Robertson, 2004).

The natural aging process, though, seems to discourage high activity levels in virtually all domains. Employment provides most people with one of the greatest opportunities for social interaction, and when individuals retire a significant portion of their social life is lost along with their career. Physical limitations also encourage disengagement. Few elderly play on intramural softball teams, and even something like poor night vision can keep a senior from being able to hop in the car and visit family. Thus, many elderly people naturally begin withdrawing from the world, both physically and socially, in response to diminished capability and opportunity, and with such disengagement comes an increase in physical and emotional problems, problems such as depression and even alcohol abuse to combat loneliness.

In addition to maintaining a healthy activity level, it is also important for the elderly to maintain good coping strategies for the challenges that lie before them. Although many of these challenges may be minimized because they are a part of the expected life course, many elderly not only face increased health problems and physical limitations, but they also must deal with multiple losses as they begin to lose friends, siblings, and even their spouse to death. Many elderly must move from their longtime home into residential care or the home of a family member, and even the loss of independence can create a situation where their mental health is determined by the veracity of their coping mechanisms.

In my own clinical practice I have found that individuals typically age in the same way that they lived. Thus if someone has poor coping abilities when they are younger, resulting in a diminished ability to manage life transitions, stress, and loss, they typically will carry these poor coping strategies into old age. If someone exercises regularly and has good social contacts, they will typically remain active, both socially and physically, during their elderly years.

Current Issues Affecting the Elderly and the Role of the Human Service Professional

In anticipation of the increase in the elderly population as well as an increase in the needs and complex nature of the issues facing many elderly, the *Older Americans Act* was signed into federal law in 1965. This act led to the creation of the *Administration on Aging,* and it funded grants to the states for various community and human service programs and provided money for age-related research and the development of human service agencies called Area Agencies on Aging (AAA) operating on the local level. The Administration on Aging also acts as a clearinghouse, disseminating information about a number of issues affecting the elderly population in the United States.

Numerous issues affect today's elderly population, including elder abuse, age-based discrimination, housing needs, biopsychological problems, (such as depression, anxiety, and alcoholism), adjustment to retirement, and grandparenting. Those in the human services field are often included in the group of professionals most likely to come into contact with the elderly population, either through direct service or through providing counseling services to a family member of an elderly individual, and therefore they must be familiar with these key issues, knowing how they affect the elderly and their family.

Ageism

Ask some typical young Americans what they think it is like to be a man of 70, and they may well tell you that an average 70-year-old man is in poor health, drifts off to sleep at a moment's notice, talks of nothing but the distant past, and unproductively sits in a rocker, rocking back and forth all day long. They might even throw in a comment or two about his general grouchy disposition. Ask if the elderly still have the desire for sexual intimacy, and you might get a good hearty laugh in response. However, this description of the elderly is a myth based on deeply entrenched negative stereotypes and can serve as a foundation of a form of prejudice and discrimination of the elderly called *ageism*.

"Ageism" was a term first coined by Robert Butler (1969), chairman of a congressional committee on aging in 1968. He defined ageism as "a systematic stereotyping of and discrimination against people simply because they are old, just as racism and sexism accomplish this with skin color and gender." Butler theorized that the basis of this negative stereotype is a fear of growing old. This fear and the resultant negative stereotyping can often result in discrimination of the elderly population in all areas of life and is the basis of many forms of elder abuse.

Ageism typically involves any attitude or behavior that negatively categorizes the elderly based either on partial truth (often taken out of context) or on outright myths of the aging process. Such myths often describe old age as involving (1) poor health, illness, and disability; (2) lack of mental sharpness and acuity, senility, and dementia; (3) sadness, depression, and loneliness; (4) an irritable demeanor; (5) a sexless life; (6) routine boredom; (7) a lack of vitality and continual decline; and (8) an inability to learn new things, and (9) the loss of productivity (Thornton, 2002).

Gerontologists caution that the promotion of such negative stereotypes of old age and the elderly not only trivialize older individuals, but also risk displacing the elderly population as communities undervalue them based on this perception that the elderly are nothing more than a drain on society. A further risk of ageism is that the elderly may internalize this negative stereotype creating a self-fulfilling prophecy of sorts (Thornton, 2002). This is similar to what happens with other vulnerable populations, such as minority groups, who internalize the negative perceptions of them held by the majority population (Snyder, 2001).

Old age has not always been something those in the United States have viewed negatively. In fact, earlier in the twentieth century, societal attitudes reflected a relatively positive view of the elderly and of the aging experience. The elderly were respected for their wisdom and valued for their experience. They were not typically perceived as being a drain on society or as a burden to the community. Yet, some time around the middle 1900s, as life expectancy began to grow and medical technology improved so dramatically, professionals such as physicians, psychologists, and **gerontologists** began discussing the elderly in terms of the *problems* they posed (Hirshbein, 2001).

Many social psychologists and gerontologists cite the media as a major source of negative stereotypes of the elderly. These critics claim that the consistent negative portrayal of the elderly in both television shows as well as commercials, portraying them as dimwitted, foolish individuals living in the past, has a dehumanizing effect on the entire elderly population and has a negative affect on the self-concept of the elderly. Yet the results of a study conducted in 2004, which reviewed television commercials from the 1950s to the 1990s, did not support this critical view of the media (Miller, Leyell, & Mazacheck, 2004). In fact, Miller and his colleagues found that the media depiction of the elderly has been relatively positive, particularly in the latter two decades.

The issue of whether stereotypes (either positive or negative) depicted in the media simply reflect social values or actually have the power to shape social values remains unclear, thus it is difficult to know the implications of this research. Are advocates of the elderly making headway in their attempt to wipe away ageism reflected in the media? Or is the media responding to the call of antiageism advocates and leading the way in the fight to see the elderly as individuals with a wide range of functioning levels, and probably more importantly as individuals with far higher capacity than negative stereotypes imply? Regardless of the answer to this question, ageism remains a real problem, particularly in the workplace.

Employment discrimination based on age has not historically attracted a tremendous amount of attention or sympathy, but has been the recent focus of concern due to the aging of the U.S. workforce. This has made age-related discrimination a hot topic among economists, human resource managers, and other concerned professionals. A 1999 article in *Fortune* magazine highlighted the problem of age discrimination in the workplace, noting that although it has long been known and even expected that those 55 years and older would likely face difficulty in finding employment, the new age ceiling for many in business is now as low as 40 years old (Munk, 1999).

Munk identifies several reasons for this trend. In the past, longevity with a company translated into financial security, yet beginning in the 1980s, companies began trimming their workforces considerably, laying off thousands of employees. This trend affected the older, more experienced workforce the hardest, as many companies reasoned that older employees could be replaced by more efficient, more productive, and far less costly younger employees. Although this practice might make good business sense in some respects, any decision to lay off older employees that is based on a negative stereotype that they are less efficient and productive constitutes ageism (Tougas, Lagacé, & De La Sablonnière, 2004).

It is vital that human service professionals make certain that they do not hold any of these misconceptions of old age. For instance, assuming that someone over the age of 70 is incapable of being productive and of learning something new, of gaining a new insight, whether in the counseling office, or in life in general, would undoubtedly affect the dynamic between the counselor and elderly client. Practitioners then must address any misconceptions they have of old age and of the elderly population in general. Practices such as talking down to elderly clients, not directly addressing difficult issues for fear that they lack the capacity to understand, will undoubtedly affect the level of investment the client makes in the counseling relationship. This type of behavior on the part of the practitioner can also encourage a self-fulfilling prophecy within elderly clients, where they begin to act the part of the incapable, unproductive, and cognitively dull individual. Making positive assumptions about elderly clients will increase the possibility of bringing out the most authentic and dynamic aspects of elderly clients.

Housing

Contrary to the common belief of many in the United States, most elderly individuals remain in their homes until death and are cared for by family members (Bergeron & Gray, 2003). But as medical technology allows people to live longer albeit not necessarily healthier lives, coupled with the fact that more women than ever are in the workforce and therefore unavailable to care for their elderly and chronically ill relatives, many seniors find themselves needing to move out of their homes once they reach a certain level of physical and/or cognitive decline. They might move into the home of a family member, which was far more prevalent when the United States was an agricultural society, and both men and women were home based in their work, or they might move into a *retirement community*, where they can still enjoy their independence while enjoying many facility-offered services to meet their needs, such as shuttle service, handicapped-accessible facilities, and child-free living.

Laguna Woods (formerly Leisure World) is a famous retirement community in Southern California. This community refers to itself as an "age-restricted" community for the active lifestyle and boasts 18,000 residents, with an average age of 78 years. The gate-guarded community offers a multitude of athletic activities including an 18 hole golf course, tennis, community dances, and yoga classes. The community center serves as a central hub organizing the activities of over 60 different clubs, including anything from a billiard or bridge club to various travel clubs. The community even has its own television station to announce the day's activities! Laguna Woods has its own bus service to transport its residents within the community as well as to local sites around the area. The community has a team of human service professionals, such as licensed counselors and social workers, who provide crisis intervention, case management, individual counseling, and support groups on topics such as caregiver support, grief, and even a group on successful aging. The catch of course is that all residences are for-sale properties (except for those homes offered for rent by owners), and in addition to the $400 monthly community fee, the house prices range anywhere from about $175,000 to about $575,000. Thus at least in Laguna Woods, successful aging comes at a high price! The reality is that the majority of the elderly living in the United States cannot afford to live in attractive retirement communities, such as Laguna Woods, that so readily support successful aging.

Government subsidized senior housing can making housing costs more affordable for the elderly population, whether in the form of a subsidy provided directly to the elderly in the form of tax credits, loans, or rental vouchers, or subsidies provided to the housing community, which then passes on this discount to the renter. One problem with many of these programs, though, is that they require the elderly residents to find their own housing in the community, much of which is older and not appropriate for elderly residents who often need special age-related accommodations. Another concern relates to government-subsidized communities that are designed for the elderly population but tend to be wrought with problems related to safety, including problems with poor physical upkeep of the property.

A 2003 longitudinal study that followed 1200 elderly individuals in their transition from independent living to age-restricted housing in 1995 found that those elderly who transitioned to more expensive communities fared the best with regard to physical health and overall life satisfaction, and those who transitioned to government-subsidized housing programs fared the worse. Although the study investigators acknowledged that levels of life satisfaction might be related to a cumulative affect of a lifetime of poverty, they concluded that overall quality of housing has a direct relationship to life satisfaction (Krout, 2003).

Elderly individuals needing more consistent care with their **activities of daily living (ADL)** sometimes enter *assisted-living facilities.* These facilities offer apartment-like living in a more structured environment. In many respects assisted-living facilities act as a bridge between independent living and nursing home care. Assisted-living facilities offer assistance with eating, bathing, dressing, housekeeping, and medication, and some even have fully functioning medical centers. Many assisted-living apartments have alarm systems in every unit, offer a restaurant-style cafeteria, a club for social activities, a hairdresser, a medical staff, home health care, and a relatively full array of human services. The services are far more intensive than in a retirement community, as residents in assisted-living facilities are there because they cannot manage their ADLs without daily assistance. Human service professionals provide many of the same services as provided in retirement communities, but at a more comprehensive level.

Homelessness and the Elderly Population

One of the opening vignettes of this chapter highlighted the issue of homelessness in the elderly community. Although the elderly are at a lower risk for homelessness than other age groups, homelessness in the elderly population is a growing concern because the percentage is expected to grow as the baby boomer generation ages. The root cause of homelessness in the elderly population is of significant interest to social scientists, who are concerned about the complex set of needs this population possesses when facing housing vulnerability.

The common causes of homelessness in the general population apply to the elderly subgroup as well, such as a lack of affordable housing, too few jobs for unskilled workers, and a reduction in human services support (Hecht & Coyle, 2001; Kutza & Keigher, 1991), but the elderly population in general has additional risk factors such as being too elderly to reasonably recover from a job loss, enter a new career, or reenter the workforce, as well as experiencing chronic illnesses that are either costly or bar the elderly individual from being self-supporting (Kutza & Keigher, 1991).

For statistical purposes, individuals above the age of 50 to 55 are usually considered in the elderly category. Homeless elderly are a particularly vulnerable subgroup because of age-related physical vulnerability, which is often exacerbated by poor nu-

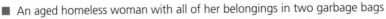

■ An aged homeless woman with all of her belongings in two garbage bags

trition and difficult living conditions either on the streets or in a homeless shelter. They are also at a much higher risk of becoming a victim of crime while living on the streets (Hecht & Coyle, 2001).

A research study based in Los Angeles found that unlike the homeless in the general population, 85 percent of the elderly population was white (versus 61 percent in the younger homeless population), and 59 percent were veterans (versus 27 percent in the younger homeless population). The elderly homeless were far more likely to be socially isolated and suffer from a physical illness, but less likely to suffer from substance abuse, mental illness, or domestic violence (Linn & Mayer-Oakes 1990). Elderly homeless between the ages of 50 and 65 are often the most vulnerable group because they are frequently the target of ageism when attempting to reenter the workforce, but too young to qualify for Medicare and Social Security benefits (Hecht & Coyle, 2001).

The differences between younger homeless and older homeless populations become important when considering programs designed to assist the elderly homeless population. Many human services homeless assistance programs focus on root causes of homelessness more common in younger populations, such as providing assistance with substance abuse and domestic violence. Any human services programs designed to assist the elderly subgroup with housing issues need to focus more on issues related to insufficient income, health concerns, and low-income housing offering supportive services to the elderly population with declining health.

Adjustment to Retirement

The concept of retirement is so common to the twenty-first century that it rarely needs explanation. When an individual comments on his or her upcoming retirement, others seem to instinctually understand that what is being discussed is the practice of leaving one's employment to permanently enter a phase of chosen nonemployment, and even though some might choose to dabble in part-time employment from time to time, the most common conceptualization of retirement involves an employee permanently surrendering his or her position, at the approximately age of 65, and drawing on a pension or retirement account that has likely been accruing for years. Of course, there are numerous variations on this theme—some people don't ever formally retire, and some people work in fields that have mandatory retirement ages, such as the airline industry, which requires that all pilots retire at the age of 60, and for some, retirement is a luxury they cannot afford. Also, it would be incorrect to assume that everyone in the workforce has accrued a pension sizeable enough to permit them to live on for years. But despite the range of retirement experiences, certain generalizations can be made about the retirement experience for the majority of those living in the United States during the twenty-first century.

Robert Atchley (1976) was one of the first researchers who attempted to describe the retirement experience for men and women. He identified five distinct, yet overlapping, stages that most retirees progress through on formal retirement. These stages are

1. The Honeymoon Phase: Retirees embrace retirement and all their newfound freedom in an optimistic but unrealistic manner.
2. Disenchantment: Retirees become disillusioned with what they thought retirement was going to be like and get discouraged with what often feels as though is too much time on their hands.
3. Reorientation: Retirees develop a more realistic view of retirement, both with regard to increased opportunities, but also with regard to increased constraints.
4. Stability: Retirees adjust to retirement.
5. Termination: Retirees eventually lose independence due to physical and cognitive decline.

There has been some controversy about whether retirees actually progress through such distinct phases, or whether there is just too much of a range of experiences among retirees in the United States to categorize experiences in a stage theory. Yet, a recent study supported Atchley's stage theory finding that retirees do experience a positive attitude about retirement for approximately six months after retiring, which is followed by a more negative attitude beginning at about 12 months, followed by a resumption of a more positive attitude at about 24 months (Reitzes & Mutran, 2004).

This study also found that individuals who had high self-esteem prior to retirement tended to have a more positive attitude about retirement, as did individuals who valued their ability to be a good friend. Reitzes and Mutran (2004) reasoned that this might be because such individuals looked at retirement as an opportunity to socialize and increase their friendship base. Factors such as a poor pension plan and poor health most often led to negative feelings about retirement. The final conclusion of this study was that good planning prepares individuals for the various ups and downs of retirement and helps them to approach this developmental phase realistically and well prepared.

Because nearly 50 percent of the U.S. population is now over the age of 50, the implications of retirement preparation and adjustment on the human services field obviously cannot be ignored. Human service professionals will likely come into contact with retired or retiring adults in many different settings, but it is important to realize that impending retirement can become an issue for someone even in middle adulthood, and therefore it is important for human service professionals to recognize that this issue can either be the direct focus of counseling or a residual issue, perhaps even being a stressor of which the client is completely unaware.

Using Atchley's model as a guide, Rhonda Jensen-Scott (1993) recommended that counselors assist retired or retiring clients in tackling four major tasks:

1. Seeking out and obtaining relevant information related to retirement
2. Adjusting to the change retirement will bring
3. Reworking personal priorities and goals to be consistent with a retired lifestyle
4. The acquisition of a new job if reentry into the workforce is necessary or appropriate

Jensen-Scott (1993) recommended asking questions similar to the following:

▶ What is a "big" change for you? What was the last "big" change you experienced in your life? What was that like for you?

▶ If you didn't have to work at your current job, what would you do?

▶ Besides a paycheck, what do you get from your job? What do you like and dislike about it?

▶ As you have progressed through your working life, are you aware of having had goals for yourself? If so, what are these goals? What parts of them have you accomplished?

▶ Make a list of the things you do in your life that are important to you (roles you play, activities you engage in, for example).

▶ Now tell me which ones are most important to you? How does your job fit into this list?

▶ How would you describe yourself?

▶ When you think of older adults or retirees, what do you think of?

▶ How do you imagine life will be when you retire? (p. 258).

It is important to remember, though, that not all retirements are planned—some employees are forced into retirement, some are "laid off" during retirement age, and some individuals are even terminated just prior to retirement so that the company does not have to fully invest in the employee's retirement plan, an unethical practice, but increasingly common. Thus the practitioner must be prepared for a wide range of experiences, as well as a wide range of feelings toward retirement.

Three primary factors significantly influence how retirement is experienced by the retiree. First, the increased life span has actually created the necessity for formal retirement because individuals in many instances are outliving their ability to work productively, at least in the same capacity as they did when they were younger. When people rarely lived beyond their forties or fifties, they often died in the midst of their careers, thus planning for retirement, both emotionally and financially, was often unnecessary. With the increased life span people are spending far more time in retirement than ever before (Reitzes & Mutran, 2004).

Second, there have been two simultaneous yet opposing trends developing, particularly in the past 25 years. The first trend involves a movement toward early retirement, with many individuals retiring in their fifties or even earlier (Kim & Moen,

2001), some to enter a second career and some to truly enjoy a more leisurely lifestyle. Yet this trend is creating a situation where retirement is a midlife experience, rather than one marking old age. Yet at the same time, the practice of employees working at the same company for 20 to 30 years and accruing an employer-sponsored retirement plan that they can draw from for the balance of their lives has become far less common as the workforce has become more transient, and companies have been forced to streamline expenses by no longer offering structured financial retirement plans (Munk, 1999).

Finally, race and gender have a significant affect on retirement experiences. Research has shown that women and minority workers often have different attitudes and experiences surrounding retirement issues due to disparity in income and education levels (McNamara & Williamson, 2004). Thus the human service professional must understand that most factors affecting a client's retirement experience are going to be influenced by the client's gender and racial background.

Ultimately, as is the case with virtually all life's transitions, one's background and previous experiences, including losses and traumas, coupled with coping skills and general personality style will all factor into how a client experiences and handles the life transitions involved with retirement. Thus, although counseling an individual through this experience can be quite complex and sometimes overwhelming, it should also be recognized as an opportunity for change, growth, and the reworking of old issues and perhaps even past losses, thus opening the doorway for higher functioning during the next stage in life.

Grandparents Parenting

The practice of grandparents raising grandchildren has increased dramatically over the past several years, signaling many problems within U.S. society that have emerged since the 1970s. Between 1990 and 1997 alone, grandparent-headed households increased approximately 20 percent (Casper & Bryson, 1998). The U.S. Congress became interested in this issue in the mid-1990s and in 1996 passed legislation that required the 2000 U.S. Census to include questions regarding whether grandparents were residing with grandchildren, whether they had primary responsibility for them, and what length of time they had acted in a parental role (i.e., revealing whether the situation was temporary or permanent).

Current figures estimate that approximately 5.8 million U.S. households (approximately 3.9 percent of the population) are comprised of grandparents coresiding with grandchildren under the age of 18; 64 percent of these are female grandparent-headed households. Approximately 2.4 million of these families involved grandparents who were the primary caregiver of their grandchildren, and of these approximately 40 percent had acted in this caregiving role for longer than five years (Simmons & Dye, 2003). This represents a 30 percent increase from 1990. About half of these grandparents are between the ages of 50 and 59, and 20 percent are over 60. Some of these households included at least one of the parents, but many of them included one or both grandparents acting in the role of surrogate parent(s).

Although the demographics of grandparent-headed households vary considerably, such households are far likelier to be an ethnic minority, poor, and undereducated. Households led by a grandmother only are far more likely to face economic hardship. Grandparent caregivers in the South and in urban areas had the highest levels of poverty and the lowest levels of education (Simmons & Dye, 2003).

Ethnic minority children are far more likely to be raised by a grandparent than Caucasian children. As Table 6.1 indicates, 10 percent of Pacific Islander grandparents are raising grandchildren compared to 8 percent each of Native American, African-American, and Latino grandparents, although Latino grandparents were far less likely to have caregiving responsibilities. Only 2 percent of Caucasian grandparents coresided with grandchildren under the age of 18 (Simmons & Dye, 2003). It is important to note though that some of these households are accounted for by multigenerational occupied households common particularly in Mexican and Asian cultures.

The issue of health-care insurance has far-reaching implications because children living with grandparents are less likely to have private health insurance, and many grandparent-headed households make too much money to qualify for Medicaid, but not enough to be able to afford a private health insurance plan (Glass & Hunnycutt, 2002). The lack of health insurance not only has a financial impact on these families, but also may affect their access to good mental health services.

Glass and Hunnycutt (2002) discussed the differences between traditional grandparenting and grandparents who parent. Grandparenting, they point out, often involves the best of both worlds where grandparents can play and have fun with their grandchildren, without daily task-related caregiving responsibilities, yet grandparents who are cast into surrogate parenting roles, whether the biological parents are present or not, must often deal with blurred boundary lines of responsibility. Thus they can no longer enjoy the fun aspects of grandparenting because they are thrust into the role of surrogate parent at the same time where they often deal with a weaker than average support system, both socially as well as financially.

The reasons why grandparents become surrogate parents are many, but the chief reasons include

1. the high divorce rate, leaving many women facing potential poverty resulting in them returning home to live with parents;
2. the sharp rise in teen pregnancies, also resulting in the mother residing with her parents for economic (and oftentimes emotional) reasons;
3. the increase in relative foster care in response to a sharp increase in child welfare intervention due to child abuse;

■ Table 6.1 Grandparents Living with Grandchildren by Race

(Data based on sample. For information on confidentiality protection, sampling error, nonsampling error, and definitions, see www.census.gov/prod/cen2000/doc/st3.pdf)

Characteristic	Total	Race							Hispanic origin		
		White alone	Black or African American alone	American Indian and Alaska Native alone	Asian alone	Native Hemalian and Other Pacific Islander alone	Some other race alone	Two or more races	Hispanic or Latino (of any race)	Not Hispanic or Latino	
										Total	White alone, not Hispanic or Latino
Population 30 years old and over	158,881,037	125,715,472	16,484,644	1,127,455	5,631,301	169,331	5,890,748	2,862,086	14,618,891	144,262,146	119,063,492
Grandparents living with grandchildren	5,771,671	3,219,409	1,358,699	90,524	359,709	17,014	567,486	158,830	1,221,661	4,550,010	2,654,788
Percent of population 30 and over	3.6	2.5	8.2	8.0	6.4	10.0	9.6	5.5	8.4	8.2	2.2
Responsible for grand-children	2,426,730	1,340,809	702,595	50,765	71,791	6,587	191,107	63,076	424,304	2,002,426	1,142,006
Percent of coresident grandparents	42.0	41.6	51.7	56.1	20.0	38.7	33.7	39.7	34.7	44.0	43.0
By duration of care (percent)[a]											
Total	100.0	100.0	100.0	100.0	100.0	100.0	100.0	100.0	100.0	100.0	100.0
Less than 6 months	12.1	12.6	9.8	13.0	13.6	12.7	15.6	13.5	14.6	11.5	12.4
6 to 11 months	10.8	11.6	9.3	10.5	11.0	8.4	11.4	11.2	11.2	10.7	11.6
1 to 2 years	23.2	23.8	21.2	22.5	25.2	23.8	26.1	23.4	25.1	22.8	23.6
3 to 4 years	15.4	15.8	14.6	13.9	17.6	11.7	15.7	16.0	15.8	15.3	15.7
5 years or more	38.5	36.3	45.2	40.0	32.7	43.3	31.1	35.9	33.3	39.6	36.6

[a]Percent duration based on grandparents responsible for grandchildren. Percent distribution may not sum to 100 percent because of rounding.

Source: U.S. Census Bureau. Census 2000, Summary File 4.

4. an increase in parents serving time in prison, primarily for drug and drug-related offenses punishable by high prison sentences due to the U.S. government's "War on Drugs";

5. the sharp increase of drug use, particularly among women of color whose use of crack cocaine has literally exploded over the past ten years; and,

6. the AIDS crisis, which has devastated many communities, leaving children orphaned and in need of permanent homes. These cases are complicated when the children have contracted the HIV virus, particularly when one considers their complex medical needs. (de Toledo & Brown, 1995)

The issues facing grandparents raising grandchildren are complex involving emotional as well as financial, legal, and physical challenges. Many grandparent caregivers are often forced to live in a type of limbo not knowing how long they will remain responsible for their grandchildren, particularly when the biological parent(s) are either in jail or are suffering from drug addiction that prevents them from resuming their primary parenting role.

The choice to act as a surrogate parent is in many instances made in a time of crisis, thus the elderly who may have been planning their retirement for years, often find themselves in a position where they either take on this parenting role in the face of the situation that rendered the biological parents unable to continue parenting or allow their grandchildren to enter the county foster care system. Parenting younger children has its unique challenges, but often comes with some level of social support, at least within the elementary school system, but this is often not the case with older children, particularly adolescents.

Parenting adolescents can often present significant challenges for grandparents, particularly those who are elderly. Parenting adolescents can be an exhausting endeavor for the young or middle-aged parent, but imagine the demands placed on someone who is elderly, has limited physical capacity, and even more limited financial means. Adolescents who have endured significant loss through death or abandonment or who have been raised in abusive homes, by parents who abuse drugs, or by parents who are serving time in prison are likely to act out emotionally and even physically, putting even greater stress on an already vulnerable family system.

Human service professionals may enter a grandparent-led family system in numerous ways—they could be the school social worker working with the children, they might be the child welfare caseworker assigned to assist the grandparents who are serving as relative foster care parents, or they might work for a human services agency offering outreach services to grandparent caregivers.

The American Association of Retired Persons (AARP), an advocacy organization for the elderly population, recommends that faith-based organizations and schools be among the organizations conducting outreach efforts to grandparent-headed households, particularly within ethnic minority communities. AARP has also highlighted the need for the development of more regional support groups focusing on important issues including respite care, parenting issues, and general emotional support, as well as the development of regional all-inclusive resource centers offering case management services to meet the comprehensive needs of grandparent caregivers.

Depression

Another significant concern affecting the elderly population is the increased incidence of depression. In fact, the National Institutes of Mental Health (NIMH) estimates that approximately 2 million individuals over the age of 65 suffer from some form of depression, and as many as 5 million more suffer from some form of depressive symptoms, although they may not meet all the criteria for clinical depression. Although prevalence rates can vary rather widely within the population, due in part to how depression is defined, these statistics indicate that at any given time anywhere between 5 to 30 percent of the elderly population may suffer from some form of depression, compared to a 1 percent prevalence rate in the general population, (Birrer & Vemuri, 2004).

Depression rates in nursing homes are even higher, with some studies finding up to 50 percent of the residents meeting the criteria for clinical depression. The elderly are also disproportionately at risk for suicide. Although individuals ages 65 years and older make up about 13 percent of the U.S. population, they account for nearly 18 percent of all those who committed suicide in the year 2001, which is the highest rates of all age groups. Surprisingly, those elderly at the highest risk for suicide are white males over the age of 85, many of whom are widowed (Birrer & Vemuri, 2004; McIntosh, 2003).

Many believe that depression is just a normal part of the aging process caused by the natural course of cognitive and physical decline and the multiple losses associated with growing old. But depression is not a natural part of growing older and can be avoided. Unfortunately, many in the medical and mental health fields, even the elderly themselves, believe that it is, and thus many in the elderly population who are suffering from depression remain undiagnosed and untreated. Misdiagnosis is also relatively common, with depression often being mistaken for dementia or some other form of cognitive impairment (Birrer & Vemuri, 2004).

Human service professionals working with the elderly community must be observant of the signs of depression. They must also be aware of the many risk factors for depression, including anxiety; chronic medical conditions such as heart disease, stroke, and diabetes; dementia; being unmarried; alcohol abuse; stressful life events; and minimal social support (Birrer & Vemuri, 2004; Lynch, Compton, Mendelson, Robins, & Krishnan, 2000; Waite, Bebbington, Skelton-Robinson, & Orrell, 2004).

A 2001 study conducted in the Netherlands found that negative life events such as the death of a significant other, a history of sexual abuse, and relational stress were all associated with depression later in life, but interestingly physical abuse, crime, disaster, and war events were *not* linked with depression later in life. The study also found that the number of negative life events throughout one's life was positively correlated with depression later in life. Thus, it appears that traumatic events have a cumulative effect that can potentially result in depression during old age. The authors of this study refer to this cumulative effect as *social poverty* and recommend that practitioners focus on helping their elderly clients in skill building and with the development of healthy social relationships (Kraaij & de Wilde, 2001).

Dementia

The American Psychiatric Society defines dementia as progressive, degenerative illnesses experienced during old age that impair brain function and cognitive ability. Dementia is an umbrella term encompassing most likely numerous disorders. Two of the most common forms of dementia are Alzheimer's disease and multi-infarct dementia (small strokes in the brain).

The general symptoms of dementia include a comprehensive shutting down of all bodily systems indicative by progressive memory loss, increased difficulty concentrating, a steady decrease in problem-solving skills and judgment capability, confusion, hallucinations and delusions, altered sensations or perceptions, impaired recognition of everyday objects and familiar people, altered sleep patterns, motor system impairment, inability to maintain ADLs (such as dressing oneself), agitation, anxiety, and depression. Ultimately, the dementia sufferer enters a complete vegetative state prior to death.

According to the NIMH, multi-infarct dementia accounts for nearly 20 percent of all dementias, affecting about 4 in 10,000 people. Even more individuals suffer from some form of mild cognitive impairment, but do not yet meet the criteria for full-blown dementia (Palmer, Fratiglioni, & Winblad, 2003). Alzheimer's disease affects approximately 4.5 million Americans, or about 5 percent of the population between the ages of 65 and 74 years of age, and the incident rate increases to 50 percent for those over 85 years of age. Diagnosis is based on symptoms, and it is only through an autopsy that a definitive diagnosis is made. The United States has experienced a dramatic increase in the incidence of dementia in the latter part of the twentieth century, primarily due to the increased human life span. It is theorized that dementia did not have an opportunity to develop prior to the 1900s, when the average life span was about 47 years. There is no known cure for dementia, thus treatment is focused on delaying and relieving symptoms.

Human service professionals may work directly with the sufferer of dementia or with the caregiver (typically a spouse or adult child) if they work in a practice setting that serves the elderly community. However, dealing with dementia as a clinical issue can occur in any practice setting because any client may have a relative suffering from one of these disorders and will therefore need counsel and perhaps even case management. Consider the practitioner who is assisting a client manage his ailing mother, questioning whether she is suffering from a cognitive impairment, grieving the slow loss of the mother she loves, and needing support in making difficult decisions such as determining when her mother can no longer live alone. Or, consider the school social worker who is counseling a student whose grandfather was recently diagnosed with Alzheimer's disease. The pressure on the entire family system will affect the student in numerous ways—academically, emotionally, perhaps even physically—and will frequently magnify any existing issues with which the student is currently struggling.

Elder Abuse

The elderly are a vulnerable population due to such factors as their physical frailty, dependence, social isolation, and the existence of cognitive impairment and as such are at risk of various forms of abuse and exploitation. The National Center on Elder Abuse (NCEA) defines elder abuse as any "knowing, intentional, or negligent act by a caregiver or any other person that causes harm or a serious risk of harm to a vulnerable adult." The specific definition of elder abuse varies from state to state, but in general can include physical, emotional, or sexual abuse, neglect and abandonment, or financial exploitation.

Although elder abuse is presumed to have always occurred, just as other forms of abuse such as child abuse and spousal abuse, it was not legally defined until addressed within a 1987 amendment of the Older Americans Act. Reports of elder abuse have increased significantly over the last several years due to an increase in reporting requirements, but also due to societal changes that are putting more older adults at risk. In 1986, there were 117,000 reports of elder abuse nationwide, and by 1996 the number of abuse reports increased to 293,000 (Tatara & Kuzmescus, 1997). By the year 2000 (the most recent reported data) the number of elder abuse reports had risen to an alarming 472,813 among all 50 states, Guam, and Washington, D.C. One reason for the rise in abuse reports is that the newest figures include not only abuse in domestic settings, but include abuse in institutional settings as well, but despite the more comprehensive data collection methods there is no escaping the fact that elder abuse is increasing within the United States (Teaster, 2000). Elder abuse is projected to continue to rise in the coming years due to the increased life span and the resultant increase in chronic illnesses, changing family patterns, and the complexity involved with contemporary caregiving.

Sixty percent of all reported abuse victims are women, 65 percent of all abuse victims are white, more than 60 percent of abuse incidences occurred in domestic settings, with about 8 percent occurring in institutionalized settings. Family members were the most commonly cited perpetrator, including both spouses and adult children (Teaster, 2000).

Every state in the United States has an adult protective services agency, although there is significant variation between states, particularly related to reporting laws and investigation methods and policies. Some states have separate agencies handling elder abuse, and some combine the protection of elderly with the protection of disabled adults of all ages. One significant difference between state policies involves who is considered a mandated reporter. Sixteen states require anyone who is aware of elder abuse to report it. About half the states require medical personnel, the clergy, and mental health personnel, including all human service professionals, to report elder abuse. Some states specify that only medical personnel are mandated reporters. Yet five states—Colorado, Delaware, New York, South Dakota, and Wisconsin—do not mandate that anyone report elder abuse (Teaster, 2000).

Elder abuse tends to be grossly underreported for several reasons, but many cite the lack of uniform reporting requirements as a primary reason. Because of the wide range of elder abuse reporting requirements, as well as differences in Adult Protective Services investigation policies and enforcement powers, it is essential that those working in the human services field be aware of the elder abuse reporting laws and requirements in their state. Many human service professionals may be in a position to protect an elderly client but may not be aware that their state has an elder abuse hotline.

Caregiver burnout is one of the primary risk factors of elder abuse. The most common scenario involves a loving family member who becomes intensely frustrated by the seeming impossible task of caring for a spouse or parent with a chronic illness such as dementia. Providing the continuous care of someone with Alzheimer's disease, for example, can be frustrating, provoking an abusive response from someone with no history of abusive behavior.

An example of such an incident is included in Bergeron and Gray's (2003) article on the ethical dilemmas facing support group facilitators. In this vignette, an elderly man is discussing the intense frustration he endures when attempting to encourage his wife, who is suffering from Alzheimer's disease, to undress at the end of the day and put nightclothes on. He describes how he starts by talking to her and asking her to please remove her blouse. He gently attempts to coax her to cooperate by helping her with a button, but she backs away from him. He then attempts to illustrate what he wants by undressing himself. She does not follow this prompt and continues to be combative and agitated, behavior consistent with Alzheimer's disease. Finally, this overwhelmed and overburdened husband admits to resorting to slapping his wife to get her to cooperate.

One of the most effective intervention strategies is *caregiver support groups*. These groups are typically facilitated by a social worker or other human services practitioner and focus on providing caregivers, many of whom are elderly themselves, a safe place to express their frustrations, sadness, and other feelings related to caring for their dependent elderly loved one. Although these support groups provide a wonderful opportunity for caregivers to share their frustrations and caregiving challenges, they can put facilitators in an ethical bind if group members disclose, either directly or inadvertently, that they are abusing their elderly charge. This issue becomes even more problematic if group members are not warned in advance of the limits of confidentiality, but are encouraged to open up and share their struggles in the safety of the support group, only to be reported for abuse after an emotional disclosure.

Bergeron and Gray recommend that human service professionals become aware of elder abuse reporting laws in their state and that they inform all group members of these laws as well as the limits of confidentiality before the group process begins. Other suggestions include developing a rapport with adult protective services personnel to coordinate services before an abuse report must be made, monitoring group member disclosures, and listening for situations that sound as though they are approaching a crisis stage. By noting comments referencing a feeling of being tempted to strike out physically, the support group facilitator can intervene and secure supportive services before the situation evolves into an abusive situation warranting protective services intervention (Bergeron & Gray, 2003).

Practice Settings Serving the Elderly

Human service professionals wishing to provide direct service to the elderly community have a wide array of choices in practice settings. Virtually all practice settings delivering services to the elderly have certain treatment and intervention goals, including the promotion of the health and well-being of the elderly, special attention to the needs of special populations such as women and ethnic minority groups, providing effective services at an affordable price, identifying the common needs of all elders, and removing existing social barriers so that elders can be empowered to seek assistance in meeting those needs.

Area Agencies on Aging (AAA), discussed earlier in this chapter, often serve as human service agencies offering direct service to the elderly community on a local level. Generally these agencies offer a multitude of services for the elderly such as nutrition programs, services for homebound elderly, low-income minority elderly, and other programs focusing on the needs of the elderly within the local community. Many AAAs also act as a referral source for other services in the area. For instance, the Mid-Florida AAA offers programs for those suffering from Alzheimer's (including caregiver respite), a toll-free elder hotline that links area elderly with resources, an emergency home energy assistance program, paralegal services, home care for the elderly, Medicaid waivers, and practitioners who work with the elderly in helping them to make informed decisions. Most AAAs offer both in-house services, many of which are facilitated by human service professionals, as well as funding off-site programs. Human service professionals working at an AAA-funded center might facilitate caregiver respite programs, or they might provide case management services for an agency that provides employment services for clients over 60 years old. Even at centers where services are primarily medical in nature, human service professionals often provide adjunct counseling and case management as a support service.

Other practice settings include adult day cares, geriatric assessment units, nursing home facilities, veterans' services, elder abuse programs, adult protective services, bereavement services, senior centers, and hospices. A human service professional will likely perform similar types of direct service, consultation, and educational services focused on assisting older clients maintain or improve their quality of life, independence, and level of self-determination. Tasks are typically performed using a multidisciplinary team approach and can include conducting psychosocial assessments, providing case management, developing treatment plans, providing referrals for appropriate services, and providing counseling to the elderly clients and their families. Services are also provided to family caregivers offering support and respite care.

Special Populations

As the frail elderly population has increased in numbers, the government has shifted its priorities and began developing programs aimed at long-term health-care needs, with a particular focus on vulnerable populations such as women, ethnic minorities, and the elderly living in rural communities. It is difficult to define who is "special" or particularly vulnerable within the elderly population because in many senses all elderly could conceivably be considered special in that they are vulnerable to social, economic, physical, and psychological harm or exploitation simply by virtue of their advancing age and corresponding dependency needs. But many gerontologists classify various subpopulations as more vulnerable for various reasons. For instance, successful aging has been linked to good economic status, good health-care, relatively low stress levels, and high levels of social connections. A 2004 study also showed a link between good health and financial stability, finding that Caucasians tend to have greater economic wealth and better health than African-American and Latino populations (Lum, 2004).

Women are often considered a special population because as a group they are more prone to depression and typically have a worse response to antidepressant medication (Kessler, 2003). Women often experience greater financial vulnerability, particularly if divorced or widowed, and are often in lower-wage jobs, undereducated, and underinsured. Widowhood is a common occurrence for women because they live an average of seven years longer than men, and although the majority of women in the United States marry, by the age of 65, 75 percent of women are unmarried. Widowhood puts women at increased risk for lower morale and other mental health problems, even though these symptoms abate with time and intervention (Bennett, 1997).

Research has also shown a link between stress and racism that affects quality of life. A study conducted in 2002 found that racism, and particularly institutionalized racism (such as government-sanctioned racism through discrimination in housing, employment, and health care), had a detrimental affect on elderly African Americans, particularly males, who tend to experience worse racial discrimination than women (Utsey, Payne, Jackson, & Jones, 2002).

Other special populations could conceivably include any subgroup that is vulnerable at any point across the life span because of physical or mental disability, veterans status, and those individuals living in isolated rural areas. Identifying special populations within the elderly population will allow the human service professional to explore issues that can potentially render the elderly client at increased risk and vulnerability during old age. For example, research has shown that veterans are at special risk for depression, PTSD, and alcohol abuse. Thus, elderly veterans will be at particular risk for these conditions. An elderly client who is developmentally disabled will also face increased vulnerability compared to those in the elderly population who have intelligence in the normal range. A human service professional who is well versed on typical risk factors for the elderly in the United States, as well as for the increased risk factors facing special populations, will be far more effective in protecting and advocating for their elderly clients.

Concluding Thoughts on Services to the Elderly

The elderly population is increasing at a dramatic rate in the United States, rendering this one of fastest growing target populations of human service agencies. As the baby boomers continue to age and as life continues to become more complex, many within the elderly population will rely on human service professionals to meet many of their basic needs. Many human service educational programs are adding the field of elderly care, or social gerontology, as an area of specialization in response to the growing need for practitioners committed to work with this population in a variety of capacities.

Future considerations include the continued effort to identify vulnerable populations, as well as addressing ongoing concerns such as the shortage of available affordable housing, the available of long-term care, health-care services directed to the elderly population, and the increased role of parenting responsibilities placed on the elderly population. Human service professionals can make a significant positive impact on the lives of the elderly and their family members by addressing both ongoing and anticipated needs of this population.

r e f e r e n c e s

American Psychiatric Association. (2000). *Diagnostic and statistical manual of mental disorders* (4th ed., Text Revision) (DSM-IV-TR). Washington, DC: American Psychiatric Association.

Arias, B. (2004). *United States life tables, 2002.* National Vital Statistics reports, 53(6). Hyattsville, Maryland: National Center for Health Statistics.

Atchley, R. C. (1976). *The sociology of retirement.* New York: John Wiley.

Bergeron, R., & Gray, B. (2003). Ethical dilemmas of reporting suspected elder abuse. *Social work, 48*(1): 96–104.

Birrer, R. B., & Vemuri, S. P. (2004). Depression in later life: a diagnostic and therapeutic challenge. *American Family Physician, 69*(10), 2375–2382.

Butler, R. N. (1969). Ageism: Another form of bigotry. *The Gerontologist, 9,* 243–241.

Casper, L. M., & Bryson, K. R. (1998). Co-resident Grandparents and their Grandchildren: Grand-parent maintained families. *Population Division Working Paper No. 26.* Washington, DC: U.S. Bureau of Statistics.

Centers for Disease Control and Prevention, National Center for Injury Prevention and Control. Injury Statistics Query and Reporting System (WISQARS) [Online]. (2004). Retrieved on October 28, 2005, from   http://www.cdc.gov/ncipc/wisqars/default.htm

Erikson, E. H. (1959). Identity and the life cycle. *Psychological Issues, 1,* 1–171.

Erikson, E. H. (1966). Eight ages of man. *International Journal of Psychiatry, 2,* 281–300.

Glass, J. C. & Hunnycutt, T. L. (2002). Grandparents parenting grandchildren: Extent of situations, issues involved, and educational implications. *Educational Gerontology, 28,* 139–161.

Havighurst, R. J. (1961). Successful aging. *The Gerontologist,* 1(1), 8–13.

Hecht, L., & Coyle, B. (2001). Elderly homeless: a comparison of older and younger adult emer-gency shelter seekers in Bakersfield, California. *American Behavioral Scientist, 45*(1), 66–79.

Hirshbein, L. D. (2001). Popular views of old age in America, 1900–1950. *Journal of American Geriatrics Society, 49,* 1555–1560.

Hoyert D. L., Kochanek, K. D. & Murphy, S. L. (1999). Deaths: Final data for 1997. *National Vital Statistics Report, 47(19).* DHHS Publication No. 99-1120. Hyattsville, MD: National Center for Health Statistics.

Jensen-Scott, R. L. (1993). Counseling to promote retirement adjustment. *Career Development Quarterly, 41(3),* 257–267.

Kessler, R. C. (2003). Epidemiology of women and depression. *Journal of Affective Disorders, 74*(1), 5–13.

Kim, J. E., & Moen, P. (2001). Moving into retirement: Preparations and transitions in late midlife. In M. E. Lachman (Ed.), *Handbook of midlife development* (pp. 487–527). New York: Wiley and Sons.

Kraaij, V. & de Wilde, J. (2001). Negative life events and depressive symptoms in the elderly life: A life span perspective. *Aging & Mental Health, 5(1),* 84–91.

Krout, J. A. (2003). *Residential choices and experiences of older adults: Pathways for life quality.* New York: Spring Publishing Company.

Kutza, E. A., & Keigher, S. M. (1991). The elderly. "New homeless": an emergency population at risk. *Social work, 36*(4), 283–293.

Levinson, D. (1978). *The Seasons of a man's life.* New York, NY: Knopf.

Levinson, D. (1996). *The Seasons of a woman's life.* New York, NY: Knopf.

Linn, G. L. & Mayer-Oakes, S.A. (1990). Differences in health status between older and younger homeless adults. *Journal of American Geriatric Society, 38*(11), 1220–1229.

Lum, Y. (2004). Health-wealth association among older Americans: Racial and ethnic differences. *Social Work Research, 28*(2): 106–116.

Lynch, T. R., Compton, J. S., Mendelson, T., Robins, C. J. & Krishnan, K. R. R. (2000). Anxious de-pression among the elderly: Clinical and phenomenological correlates. *Aging and Mental Health, 4*(3), 268–274.

McIntosh, J. L. (2003). *U.S.A. suicide: 2001 official final data.* Retrieved on October 28, 2005, from http://www.suicidology.org/associations/1045/files/2001datapg.pdf.

McNamara, T. K., & Williamson, J. B. (2004). Race, Gender, and the Retirement decisions of people ages 60 to 80: Prospects for age integration in employment. *International Journal of Aging and Human Development*, 59(3), 255–286.

Miller, D., Leyell, T. & Mazacheck, J. (2004). Stereotypes of the elderly in U.S. television commercials from the 1950s to the 1990s. *International Journal of Aging and Human Development*, 58(4), 315–340.

Munk, N. (1999, February). Finished at forty. *Fortune*, 139(2), 50–66.

National Institute of Mental Health. (2003). *Older adults: Depression and suicide facts.* (NIH Publication No. 99-4593). Bethesda, MD: National Institutes of Health.

Office of Statistics and Programming, NCIPC, CDC. *Web-based Injury Statistics Query and Reporting System* (WISQARS™). http://www.cdc.gov/ncipc/wisqars/default.htm

Palmer, K., Fratiglioni, L. & Winblad, K. (2003). What is mild cognitive impairment? Variations in definitions and evolution of nondemented persons with cognitive impairment. *Acta Neurologica Scandinavica, 107*(179), 14–20.

Reitzes, D. C. & Mutran, E. J. (2004). The transition to retirement: Stages and factors that influence retirement adjustment. *International Journal of Aging and Human Development*, 59(1), 63–84.

Senate Special Committee on Aging: Written testimony of Robert V. Butter, M.D.

Simmons, T. & Dye, J. L. (2003, October). Grandparents living with grandchildren: 2000. Washington DC: U.S. Bureau of the Census.

Snyder, M. (2001). *Self and society.* Malden, MA: Blackwell Publishers.

Tatara, T. (1997). Summaries of the statistical data on elder abuse in domestic settings. *National Center on Elder Abuse,* Washington, D.C.

Teaster, P. B. (2000). A response to the abuse of vulnerable adults: A 2000 survey of state adult protective services. *The National Center on Elder Abuse,* Washington, D.C.

Thornton, J. E. (2002). Myths of Aging or Ageist stereotypes. *Educational Gerontology,* 28, 301–312.

Tougas, F., Lagacé, M. & De La Sablonnière, R. (2004). A new approach to the link between identity and relative deprivation in the perspective of ageism and retirement. *International Journal of Aging & Human Development*, 59(1), 1–23.

Utsey, S. O., Payne, Y. A., Jackson, E. S., & Jones, A. M. (2002). Race-related stress, Quality of Life Indicators, and life satisfaction among elderly African Americans. *Cultural Diversity and Ethnic Minority Psychology*, 48(3), 224–233.

Waite, A., Bebbington, P., Skelton-Robinson, M. & Orrell, M. (2004). Life events, depression and social support in dementia. *British Journal of Clinical Psychology*, 43, 313–324.

Warr, P., Butcher, V., & Robertson, I. (2004). Activity and Psychological well-being in older people. *Aging & Mental Health*, 8(2), 172–183.

suggested reading

Bergling, T. (2004). *Reeling in the years: Gay men's perspectives on age and ageism.* Binghamton, NY: Southern Tier Editions.

Davis, R. (1989). *My journey into Alzheimer's disease.* Wheaton, IL: Tyndale House.

de Toledo, S. & Brown, D. E. (1995). *Grandparents as parents: A survival guide for raising a second family.* New York: The Guildford Press.

Kaye, L. W. (2005). *Perspectives on productive aging: Social work with the new aged.* Washington, DC: NASW Press.

McGowin, D. F. (1994). *Living in the labyrinth: A personal journey through the maze of Alzheimer's.* New York: Delta Books.

Osborne, H. (2002). *Ticklebelly hill: Grandparents raising grandchildren.* Bloomington, IN: Authorhouse.

Rosenthal, E. R. (1990). *Women, aging and ageism.* Binghamton, NY: Huntington Park Press.

i n t e r n e t   w e b   s i t e s   r e l a t e d   t o   a g i n g

Alzheimer's Disease Education & Referral Center: **http://www.alzheimers.org**

AARP: **http://aarp.org**

Arthritis Foundation: **http://www.arthritis.org**

Elder Hostel: **http://www.elderhostel.org**

The Grandparent Foundation: **http://www.grandparenting.org**

National Indian Council on Aging: **http://www.nicoa.org/**

chapter 7

Mental Health and Mental Illness

Every society has its mentally ill—those members whose behavior is considered outside what is normal and appropriate. Each society has also developed ways in which to handle or manage such individuals so that healthy societal function is not disrupted. But because the criteria for what is considered *normal behavior* changes from era to era, as well as from culture to culture, it is important to keep cultural mores and generational issues in mind when characterizing someone's behavior as abnormal or unhealthy.

It would be difficult to imagine any human service professional who does not at some point in his or her career come into contact with clients suffering from some form of mental illness. Mental illness is a term that, in its broadest sense, refers to a wide range of mental and emotional disorders, such as depression and anxiety disorders and in its most narrow sense refers to those individuals who suffer from severe and chronic mental illness, requiring at least intermittent **custodial care.** Because of the broadness of this term it can be challenging to reach a consensus on just how many people suffer from mental illness at any one time within the United States.

A recent comprehensive study on mental illness found that approximately 26 percent of the U.S. adult population suffers from some diagnosable mental disorder, most of which are relatively minor not requiring formal psychological intervention. But of this percentage, 6 percent suffer from one or more severe mental disorders significantly limiting their ability to function (Kessler, Berglund, & Demler, 2005).

The term *severely mentally ill* typically refers to those individuals suffering from schizophrenia, bipolar disorder, severe and recurrent depression, and other mental disorders that prevent normal functioning such as maintaining employment or performing activities of daily living. Individuals suffering from severe mental illness are often unable to consistently provide self-care, think clearly, reason, relate to others, and cope with the demands of daily life.

The History of Mental Illness: Perceptions and Treatment

To understand the current climate with regard to perceptions of mental illness as well as treatment paradigms commonly used in the United States, it is important to have some understanding of the historic treatment of the severely mentally ill. It has been said that the measure of a truly civil, ethical, and compassionate society is reflected in how it treats its most vulnerable members. The mentally ill, particularly the severely and chronically mentally ill, certainly fall into this category, and if this statement is in fact true, then the U.S. society has undoubtedly gone through some periods that were uncivilized, unethical, and compassionless.

Early in human history, mental illness, or madness as it was often called, was commonly believed to be caused by demonic possession. Skulls dating back to at least 5000 BCE were found with small holes drilled throughout, presumably to allow the in-dwelling demons to escape. Demonic possession and witchcraft were still thought to be the cause of insanity and "lunacy" throughout the Middle Ages and well into the seventeenth and eighteenth centuries. A common "cure" for madness in the Middle Ages involved tying the suspected witch or demon-possessed person up with a rope and lowering them into freezing cold water. If they floated, they were believed to be witches and were then killed in some horrible way. If they sunk they were not witches, but the cold water was believed to be a cure for madness, so either way the problem of insanity was resolved (Porter, 2002).

During colonial times the problem of the insane and "feebleminded" was con-sidered a family matter, but as populations in the cities grew, those suffering from some form of mental illness increasingly became a problem for the community. Almshouses, typically used as poorhouses or workhouses for those unable or unwill-ing to find work on their own, were often used to house the insane as well. By the mid-1700s many towns in Colonial America were following the trend in Europe of building separate almshouses and even specialized hospitals for the insane (Torrey & Miller, 2001). Yet reports of mistreatment were common. In fact, the trend of abuse noted in the Middle Ages continued throughout the nineteenth century, where members of so-ciety whose behavior was not in line with social mores and the general expectations of society were subjected to public beatings, incarceration, and sometimes death, partic-ularly if their strange behavior was perceived as particularly threatening. Typical "treat-ment" in asylums, almshouses, and even in the new state hospital system included, among other things, beatings with chains and rods. Chains were also used to contain patients in insane asylums—some for most of their lives (Torry & Miller, 2001).

By early in the eighteenth century mental health reform had begun, led in part by Philippe Pinel of France, who when appointed chief physician at a hospital for the incurably mentally insane, was appalled at the barbaric conditions of the hospital. He found patients chained to walls, some for up to 40 years, and a system where community residents could pay an admission fee to see the insane patients as if they were animals in a zoo. In 1792 Pinel was memorialized for his decision to unchain up to five thousand patients. This event marked the beginning of the era of "Moral Treatment" of the mentally ill. Pinel later became chief of another hospital in Paris, where he consistently pushed for reform for more compassionate care.

Dorothea Dix, a U.S. social activist, was a leader in advocating for more compassionate treatment of the mentally ill in insane asylums. Her plea to the Massachusetts state legislature in 1843 poignantly described the deplorable conditions those with mental illness were forced to endure, including being held in cages by chains, often naked, beaten with rods, and whipped to ensure obedience. Dix pleaded for the legislators to intercede on behalf of society's most vulnerable members. Dix's efforts

■ The mentally ill were often housed in inhumane conditions, sometimes restrained for extended periods of time.

resulted in an improvement in the conditions of both hospitals and asylums (Torrey & Miller, 2001).

By the beginning of the twentieth century most of the almshouses and insane asylums had closed, and state mental institutions became the primary facilities housing the mentally ill. Yet although institutionalized care was considered revolutionary, compassionate, and far better than the plight of the mentally ill in former generations, rampant abuses involving cruel treatment, neglect, and physical and emotional abuse were increasingly reported throughout the early 1900s.

Clifford Beers, an Ivy League–trained businessman who enjoyed a privileged life, served as one of the initial sparks in what ultimately led to a radical change in the way the mentally ill were perceived in the United States. In 1900 Beers suffered a serious breakdown after enduring a family trauma. He was ultimately hospitalized in several different mental hospitals, each one more abusive than the next. In his 1908 autobiography entitled *A Mind that Found Itself,* Beers chronicled his descent into mental illness, as well as the cruel and often inhumane treatment he received at the hands of those charged with the responsibility for his care. His book ultimately led to the creation of the National Committee for Mental Hygiene (currently the National Mental Health Association), which developed model commitment goals, including improving the treatment of the mentally ill, developing better prevention methods, and reducing the stigma and negative attitudes toward mental illness and the mentally ill. As a result of Beers's advocacy many states ultimately incorporated these goals into their own state statutes.

The Deinstitutionalization of the Mentally Ill

Although horrible abuses in state and private mental hospitals were well documented through the mid-1900s, institutionalized care remained the primary method of treatment for the seriously mentally ill for another 50 years. The U.S. government's first legislative involvement in the care of the mentally ill occurred in 1946, when President Harry Truman signed the *National Mental Health Act* into existence. The signing of this act allowed for the creation of National Institutes of Mental Health (NIMH) (one of the first four institutes under the National Institutes of Health) in 1949.

In 1955 the Mental Health Study Act was passed, which directed the convening of the *Joint Commission on Mental Health and Illness* (under the auspices of the NIMH), charged with the responsibility of analyzing and assessing the needs of the country's mentally ill, as well as making recommendations for a more effective and comprehensive national approach to their treatment. The committee was comprised of professionals in the mental health field, such as psychiatrists, psychologists, therapists, educators, and representatives from various professional agencies, including the American Academy of Neurology, American Academy of Pediatrics, the American Psychological Association, National Association of Social Workers, and National Association for Mental Health.

In general, in addition to making recommendations for increasing funding for both research and training of professionals, the committee recommended transitioning from an institutionalized treatment model, to an outpatient community mental health model, where patients were treated in the *least restricted environment* within the community. This report led to the creation of *The Community Mental Health Centers Act of 1963*, which was passed under the Kennedy administration. This act enabled funding of a new national mental health care system focusing on prevention and community-based care, rather than on institutionalized custodial care (Feldman, 2003). The passage of the Community Mental Health Centers Act (CMHC) set the de-institutionalization movement into motion, prompted by an overall dissatisfaction with public mental hospitals in general, the development of new psychotropic medications, and a new focus on the brain–behavior connection that fostered a sense of hope and optimism among those in the mental health field (Mowbray & Holter, 2002).

Several decades after President Kennedy described the CMHC program as a "bold new approach" to dealing with mental illness, many in the mental health field cite frustration and discouragement with what many perceive as numerous failures of the program. The replacement of hope with discouragement is in part due to the reality that mental illness was been a far more worthy opponent than early advocates for change suspected. Early proponents of deinstitutionalization had hoped that through early detection, increased research, psychotropic medication and better intervention strategies, mental illness could be greatly reduced and perhaps even eliminated. Yet, mental illness remains a pervasive problem in today's society regardless of significant efforts to curb its devastating impact on individuals, families, and society. The most serious criticisms are leveled at the federal government, which many claim fell short of funding commitments, resulting in far fewer community mental health centers being opened across the county, which in turn resulted in the burden of care for the country's mentally ill shifting from the public mental hospital system to nursing homes, the streets, and the prison system (Sullivan, 1992).

Common Mental Illnesses and Clinical Issues

Human service professionals may encounter mental illness directly when clients seek therapy for previously diagnosed disorders, or they may encounter mental illness indirectly when a client seeks services from a human service agency for reasons unrelated to their mental health, and symptoms of mental illness begin to surface in the midst of the counseling relationship. Whether clients present with prior diagnoses or have no previously identified mental health issues, practitioners must be able to recognize the common signs and symptoms of mental illness in their clients.

In the United States individuals are diagnosed using the DSM-IV-TR (described in chapter 4), which categorizes mental disorders in a manner similar to physical disorders. Certain criteria must be met to diagnose someone with a particular mental or emotional disorder. It is important to remember, though, that mental and emotional disorders are diagnosed based on symptoms, not causes or etiology, as with medical illness. There is some controversy surrounding the possibility that the DSM-IV-TR contributes to pathologizing people rather than focusing on their strengths, but it is to date the most effective system we have for assessing individuals in a systematic, organized, and universal manner.

The first two axes of the DSM-IV-TR are the ones most commonly used by clinicians in diagnosing clients. Clinical or mental disorders are diagnosed on Axis I, in 14 different categories. Disorders such as anxiety disorders, eating disorders, mood disorders (depression and bipolar disorder), and substance-related disorders are all diagnosed on Axis I. Many clinical disorders are amenable to treatment through psychotherapy and psychotropic medication, but they are diagnosed on the first axis because they are serious enough to warrant clinical attention.

Axis II is reserved for personality disorders and mental retardation. Personality disorders differ from clinical disorders in many respects, but most notably many clinicians believe that personality disorders can be resistant to treatment because most of the problems that individuals with personality disorders experience are by definition ingrained in their personalities, thus authentic change is challenging because changing one's personality requires pervasive transformation. Examples of personality disorders include antisocial personality disorder (sociopathy), borderline personality disorder, and narcissistic personality disorder.

Serious Mental Disorders Diagnosed on Axis I

The following section includes some of the more serious mental illnesses that human service professionals often encounter in clients who are functionally impaired and in need of extensive case management and counseling services. Depending on the severity of their illness, these individuals might be in and out of inpatient psychiatric facilities, referred through the court system, or even living on the streets. It is important, then, that even entry-level human service professionals be generally familiar with these disorders so that their cases can be as effectively managed as possible and referred for appropriate services.

Psychotic Disorders

Psychotic disorders include a number of illnesses where contact with reality is severely impaired. Common symptoms of a psychotic disorder include hallucinations, delusions, and generally bizarre and eccentric behavior.

The most common psychotic disorder is *schizophrenia*, which is actually an umbrella term referencing what is theorized to be a number of disorders with similar symptoms, but with many different causes, such as genetic anomalies, brain chemistry disturbances, and brain damage. Recent research has even suggested that some forms of schizophrenia may be caused by exposure to the Borna virus (Terayama et al., 2003). Schizophrenia usually manifests during the teen and early adulthood years. Schizophrenia is *not* a split personality, and a diagnosis of schizophrenia does not automatically mean that someone will become violent (despite sensationalized media reports). Schizophrenia is not caused by a bad childhood, although stress and trauma can trigger a psychotic episode (NIMH, 1999).

Symptoms of schizophrenia can include

1. *Delusions:* false beliefs or misperceptions, many of which could not possibly be true, such as believing that the government is monitoring one's activities through the television set, or that one has special powers, such as speaking to others through mental telepathy.

2. *Hallucinations:* sensations that are experienced but do not exist, such as hearing voices, or seeing things that are not there, smelling smells that do not exist, or feeling sensations when nothing is present.

3. *Disorganized thinking and speech:* the frequent trailing off into incoherent talk often referred to as "word salad." Speech often reflects thinking that makes no sense. Someone with schizophrenia may even make up his own words, and some will stop speaking all together (as is the case with catatonia).

4. *Negative symptoms:* the absence of normal behavior such as the *lack* of emotion (often referred to as affective flattening), alogia (complete *lack* of any speech), and extreme apathy (complete *lack* of interest or drive).

Treatment used to consist solely of custodial care and heavy tranquilizers to minimize symptoms, particularly destructive ones. Antipsychotic medication has been available since the mid-1950s, but negative side effects such as sexual impotence, tardive dyskinesia (involuntary jerking spasms of the muscles), and tranquilizing effects kept many individuals with schizophrenia from taking their medication consistently. Yet new "atypical" antipsychotic drugs, such have Risperdal® have shown great promise in significantly reducing schizophrenic symptoms such as hallucinations and delusion without nearly the number of side effects.

Affective Disorders

Affective disorders include disorders of one's mood and emotions and include depression and bipolar disorder.

Clinical Depression includes symptoms such as

1. Persistent sad, anxious, or "empty" mood
2. Feelings of hopelessness and pessimism
3. Feelings of guilt, worthlessness, and helplessness
4. Loss of interest or pleasure in hobbies and activities that were once enjoyed

5. Decreased energy and fatigue

6. Difficulty concentrating, remembering, and making decisions

7. Insomnia, early-morning awakening, or oversleeping

8. Appetite and/or weight loss or overeating and weight gain

9. Thoughts of death or suicide; suicide attempts

10. Restlessness and irritability

11. Persistent physical symptoms that do not respond to treatment, such as headaches, digestive disorders, and chronic pain (NAMI, 1999).

The National Institute of Mental Health (2000) estimates that at any given time 9.5 percent of the U.S. population, representing roughly 18.8 million people, are suffering from psychological depression, making this disorder a significant public health issue in America. The World Health Organization has projected that depression will continue to be widespread globally, becoming a leading cause of disability by 2020 (Michaud, Murray & Bloom, 2001).

References to depression date back to the beginning of recorded time. Hippocrates wrote about melancholy in the fourth century, citing an imbalance in the body's "humors" or liquids (blood, bile, phlegm, and black bile) as the cause of melancholy. Everyone feels sad at times, and grieving over a loss is perfectly normal and in fact healthy, despite the pain and discomfort involved. A productive depression can motivate people to change both themselves and their circumstances, where complacency might otherwise keep someone in an unhealthy situation. But debilitating depression is rarely productive and can leave people feeling ashamed, particularly in a productivity-oriented society such as the United States. Such shame and guilt just serves to add an increased burden to the depressed person, exacerbating depressive symptoms and often leading to a downward emotional spiral.

Although the existence of depression might not be new, theories of what causes depression are being developed all the time. Hippocrates believed that melancholy (depression) was caused by an imbalance in the humors of the body. Freud believed that melancholy was caused by unresolved grief, where the sufferer denied the real loss they experienced and then turned the grief onto themselves in the form of internalized aggression (Freud, 1917). This theory attempted to explain the intermittent anger that many depressed people often express, as well as their loss of self-esteem.

Theories based on behaviorism theorize that individuals become depressed because their depressive behavior is reinforced and rewarded as children, and more productive behavior was not. A popular theory of depression is the cognitive-behavioral theory, which is somewhat of a hybrid model (incorporating aspects of both Aaron Beck's cognitive theory of depression and behaviorism). This theory hypothesizes that depression is related to negative or irrational thinking. Thoughts such as "I'm a horrible person," or "Nothing good will ever happen to me, I will always fail" if thought consistently enough can ultimately lead to feelings of sadness, despair, and hopelessness (Beck, 1964).

Another popular theory, particularly with human service professionals and social workers, is a social-contextual model of depression in which environmental conditions such as negative life events, racial discrimination, and poverty impacting an individual is believed to contribute to depression, particularly if the depressed individual does not have the coping skills to deal with them in a positive manner (Swindle, Cronkite & Moos, 1989).

In the last several decades a biological model of depression has emerged in which a predisposition to depression is believed to be genetically related, and depressive symptoms are believed to be caused by neurohormonal irregularities, such as problems with neurotransmitter functioning. Most human service professionals embrace a biopsychosocial model of depression that recognizes the biological basis of many depressions, the emotional nature of depression, and the impact that one's environment, including such factors as an abusive childhood, and even social oppression can have on depression.

Because depression often *co-occurs* with other disorders, such as anxiety, eating disorders, substance abuse disorders, and even psychotic disorders, it is essential that all human service professionals involved in direct service be able to screen for depression, even if a client is not seeking services for this purpose.

Bipolar depression (formerly manic depression) involves both depressive episodes as well as manic episodes, which involve racing thoughts, increased energy, euphoric mood, poor judgment, impulsive behavior, and risk-taking behavior such as unrestrained sexual activity, going on spending sprees, or acting in an aggressive manner. Cycles between depressive and manic episodes vary greatly, with rapid cycling often occurring as the disorder advances. Some individuals even experience depressed and manic episodes within the same day, whereas others might experience such episodes on only a few occasions per year.

Although researchers strongly believe that bipolar disorder is biologically based, no singular biological cause has been identified. In other words, there is no single gene that is responsible for bipolar disorder, and individuals can't take a blood test to see if they have the disorder. Brain imaging studies have shown some differences in the brains of individuals with bipolar disorder, strengthening the theory that this is a biologically based disorder. Yet to date, bipolar disorder is diagnosed based on symptoms. For this reason, if a client comes into an agency with a former diagnosis of bipolar disorder, the human service professional should consider the past diagnosis, but should not rely solely on another clinician's observations. I have had numerous clients come into my practice citing a long list of various diagnoses, but I did not diagnose them in a similar manner because I did not note the same symptoms during my evaluation.

Thus, there is a certain amount of subjectivity involved in the diagnostic process, particularly with regard to how strictly DSM-IV-TR criteria are applied, and although this does not mean that one clinician is right and the other wrong, it does mean that each clinician should rely on his or her own clinical assessment skills. This is particularly important when confronting disorders such as bipolar disorder, because overdiagnosis has been noted as a potential problem, particularly in the child and adolescent population (Geller et al., 2002; Hutto, 2001).

Treating individuals with bipolar disorder can be challenging because many clients with this disorder claim to enjoy the mania because the feeling of euphoria, increased energy, and quick thinking makes them feel powerful and alive; thus if they experience breakthrough mania while on medication, this can often lead them to stop taking their medication, leading some clients into a seemingly never-ending cycle of going on and off their medication. Many individuals with bipolar disorder can live relatively normal and functional lives if they can comply with treatment, such as consistently taking their prescribed medication.

Serious Mental Disorders Diagnosed on Axis II

Personality disorders include generally rigid and inflexible patterns of inner experience and outward behavior. Personality disorders often involve unhealthy and maladaptive patterns of perceiving things, difficulty controlling or regulating emotions, and difficulty controlling emotional impulses. Someone with a personality disorder will often perceive things differently than others and often misperceive another's behavior and intentions. Up to 30 percent of all individuals seeking mental health care services have at least one personality disorder (Dingfelder, 2004).

But just because someone has personality traits that are irritating or somewhat eccentric it does not mean that they have a personality disorder. One of by best friends can be defensive if someone is criticizing her children. She often misperceives innocent comments as slights or criticism of her parenting. But does this mean that she has a personality disorder? Of course not. But what if her defensiveness was so intense that she started arguments constantly with friends and family members? What if she could not enjoy going out socially because all she could think about was protecting her children? What if she perceived insults everywhere and could not get along with anyone, including her children's teachers? This behavior might then push her in the direction of a personality disorder—a collection of maladaptive and rigid personality traits that are exhibited across different contexts and interfere with one's ability to function effectively in life, including interfering with one's ability to enjoy reasonably healthy relationships with others.

For instance, it might be perfectly normal for a woman to feel emotionally attacked whenever she gets into an argument with her husband if he has an attacking way of expressing his needs and frustrations. But it is not necessarily healthy or normative for a woman to feel emotionally attacked whenever she receives constructive feedback that she perceives as criticism from her husband, friends, family, coworkers, supervisor, teachers, and children. It also might be perfectly healthy for someone to consistently focus on himself in certain situations where perhaps he feels somewhat insecure, such as in large social environments. But it might not be considered healthy if this person excessively focused on himself in virtually all areas of his life—at home, at work, with family, in social situations large and small, often at the expense of others.

The relative level of health or adaptive aspects of one's personality traits are judged on a continuum, like so many other mental and emotional conditions. If someone is a bit on the rigid side with certain issues, it wouldn't necessarily be appropriate to diagnose this person with a personality disorder. Yet if someone gets far enough out on the continuum with regard to rigidity, for example, so that it interferes with an ability to function at work, with family, or with social situations, then this person might have what is considered a disordered personality. The key difference according to the DSM-IV-TR (APA, 2000) is that a personality disorder must cause distress and impairment of functioning in several important areas of functioning.

The DSM-IV-TR categorizes personality disorders into three groups or clusters with three to four personality disorders in each cluster. Table 7.1 includes a list of these clusters and the disorders within those clusters. Although all personalities share some factors in common such as misperception, rigidity, pervasive problems in interpersonal relationships, and with emotional regulation, each cluster of personality disorders varies considerably both with symptoms as well as cause. For instance, many of the Cluster A personality disorders, such as schizoid personality disorder, is strongly believed to be a precursors for psychotic disorders. Obsessive compulsive personality disorder is also theorized to be obsessive compulsive disorder in the early stages. Yet the Cluster B and C personality disorders such as borderline personality disorder and dependent personality disorder are theorized to have some biological influences, but are believed to be related to abuse in childhood, particularly sexual and physical abuse (Bandelow et al., 2005).

Because of the impulsivity and difficulty in managing emotions common among various personality disorders, such individuals might come into counseling at a human service agency voluntarily in response to some crisis (such as a spouse threatening to leave if they do not get help), or they may be mandated for services either through the court system or through county child protective services. Treatment of personality disorders can be challenging as well as frustrating because by definition those with disordered personalities typically lack the insight and awareness to see that anything is wrong with them. In fact, many times such individuals come into counseling wanting assistance in learning how to cope with the vast number of people in their lives they perceive as being unhealthy! Many times these clients are fragile beneath a surface of bravado and seeming self-confidence but when challenged in any manner, they may withdraw or become defensive in a self-protective manner.

Individuals with personality disorders in clusters B and C often come into counseling due to a crisis, but often do not remain once the crisis subsides, opting for

■ **Table 7.1   DSM-IV-TR Criteria for Personality Disorders**

Cluster A (odd, eccentric)

Paranoid personality disorder: Individuals with this disorder display pervasive distrust and suspiciousness.

Schizoid personality disorder: This type of personality disorder is uncommon in clinical settings. A person with this disorder is markedly detached from others and has little desire for close relationships. This person's life is marked by little pleasure in activities. People with this disorder appear indifferent to the praise or criticism of others and often seem cold or aloof.

Schizotypal personality disorder: People with this disorder exhibit marked eccentricities of thought, perception, and behavior.

1. Cluster B (dramatic, emotional)

Antisocial personality disorder: Individuals with antisocial personality disorder display a pervasive pattern of disregard for and violation of the rights of others and the rules of society. Onset must occur by age 15 years.

Borderline personality disorder: The central feature of borderline personality disorder is a pervasive pattern of unstable and intense interpersonal relationships, self-perception, and moods. Impulse control is markedly impaired. Transiently, such patients may appear psychotic because of the intensity of their distortions. Borderline personality disorder is one of the most commonly overused diagnoses in *DSM-IV-TR*.

Histrionic personality disorder: Patients with histrionic personality disorder display excessive emotionality and attention-seeking behavior. They are dramatic and often sexually provocative or seductive. Their emotions are labile. In clinical settings, their tendency to vague and impressionistic speech is often highlighted.

Narcissistic personality disorder: Narcissistic patients are grandiose and require admiration from others.

2. Cluster C (anxious, fearful)

Avoidant personality disorder: Avoidant patients are generally shy. They display a pattern of social inhibition, feelings of inadequacy, and hypersensitivity to rejection. Unlike patients with schizoid personality disorder, they actually desire relationships with others but are paralyzed by their fear and sensitivity into social isolation.

Dependent personality disorder: Although many people exhibit dependent behaviors and traits, people with dependent personality disorder have an excessive need to be taken care of that results in submissive and clinging behavior, regardless of consequences.

Obsessive-compulsive personality disorder: People with obsessive-compulsive personality disorder are markedly preoccupied with orderliness, perfectionism, and control. They lack flexibility or openness. Their preoccupations interfere with their efficiency despite their focus on tasks. They are often scrupulous and inflexible about matters of morality, ethics, and values to a point beyond cultural norms. They are often stingy as well as stubborn.

Note: From DSM-IV-TR (APA, 2000)

superficial solutions to their problems rather than anchoring themselves in a counseling relationship where they must do the difficult, slow work of unearthing long-held unhealthy beliefs and behavioral patterns. They might also stick with counseling as long as they perceive that the practitioner is on their side, but once the practitioner gives them honest feedback or challenges them on irrational, one-sided, or distorted thinking, they often quit, arguing that even the practitioner is now against them.

Counseling individuals with personality disorders is often frustrating for practitioners because progress is slow, and clients are often resistant to change. Yet, many new counseling techniques are being developed, some with significant success, but progress is always slow because authentic change requires that clients actually change the entire way they perceive the world, and themselves within it. They must also learn how to "sit with their emotions" rather than act on them and to control their impulses rather than indulging them. Thus, teaching self-discipline is a significant component of counseling most individuals with personality disorders. Antidepressant and antianxiety medication can help with the co-occurring depression and anxiety common with many personality disorders.

Mental Health Practice Settings and Counseling Interventions

Human service professionals involved in the practice of caring for the mentally ill was formally marked by involvement in the *aftercare movement* of the late 1800s and early 1900s. Aftercare, a social reform issue of the time, involved the short-term care of the formerly "insane" and "lunatics" (Vourlekis, Edinburg, & Knee, 1998). Aftercare was typically managed by private charitable societies who offered temporary assistance and housing for those coming out of the state asylum system. Social workers were on the forefront of this helping model, which was really before its time because this type of "continuum of care" was not a part of the psychological mainstream during that era. It wasn't long before aftercare programs were considered the sole domain of social workers, who were paid by the state, and ultimately by public or private hospitals. This program set the foundation for the contemporary role of those in the human services field who provide both advocacy and direct service to those who suffer from mental illness.

According to the NASW social workers provide the majority of the mental health services in the United States, whether providing case management, counseling services, or advocacy either on a micro or macro level. Social workers and other human service professionals work in a variety of practice settings including human service agencies; military and veterans services agencies; psychiatric in-patient or day-treatment programs; police departments and criminal justice agencies, such as police departments, probation departments, and county prosecutor offices;

hospitals and skilled nursing facilities; private practices; and community mental health centers.

Historically, human service professionals have had somewhat of a love–hate relationship with providing direct service to the mentally ill. A century ago social workers and other professionals in the mental health field opted for practice settings with more functional clients so they could actually use their advanced training, often not required with those needing only custodial care. Unfortunately a survey conducted in 1985 revealed that human service professionals, including social workers, had similarly negative attitudes about working with the chronically mentally ill population (Mirabi, Weinman, & Magnetti, 1985).

This trend might be changing, though, indicated by a more recent survey revealing more positive attitudes among students regarding working with the seriously mentally ill population. Also, a 2004 study of NASW members found that attitudes among human service professionals with master's level training was improving, and a great majority of those queried expressed a strong commitment to working with vulnerable populations, including the severely mentally ill. In fact, the primary frustration among human service professionals, including social workers, was not working with high-need clients, but rather, working within a system that is wrought with treatment barriers and inconsistencies barring practitioners from providing the best service possible for their clients (Newhill & Korr, 2004).

Intervention Strategies

A chief complaint of many in the human services field is the mental health community's general tendency to approach mental illness from a pathological perspective. This inclination to see human behavior in what often amounts to polarized terms of good and bad, acceptable and unacceptable, desirable and undesirable has only served to promote the social stigma of mental illness. Viewing mental illness through the lens of biology can also contribute to the tendency to pathologize the mentally ill where individuals are seen as "sick" and "broken." So although the discovery that many forms of mental illness have biological roots can relieve the mentally ill and their family of unnecessary guilt, it also suggests limited potential on the part of the mentally ill, increasing both social stigma and social rejection (Sullivan, 1992).

An alternative approach to viewing mental illness is to use a *strengths perspective,* a model commonly used in the human services field. This theoretical perspective encourages the practitioner to recognize and promote a client's strengths, rather than focusing on deficits. A strengths perspective also presumes a client's ability to solve his or her own problems through the development of self-sufficiency and self-determination. Although there are several contributors to strengths-perspective research in the human services field, Saleebey (1996) has developed several principles for practitioners to follow that can help the client experience a sense of empowerment in their lives. Saleebey encourages practitioners to recognize that all clients:

1. Have resources available to them, both within themselves and their communities
2. Are members of the community and as such are entitled to respect and dignity
3. Are resilient by nature and have the potential to grow and heal in the face of crisis and adversity
4. Need to be in relationship with others in order to self-actualize
5. Have the right to their own perception of their problems, even if this perception isn't held by the practitioner

Sullivan (1992) was one of the first theorists to apply the strength perspective to the area of chronic mental illness where clients suffering from mental illness are encouraged to recognize and develop their own personal strengths and abilities. Sullivan compared this approach to one often used when working with the physically challenged, where focusing on physical disabilities is replaced with focusing on and developing one's physical abilities. Sullivan claimed that by redefining the problem (rather than continuing to search for new solutions), by fully integrating the mentally challenged into society, and by focusing on strengths and abilities rather than solely on deficits, an environment can then be created that is truly consistent with the early goals of mental health reforms who sought to remove treatment barriers promoting respectful, compassionate, and comprehensive care of the mentally ill. Operating from a strengths perspective is important regardless of what intervention strategies a human service professional uses in direct practice.

Human service professionals utilize many tools and interventions when working with mentally ill clients. Some of these intervention strategies include *insight counseling,* where clients develop self-awareness skills intended to help them cope more effectively with their various mental health–related challenges. *Group counseling* assists mentally ill individuals gain strength and support from others in similar situations— some a few steps ahead of them and some a few steps behind. *Psychotropic medication* based on recent brain research offers many clients with the hope of controlling the often debilitating symptoms common to many serious mental illnesses.

Psychiatric rehabilitation focuses on skill building, where human service professionals help seriously mentally ill clients function to the best of their abilities within the community (Stromwall & Hurdle, 2003). Clients are empowered, as they develop skills giving them a sense of competence as they learn important skills enabling them to work and live within the community, interact appropriately with others, and provide necessary self-care. Skills development focuses on areas related to budgeting, parenting, social skills, stress management, time management, and symptom management. The skill level targeted is dependent on the functioning level of the client. Clients functioning at a higher level will develop higher level skills such as learning effective parenting techniques, whereas lower functioning clients might focus on more rudimentary skills such as the importance of daily personal hygiene, such as showering and brushing one's teeth. The guiding principles of psychiatric rehabilitation of personal empowerment and competence uses the strengths perspective previously discussed by assisting clients achieve their highest level of functioning on both a personal and social level.

These are just a few of the wide range of intervention strategies that human service professionals use, and successful programs often utilize all these strategies in combination with case management services. Providing a variety of services for mentally ill clients addresses not only the wide range of issues often confronted by such clients, but they also effectively manage the cyclical nature of serious mental illness because the continuum of services can be adapted to fit the needs of the client at any given time.

Common Practice Settings

Human service professionals working with the mentally ill population do so in a variety of practice settings, including outpatient mental health clinics, not-for-profit agencies, outreach programs, job training agencies, housing assistance programs, prisoner assistance programs, government agencies, such as departments of mental health, human services, and probation programs. Human service professionals might be case managers responsible for conducting needs assessments and coordinating the mental health care of clients, they might be providing psychotherapy services on an individual and/or group basis, or they may provide more concrete services such as job training. In truth, a human service professional will likely encounter clients with serious mental illnesses in just about any practice setting, but in this section I will focus on those settings where the seriously and persistently mentally ill is the target population.

Community Mental Health Centers (CMCH) provide direct services to the seriously and chronically mentally ill population. They are typically licensed by the state, and designated to serve a certain catchment area within the community. Services offered often include outpatient services for adults and children, 24-hour crisis intervention, case management services, community support, psychiatric services, alcohol and drug treatment, psychological evaluations, and various educational workshops. They might also offer partial hospitalization and day treatment programs. Although most CMHCs operate on a sliding scale, CMHCs cannot turn away clients who have no ability to pay, thus they are highly reliant on public funding.

Another practice setting that often encounters the seriously mentally ill is the *full-service human service agency.* It is difficult to define "human service agencies" because they come in all shapes, sizes, and colors, but essentially a full-service human or social service agency is a not-for-profit organization, meaning that any financial profits must be reinvested in the agency. This distinction also means that the agency is exempt from paying state and federal taxes, allowing more money to be directed back into the agency. Human services agencies typically offer an array of services aimed at various target populations, including the seriously mentally ill. The agency might provide general counseling services or might target more specific services, such as providing job skills training, housing assistance, or substance abuse counseling.

A human service professional might work in a number of capacities within a human services agency, depending in large part on what types of programs the agency offers. For instance, a human services worker might offer general case management services coordinating all the care the client is receiving and act as the point person for the psychologist, psychiatrist, and any other service providers involved. They might provide direct counseling services or run support groups focusing on a number of psychosocial and daily life issues. If the agency provides outreach services, the human services worker might be out in the community providing emergency crisis intervention services for the local police department or other emergency personnel. Obviously the list of program services is almost endless, particularly because a part of the role of the human services worker and agency is to identify needs within a community and fulfill those needs if not otherwise met.

An alternative to inpatient hospitalization is *partial hospitalization* or *day treatment programs.* These programs, often operated within a hospital setting, are intensive and offer services for individuals who are having difficulty coping in their daily lives, but are not at a point where in-patient hospitalization is a necessity. Clients attend the program five days a week, for approximately seven hours a day, and typically work with a multidisciplinary team of professionals, including a psychiatrist, psychologist, and social worker. Family involvement is highly encouraged. Certain partial hospitalization programs narrowly focus on specific issues, such as eating disorders, self-abuse, or substance abuse, whereas others focus on a wider range of clinical issues such as severe depression, anger management, and past abuse issues. The nature of the program will also vary depending on whether the target population is adults, adolescents, or children. These structured programs can either serve as an alternative intervention to in-patient hospitalization or they can be utilized in the transition from in-patient hospitalization.

Although deinstitutionalization of the mentally ill has resulted in a dramatic reduction in long-term hospitalization of the severely mentally ill, some individuals who are acutely disturbed or suicidal are hospitalized on a short-term basis for diagnostic assessment and stabilizing in in-patient or *acute psychiatric hospitals.* Psychiatric units are typically locked for the safety of the patients who are often either actively psychotic or are a danger to themselves or others. Again, services are focused on assessment and stabilizing with focus on discharge planning. Licensed social workers, counselors, and psychologists often provide case management and discharge planning services in in-patient settings providing adult services and will likely provide more intensive counseling services such as facilitating individual and group counseling, as well as behavioral management if the program is focused on children and adolescents.

Another successful practice setting based on a human services model of empowerment is called the *clubhouse model program.* Clubhouses were first developed in the mid-1950s, but have gained in popularity since deinstitutionalization. This model of service delivery has been compared to the settlement house model of a century ago where the mentally ill are called members, not patients, and meeting the needs of the whole person is seen as the key to recovery. At the foundation of the clubhouse model is its philosophy, which is based on the tenets of mutual respect and personal empowerment, a focus on accepting responsibility, and recognition of the members' strengths and abilities.

Clubhouses are designed to provide a sense of community to mentally ill members who are valued for their personhood and not defined by their mental illness. Services are coordinated through clubhouse staff, and members are responsible for contributing to the overall function of the clubhouse. Clubhouses are open at least five days a week, during normal business hours, and members who are not working outside the clubhouse are given transitional employment within the clubhouse, thus they feel both productive and valued because they have a place to go everyday, where they have valuable work waiting for them. Other services include basic tutoring, including high school equivalency courses, counseling referrals, general advocacy, employment placement, and transitional housing. Members and staff prepare meals together, clean together, and work as a team in ensuring that all clubhouse services and activities run smoothly, including reaching out to new members.

One of the most important values members gain at a clubhouse setting is a sense of social connectedness and cohesion. Each member has assigned responsibilities, which allows them to feel valued and needed. Clubhouses also have reciprocal agreements with various organizations and businesses in the community to assist members in obtaining work, shelter, and other needed services and activities (Jackson, Purnell, Anderson, & Sheafor, 1996).

The clubhouse model is used as an alternative to day treatment programs and partial hospitalization programs, which became popular once long-term hospitalization was phased out after deinstitutionalization. Human service professionals make ideal staff members in clubhouses because of the emphasis on generalist skills, client participation and empowerment, and a philosophy that embraces the ecological perspective, attending to the individual, the community, and the larger society, and understanding how all these levels work together to affect the client. Human service professionals working in a clubhouse setting are constantly engaging client members, promoting their strengths and values, both within the clubhouse as well as within the community, providing both counseling and case management by acting as a liaison with community partners and clients, and most importantly, creating a homelike atmosphere for individuals who often have little or no other family or place to call home.

Mental Illness and Special Populations

Mental Illness and the Homeless Population

One unanticipated consequence of deinstitutionalization was the shifting of literally thousands of mentally ill patients from institutions to the streets. In fact, a 2005 study found that nearly one in six mentally ill individuals is homeless (Folsom, Hawthorne, & Lindamer, 2005). Such individuals would have previously been hospitalized, but with the closing of the majority of public mental hospitals and the transitioning of most psychiatric units to a focus on short-term stays, the severely mentally ill who do not have a network of supportive and able family members are often left with no place to live. Even individuals who do have supportive families will often live on the streets due to the nature of psychosis, which clouds judgment and impairs the ability to think without distortion, leading some individuals to disappear for literally years at a time.

This link between homelessness and mental illness is not solely related to deinstitutionalization. Certainly warehousing the mentally ill kept them off the streets, but the nature of this link is far more complex and likely reciprocal in nature, meaning that severe mental illness leaves many incapable of providing for their basic needs, and the stressful nature of living on the streets, not knowing where one will lay their head at night, dealing with exposure to violence as well as inclement weather, and not knowing where their next meal will come from would put the healthiest of individuals at risk for developing some mental illness.

Government sources estimate that approximately 20 to 30 percent of the homeless population is suffering from a serious mental illness (U.S. Mayor's Survey, 2003), and if mental illness is broadened to include clinical depression and substance abuse disorders (often used to self-medicate), that percentage jumps to an astounding 50 to 80 percent, and this number is continuing to rise (North, Eyrich, Pollio, & Spitznagel, 2004; Shern et al., 2000). The mentally ill homeless population is a somewhat diverse group, but African-American single men and veterans are most likely to be homeless and suffering from mental illness (Folsom et al., 2005; Koerber, 2005; Shern et al., 2000). Although deinstitutionalization is credited for being the primary cause of this increase in the homeless population, the increase in homelessness did not occur until the 1980s, thus other issues are at play as well, including a shortage in affordable housing and again a lack of funding of housing assistance programs targeted to middle-aged men and veterans.

One of the biggest challenges in getting individuals with mental illness off the streets is engaging them in treatment. One of the problems noted after deinstitutionalization was the common difficulty of mentally ill individuals exercising their newly won right to refuse treatment. But a deeper look into this issue reveals that it may not be as simple as individuals in need not wanting help, but rather may be far more related to the difficulty and complexity of *accessing* needed services (Shern et al., 2000).

Barriers to accessing services often include difficulties in applying for government assistance such as Medicaid and Medicare to pay for both treatment and medication. Another barrier involves the actual service delivery model most popular in counseling and mental health centers, where the client comes to the psychologist. History clearly reveals that this model simply does not work with seriously mentally ill individuals, particularly those living on the streets. Such individuals are often confused, disoriented, and frequently distrusting of others, particularly if they are suffering from some sort of paranoid disorder. To expect a person who is homeless and suffering from some mental illness to remember a weekly appointment and somehow figure out how to navigate transportation is clearly unrealistic.

The treatment models commonly used within the human services are far more successful in engaging the seriously mentally ill homeless population. This model involves the human service professional going out into the community to meet the client in the client's environment. Thus, rather than sessions occurring in the comfort of the practitioner's office, they occur on park benches, or curbs, or in homeless shelters. The value of this model lies not only in its practical approach to reaching psychologically unstable and marginalized clients, but in addition, clients are not as likely to be intimidated by entering an environment where they likely will feel they do not belong. Finally, human service professionals will undoubtedly learn more about the lives of their seriously mentally ill clients by spending time with them where they live.

Another barrier to seeking treatment involves the many stipulations and requirements common in standard treatment models used by many CMHCs. Most standard mental health programs have strict participation requirements, particularly related to behavioral issues such as maintaining sobriety to remain in a housing assistance program, or program requirements such as requiring clients to participate in weekly counseling support groups to receive other services. In fact, most standard programs are directive with seriously mentally ill clients, often determining treatment goals and interventions for the client, rather than empowering clients to assist in determining their own treatment goals and interventions (Shern et al., 2000).

A study conducted in 2000 tested a pilot program that differed significantly from standard mental health programs targeting the homeless mentally ill population. The experimental program called *Choices* offered comprehensive mental health services including (1) outreach and engagement of "street-dwelling" mentally ill individuals; (2) a Choices center that offered desirable services such as food and showers, as well as more structured services such as case management, mental health services, and rehabilitation services; (3) **respite housing;** and (4) in-community and on-site assistance in locating community-based housing.

The key difference between the experimental program and standard mental health programs were an extensive focus on outreach and community engagement, low-demand program requirements that increased client self-determination, and increased integration and streamlining of services because all programs were offered under the umbrella of the Choices program. The results of this study clearly indicate that participants in the Choices program were better served in all areas compared to the participants in traditional mental health programs. These results support the theory that rejection of services is likely not the primary reason why the homeless mentally ill population is underserved, but rather, issues related to barriers to accessing services such as complicated coordination of services and programs with mandatory participation requirements and stipulations that might be unrealistic for the target population are more likely to blame (Shern et al., 2000).

It is clear, then, that any program designed to engage the seriously mentally ill must include intensive case management that effectively engages clients and keeps them engaged, regardless of where they are in the cycle of their mental illness (i.e., stable, or actively psychotic). The issue of homelessness is always a relevant concern because the majority of seriously mentally ill individuals are at a high risk for homelessness. Empowering the client to feel they are an active part of treatment is also essential, as is making sure that all levels of service, particularly those offered by networking agencies, are sufficiently integrated so clients do not lose touch with service providers when transitioning from one level of treatment to another. For instance, close coordination between human services workers from inpatient hospitals and outpatient programs will ensure that discharged patients are closely tracked and seen at a community-based outpatient center within days of being released from an inpatient setting.

The problem of homelessness among the mentally ill population will not be resolved until sufficient long-term housing assistance can be provided. Housing assistance programs typically have long waiting lists and often allow only women with children accelerated access to the program. Because African-American men and veterans are overrepresented in the mentally ill homeless population, more programs need to be developed that target these populations most at risk for homelessness. Such programs must also be designed to address issues related to alcohol and substance abuse problems as well because many within the mentally ill homeless population have cooccurring substance abuse problems.

Mental Illness and the Prison Population: The Criminalization of the Mentally Ill

Another unintended by-product of deinstitutionalization is what has effectively amounted to the inadvertent shifting of chronically mentally ill patients from public hospitals to jails and prisons. In fact, many mental health advocates have argued that prisons have now become one of the primary institutions warehousing the United States' most severely mentally ill individuals (Palermo, Smith, & Liska, 1991; Torrey, 1995). Thus, although this was never the intention of policy changers and proponents of deinstitutionalization, it appears that the United States has in many respects returned to the era where the mentally ill were locked away in almshouses.

■ **Table 7.2**   Estimated Number of Mentally Ill Inmates
and Probationers—1998

	Estimated number of offenders[*]			
	State prison	Federal prison	Local jail	Probation
Identified as mentally ill	179,200	7,900	96,700	547,800
Reported a mental or emotional condition	111,300	5,200	62,100	473,000
Admitted overnight to a mental hospital	118,300	5,000	60,500	281,200

[*]Based on midyear 1998 counts from the National Prisoner Statistics and Annual Survey of Jails and preliminary year-end 1998 counts from the Annual Probation Survey.

Source: Ditton, P. (1999). Bureau of Justice Statistics, Special Reports

The U.S. Department of Justice estimates that over a quarter of a million mentally ill individuals are currently incarcerated in the U.S. state and federal prison system constituting between 8 and 17 percent of the entire prison population (Table 7.2). In addition, well over a half million mentally ill individuals are currently on probation (Ditton, 1999). Twenty percent had no prior criminal history, and over 50 percent were incarcerated for a violent crime. Over 60 percent of these mentally ill offenders admitted that they were high on alcohol or drugs at the time of their offense, and between 20 to 30 percent were homeless at the time of arrest (Belcher, 1988).

The National Alliance for the Mentally Ill (NAMI) estimates that approximately 40 percent of the mentally ill population will come into contact with the criminal justice system at some point in their lives (NAMI). At least 20 percent of juveniles involved in the criminal justice system meet the criteria for a serious mental illness (Ditton, 1999). Caucasian women are particularly overrepresented in the prison population with approximately 29 percent of white women in state prisons suffering from some form of serious mental illness (Table 7.3). Most mentally ill prisoners are poor and were either undiagnosed prior to their incarceration or untreated in the months prior to entering the prison system. Mentally ill inmates were twice as likely to have a history of physical abuse and four times as likely to have been the victim of sexual abuse. In fact, almost 65 percent of mentally ill female inmates reported having been physically and/or sexually abused prior to going to prison (Ditton, 1999).

But what does this really mean? Could it simply mean that some mentally ill individuals break the law more than mentally healthy individuals? Couldn't it be argued that one must certainly be mentally ill to kill a string of women or one's entire fam-

■ **Table 7.3** Inmates and Probationers Identified as Mentally Ill, by Gender, Race/Hispanic Origin, and Age

Offender Characteristics	Percent identified as mentally ill			
	State inmates	Federal inmates	Jail inmates	Probationers
Gender				
Male	15.8%	7.0%	15.6%	14.7%
Female	23.6%	12.5%	22.7%	21.7%
Race/Hispanic origin				
White*	22.6%	11.8%	21.7%	19.6%
Black*	13.5%	5.6%	13.4%	10.4%
Hispanic	11.0%	4.1%	11.1%	9.0%
Age				
24-year or younger	14.4%	6.6%	13.3%	13.8%
25–34	14.8%	5.9%	15.7%	13.8%
35–44	18.4%	7.5%	19.3%	19.8%
45–54	19.7%	10.3%	22.7%	21.1%
55 or older	15.6%	8.9%	20.4%	16.0%

*Excludes Hispanics

Source: Ditton, P. (1999). Bureau of Justice Statistics, Special Reports

ily? After all, what sane person sexually abuses children? Depending on how mental illness is defined, it could be argued that those who commit heinous crimes are by definition mentally ill, and their mental illness does not and should not negate the appropriateness of sending them to prison for their crimes. But even in situations where offenders clearly should be incarcerated, a retrospective look at their mental health histories might reveal a history of poor service utilization, treatment refusal, or an outright inability to access much needed mental health treatment.

It seems as though all one needs to do is turn on the television set to be barraged with media reports of disturbed and deranged individuals who showed up at work with a gun or ran their car into a day care center, or killed their entire family. Many times it is reported that the offenders of these horrible crimes were seriously mentally ill. Yet it would be incorrect to assume that the majority of violent crimes committed by mentally ill offenders are as atrocious as these. In fact, the majority of violent crimes committed by the mentally ill may be legally categorized as "violent," but are relatively minor in nature, often resulting in misdemeanor charges.

Of the 53 percent of mentally ill prisoners incarcerated for violent offenses, 13 percent committed murder, 12 percent committed sexual assault, 13 percent committed robbery, and 11 percent committed assault. Government statistics show that those individuals committing the more serious violent offenses suffered from various forms of schizophrenia, often paranoid schizophrenia. But even more telling is the fact that many of the mentally ill inmates in county jails committed relatively minor crimes such as property offenses and disorderly conduct offenses yet are serving disproportionately long jail sentences often because they cannot pay bail or do not have private legal counsel (Ditton, 1999).

Clearly the relationship between mental illness and violent behavior is complex involving more factors than simply a propensity on the part of some mentally ill individuals for harming others. For instance, disorientation and mental confusion common in psychosis can cause some psychotic individuals to believe that others are behaving in a threatening manner toward them, thus they respond in what they perceive to be self-defense. Consistent with this theory, many assault cases involve mentally ill individuals who resist police either because the arresting officers are not sufficiently trained in how to diffuse situations involving the mentally ill or because the mentally ill defendant becomes combative in a defensive nature when the police attempt to restrain them.

A related problem commonly ignored by those in the criminal justice system and the media, as well as by the general public, is the increased risk of violence against the mentally ill both within the community as well as within the criminal justice system. Although crime vulnerability among the mentally ill population is not a topic that has received much research interest, studies that have been conducted on this issue have clearly shown that mentally ill individuals are targets for victimization such as assault, robbery, and sexual assault, both on the streets as well as in prison and at a much higher rate than the general population (Marley & Buila, 2001). Far too often mentally ill prisoners, particularly those in the general prison population, are the consistent targets of victimization, particularly sex-related crimes, many of which go unreported.

The incarceration of the mentally ill is not a simple problem, thus it has no simple answers. Mental health and prison advocates cite barriers to accessing mental health services and problems with early intervention as direct causes of seriously mentally ill individuals ending up in the penal system, rather than in psychiatric facilities. Once again the controversial issue of an individual's right to refuse treatment is relevant in this matter as well evidenced by the many family members of the mentally ill who consistently complain that the courts have refused to order involuntary treatment, only to have their mentally ill family member commit a violent crime some time later. What is so unfortunate in these incidences is that the majority of mentally ill defendants are amenable to treatment, but many were not receiving any treatment at the time of their incarceration (Marley & Buila, 2001).

Mental Health Courts

Many steps are currently being taken by those in the criminal justice system and mental health and human services fields to address the issue of the incarceration of the mentally ill, or what is often termed the *criminalization of the mentally ill.* The development of mental health courts program is an example of a significant step in the right direction. The Mental Health Courts Program was developed pursuant to the America's Law Enforcement and Mental Health Project (Public Law 106–515 passed in November of 2000) and is administered under the Bureau of Justice Assistance (BJA), a component of the U.S. Department of Justice, in cooperation with the Substance Abuse and Mental Health Services Administration (SAMHSA).

The goal of the BJA is to encourage, lead, and fund the development of comprehensive programs run by criminal justice systems across the country that offer alternatives to incarceration as well as helping to avoid future court involvement. Examples of program elements include

▶ Ongoing court monitoring of defendants of misdemeanor crimes and/or nonviolent offenses with mental illness and mental retardation who may or may not have a substance abuse disorder

▶ Mental Health services, which includes

• Specialized training of those working in the criminal justice who might come into contact into contact with the mentally ill population, focusing on ways to identify mental illness and effective intervention strategies based on the unique needs of the mentally ill and mentally disabled populations

• Voluntary outpatient or inpatient mental health treatment, in the least restrictive environment designed to be offered in lieu of criminal charges or a reduced sentence if mentally ill defendants successfully complete the recommended treatment

• Case management services of all cases involving mentally ill or mentally disabled defendants (including probation violations) and the coordination of all mental health treatment and social services, such as life skills training, counseling, and relapse prevention

Mental health courts are modeled after drug courts and are designed to divert appropriate mentally ill defendants to community-based treatment programs that are supervised by the courts. Participation is voluntary, and defendants are screened for appropriateness. Human service professionals are involved in all aspects of mental health courts, including assessment and program placement, development of treatment plans, and facilitation of treatment interventions and case management.

Mental health courts are relatively new, thus little research has been conducted to determine their success. In fact, even though the goal is for all court jurisdictions to have a mental health court, as of 2004, only 90 mental health courts were in existence across the United States But their numbers are growing, and preliminary research indicates that they are successfully diverting the mentally ill from jail to programs offering much needed services. One study researching one of the first mental health courts (located in Broward County, Florida) found that participants spent 75 percent less time in jail, received needed mental health services on a more frequent basis, and were no more likely to commit a new crime, compared to mentally ill defendants who proceeded through the traditional court process (Christy, Poythress, Boothroyd, Petrila, & Mehra, 2005).

But no new program can exist without some criticism. Some critics cite that the primary reason the mentally ill end up in the court system in the first place is because appropriate low- or no-cost mental health treatment simply is not available, at least not without a lengthy waiting list. Thus, some have questioned the rationale of diverting mentally ill defendants to unavailable services, a particularly ironic response because many argue that if the services had been available in the first place, many of these individuals would never have ended up in the criminal justice system (Powell, 2003). Thus for these programs to be truly successful, efforts must continue on a policy level to ensure that funding, either through grants or government Medicare programs, continues to keep pace with demand.

Passage of the Mentally Ill Offender Treatment and Crime Reduction Act of 2004 will significantly assist in the effort to fund these much-needed programs as long as future funding remains available. This act works in concert with the efforts of the Department of Justice and the BJA by allowing for the funding of grants totaling $50 million in 2005 alone to assist criminal justice agencies in jurisdictions across the country to develop mental health courts and more importantly, fund the much needed treatment options.

Multicultural Considerations

Early studies have shown that ethnic minority populations are often poorly served in mental health centers because of a lack of culturally competent counselors and bilingual counselors (Sue, 1977). Other early studies showed that whereas those in the Latino and Asian populations were underrepresented in community mental health center settings, those within the African-American and Native American populations were overrepresented (Sue & McKinney, 1975). This pattern may be partly due to cultural acceptance or rejection of psychotherapy within different cultural groups, and it might also be related to the relative complexity of issues facing the populations served, particularly Native Americans, who traditionally have high rates of substance abuse and depression and often reside in remote areas (Patterson, 1996).

A 1997 study found that African-American caregivers of mentally ill individuals face a number of barriers making it difficult for them to be involved in their family member's treatment, including a failure on the part of practitioners to recognize them as an integral part of the treatment team. Mental health clinicians need to partner with the family members of mentally ill clients and keep an open line of communication so that family caregivers do not feel marginalized in the treatment process. The authors of the study suggested that by working hard to engage family caregivers in treatment, common negative assumptions of family members of African-American clients can be countered and overcome (Biegel, Johnsen, & Shafran, 1997).

It is important that human service professionals be aware of their negative biases, whether they are toward people of color, sexual orientation, or socioeconomic status. Most people, particularly within the majority culture, deny having negative or stereotypical biases toward cultures different than their own, because few want to be characterized as racist, homophobic, or elitist, but all individuals possess some negative biases, and if not directly confronted through both personal awareness as well as in clinical supervision within their agency, even subtle biases will unfold within the counseling relationship.

Consider the bias that many in the United States have about time. The U.S. culture tends to highly value time and promptness. When someone is timely, they are often considered to be respectful, considerate of others, and organized. Conversely, those who are consistently late are often presumed to be disrespectful, inconsiderate of others, disorganized, and perhaps even lazy. Yet, not all cultures value time in the same manner, and a stereotyped bias is that individuals from these cultures (Latino and East Indian cultures, for example) are lazy, disrespectful, and disorganized. Counselors who have been enculturated in U.S. values might not even realize that they hold this stereotype and might unconsciously attribute negative traits to clients who consistently show up late to their appointments. Thus, although it might be worth exploring whether this pattern is related to lacking motivation, it may be racist to make negative assumptions about a client's character based solely on the fact that the client is from an ethnic culture that does not value time in the same way manner as those embracing U.S. values.

Hence, although rarely is someone eager to admit holding negative stereotypes about certain races, cultures, or lifestyles, it is imperative, particularly when working with the seriously mentally ill population, that these negative stereotypes are explored, challenged, and discarded. Otherwise they will remain powerful forces in how human service professionals subtly or overtly evaluate and assess client actions and motivations, strengths, and deficits, including assessing accountability and causation for their life circumstances.

Current Legislation Affecting Access to Mental Health Services

Mental Health Parity Act of 1996

Some mental illnesses take a lifetime to develop. Others seem to hit out of nowhere, such as schizophrenia. Mental illness cuts across all socioeconomic, racial, and gender lines; in fact, one could say that mental ill is an "equal opportunity" affliction. I have worked with both the lower-income and undereducated population, as well as the upper-income and highly educated population, and my only observation about the difference regarding these two groups is that oftentimes those on the upper end of the income/education continuums do a better job at hiding their mental illnesses and emotional disorders, at least for a time. For this reason, as well as the increasing evidence of the biological basis of many mental illnesses formerly believed to be solely psychological in nature, most mental health advocates argue the importance of requiring health insurance companies to cover mental health conditions in the same manner as they cover general medical conditions. Yet in the 1980s, when managed care became the norm in health insurance coverage, many advocates complained that managing costs became synonymous with limiting much-needed benefits, particularly in the area of mental health coverage.

Through bipartisan efforts, the *Mental Health **Parity** Act* was passed in 1996 barring employee-sponsored group health insurance plans from limiting coverage for mental health benefits on a greater basis than for general medical or surgical benefits. The somewhat watered-down version of the bill removed annual and lifetime dollar limits commonly used by insurance companies to limit mental health benefits. Unfortunately, the majority of health insurance companies have found loopholes around this legislation.

First, it is important to note that the law does not require insurance companies to provide mental health insurance coverage unless a beneficiary already had this type of coverage. Thus this legislation essentially acts as a disincentive for companies to offer mental health coverage for new policy holders. But the biggest loophole found by insurance companies involves increasing deductibles and copays, which most insurance companies have in fact done. Some insurance companies have even manipulated the definition of "medical need," which in the human services and counseling fields essentially means that insurance companies are asserting that some diagnoses qualify for reimbursement and some do not.

Overall, research has shown that parity laws have not been particularly effective in making behavioral health services more readily available and affordable. Yet even though the act that passed wasn't nearly as stringent as the original authors intended, it was viewed by many as the first step in what is hoped to be many on the way to having a truly comprehensive insurance program that recognizes mental illness, particularly serious mental illness, as disorders in need of insurance coverage (Kjorstad, 2003).

The President's New Freedom Commission on Mental Health

Over 40 years after a dramatic and complete overhaul of the mental health delivery system in the United States, the country is in the midst of another major overhaul. On February 1, 2001, President George W. Bush announce the establishment of the New Freedom Initiative designed to identify and remove barriers to community living for all individuals with mental disabilities and long-term mental illness. This initiative led to the formation of the Commission on Mental Health on April 29, 2002. The commission was charged with the responsibility of studying the current mental health delivery system and making recommendations on ways for adults and children with serious mental illnesses to integrate into their communities as fully and as effectively as possible. Referring to the current system as offering a "piecemeal" approach to mental health care, the commission made recommendations for change based on the contention that people can recover from mental illness and are not destined to accept a life of long-term disability. The President's Commission on Mental Health promised to transform mental health care in America by promoting access to educational and employment opportunities to individuals with mental disabilities, as well as promoting full access to community life (President's New Freedom Commission on Mental Health, 2003).

The President's New Freedom Initiative Act identified three primary obstacles to receiving effective mental health care: (1) the stigma associated with mental illness; (2) unequal treatment, limitation of benefits, and other financial requirements placed on mental health care reimbursement by private health insurance companies; and (3) a fragmented and piecemeal mental health care delivery system.

One of the chief complaints of the commission's report is that the current system does not offer much hope for recovery to those suffering from a mental illness. In addition, the commission noted that it took sometimes years for new treatment strategies discovered at research institutes to be used in clinical settings. Thus although thousands of government dollars are being spent identifying new treatment modalities, those suffering from mental illness often do not benefit from these discoveries, due to many factors, including poor communication between research facilities and clinical settings. The commission then made several recommendations for removing barriers to treatment and lifting the stigma often associated with mental illness (Table 7.4).

Ironically the final report for the committee studying the community mental health center program in 1963 had goals that were similar in nature and just as admirable as these goals, yet clearly the implementation of those goals did not unfold as anyone had hoped or planned. The current administration is planning on carrying out its plan to improve the mental health care system in several ways, including making recommendations to states to assist in the development of a more effective mental health delivery system, but the most powerful way that the federal government can influence policy and program development is through sufficient funding. One of the chief complaints about the many failures of deinstitutionalization was the lack of federal funding, which fell far short of original plans due to administration changes and shifting priorities. Thus the success or failure of this new attempt at mental health care reform remains to be seen and is dependent on government financial commitment.

President Bush has pledged approximately $2.2 billion over a five-year period beginning in 2006 for programs related to the New Initiative Freedom Act and the mental health transformation programs operated in response to this act. This sounds

■ **Table 7.4** Goals of New Freedom Commission on Mental Health

GOALS

In a Transformed Mental Health System . . .

GOAL 1	Americans understand that mental health is essential to overall health.
GOAL 2	Mental health care is consumer and family driven.
GOAL 3	Disparities in mental health services are eliminated.
GOAL 4	Early mental health screening, assessment, and referral to services are common practice.
GOAL 5	Excellent mental health care is delivered and research is accelerated.
GOAL 6	Technology is used to access mental health care and information.

Source: President's New Freedom Commission on Mental Health Achieving the Promise: Transforming Mental Health Care in America, Executive Summary (www.mentalhealthcommission.gov./reports/FinalReport/FullReport.htm)

impressive until a deeper look at the administration's proposed budget projected to 2016 reveals dramatic cuts in virtually all programs related to the nation's mental health delivery system amounting to billions of dollars. Despite increases in certain VA and HUD programs, most programs related to mental health services will undergo billions of dollars in cuts through 2016 according to President George W. Bush's 2006 federal budget. Programs experiencing significant funding cuts include Medicaid (the primary funding source of mental health services for low- and no-income individuals), NIH research grants, SAMHSA, and housing programs. One of the most disappointing of all budget cuts includes the cutting of all funding of programs related to the Mentally Ill Offender Crime Reduction Act of 2004 that funds mental health courts; thus, unless private or local funding can be raised the future of mental health courts is uncertain.

Some human service professionals might question the importance of understanding federal trends in funding programs designed to meet the needs of the mentally ill, yet virtually all human service professionals will be affected one way or another if these budget cuts are successfully implemented. Attempting to facilitate much needed-mental health–related programs without proper funding can involve everything from understaffing and high case loads, to inadequate office space and the general inability to meet the comprehensive needs of the chronically mentally ill. Thus although human service professionals involved in direct practice may prefer to steer clear from administrative and policy concerns, such involvement particularly on an advocacy level is important because the effective facilitation of vital mental health programs is dependent on appropriate funding.

Concluding Thoughts on Mental Health and Mental Illness

The field of mental health is a dynamic practice area for the human service professional for many reasons. Human service professionals have the ability to truly make an impact while working with some of society's most vulnerable members. Because mental illness is such a broad term, encompassing such a wide array of psychological, emotional, and behavioral issues, the human service professional works as a true generalist whether in a direct service capacity or whether providing advocacy within the community. The United States has experienced dramatic shifts in its mental health delivery system during the past 50 years and will no doubt continue to experience future changes, some intended and some unintended. Human services workers are on the front lines of these intended changes lobbying for increased funding, developing new programs to meet the complex needs of the severely and chronically mentally ill population.

r e f e r e n c e s

American Psychiatric Association. (2000). *Diagnostic and Statistical Manual of Mental Disorders* (4th ed, Text Revision) (DSM-IV-TR). Washington, D.C.: American Psychiatric Association.

Bandelow, B., Krause, J., Wedekind, D., Broocks, A., Hajak, G., & Rüther, E. (2005). Early traumatic life events, parental attitudes, family history, and birth risk factors in patients with Borderline Personality Disorder and healthy controls. *Psychiatry Research, 134(2)*, 169–179.

Beck, A. T. (1964). Thinking and depression: 2. *Theory and therapy. Archives of General Psychiatric,* No. 561–57.

Beers, C. (1981). *A mind that found itself: An autobiography.* Pittsburgh: University of Pittsburgh Press.

Belcher, J. R. (1988). Are jails replacing the mental health system for the homeless mentally ill? *Community Mental Health Journal, 24(3)*, 185–195.

Biegel, D. E., Johnsen, J. E., & Shafran, R. (1997). Overcoming barriers faced by African-American families with a family member with mental illness. *Family Relations, 46(2)*, 163–178.

Christy, A., Poythress, N. G., Boothroyd, R. A., Petrila, J., & Mehra, S. (2005). Evaluating the efficiency and community safety goals of the Broward county mental health court. *Behavioral Sciences and the Law, 23*, 227–243

Diala, C. C., Muntaner, C., Walrath, C., Nickerson, K., LaVeist, T., & Leaf, P. (2001). Racial/ethnic differences in attitudes toward seeking professional mental health services. *American Journal of Public Health, 91(5)*, 805–807.

Dinofelder, S. (2004). Treatment for the untreatable. *Monitor in Psychology, 35*(11), 48–49.

Ditton, P. M. (1999). *Mental health and treatment of inmates and probationers* (Special report NCJ 174463). Washington, DC: U.S. Department of Justice, Office of Justice Programs, Bureau of Justice Statistics.

Feldman, S. (2003). Reflections on the 40th anniversary of the U.S. Community Mental Health Centers Act. *Australian and New Zealand Journal of Psychiatry, 3*, 662–667.

Folsom, D. P., Hawthorne, W., & Lindamer, L. (2005). Prevalence and risk factors for homelessness and utilization of mental health services among 10,340 patients with serious mental illness in a large public mental health system. *American Journal of Psychiatry, 162(2),* 370–376.

Freud, S. (1917). *Mourning and Melancholia,* Standard Edition, 14, 73–102.

Geller, B., Zimerman, B., Williams, M., DelBello, M. P., Frazer, J., & Beringer, L. (2002). Phenomenology of prepubertal and early adolescent *bipolar disorder:* Examples of elated mood, grandiose behaviors, decreased need for sleep, racing thoughts and hypersexuality. *Journal of Child & Adolescent Psychopharmacology, 12(1),* 3–9.

Hutto, B. (2001). Potential overdiagnosis of bipolar disorder. *Psychiatric Services, 52(5),* 687.

Jackson, R. L., Purnell, D., Anderson, S. B., & Sheafor, B. W. (1996). The clubhouse model of community support for adults with mental illness: An emerging opportunity for social work education. *Journal of Social Work Education, 32(2),* 172–180.

Kessler, R. C., Berglund, P., & Demler, O. (2005). Lifetime prevalence and age-of-onset distributions of DSM-IV-TR disorders in the national comorbidity survey replication. *Archives of General Psychiatry, 62(6),* 593–602.

Kjorstad, M. C. (2003). The current and future state of mental health insurance parity legislation. *Psychiatric Rehabilitation Journal, 27(1),* 34–32.

Koerber, G. (2005). Veterans: One-third of all homeless people. *National Association of the Mentally Ill,* Issue Spotlight. Retrieved online June 1, 2005, from http://www.nami.org/Template.cfm?Section=Issue_Spotlights&template=/ContentManagement/ContentDisplay.cfm&ContentID=26958

Marley, J. A., & Buila, S. (2001). Crimes against people with mental illness: Types, perpetrators, and influencing factors. *Social Work 46(2),* 115–124.

Michaud, C. M., Murray, C. J., & Bloom, B. R. (2001). Burden of disease—implications for future research. *Journal of the American Medical Association, 285*(5), 535–539.

Mirabi, M., Weinman, M. L., & Magnetti, S. M. (1985). Professional attitudes toward the chronic mentally ill. *Hospital & Community Psychiatry, 36(4),* 404–405.

Mowbray, C. T., & Holter, M. C., (2002). Mental health & Mental illness: out of the closet? *Social Service Review,* University of Chicago.

National Institute of Mental Health. (2000). Depression. *National Institute of Health.* Retrieved on April 4, 2006 from http://www.nimh.nih.gov/publicat/cep.cfm

New Freedom Commission on Mental Health. (2003). *Achieving the promise: transforming mental health care in America. Final Report.* [DHHS Pub. No. SMA-03–3832]. Rockville, MD: Author.

Newhill, C. E., & Korr, W. S. (2004). Practice with people with severe mental illness: Rewards, challenges, burdens. *Health & Social Work, 29(4),* 297–305.

North, C. S., Eyrich, K. M., Pollio, D. E., & Spitznagel, E. L. (2004). Are rates of Psychiatric Disorders in the homeless population changing? *American Journal of Public Health, 94*(1), 103–108.

Palmermo, G. B., Smith, M. B., & Liska, F. J. (1991). Jails versus mental hospitals. A social dilemma. *International Journal of Offender Therapy and Comparative Criminology, 35*(2): 97–106.

Patterson, C. H. (1996). Multicultural counseling from diversity to universality. *Journal of Counseling Development,* 74, 227–236.

Powell, J. (2003). Letter to the editor. *Issues in Mental Health Nursing, 24(5),* 463.

Saleebey, D. (1996). The strengths perspective in social work practice: Extensions and cautions. *Social Work, 41(3),* 296–305.

Shern, D. L., Tsemberis, S., Anthony, W., Lovell, A. M., Richmond, L., Felton, C. J., Winarski, J., & Cohen, M. (2000). Serving street-dwelling individuals with psychiatric disabilities: Outcome of a psychiatric rehabilitation clinical trial. *American Journal of Public Health, 90(12),* 1873–1878.

Stromwall, L. K., & Hurdle, D. (2003). Psychiatric rehabilitation: An empowerment based approach to mental health. *Health & Social Work, 28(3),* 206–213.

Sue, S. (1977). Community mental health services to minority groups: Some optimism, some pessimism. *American Psychologist, 32,* 616–624.

Sue, S., & McKinney, H. (1975). Asian Americans in the community mental health system. *American Journal, 45,* 111–118.

Sullivan, W. P. (1992). Reclaiming the community: The strengths perspective and deinstitutionalization. *Social Work, 37(3),* 204–209.

Swindle, R. W., Cronkite, R. C. & Moos, R. H. (1989). Life stressors, social resources, coping, and the 4-year course of unipolar depression. *Journal of Abnormal Psychology, 98(4),* 468–477.

Terayama, H., Nishino, Y., Kishi, M., Ikuta, K., Itoh, M., & Iwahashi, K. (2003). Detection of anti-Borna Disease Virus (BDV) antibodies from patients with schizophrenia and mood disorders in Japan. *Psychiatry Research, 120(2),* 201–206.

U.S. Conference of Mayors. (2003). *A Status Report on Hunger and Homelessness in America's Cities.* 1620 I st. NW, 4th Fl, Washington, D.C. 20006–40005.

U.S. Department of Health and Human Services. (1999). *Mental health: A report of the surgeon general—executive summary.* Rockville, MD: U.S. Department of Health and Human Services, Substance Abuse and Mental Health Services Administration, Center for Mental Health Services, National Institutes of Health, National Institute of Mental Health.

Vourlekis, B. S., Edinburg, G., & Knee, R. (1998). The rise of social work in public mental health through aftercare of people with serious mental illness. *Social Work, 43(6),* 567–575.

suggested reading

Kreisman, J. J., & Straus, H. (1991). *I hate you, don't leave me.* New York: Avon.

Lachenmeyer, N. (2001). *The outsider: A journey into my father's struggle with madness.* New York: Broadway.

Mason, P. T., & Kreger, R. (1998). *Stop walking on eggshells: Taking your life back when someone you care about has Borderline Personality Disorder.* Oakland, CA: New Harbinger Publishing.

Porter, R. (2002). *Madness: A brief history.* New York: University Press.

Torrey, E. F., & Miller, J. (2001). *The invisible plague: The rise of mental illness from 1750 to the present.* New Brunswick, NJ: Rutgers University Press.

internet web sites related to mental health

Affective disorders: **http://www.pendulum.org/**
Anxiety Disorders Association of America: **http://www.adaa.org/**
Borderline personality disorder: **http://www.bpdcentral.com/**
Children and adults with hyperactivity disorder: **http://www.chadd.org/**
Depression central: **http://www.psycom.net/depression.central.html**
Eating disorders: **http://www.something-fishy.org/**
Internet mental health: **http://www.mentalhealth.com/**
Personality disorders: **http://personalitydisorders.mentalhelp.net/**
PsyWeb Mental Health Site: **www.psyweb.com**
Schizophrenia: **http://www.schizophrenia.com/**

chapter 8

Homelessness

The Nature of Homelessness: How Many People are Homeless and Why

For as long as there have been established residential settlements, there have been those within the population who have either by choice or life circumstances been homeless. To address the problem of homelessness, it is important to first understand the nature of this social condition, including developing an understanding of the extent of the homeless problem, determining who is most vulnerable to becoming homeless, as well as discovering the root causes of homelessness. It is only through understanding the demographic nature and common reasons for homelessness that social programs can be developed to assist members of society in obtaining permanent, stable housing, as well as developing preventative measures to protect against homelessness in the future. Many homeless advocates believe that significantly reducing the homeless population is a reasonable goal, and in fact it truly does seem plausible to assume that one of the wealthiest countries in the world would have enough resources to wipe out homelessness all together.

Homelessness is increasing in the United States, particularly among families with children. In fact, most urban cities reported that they have turned away homeless individuals and families due to a lack of resources (U.S. Conference of Mayors, 2004). The rate of homelessness began to increase between 1970 and 1980 due to a decrease in affordable housing and an increase in poverty (National Coalition for the Homeless, 2005).

To confront the problem of homelessness it must first be determined *who* is homeless. This is a challenge due to the difficulty in defining homelessness as well as the transient nature of the homeless population. There is currently no universally agreed upon definition of "homelessness" although the federal government defines homelessness as

> An individual who lacks a fixed, regular, and adequate nighttime residence; and an individual who has a primary nighttime residence that is supervised publicly or privately operated shelter designed to provide temporary living accommodations

(including welfare hotels, congregate shelters, and transitional housing for the mentally ill); an institution that provides a temporary residence for individuals intended to be institutionalized; or a public or private place not designed for, or ordinarily used as, a regular sleeping accommodation for human beings. (U.S. Code, 2005)

When homelessness is defined using the federal definition there are on average 650,000 individuals who experience homelessness on any given night in the United States (Urban Institute, 2000). But this definition is often criticized because its narrow parameters omit the majority of the homeless population who are difficult to count either because they are not living in traditional emergency shelters, or because they do not want to be counted. The "hidden homeless" may include those living in motels, automobiles, abandoned buildings, and who frequently "double up" with friends or relatives on a temporary basis. When homelessness is defined in a more inclusive manner, homeless estimates jump to about 3.5 million individuals nationally (Urban Institute, 2000).

The second problem in determining the scope of the homeless problem relates to the transient nature of the homeless population. Most individuals who have experienced homelessness have done so on an intermittent basis where homelessness occurs in an ongoing cycle of temporary or tenuous housing leading to eventual homelessness due to economic instability. Thus as aggressive as any count might be, the number of homeless individuals will range dramatically on any given day.

Despite the difficulty in obtaining an accurate "head count" of the homeless population due to the difficulty in defining homelessness and the temporary and nomadic nature of the homeless population, in 1987 researchers in Chicago attempted one of the first comprehensive homeless census campaigns to date by sending plainclothes police officers out into the community to interview potential homeless individuals, including interviewing people who appeared to be living in their cars or were loitering in alleyways. The study was later harshly criticized for its aggressive tactics, as well for underreporting those who hid their homelessness due to shame and embarrassment or those who were staying with friends or relatives on a temporary basis. Despite these criticisms, this study remains one of the most comprehensive attempts to conduct an accurate census of the homeless population to date (Shlay & Rossi, 1992).

Unfortunately, because of the methodological challenges involved in attempting to accurately count the homeless population, many of which were illustrated by the 1987 Chicago study, most demographic studies now use homeless estimates based on indirect counts obtained by surveying professionals working with the homeless population. This reporting method is wrought with problems, though, including underreporting because this method, as other reporting methods, does not include those who are not seeking assistance for homelessness.

One of the most significant concerns with the underreporting of the homeless population due to these methodological challenges relates to the fact that government grant money is often directly linked to census numbers, thus underreporting leads to less money, which in turn leads to fewer services. For this reason as well as others, in 2004 Congress directed the Housing Urban Development agency (HUD) to collect comprehensive data on the homeless population in the United States This will be the first attempt to conduct a direct count of the homeless population since the 1987 Chicago census. HUD responded to this mandate by developing the Housing Management Information System (HMIS), which provides technical assistance to the states in their data collection efforts.

The Causes of Homelessness

Determining the root causes of homelessness is equally challenging but essential, particularly for human service professionals who are committed to advocating for and assisting those who experience poverty and homelessness. Equally important is the task of identifying common biases and stereotypes of the poor and homeless population that dramatically influence the general perception of the poor and homeless, which in turn influences the types of assistance programs that will be supported by state and federal policy makers as well as the voting public.

In general, most people's attitudes toward the poor and the homeless are negative, and the stigma that has always been associated with poverty seems to increase when the poor become homeless. The reasons for this negative bias are likely related to the public nature of homelessness, where those without permanent homes are forced to live out in the open, such as on the streets, alleyways, parks, or in automobiles where good hygiene is virtually impossible and begging for money and food is often the only means of survival (Phelan, Link, Moore, & Stueve, 1997).

The common association of mental illness and substance abuse with poverty and homelessness also contributes to the negative stigma associated with being homeless, and many experts suspect that the general public assumes that virtually all homeless individuals abuse drugs and alcohol, do not shower, live on the streets, and aggressively beg for money (to buy drugs and alcohol), adding to a sense of perceived dangerousness of the homeless population, particularly those believed to be mentally ill (Phelan et al., 1997).

This increased negative attitude toward those who are poor and homeless is reflected in several studies and national public opinion surveys. Generally, it appears as though most people blame the poor for their bad lot in life. For instance, one older national survey conducted in 1975 found that the majority of those in the United States attributed poverty and homelessness to personal failures such as having a poor work ethic, poor money management skills, a lack of any special talent that might translate into a positive contribution to society, and low personal moral values. Those questioned ranked social causes such as poverty, racism, poor schools, and the lack of sufficient employment the lowest of all possible causes (Feagin, 1975).

More recent surveys conducted in the mid-1990s reveal an increase in the tendency to blame the poor for their poverty (Weaver, Shapiro & Jacobs, 1995), even though a considerable body of research points to social and structural issues as the primary cause of poverty, such as shortages in affordable housing, recent shifts to a technologically based society requiring a significant increase in educational requirements, long-standing institutionalized oppression and discrimination against certain racial and ethic groups, and a general increase in the complexity of life (Wright, 2000).

The general public's perception of social welfare programs seems to be based in large part on this negative stigma of poverty as well. In several studies during the 1980s and 1990s those surveyed claimed support for the general idea of helping the poor, but when asked about specific programs or policies, most became critical of governmental policies, specific welfare programs, and welfare recipients in general. In fact, a 1987 national study found that 74 percent of those surveyed believed that most welfare recipients were dishonest and collected more benefits than they deserved (Kluegal, 1987). In general, though, compassion for poverty-related homelessness tends to be greater during difficult economic times and lower during economic booms, and general compassion for homeless individuals such as families, who are unlike the stereotypical **skid row alcoholic,** tends to be greater as well.

Based on these studies it appears as though the general public is not overwhelmingly compassionate toward the poor and even less compassionate toward those who are homeless. When the homeless suffer from some form of mental illness, there is a slight increase in compassion, but this is balanced by a general perception of dangerousness among those who are severely mentally ill (Phelan et al., 1997). Although perceptions of the homeless on an individual basis are not as negative as perceptions of specific subgroups within the homeless population (for example, single men, certain racial groups, alcoholics, migrant farm workers), possible reasons for the overall negative perceptions of the homeless may relate to the *fundamental attribution error,* where people tend to attribute their own personal failures or the failures of people they know well and like to situational factors, but attribute the failures of those they do not know or do not like to personal or dispositional factors. Thus, according to the fundamental attribution error the average person would assume that those whom they did not know were homeless due to their own personal shortcomings. Yet if someone they knew became homeless, they would attribute the homelessness to situational causes, such as being laid off, or abruptly leaving an abusive marriage.

Human service professionals must understand the **stigma** associated with homelessness because unless these negative attitudes are acknowledged and challenged, human service professionals may even embrace them, significantly influencing their perceptions of their clients suffering from poverty and poverty-related homelessness. Understanding homelessness from a historical perspective is also useful in understanding the nature of this long-standing social problem so that situational forces can be acknowledged.

History of Homelessness in the United States

The types of people who have experienced homelessness and the reasons for their misfortune have changed significantly throughout the years. Prior to the Middle Ages (from about the fourteenth to the seventeenth centuries), the early church was responsible for the care of the poor, including those without homes. The monasteries embraced this responsibility as one given by God. Thus at least the "deserving poor" (those who were poor through no fault of their own) were considered blessed, and it was considered a blessing to care for them.

Throughout the Middle Ages the homeless population consisted primarily of the wandering poor—those individuals, most commonly men, who migrated for employment, either working someone's land or selling goods. The English Poor Laws (discussed in chapter 2), which were adopted by many of the American colonies, included harsh measures for dealing with the poor and destitute adding to the overall negative social stigma associated with poverty. For example, most communities enforced strict residency requirements designed to discourage the wandering poor from settling in more affluent districts to collect social welfare intended to serve longtime residents who had contributed to the community before falling on hard times. This policy, as well as others against vagrancy and even unemployment, is reflective of the overall negative sentiment held of the homeless population in general, particularly when it could be assumed that one was homeless either through choice or some personal failing.

Distinguishing the deserving from the undeserving poor was practiced throughout the Middle Ages (in fact many argue that U.S. policy continues this practice even today). Under English Poor laws many of the undeserving poor and homeless were sent to work camps or almshouses, where they were forced to perform demeaning work for excessively long hours in what amounted to slave labor. This practice continued to play into the overall stigma of poverty and homelessness by stripping the poor and destitute of their self-determination, their family, and their freedom. Even the "deserving poor" who received public assistance were often forced to wear badges or some marking signifying that they were receiving public assistance (Phelan et al., 1997).

Throughout the nineteenth and early twentieth centuries the homeless population still consisted of primarily men, either vagrants (men who were unemployed for a variety of reasons, including mental illness or alcoholism) or migrant workers such as men who were making their way out West to work in the gold mines, the railroads, or the fields. Hobos, for instance, were often counted among the homeless population. Hobos were men of European descent, typically Germany or Scandinavian countries, who were migrating laborers and were often treated with mistrust and contempt despite the fact that they were an integral part of the labor force throughout the nineteenth century (Axelson & Dail, 1988).

It was not until the Great Depression in the mid-1930s that families began to appear on the homeless scene in significant numbers. The failure of the financial markets, the closings of many banks, and rampant unemployment resulted in many families losing their homes and wandering the streets in search of sustenance and shelter. Because the Great Depression hit just about everyone in the United States, there was increased compassion for the homeless population and for those suffering from poverty in general. The Great Depression brought most people back to a

■ The Great Depression left the majority of mainstream Americans financially destitute forcing many to sell off all of their personal belongings on the streets in order to survive.

■ An impoverished family of nine on the New Mexico highway during the Depression Era.

pre-Protestant ethic time, where people recognized and acknowledged that poverty and homelessness could be caused by circumstances beyond one's control. Thus although the Protestant ethic and social Darwinism might have had many people believing that falling on hard times was a result of laziness, the Great Depression reminded most everyone that sometimes, no matter how hard one works or is willing to work, circumstances occur that render someone destitute and impoverished. Unfortunately this spirit of empathy and compassion for society's poor and homeless did not last much past the next economic boom. Apparently, a by-product of personal good fortune may just be a reduction in one's ability to empathize with those less fortunate.

The Contemporary Picture of Homelessness: The Rise of Single-Parent Families

After the Depression, the homeless landscape returned to its former demographic picture, with the majority of the homeless population consisting primarily of single, white men. Yet another significant change was on the horizon. The 1970s and 1980s saw a dramatic increase in the homelessness of families. Yet the difference between the homeless families of the Great Depression era and homeless families of late is that the latter consist primarily of single parents with children. In fact, a study conducted in 1999 found that of all homeless families, about 80 percent were headed by a single parent, and of these approximately 95 percent were female (Nunez & Fox, 1999). Regardless of how these statistics are broken down, it is important to note that estimates now put single mothers with children at anywhere between one-third to three-fourths of the entire U.S. homeless population (Axelson & Dail, 1988; Reyes & Waxman, 1987).

There is a tendency among policy makers to oversimplify the causes of homelessness, perhaps because a simple cause would warrant a simple solution, and multifactor causes often call for overwhelming responses. But most single-parent families become homeless as a result of a complex set of circumstances, as illustrated in the vignette about Patricia later in this chapter. There are some common themes among single-parent homeless families. The great majority of homeless single mothers are approximately 25 years of age, with two to three children in the preschool to six years of age range. The majority of these single mothers are U.S. citizens, native born, and fluent English speakers. Even states that border Mexico have a relatively low percentage of homeless immigrants. African Americans are highly overrepresented in the homeless population, particularly in urban areas, making up about 50 percent of the general homeless population according to the 2004 U.S. Conference of Mayors. Native Americans and Latinos are also overrepresented in the homeless population (U.S. Conference of Mayors, 2004; Wright, 2000).

Most homeless single mothers have never been married, and although many are high school graduates, a significant majority of single moms never established a solid work history for many reasons. Most cite either never having had stability in their housing situations or having experienced unstable housing for several years prior to becoming homeless. Most have experienced homelessness chronically on a cyclical basis, securing housing for a short time only to experience a financial crisis, such as a job loss, which results in a domino-effect of negative life events and ultimately another incident of homelessness. Most homeless single mothers are unemployed, the majority citing the inability to pay for child care as the primary barrier to finding employment, but others cited being undereducated and an inability to secure employment that would pay for market rent.

Historically, only about 20 percent of homeless individuals have been on any form of public assistance, even though the majority of these individuals would have qualified for some form of assistance (Shlay & Rossi, 1992). Although single mothers qualify for more aid than single homeless men and single homeless women, as a group they still tend to underutilize public assistance programs (Roll, Toro & Ortola, 1999). In addition, the availability of public assistance has sharply declined since the passage of federal welfare reform legislation in 1996, which effectively ended the Aid to Families with Dependent Children (AFDC) program, and initiated Temporary Assistance to Needy Families (TANF), a program that provides assistance at one-third of the federal poverty level (Nickelson, 2004). To add to the dilemma of shrinking public assistance programs, aid that is provided in the form of block grants or aid packages may have long waiting lists for certain types of assistance. For instance, in the county where I practice, I recall numerous clients being told that waiting lists for child care subsidies and housing vouchers were several years long, or applications were not being accepted at all, even when these clients qualified for the services and women with children received priority status.

Another contributor of homelessness in single-parent families may relate to the bad childhoods many homeless women appear to experience. Many single mothers report unstable childhoods filled with physical and sexual abuse. In fact, it appears as though many of these women proceeded to recreate these patterns of abuse in their adult lives because approximately three-quarters of all homeless single mothers who were married prior to becoming homeless cited domestic violence as the primary reason for leaving their marital home and moving into a shelter with their children. Other reasons include having a child early, either during adolescence or early adulthood, which interrupts the development of educational and career goals (Nunez & Fox, 1999). Other personal vulnerabilities include having a substance abuse disorder or mental illness (although some research suggests that the trauma of homelessness is actually a risk factor for substance abuse and mental disorders, such as depression, and not typically the cause of homelessness in single-mother families), having grown up in the state foster care system, and having a poor or absent social support system.

Some structural causes of the recent dramatic increase in homeless single-parent families include the failure of many courts to enforce child support orders, dramatic cutbacks in federal housing programs in the 1980s, and the failure of public welfare to keep pace with inflation and increases in the cost of living. Further increases in homeless families are expected particularly now that welfare benefits are limited to only two to five years (depending on the state), rather than providing long-term benefits on a case-by-case basis.

It is important to discuss the strengths that many of these single mothers exhibit as well, particularly because human service professionals will need to identify such strengths and work with the single-parent client to enhance and build on existing strengths. A 1994 study found that single mothers living in shelters had an amazing amount of determination, a sense of personal pride, and an ability to confront their problems directly. Many of the single mothers interviewed exhibited a strong commitment to the welfare of their children (particularly those who chose homelessness over remaining in an abusive relationship), had strong moral values that acted as a guide in decision making, and many had deep religious convictions that provided them with a sense of purpose and meaning. Despite being homeless many of these single mothers maintained a commitment to helping others in need (Montgomery, 1994). Many also overcame what seemed to be insurmountable odds to keep their children with them rather than have them placed within the state foster care system, despite harsh living conditions.

Homeless Shelter Living for Families with Children

This dramatic increase in single mothers with children becoming homeless has resulted in the need for significant changes in social welfare policy regarding how homelessness is managed on local, state, and federal levels. When the homeless population was more homogeneous consisting primarily of single men living in **Single Residence Occupancy (SRO)** or on skid row, the community response was less complex focusing on low-cost housing and substance abuse counseling. But this new homeless population presents more complex problems requiring a more multifaceted approach. For instance, the traditional homeless person typically resided on the streets, whereas families often avoid street dwelling opting for shelter living instead. Yet many emergency shelters are not equipped to serve families.

Elizabeth Lindsey (1998) interviewed single mothers who had lived in homeless shelters with their children and asked them about their experiences in shelters and the impact it had on their family life. Many shelters would not allow boys as young as eight to sleep in the same area as their mothers, requiring them to either stay on the men's side of the shelter alone, stay with relatives, or in some cases, even enter the foster care system.

Other shelters applied the same rules to families as they did to singles, forcing single mothers to leave the shelter at 7 AM, even if they had infants or preschool-aged children, and not allowing them to return to the shelter until 5:00 or 6 PM, regardless of weather conditions or the safety of the community where the shelter was located. Many single mothers complained that there was no way to look for a job when they had to stay out of the shelter with their kids for 9 to 10 hours a day. Other complaints included staff who seemed insensitive to children's needs, such as enforcing rules against children running around and playing creating difficult situations for parents who were mandated to keep their children quiet at all times, with no distractions, such as television or toys, to assist them.

But by far the most difficult aspect of shelter life according to these women involved staff who would override their parenting decisions, such as correcting a parent in front of the child and other shelter residents for how she was disciplining her child. Mothers complained that their authority was often diminished by shelter rules and interfering shelter staff. Other shelter rules that make parenting difficult include rules prohibiting anyone from eating in the shelter at any time other than during designated meal times, including prohibiting mothers from even bringing snacks into the shelter for their young children.

Research studies have shown that such shelter rules and policies, not necessarily created with families in mind, have a powerfully devastating affect on the parent–child relationship, as mothers find themselves no longer the "head of household" with the power to make parenting decisions in the best interest of their children—even basic decisions such as when to bathe and feed their children. Instead, their children are cared for on the shelter's time frame. These issues might seem like minor inconveniences and relatively innocuous in light of the other major crises going on in the lives of homeless mothers, but researchers noted that the disintegration of the mother–child relationship is not just temporarily disruptive, but this disruption essentially further degrades and disempowers parents who are already feeling shamed and powerless by their homeless status leading to an increase in parental distress and depression, which in turn often leads to an increase in child misbehavior and acting out (Lindsey, 1998).

Homeless Children: School Attendance and Academic Performance

Children are the fastest-growing segment of the homeless population, which creates new challenges for shelters and other social welfare responses, particularly when these children are school-aged. Developing effective programs designed to keep homeless children in school and succeeding academically is essential, otherwise all these homeless children will be at risk for continuing the cycle of homelessness in the next generation, having never experienced physical or emotional security in their own childhoods.

Between the chronic and cyclical nature of homelessness and the fact that most emergency shelters limit the amount of time residents can stay, ranging anywhere from 1 to 30 days, a significant problem for school-aged children was switching schools everytime their families were forced to move to a new shelter. I recall when I was working as a school human service professional in the inner city of Los Angeles having several school-aged children who were homeless on my caseload. No sooner did these children get settled and acclimated to their classroom and start the long process of building a trusting relationship with me than they would literally disappear one day. I would typically learn at some point later that the family was forced to move to a different shelter, and even if remaining at their school of origin was a legal possibility, it was not a realistic one because there was no guarantee that the next shelter would be anywhere close to the children's current school.

A 2000 report to Congress stated that only 87 percent of homeless children were enrolled in school, and of these only 77 percent attended school regularly (U.S. Department of Education, 2001). Many school districts attempted to resolve this issue by creating special schools or programs for homeless children, but these programs have been criticized by many because it segregated homeless children, increasing their social stigma and sense of rejection they no doubt already experienced. Federal legislation discussed later in this chapter was designed to address this issue and put a stop to poor attendance and student retention and poor academic performance related to homelessness.

Runaway Youth

No one is certain just how many adolescents are homeless and living on the streets, but some estimates put that number as high as 2 million in the United States alone. This is a unique population among the entire homeless population because the reasons, risk factors, and intervention needs are considerably different. Adolescents are far more likely to be living on the streets than in a shelter. They are also far more likely to participate in dangerous behaviors such as drug abuse (including needle sharing), panhandling, theft, drug abuse, and survival sex (sex for food, money, and shelter). These risky behaviors put homeless adolescents at risk for HIV, Hepatitis B and C, and sexually transmitted diseases (Beech, Meyers, & Beech, 2002). These teens are also at high risk for physical and sexual violence, both by other teens and by adults.

Most homeless adolescents are living on the streets because they have either run away from an abusive home, or they have been kicked out of their homes by parents who no longer wish to take care of them. In fact the majority of homeless adolescents interviewed in various research studies reported a history of both physical and sexual abuse, which served as a primer for being similarly victimized on the streets (Whitbeck, Hoyt, & Ackley, 1997). Another study of over 600 runaway youth found that sexual abuse was the chief reason adolescents chose to live on the streets rather than remaining in their homes (Yoder, Whitbeck & Hoyt, 2001). The fact that many of these teens will continue to experience sexual exploitation while living on the streets, whether through outright attacks or through survival sex, is certainly a tragedy, and one that can be addressed by those in the human services field.

One study that interviewed homeless youth found that in most urban cities homeless adolescents often operate as a somewhat cohesive group on the streets, protecting each other and helping one another survive. In fact, this study found that the more seasoned adolescents would often take new homeless teens under their wings, teaching them survival tactics and welcoming them into the "fold." Newer homeless youth who were interviewed talked about what a relief it was to have someone essentially mentor them into the ways of surviving street life. But without glamorizing this life, most teens, both boys and girls, talked of the horrors of having to participate in prostitution to survive. In fact, the adolescents who were interviewed talked about many ways in which they felt exploited, both by older teens, but often by adults who forced them into drug dealing and prostitution (Auerswalk & Eyre, 2002).

Ironically, many teens reported having a strong belief in God, who they believed watched out for them and kept them alive. One teen stated that when they were not really in need, they would often get no offer of food and little money while panhandling. Yet when they were really in need, having gone without food for a few days, then whatever they needed would just come to them. He attributed this to God knowing what they needed and providing for them when they needed it the most (Auerswalk & Eyre, 2002). In fact, in one study researchers found that over half of all homeless youth interviewed cited faith in God as the primary motivation for survival (Lindsey, Kurtz, Jarvis, Williams, & Nackerud, 2000).

Yet even with this surprisingly high percentage of faith-seeking homeless teens, an estimated 40 percent of homeless youth attempt suicide (Auerswalk & Eyre, 2002). They are also at high risk for posttraumatic stress disorder (PTSD), anxiety disorders, and depression. Many homeless adolescents report losing all contact with people in their former lives, even siblings, extended family, and those who had been supportive of them in the past. Most also talked of feeling extremely lonely and distrustful but in desperate need of love and affection. Because the majority of homeless adolescents have run away from abusive homes, it seems likely that many were suffering from some form of emotional disturbance even prior to entering street life (Kidd, 2003).

Unfortunately many of the adolescents interviewed were highly suspicious of all adults, including outreach workers with human services agencies providing assistance to the homeless adolescent population. The overall perspective of these outreach agencies were negative, and adolescents who accepted assistance from these agencies were considered "sellouts" and foolish. The prevailing belief was that human services organizations would force the teens to return to an abusive home environment, or they'd be turned over to the police. Knowing these attitudes, though, can aid human services agencies in developing outreach efforts and other services designed to overcome these negative perceptions.

Any successful intervention program is going to have to address the issue of the teens feeling like outsiders. In fact, research studies have found that homeless adolescents are acutely aware of their outsider status, and many of them manage this through incorporating this outsider status into their identity. By embracing being an outsider, through multiple piercings, for example, they take control of something that could potentially make them vulnerable (Auerswalk & Eyre, 2002).

Many human service experts strongly recommend that any intervention program be targeted at identifying the adolescents' strengths. But this is challenging when most intervention systems view homeless youth in a deviant manner, first because they are "runaways," and second, because many of the behaviors they engage in while living on the streets are criminal. Even the classification of their behavior is in pathological terms, such as diagnosing them with conduct disorder. This can be humiliating and shaming to an adolescent who is likely acting out in response to being victimized in their family of origin. Most homeless youth have been both physically and verbally abused and degraded in their homes, thus in many respects they are living up to their parents' negative expectations of them by dropping out of high school and living on the streets. To then enter into the juvenile justice system that continues to pathologize their behavior and responds in punitive measures rather than supportive ones only adds to their feelings of victimization.

Human service professionals working with this population must provide consistent encouragement, compassionate care, and understanding that promotes both self-esteem and self-efficacy (a sense of competence) in these emotionally broken and bruised teens. This can be accomplished while focusing on basic needs such as providing food, shelter, and good health care. Yet again the barrier that human services agencies must overcome is significant because so many homeless youth have been so horribly rejected and abandoned by their families, and then further exploited and abused by adults on the streets, that to trust any adult seems foolish and risky.

Developing one-on-one relationships where trust can grow slowly is one method of intervention that may be more successful than more traditional outreach efforts, but the ratio of outreach workers to homeless youth renders this approach challenging. Regardless, any intervention must allow the teen to feel safe and empowered in seeking services.

Single Men, the Mentally Ill, and Substance Abuse

Although single-parent families now comprise the majority of the homeless population, just less than 50 percent of the homeless population consists of men, many of whom are single, some of whom are mentally ill, some of whom have substance abuse issues, and some of whom are veterans. Of course these are overlapping categories in many instances. Reasons for homelessness often vary, and some are similar to the causes noted in single-parent families—childhood histories of abuse, growing up in the foster care system, having little or no family or social support, being undereducated and stuck in minimum wage jobs, substance abuse, and mental illness. Social causes include institutionalized racism and oppression, suffering from PTSD after having served during wartime, and changes in the economic infrastructure leading to fewer well-paying jobs.

Veteran's services address many of these issues in programs designed to meet the complex needs of the homeless population who were enrolled in the armed services. Human service professionals working for the Veterans Administration (VA) provide both in-house and outreach services and are trained on PTSD recovery and the unique needs of this special population.

The Elderly Homeless

Chapter 7 touched briefly on the issue of the elderly and homelessness, but it will be explored again somewhat briefly in this chapter because although rates of homelessness among the elderly are significantly lower than younger individuals, it is still an important issue worth exploring in some depth, particularly because the number of homeless elders is expected to increase as the baby boomer generation ages.

Differences exist between elder homelessness and homelessness among younger persons, both in terms of the root causes of homelessness as well as in effective responses. Younger homeless individuals report higher levels of domestic violence as a reason for becoming homeless, and being released from prison is also cited far more frequently by younger persons who are homeless. Both groups report equal difficulty in finding affordable housing, and both groups report equivalent rates of alcohol and substance abuse as reasons for homelessness, with 4 percent of younger individuals reporting this as a reason and just over 6 percent of elders reporting substance abuse as the primary reason for their homelessness. Yet in light of the nature of substance abuse and the tendency for alcoholics and drug addicts to minimize or deny the impact of their addiction, these percentages might be underreported.

Elderly homeless persons report being without shelter for far longer periods than younger individuals, with elder men reporting an average homeless episode lasting over 60 days, and younger homeless men averaging about 14 days. Elderly men also reported far longer episodes without a permanent shelter, some reporting homeless episodes of over two years, whereas younger men reported being homeless an average of 11 months (Hecht & Coyle, 2001). This is likely due to fewer social supports and the difficulty in either moving in with a roommate or living with family, often due to caretaking issues related to common age-related physical problems.

Even though there are more similarities than differences between elderly and younger homeless persons, the response to elders who are homeless must be vastly different due to all of the variables associated with their advanced age. One variable mentioned in the previous paragraph relates to the diminished capacity of the elderly in getting back on their feet by finding new employment opportunities or entering a reeducation program to enter a new career, thus the possibility of regaining financial independence is greatly diminished in the elderly population.

Other issues affecting the elderly population includes their increased vulnerability—both physically and psychologically, leaving them open to physical and financial victimization. Physical disability and illness are also complicating factors in meeting the needs of the elderly homeless population.

Although there is increased funding for elderly services, most economic support is not available until the age of 65. Self-sufficiency models designed for the general homeless population do not work with the elderly population for the reasons mentioned earlier, thus some experts suggest responding to the elderly homeless population by developing aid-assisted low-cost housing with social services to assist the elders with financial, physical, and psychological support to deal with the trauma of becoming homeless.

Current Policies and Legislation

Governmental policies designed to meet the needs of the homeless population are often targeted to subgroups, such as single-parent families and veterans, or toward particular issues that make one more vulnerable to homelessness, such as substance abuse and mental illness. But some legislation has been passed intended to address the homeless problem directly. The McKinney-Vento Homeless Assistance Act of 1987 is probably one of the most important pieces of legislation passed for those suffering from homelessness or who are at-risk for homelessness, and prior to the passage of this act, the majority of homeless services were facilitated at the grassroots level. This act guaranteed government assistance for the homeless and homeless services. Funding included $180 million in 1987 and increased to 1.8 billion by 1994. Talmadge Wright (2000) points out that when this increase in funding did not abate the increasing numbers of people becoming homeless, general attitudes toward the homeless and their plight hardened considerably as did attitudes of local politicians who increased criminalizing measures such as laws against loitering, panhandling, and camping. Wright cautions that although such criminalization might make it appear that homelessness is a thing of the past, in reality the homeless population either goes into hiding or to jail so that the general population, including tourists, are not negatively affected by the ugliness of social poverty.

Other legislation although not directly aimed at preventing homelessness has certainly had an impact on the homeless population. In the 1990s the United States made the transition from a long-term welfare program (AFDC) to a temporary social welfare program (TANF). Welfare reform had tremendous support within the U.S. society, the reasons for which have been discussed in this chapter and include negative attitudes toward the poor in general and the belief that those on welfare are dishonest about their needs. But there was also a prevailing belief that long-term aid to low-income families encouraged dependency, and even though research clearly shows that the majority of women on welfare did not continue to have more children while receiving public assistance, the majority of people believed that they did. Certainly, offering aid to only single-mother heads of households discouraged marriage, which had a devastating impact on those populations most likely to receive public assistance.

TANF is designed to encourage women on public assistance to reenter the workforce, either through obtaining more education or entering into an internship program that will make aid recipients more employable. This program has been successful for many women, leading them to experience a greater amount of financial independence. Yet many social welfare experts cite TANF with contributing to the dramatic increase in homeless families as aid packages are reduced and barriers to employment and financial independence continue unabated. Since 1995 the economy has suffered a recession, companies have laid off thousands of employees, incomes have either remained fixed or been reduced, and those at the bottom of the financial ladder have suffered the most.

The special challenges associated with homeless families with school-aged children were discussed earlier in this chapter. The McKinney-Vento Education for the Homeless Children and Youth Program, operated under the No Child Left Behind Act of 2001 originally passed in 1987, is designed to address many of the problems experienced by homeless students. Through this act, states can apply for funding to assist them in managing the many academic challenges associated with a student being homeless. Problems related to enrollment, attendance, and academic achievement are all addressed in this act, and states applying for funds must abide by certain standards and meet various criteria in meeting the complex needs of homeless students. For instance, according to the McKinney-Vento, program schools:

► Must provide the same educational opportunities to homeless children and youth that are available to nonhomeless children and youth.

► Must not segregate homeless children from the mainstream school environment for reasons based solely on their state of homelessness.

► Cannot educate children off-site, such as at a shelter, but must educate them alongside their peers, in a regular classroom setting.

► Must make school placement decisions based on the best interest of child, not on the physical location of the shelter. Thus, whenever possible, the child must be allowed to remain in the school of origin, and the school district must make arrangements for the child to be transported to school, if transportation is an issue.

► Must designate a liaison to identify homeless students and assist them and their families in addressing barriers to enrollment, attendance, and academic achievement.

► Must immediately enroll homeless students, even if they do not have immunization records, birth certificates, or proof of residency. The liaison must then work with the family and the former school in obtaining these records in a timely fashion. Schools are also required to transfer school records immediately when a homeless student transfers to a different school.

► Provide transportation for homeless students so that they may remain in their school of origin.

► Allow "unaccompanied youth" (students who for a variety of reasons, including **emancipation,** do not have a legal guardian) to enroll in school even if they do not have a parent or legal guardian to sign admittance forms for them.

► Make a determination of homelessness on a case-by-case basis according to the McKinney-Vento definition of "fixed, regular, and adequate nighttime residence."

This legislation goes a long way in addressing the many challenges facing homeless families with school-aged children, yet much more must be done. School human service professionals, for instance, can be utilized to assist in the identification of homeless youth because a great number of families are too overwhelmed and embarrassed to come forward and report their homeless status. In addition, many homeless parents are simply unaware of their children's educational rights, and even though the McKinney-Vento act requires that school liaison's inform students and their families of these rights, school human service professionals are often the link between the families, students, liaison, and school administration and can therefore be extremely instrumental in ensuring that these kids remain in school, without disruption, despite the immense level of instability homelessness causes.

The Role of the Human Service Professional: Working with the Homeless Population: Common Clinical Issues

Working with the homeless population is as challenging as it is meaningful. Whether a homeless client is a grown man, an elder, a child, or an entire family, being homeless is traumatic, degrading, and for many actually terrifying as one's foundation slips away without any sort of safety net to stop the fall. For many people homelessness is not an isolated incident, but is a way of life, and even when employed and residing in a permanent home, for many people homelessness is only one unexpected financial crisis away.

Many believe that there is a reciprocal relationship between many mental and emotional disorders and homelessness. The process of becoming homeless, which typically comes on the heels of months or years of financial and residential instability, is extremely stressful and often leads to anxiety disorders, depression, loss of self-esteem, substance abuse, and even personality disorders as individuals respond to the harshness of life in various maladaptive and defensive ways.

Research indicates that children who have experienced extreme poverty and homelessness are at risk for higher rates of physical illnesses, depression, anxiety, behavioral problems, learning problems, and low self-esteem (Davey, 2004). Children who live in shelters are often negatively affected as they watch their parent's caretaking roles and responsibilities taken over by shelter staff and human service professionals. Thus working with the homeless population, whether directly at a emergency or domestic violence shelter, transitional housing program, at a school as a homeless liaison or other human services program, or indirectly as a school human service professional, general counselor, child welfare worker, or in some other capacity where homeless clients might seek services, will involve working with an extremely wide range of clients and clinical issues.

Human service professionals provide counseling services to homeless adults and children, facilitate support groups, and provide individual counseling. But one of the most significant roles that human service professionals play is advocating for the homeless population, both on a personal case-by-case basis as well as on a community level by influencing policy and the development of legislation designed to aid the homeless population. Human service professionals also supervise shelters residents and provide case management services for adult and child residents, assisting them in connecting to a wide array of human services that will help them obtain economic and housing stability.

One of the underlying principle values of the human services field is to empower clients by plugging them into a variety of social support systems moving them toward a state of self-sufficiency. This is particularly important when working with the homeless population and those suffering from severe poverty, thus networking with other human service providers to provide a comprehensive continuum of care is a powerful intervention tool for human service professionals. The effective human service professional will not attempt to meet all of a homeless client's needs alone, but will depend on the services provided by other governmental and not-for-profit agencies in the area. Even many churches offer services for homeless individuals, including providing respite care for children, job training and networking, and financial assistance.

Many clients facing or experiencing homelessness tend to have multiple problems, which the human service professional might find challenging to address. Single-parent families that are either homeless or are on the verge of homelessness are particularly challenging because the human service professional must address the needs of the children as well as the parent, and these needs might conflict with one another. For instance, consider the young, overwhelmed single mother with two young children and absolutely no one to help her with her child care responsibilities. Life in the shelter is depressing and difficult, her children are acting out more than ever because they miss their home and do not understand why they have to live in a shelter with so many strangers and so many odd and confusing rules. It is perfectly understandable for this mother to desperately need some time alone without her children, yet the tremendous amount of instability and the trauma associated with being homeless causes the children to need her more than ever. This dynamic can result in increased frustration on the part of the mother, which in turn creates increased fear and insecurity in the children. The human service professional can work with the mother to help her recognize this relationship interaction and take steps to resolve it through intermittent child care respite and counseling the family so that each member better understands the impact homelessness has on each other as well as themselves.

In light of the burden and stress placed on the single mother, who never enjoys a break from the frightening stressors and responsibilities she experiences living on the streets and in shelters with her children, it is no wonder that many women rush into romantic relationships believing promises of never-ending love and rescue. And although it would be tempting for anyone so completely overwhelmed with life to believe a man's offer to take over the control of one's life and the lives of her children, a relationship that moves too quickly will often result in domestic violence.

Many single mothers make decisions to move in with a man they barely know after a whirlwind romance believing that they can finally provide the stability of an intact family for their children, only to find out a short time later that they have entered into yet another abusive relationship with someone who wants to control them and becomes violent if not successful. The shame these women feel is immense and sometimes results in their choice to remain in the abusive relationship because it seems better than facing homelessness again and having to admit that they made yet another devastating mistake. Yet all this accomplishes is to further lower their self-esteem, and change is rarely possible when one cannot move past the shame. In light of the fact that so many homeless single mothers experienced physical and verbal abuse growing up and then repeat this pattern in adult relationships, it is no surprise that many will eventually believe the horrible things being said to them causing them to further doubt whether they have the ability make good choices for themselves and their children.

Many people, including human service professionals, become critical and frustrated with single mothers who enter into a string of relationships with abusive men, sometimes becoming pregnant, but I have often challenged people to consider how they might respond if they had no one in the world to help and support them, had no one to share the burdens and difficulties of life with, and did not have the luxury of taking their time to build a truly loving and healthy relationship because they had never enjoyed a solid foundation of love and security in their childhoods, causing them to enter into an adult world desperate for someone to love them and provide for them. I strongly believe this would make anyone impulsive in jumping into a relationship that looked good at first glance, because when you are desperately alone in the world anything looks good—in fact, it is a little like living in a desert with no water and thinking seawater tastes absolutely wonderful, only to find out later that rather than saving you, it will kill you! Consider the following Case Study about Patricia, paying particular attention to the complexity of her problems and issues, as well as the "domino effect" occurring in this single mother's life.

case study 8.1

Case Example of a Homeless Single Mother

I met Patricia when she was homeless and looking for permanent housing and attempting to put the pieces of her life together. Patricia was raised in an unstable and abusive home environment where she had been told repeatedly throughout her childhood that she was worthless and that no one would ever love her. Her every move was criticized and served as proof that she was no good. She had the natural need and desire to be loved and accepted, and by the time she was 17 this need peaked to a point that she could not resist the affections of an older man who promised her the world. Although she initially resisted his attempts to become sexual with her, he eventually convinced her that the only way he would know she loved him was if they had sex, and if she refused he would leave her. Patricia's immense insecurities and her deep need to be cared for made her vulnerable to his manipulative threats, so she relented and agreed to become sexual with him, believing that she had finally found someone who truly loved and accepted her. Yet when she became pregnant, he became abusive and used many of the same abusive statements she had confided that her father had used to manipulate and control her. She believed that her father must have been right all along, because how else could she explain yet another man seeing such ugliness in her? Ultimately he abandoned her and her unborn child, and when her father learned of her pregnancy he kicked her out of the house and refused to allow her to return.

For the next four years she was intermittently homeless, finding temporary stability through various transitional housing programs that helped her secure employment and an apartment, but any crisis put her on the streets again, such as the time her son got the chicken pox, resulting in her needing to stay home with him for two weeks. Patricia got fired even though she had medical verification of his illness. This led to yet another financial downward spiral and another episode of homelessness. By the time her son was five, he was acting out considerably adding to her sense of frustration and burden. So when she met a new man who showered her with attention and compliments, all she could think of was that she had finally met the man of her dreams. He said all the right things, offered to let her and her son move in with him, and offered to manage every part of her life. He even told her that she would not have to work and could stay home with her son, so she gladly quit her job and embraced being a stay-at-home mom at last—something she had wanted to do for years.

Patricia wanted desperately to believe this was real and accepted his seemingly generous offers because she believed that to do otherwise would mean robbing her son of his only opportunity for a real home and family. When her new boyfriend told her that she was the first woman he ever wanted to have a baby with, she was so flattered she agreed immediately to get pregnant. She believed with all her heart that she finally had it all, and that all the years of suffering were behind her.

Patricia became pregnant quickly and dreamed of her new life with her new boyfriend. Although she would have preferred they got married, he claimed to not be ready yet, and because she did not want to create waves in the relationship, she did not push the subject. She talked endlessly to her son about their good fortune in finding this man who was going to take care of them forever. When her new boyfriend hit her for the first time she convinced herself that it was a one-time incident caused by the stress of having a new family. When she noticed that he drank too much alcohol and seemed impatient with her son, she convinced herself that he needed time to adjust to having an instant family. Then one day he did not come home from work, and when a few days had gone by and he still did not return with her car, she came to the agency where I worked asking for financial assistance because she had no money to pay for the rent due in a few short days.

Unfortunately we learned that this man had a pattern of treating women in this way, and this was not the first time he had encouraged a single mom to depend on him only to flee when the good feelings ended. Equally unfortunate was the fact that she had absolutely no recourse against him, even for taking her car, because to make insurance matters easier, she had agreed to put his name on the title, a decision that seemed foolish now, but in light of all that he was offering her it seemed the least that she could do. Now she had no money, no job, no car, a devastated, hurt, and angry child and a baby on the way, and she would be homeless again within the month.

Adding to her burden was the intense sense of humiliation she felt when she realized that she had once again been taken advantage of. She firmly believed that she deserved this treatment and argued that there must be something terribly defective about her because these things kept happening to her. She was devastated that she was so horribly abandoned in the wake of breathing her first sigh of relief in years. She was extremely depressed, which made her at risk for either inadvertently abusing her child or neglecting him in some way, particularly when he expressed anger at her for driving his new daddy away. And, her additional loss of self-esteem left her in no shape to problem solve by gaining employment, finding low-cost housing, and searching out assistance programs, most of which would require her to disclose her reasons for becoming homeless, forcing her to repeat her failures and leaving her vulnerable to the criticisms of others. Although she should have been hospitalized for severe depression and risk of suicide, she refused because it would mean placing her son in temporary foster care.

Ultimately she managed to piece her life back together, and it was the security of an authentic counseling relationship that enabled her to resist getting into another whirlwind romance and allowed her to see that saying no to a man was not saying no to a secure future, but likely saying no to another abusive and exploitative relationship. Virtually all my guidance meant her acting in a counterintuitive manner. She was desperate for love and companionship, yet I cautioned her to resist getting into a relationship until she was out of crisis. She desperately wanted to avoid revisiting old wounds from her childhood, yet I encouraged her to delve into her early experiences drawing parallels with relationships in her adult life and helping her to see the patterns she seemed helpless to escape. It would be difficult to imagine my client developing the wisdom to respond to her psychological issues and her current life crisis without the benefit of the objective and unconditional support of a human service professional trained to understand and respond to suffering from a social systems perspective—embracing, encouraging, supporting, and guiding in a nonjudgmental manner. ■

Although Patti's life sounds complicated, it is not at all unique. Understanding the dynamics involved in intergenerational abuse and poverty helps one to understand how and why people repeatedly make what often turns out to be unhealthy choices that when combined with social and structural factors leave them vulnerable and at risk for severe poverty and homelessness. Thus, although it might be easy to sit in the comfort of one's stable and healthy home environment and criticize the immoral lifestyle of single mothers who jump from relationship to relationship getting pregnant along the way, once all the situational factors are known and someone takes the time to truly look at the world through the eyes of someone suffering and alone, it becomes far easier to understand how someone could make the choices my client did. One of the saddest statements of humankind is that it seems as though for every vulnerable and hurting person, there is someone waiting to exploit him or her. Fortunately there are just as many people waiting to lend them an accepting, nonjudgmental, and helping hand as well.

Common Practice Settings for Working with the Homeless Population

Programs designed to aid the homeless population are offered in three levels of service. The first includes *emergency shelters,* and *daytime drop-in centers.* Both offer short-term solutions to a long-term problem. Although emergency services are definitely needed particularly when dealing with a population that might experience a crisis resulting in sudden homelessness, many emergency shelters are sharply criticized for their often unsafe and inflexible environment where residents can stay for as short as one night to as many as 30 days. Another area of criticism is that far greater amounts of funding are appropriated for emergency services rather than for long-term programs and services (Shlay & Rossi, 1992).

The second level of service includes *transitional housing programs.* These programs offer temporary housing for anywhere between six months to two years, with most programs offering a one-year program. Housing is only one part of the program package, though, and residents are typically required to participate in a wide range of adjunct social services such as job training, budgeting classes, adult literacy, substance abuse treatment, and parenting training. Other support services may include child care, job placement, and medical care. Most transitional housing programs focus on a specific target population, such as victims of domestic violence, single-mother families, single men suffering from substance abuse, adolescents, or the elderly. These programs tend to be more successful because they provide a wide range of intensive services aimed at addressing the root causes of extreme poverty and homelessness, but they are also challenging to facilitate due to the complexity of the issues being addressed and the cost associated with administering programs offering comprehensive services, particularly because one of the primary root causes of homelessness is the unavailability of low-cost housing. Thus to secure housing for homeless clients is just as expensive for the administering agency. Unfortunately, transitional housing programs have not garnered the majority of governmental funding.

A type of homeless service that is actually a combination of levels one and two includes domestic violence shelters. Because domestic violence is such a significant issue in the prevalence of single-parent families becoming homeless, shelters specialize in meeting the needs of individuals, most commonly women and children, who are fleeing from dangerous domestic relationships. Although there is some variation, the most common scenario involves a woman with children fleeing from a boyfriend or husband who is physically, emotionally, and verbally abusive. Domestic violence shelters operate on a 24-hour emergency basis, providing safe houses whose locations remain confidential.

Most domestic violence shelters have various homes and apartments spread throughout the community, each shared by a few women and children. Shelter stays range from one month to several months, and residents and their children participate in a broad range of services, including support groups for the mothers and the children. Human service professionals provide counseling, case management, and advocacy services including assisting clients obtain orders of protection through the court system and advocating for them during any criminal or civil court hearings. Support groups focus on empowerment issues and educating the women on the nature of domestic violence, parenting from a perspective of strength, and developing better boundaries in relationships. Services may also include providing job training skills and job networking, locating child care, referral for substance abuse treatment, and assistance in locating permanent housing. In general human service professionals provide as many services as are needed by the client.

Issues related to domestic violence will be explored in greater depth in chapter 11 on violence, but it is important to understand that working with domestic violence victims can be challenging for a variety of reasons, but one of the most difficult aspects of working with this population is the cyclical nature of domestic violence where victims often return to their batterers when promises are made to authentically change.

The third level of service involves the provision of low-cost or *public housing projects* provided by the federal department of Housing and Urban Development (HUD), which theoretically provides a permanent solution for the problem of homelessness. Unfortunately this solution is the most difficult to provide and does not have a good track record of providing effective resolution to the homeless problem because traditional public housing units mostly built in the 1950s were developed as high-rise units in low-income neighborhoods, essentially creating segregated societies of the poor, not only producing dangerous neighborhoods but also further adding to the general negative stigma associated with poverty. Gang activity, drug dealing, and other crimes often associated with the urban inner city were common in what is often casually referred to as "the projects."

Once government policy makers realized that housing projects of this type were likely causing more harm than good, an organized attempt was initiated to close the projects down, particularly in large cities such as Chicago and Philadelphia, and transition residents to new low-rise housing units scattered throughout the city. Yet **squatting** became a significant problem, with some squatters even using the empty units as drug labs or gang hideouts.

A more current form of permanent low-cost housing includes governmental voucher programs facilitated by HUD. HUD's Section 8 housing voucher program designed for the general population and Section 811 designed for individuals suffering from disabilities (including mental illness) involve qualified individuals or families applying for the program when it is accepting applications (which may only be a few short periods throughout the year) and having their benefits determined. The voucher beneficiary must then locate a landlord who is willing to accept a government rent voucher as rental payment.

Theoretically the voucher can be used with any rental, but either through bias or because of a competitive rental market, many landlords in more expensive communities will not accept Section 8 or 811 rental vouchers. Thus, even though one intention of this program was to avoid the isolation and segregation created by high-rise congregated public housing, in many communities the result is still much the same because it is not the individual landlord of units scattered throughout the city that is most likely to accept a rental voucher, but the owners of large apartment complexes in low-income areas where occupancy rates run high who are the most likely to accept rental vouchers, creating the same sort of isolated high-crime environment experienced with public housing high-rises.

There is good news on the horizon, though. Section 8 and 811 housing programs have the potential to be successful, and if benefits keep pace with rental prices, beneficiaries can feel a sense of empowerment because they can choose for themselves where they want to live, and stigma is reduced because neighbors are not necessarily going to know that the rent in a particular apartment, townhouse or single family home is being subsidized by the government. But the Section 8 and 811 housing programs have experienced significant funding shortages in recent years, and according to the current and future federal budget it appears that nothing is going to improve in the near future. For this program to be successful the federal government must make a firm commitment to subsidized housing that will be reflected in funding these programs appropriately.

Another piece of good news relates to the relative success of a new pubic housing paradigm where rather than building public housing in high-rises concentrated in low-income or inner-city communities, federal housing developments are scattered throughout the city. These housing projects are far less descriptive, thus residents can enjoy their anonymity without having to worry about being identified as a resident of a high-rise, high-crime housing project.

Concluding Thoughts on Homelessness

Homelessness is a complex social problem with multifaceted causes, including several root causes that lie in the personal domain (such as domestic violence, substance abuse, and teen pregnancy), as well as social causes such as institutionalized racism and oppression and structural causes related to the U.S. changing economy.

Structural issues related to a capitalist society include declining salaries, particularly for the poor, and escalating housing prices, which when combined creates an abundance of low-income renters competing for fewer affordable housing units. The development of affordable housing, although a good idea in theory, is challenging due to the high cost of land and housing in safer areas. In addition, most people who are at risk of homelessness often cannot afford to pay a significant portion of their own rent and many cannot afford to pay any rent at all. Thus regardless of how the rental subsidies are structured, focusing on affordable subsidized housing as the primary resolution to the homeless problem essentially requires permanent governmental support, and unless adjunct services are provided, some argue that permanent subsidized housing programs may encourage dependency rather than fostering independence (Wright, 2000).

It appears then that programs offering a wide array of social services focusing on the personal root causes of homelessness while at the same time addressing structural causes such as declining incomes and escalating housing costs will have the greatest likelihood of successfully addressing the homeless problem with long-term solutions in mind. Human services agencies are on the front lines of developing such programs designed to promote self-sufficiency and personal security.

r e f e r e n c e s

Auerswalk, C. L., & Eyre, S. L. (2002). Youth homelessness in San Francisco: A life cycle approach. *Social Science and Medicine, 54,* 497–1512.

Axelson, L. H., & Dail, P. W. (1988). The changing character of homelessness in the U.S. *Family Relations, 37(4),* 463–469.

Beech, M., Meyers, L., & Beech, D. J. (2002). Hepatitis B and C infections among homeless adolescents. *Family Community Health, 25(2),* 28–36.

Davey, T. L. (2004). A multiple-family group intervention for homeless families: The weekend retreat. *Health & Social Work, 29(4),* 326–329.

Feagin, J. R. (1975). *Subordinating the poor.* Englewood Cliffs, NJ: Prentice Hall.

Hecht, L., & Coyle, B. (2001). Elderly homeless: A comparison of older and younger adult emergency shelter seekers in Bakersfield, California. *American Behavioral Scientist, 45(1),* 66–79.

Kidd, S. A. (2003). Street youth: Coping and interventions. *Child and Adolescent Social Work Journal, 20(4),* 235–261.

Kluegal, J. R. (1987). Macro-economic problems, beliefs about the poor and attitudes toward welfare spending. *Social Problems, 34,* 82–99.

Lindsey, E. W. (1998). The impact of homelessness on family relationships. *Family Relations 47(3),* 243–252.

Lindsey, E. W., Kurtz, D. P., Jarvis, S., Williams, N. R., & Nackerud, L. (2000). How runaway and homeless youth navigate troubled waters: Personal strengths and resources. *Child and Adolescent Social Work Journal, 17(2),* 115–140.

Montgomery, C. (1994). Swimming upstream: The strength of women who survive homelessness. *Advances in Nursing, 16(3),* 34–45.

National Coalition for the Homeless. (2005). *How many people experience homelessness?* NCH Fact Sheet 2. National Coalition for the Homeless Publisher: Washington, DC. Retrieved online, October 7, 2005 from http://www.nationalhomeless.org/publications/facts/How_Many.pdf

Nickelson, I. (2004). *The district should use its upcoming TANF bonus to increase cash assistance and remove barriers to work.* D.C. Fiscal Policy Institute. Retrieved online December 22, 2005, from http://www.dcfpi.org/9-29-04tanf.htm

Nunez, R., & Fox, C. (1999). A snapshot of family homelessness across America. *Political Science Quarterly, 114(2),* 289–307.

Phelan, J., Link, B. J., Moore, R. E., & Stueve, A. (1997). The stigma of homelessness: The impact of the label "homeless" on attitudes toward poor persons. *Social Psychology Quarterly, 60(4),* 323–337.

Reyes, L., & Waxman, L. (1987). *The continued growth of hunger, homelessness and poverty in America's cities.* Washington DC: U.S. Conference of Mayors, 1996.

Roll, C. N., Torro, P. A., & Ortola, G. L. (1999). Characteristics and experiences of homeless adults: A comparison of single men, single women, and women and children. *Journal of Community Psychology, 27(2),* 189–198.

Shlay, A. B., & Rossi, P. H. (1992). Social science research and contemporary studies of homelessness. *Annual Review of Sociology, 18,* 129–160.

U.S. Code, Title 42, Chapter 119, Subchapter I, § 11302. General Definition of Homeless Individuals.

U.S. Conference of Mayors. (2004). *A status report on hunger and homelessness in America's cities.* 1620 Eye St., NW, 4th Floor, Washington, DC, 20006–4005.

U.S. Department of Education. (2001). *Report to Congress Fiscal Year 2000.* Washington, D. C.: U.S. Department of Education.

U.S. Department of Education, Office of Elementary and Secondary Education, Education for Homeless Children and Youth Program. (2000). *Report to Congress: Fiscal Year 2000* (page 8). Washington, DC: Author.

The Urban Institute. (2000). *A new look at homelessness in America.* Retrieved on October 15, 2005, from http://www.urban.org/url.cfm?ID=900302

Weaver, R. K., Shapiro, R. Y., & Jacobs, L. (1995). Trends: welfare. *Public Opinion Quarterly, 59(4):* 606–627.

Whitbeck, L. B., Hoyt, D. R., & Ackley, K. A. (1997). Abusive family backgrounds and later victimization among runaway and homeless adolescents. *Journal of Research on Adolescents, 7(4),* 375–392.

Wright, T. (2000). Resisting homelessness: Global, national and local solutions. *Contemporary Sociology, 29(1),* 27–43.

Yoder, K. A., Whitbeck, L. B., & Hoyt, D. R. (2001). Event history analysis of antecedents to running away from home and being on the street. *American Behavioral Scientist, 45(1),* 51–65.

suggested reading

Jencks, C. (1995). *The homeless.* Cambridge, MA: Harvard University Press.

Kozol, J. (1988). *Rachel and her children: Homeless families in America.* New York: Ballantine Books.

Liebow, E. (1995). *Tell them who I am: The lives of homeless women.* East Rutherford, NJ: Penguin Books.

Stephen, B. (2000). *Street crazy: America's mental health tragedy.* Redondo Beach, CA: Westcom Associates.

internet web sites related to homelessness

Homeless Advocacy Project: **http://www.homelessadvocacyproject.org/**
Housing and Urban Development (HUD):   **http://www.hud.gov/**
National Coalition for the Homeless: **http://www.nationalhomeless.org/**

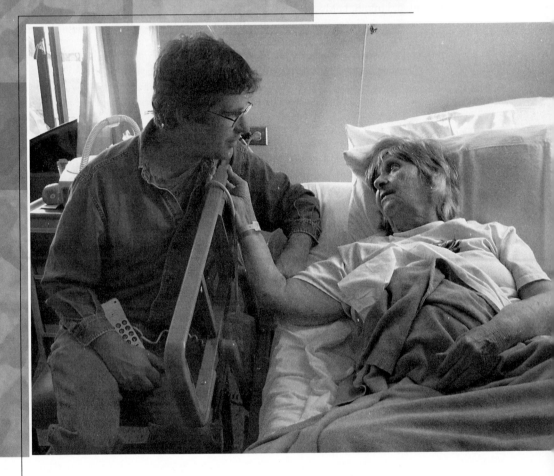

chapter 9

Healthcare and Hospice

Human Services in Hospitals

At 9 AM Glenn is called to the labor and delivery department of a large hospital where he tries to talk with a teenaged girl who just had a baby. The young girl holds her new infant as Glenn initiates a conversation with her. He explains that he is visiting her because it is hospital policy for the social worker to visit with all adolescents who have just had babies. He asks the young mother a few basic questions, such as whether she has a place to live once she and her infant leave the hospital, whether her parents knew about her pregnancy, whether the father of the baby is involved, and whether she has a plan for raising her child. The young mother admits that her parents knew nothing of her pregnancy, as she managed to hide it by wearing large clothing and spending a lot of time in her room. She admits she is frightened that if she shares the news with them they will force her to leave their home. And she admits that the father is no longer in her life, and that she has no ability, nor any real desire, to raise a child. Glenn understands that this mother's ambivalence about raising her child is far more related to her age than her character. After some further discussion, Glenn asks her if she'd be interested in talking with a counselor who can assist her sorting through all the options available to her. After learning that her parents were generally supportive and loving people, he offers to call them for her so that they can help her decide how to best manage this unplanned pregnancy. The young mother appears relieved and admits that she considered just leaving the hospital without her baby because she was so desperately frightened and didn't know what else to do. When Glenn returns to his office, he makes the call to the parents; after a 20-minute emotional phone call he makes plans to meet them in 30 minutes in their daughter's hospital room. After meeting with the entire family, he supplies them with several names of counseling agencies that can assist the young mom in either parenting or placing her infant for adoption.

While walking out of the hospital room Glenn is paged to the emergency room. When he arrives he finds the entire unit in chaos. Three cars collided, and many people were injured. After talking to the emergency room nurses and physicians, Glenn learns that one of the cars had several children in it, many of whom were seriously injured. Glenn gets to work right away collecting identifying information, making sure that each child's parent is accounted for, and obtaining numbers of parents who need to be notified of the accident and their child's condition. After obtaining all necessary information Glenn makes himself available to the parents who had children in surgery, the parents who were not in the accident, who he recently called to the hospital, and the children who are not seriously injured but had parents who were. He offers to contact friends and family for support. After contacting spouses and two family pastors, Glenn sat with one family who had two seriously injured children and provided crisis counseling so that they could be calm enough to understand all that was going on with their children. Glenn also offers to be the conduit between the waiting families and the medical team, so for over an hour he goes back and forth between the medical personnel working on the injured and delivering any new information to the family members. Two hours later, all parties were out of crisis and had support systems by their sides, and Glenn was cleared to return to his office.

Next, Glenn began working on several discharge planning cases for various patients who were scheduled to be released from the hospital within the next two days. One was an elderly patient who was not healthy enough to return to home, and it was Glenn's responsibility to assist the family in finding either appropriate alternate housing or in-house services that would enable the patient to remain in his home. Another case involved a survivor of a serious car accident who needed continued therapy, but could no longer remain in the hospital. Glenn's job was to locate a rehabilitation center close to family that would be covered under his insurance plan.

As Glenn's day was coming to a close he was paged again to the emergency room, where he learned there was a potential victim of sexual assault. Glenn asked the victim if she was comfortable talking to him, but she stated that she was not—she preferred a female counselor. Glenn then called the local county rape crisis center and asked for a volunteer to come to the hospital immediately to counsel and support a sexual assault victim.

On his way out of the emergency room he was asked to consult on a potential child abuse case. Glenn interviewed the parents of a six-year-old boy who suffered a spiral fracture of the arm. Glenn became concerned when he interviewed each parent separately and their stories differed significantly. Because of this and the child's inability to describe in detail how he injured his arm, Glenn felt the case warranted a call to Child Protective Services (CPS). He explained to the parents that he would be making an abuse allegation report and that the child would not be released until a CPS caseworker came to the hospital and interviewed everyone in the family.

Prior to Glenn leaving for the day, he was asked to visit with a patient and her adult son who just learned of her terminal diagnosis. Glenn provided both with some crisis counseling and made a referral to a local hospice agency. He offered to meet with them again tomorrow and to meet with them and the hospice team if they wished.

Glenn's last case for the day was to provide counseling to a 60-year-old man who recently underwent a liver transplant and was about to be released from the hospital. Research indicates that transplant patients often experience depression after being released from the hospital, thus Glenn's focus was to help this patient adjust to the realities of being a transplant patient, as well as preparing him for experiencing some depression in the coming weeks. He made sure this patient left armed with names of counselors who had experience working with transplant patients.

This is a typical day of a hospital or medical social worker, and although this description is realistic, it is probably more realistic to state that there is no such thing as a "typical" day for a social worker in a hospital setting! In fact, someone interested in a career in the human services field who is looking for structure and predictability would probably not fare well in a health-care center, where the broad range of patient issues determines the range of issues dealt with by the hospital social worker team.

Medical social workers traditionally worked in hospital settings, yet as the health-care field branched out to other arenas, including community-based health-care centers, primary care full-service clinics, and specialized health centers serving special populations (such as AIDS/HIV patients, women, or those suffering from cancer), medical social workers can now be found in a variety of health-care-related practice settings.

Health care is one field where most professionals working in human services are required to be licensed social workers. There is some variation from state to state, but health-care settings are highly regulated fields and as such the professionals working in these environments are typically required to have both advanced degrees as well as state licensing.

Medical social workers are true generalists: they must be flexible and able to deal with a variety of issues, often in a setting wrought with crisis and trauma. But despite their broad generalist functions, the NASW Commission on Health and Mental Health and the Society for Hospital Social Work Directors (National Association of Social Workers [NASW], 1990) outlined the scope of social worker functions in health-care and hospital settings. These include

▶ Conducting psychosocial assessments on patients as needed

▶ Providing information and referrals for patients

▶ Preadmission planning

▶ Discharge planning

▶ Psychosocial counseling

▶ Financial counseling

▶ Health education

▶ Postdischarge follow-up

▶ Consultation with colleagues

▶ Outpatient continuity of care

▶ Patient and family conferences regarding health status, care, and future planning

▶ Case management for patients

▶ Facilitation of and referral to self-help and emotional support groups for patients and families

▶ Patient and family advocacy

▶ Trauma response

In addition to performing these various functions, some of the issues addressed by a medical social worker include addressing patient problems related to activities of daily living, assisting patients and their families in dealing with illness adjustment, assessing possible physical and sexual abuse, including child abuse and domestic violence, and assessing patients with potential mental health problems (NASW, 1990).

Crisis and Trauma Counseling

A large part of a medical social worker's role is to provide crisis and trauma counseling to patients and their families. In fact, when the hospital has notified the family of a patient who has been seriously injured either through illness or accident, it is the medical social worker who meets the family at the emergency room doors.

A good model for how to approach an individual or family in crisis is one developed by Abraham Maslow. Maslow (1954) created a model focusing on needs motivation. As Figure 9.1 illustrates, Maslow believed that people are motivated to get their most basic physiological needs met first (such as the need for food and oxygen) before they attempt to meet their needs safety (such as the security we find in the stability of our relationships with family and friends). According to Maslow, most people would find it difficult to focus on higher level needs related to self-esteem or self-actualization when their most basic needs are not being met. Consider anyone you know who suffers from low self-esteem and then consider how he might react if a war suddenly broke out and his community was under siege. Maslow's theory suggests that thoughts of low self-esteem would quickly take a back seat as worries about mere survival took hold.

When individuals are facing a significant crisis, they often feel compelled to get their most basic needs met. In situations where family members or close friends have been called to the hospital in response to a loved one having been in a serious accident or is suffering from some life-threatening illness, their first priority is often to obtain information about the medical status of the patient (Silverman, 1986), and it is very important for the medical social worker to avoid escalating in panic or anxiety along

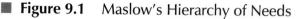

■ **Figure 9.1** Maslow's Hierarchy of Needs

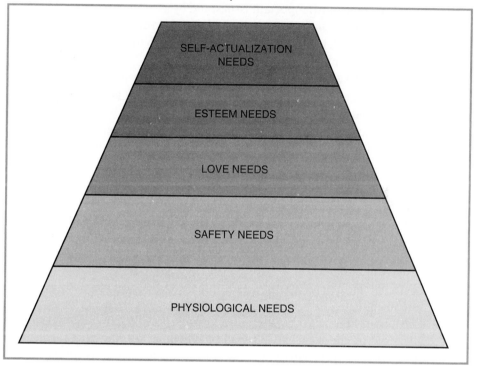

with the family. In fact, it is vital that professionalism be maintained in the midst of the crisis so that amidst crying, screaming, and perhaps even misplaced anger the medical social worker can serve as a calming influence that the family can rely on as they attempt to regain their composure.

Each family handles crises differently, though, thus it is important for the social worker to quickly recognize the family's coping style. Some families will focus on mundane details, such as asking how long their loved one will be in the hospital when the patient has not even emerged from emergency surgery, and some families will focus directly on important issues, such as repeatedly asking whether the patient will survive the surgery, even though there might be no way to answer such a question until the patient is out of surgery. Regardless of these individual coping styles, the medical social worker must be able to read between the lines recognizing that a family confronted with the shocking news of a loved one having a life-threatening condition often leaves them feeling dazed and powerless, and many of the questions or actions are rational or irrational attempts to recover some sense of control over the situation. By understanding this dynamic the social worker can take concrete steps to assist the individual family members in gaining as much control as possible by acting as the conduit between the medical staff and the family, by helping the family focus on the most important issues, and by assisting them in developing a plan of action that might include finding child care for younger children, having someone go to the patient's house to care for pets, and notifying friends and employers on behalf of the patient.

The social worker's role continues with the family as the situation progresses, but takes on a different role, including assisting the patient and family adjust to any limitations posed by the patient's condition or injury, finding necessary resources, and conducting discharge planning when the patient is well enough to leave the hospital. The social worker will even follow up with the patient and family after discharge to check on their progress.

Working with Patients with HIV/AIDS

Medical social workers and other human service professionals commonly work with various health-related **epidemics** or **pandemics.** The HIV virus, which causes AIDS, is an example of such a pandemic. HIV (human immunodeficiency virus) and AIDS (acquired immune deficiency syndrome) were first discussed in the medical literature in 1981 (Gottlieb, et al., 1981). Medical treatment during these early years typically occurred in a crisis setting when patients presented in the emergency room with advanced or end-stage AIDS infections, such as *Pneumocystis Carinii* pneumonia (PCP) and Kaposi's sarcoma, both opportunistic infections common in end-stage AIDS patients. In August 1981, 108 AIDS cases were reported in the United States by the Centers for Disease Control (CDC). By 1986 the CDC reported 16,458 cases of AIDS in the United States and 8,361 deaths, and just two years later those numbers rose to 72,024 cases with an estimate that 1 to 1.5 million Americans were infected with HIV (Centers for Disease Control, 1988).

During the early years of the AIDS crisis the role of the medical social worker or human service professional focused almost exclusively on the crisis of receiving a terminal diagnosis and included conducting emergency discharge planning, death preparation, arranging for acute care, and initiating hospice services. By the 1990s education efforts led to earlier diagnoses and better medical treatment for those who could afford it (CDC, n.d.), and clinical intervention focused more on the psychosocial issues involved with having a chronic, debilitating, and sometimes terminal disease that carried a stigma with it. These psychosocial issues typically included a fear of discrimination, concerns about receiving quality medical care, job accommodations and other income sources, and housing accommodations when physical health begins to decline (Kaplan, Tomaszewski & Gorin, 2004).

When AIDS first emerged in the United States there were no medical treatments available to address the actual disease process (other than symptomatic relief), but through **grassroots efforts** (that led to significant fund-raising efforts for medical research) significant medical advances were gained throughout the 1990s until AIDS is now being considered more of a chronic, rather than terminal, disease—for those individuals fortunate enough to have access to expensive antiviral therapy. Despite these medical advances, however, the treatment of HIV/AIDS remains a serious public health concern, particularly for those individuals who have no access to advanced medical treatment or who do not respond positively to the most aggressive antiviral therapies, commonly referred to as the "AIDS cocktail."

The most recent statistics available from the CDC indicate that in 2003 there were between 1,039,000 and 1,185,000 persons in the United States who were living with HIV/AIDS, one-quarter of whom are unaware they are infected (Glynn & Rhodes, 2005). The CDC estimates that there will be approximately 45,000 new cases of HIV every year, with minority groups being the most significantly affected. Thus, what began as a disease that was often considered a disease that affected primarily "white gay men" is now decimating many minority communities, including women, children, and the elderly (Centers for Disease Control, 2004). In fact, African-American and Latina women as well as Native Americans (both men and women) are significantly overrepresented among those infected with HIV (Kaplan, Tomaszewski, & Gorin, 2004; Weaver, 1999). The significance of this trend is that medical social workers and human service professionals are increasingly relied on to participate in prevention and outreach efforts within the African-American, Latino, and Native American communities, both through direct service as well as through prevention programs and public education campaigns.

This change in the demographics of AIDS patients has led to many changes in the psychosocial needs of the HIV/AIDS population, which has had an impact on the roles and functions of medical social workers and other human service professionals working with this population (see Table 9.1 and Figure 9.2). There is still considerable social stigma associated with an HIV/AIDS diagnosis, particularly in light of the uninformed belief that it is a disease primarily affecting the homosexual population. But because HIV/AIDS was a disease that affected primarily Caucasians when it first surfaced in the United States, racial discrimination was not a central psychosocial issue. Because this disease is now affecting many minority communities, racial discrimination has now been coupled with the existing social stigma that often presumes immoral behavior, such as sexual promiscuity and drug abuse. Despite aggressive public awareness campaigns in both the general public and the professional community designed to increase general awareness and remove stigma, many individuals with the HIV/AIDS virus are forced to endure numerous barriers to getting basic needs met—some of which are related to the stigma, some related to institutionalized racial discrimination, and some related to a combination of both (Kaplan, Tomaszewski, & Gorin, 2004).

For instance, quality medical care is lacking on most Native American reservations, and native advocates argue that reasons for this relate to racial disparity and historic

■ **Table 9.1**   Estimated Number of Cases and Rates (per 100,000 Population) of AIDS, by Race/Ethnicity, Age Category, and Sex, 2004—50 States and the District of Columbia

| | Adults or adolescents | | | | | | Children (<13 yrs) | | Total | |
| | Males | | Females | | Total | | | | | |
Race/ethnicity	No.	Rate	No.	Rate	No.	Rate	No.	Rate	No.	Rate
White, not Hispanic	10,118	12.3	1,860	2.1	11,978	7.1	7	0.0	11,985	6.0
Black, not Hispanic	13,398	99.4	7,395	48.2	29,793	72.1	29	0.4	20,822	56.4
Hispanic	6,041	37.9	1,643	11.1	7,684	25.0	7	0.1	7,691	18.6
Asian/Pacific Islander	392	7.5	92	1.6	484	4.4	1	0.1	486	3.7
American Indian/ Alaska Native	128	13.5	64	6.4	192	9.9	1	0.2	193	7.9
Total*	30,203	25.6	11,109	9.0	41,312	17.1	46	0.1	41,359	14.1

Note: These numbers do not represent reported case counts. Rather, numbers are point estimates, which result from adjustments of reported case counts. The reported case counts are adjusted for reporting delays. The estimates do not include adjustment for incomplete reporting.

Source: CDC, *HIV/AIDS Surveillance Report*, 2004, Vol. 16.

mistreatment and oppression. When reservations were first confronted with a rapidly increasing incidence of HIV/AIDS, elders complained that the medical neglect experienced on most reservations was yet another form of racial discrimination and oppression, evidenced by the fact that the federal government was not allocating sufficient funding to address this issue on the reservations (Weaver, 1999).

Human service professionals working within the medical field must be aware of the various ways that racial prejudice plays out within the community, whether such discrimination be direct and overt or institutionalized (such as where federal monies are allocated). This awareness can then translate into advocacy and outreach as well as increased sensitivity as practitioners challenge their own perception of the HIV/AIDS crisis, including their attitudes about those populations that are currently being most significantly affected by this disease.

When confronting the HIV/AIDS crisis, human service professionals engage in a four-pronged approach to psychosocial care including prevention and educational awareness (such as the practice of **"safe sex"**), client advocacy, and case manage-

■ **Figure 9.2** Bar Graph Comparing Rates (per 100,000 Population) of AIDS, by Race/Ethnicity, 2004, 50 States, Including District of Columbia

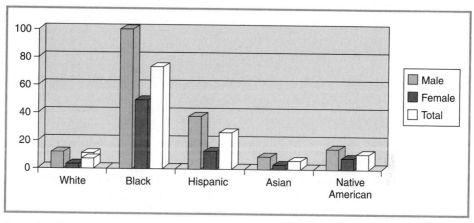

Source: Based on statistics from CDC, *HIV/AIDS, Surveillance Report,* 2004, Vol. 16.

ment/counseling. Human service professionals are actively involved in both practice and policy aspects of the HIV/AIDS pandemic, including meeting the psychosocial needs of those diagnosed with HIV/AIDS, as well as being on the front lines of prevention efforts, community and patient educational and awareness campaigns, advocacy for increased funding of intervention and treatment programs, and participating in lobbying efforts advocating for the passage of laws designed to protect the privacy and legal rights of those diagnosed with HIV/AIDS.

Medical social workers and other human service professionals assist those with HIV/AIDS in obtaining necessary medical services, obtaining the necessary funding for treatment, and providing counseling for those infected individuals, their families, and caregivers. The nature of the counseling will change depending on the progression of the virus. Clients newly diagnosed will need counseling focusing on acceptance of a potentially terminal disease, whereas other clients will need counseling focusing on living with a chronic illness, accepting a life of potential disability, of multiple medication taken on a daily basis, and learning to live with the consequences of stigmatized disease.

Depending on the demographic nature of the patient, the human service professional may help secure child care, help the patient apply for financial assistance, obtain home health care, maintain or obtain employment, housing, and medical care, including care for other health-related issues, such as substance abuse, and finally help the patient and family contend with the various stressors involved with having a stigmatized illness (Galambos, 2004).

The Hospice Movement

Hospice care is a service provided to the terminally ill that focuses on comprehensive care addressing their physical, emotional, social, and spiritual needs. Although hospices have existed since about the fourth century, the biblical and Roman concepts of hospice involved providing refuge for the poor, sick, travelers, and soldiers returning from war. Hospice as a refuge or service for the terminally ill was not developed until the mid-1960s.

The modern hospice movement emerged from the general dissatisfaction with how dying individuals were being treated by the established medical community. Western medicine is curative by design with a focus on restoring individuals back to a state of healthy functioning. This model left the majority of the traditional medical community at a loss as to how to treat those who were beyond the hope of recovery. Dying patients often felt neglected and isolated in depersonalized hospital settings where they were typically subjected to needless and futile medical interventions. The hospice movement challenged the treatment provided by the traditional medical community that often failed to address pain management effectively and often neglected the psychosocial and spiritual needs of the dying patient.

The History of Hospice: The Neglect of the Dying

Dame Cicely Saunders, the founder of the modern hospice movement, recognized this lapse of appropriate care for the dying and set about to make significant changes that would affect how the world viewed the dying process. Originally trained as a nurse, Saunders eventually earned her degree in medicine and quickly challenged what she saw as the medical community's failure to address the comprehensive needs of terminally ill patients. Saunders was passionate about the care of the terminally ill and in 1958 wrote her first paper, entitled *Dying of Cancer,* addressing the need to approach dying as a natural stage of life. Through her work with the terminally ill Saunders recognized that dying patients required a far different approach to treatment than the traditional one that tended to see death as a personal and medical failure.

In Saunders's personal letters she describes in detail her discussions with terminally ill patients in the hospice where she worked, as well as her dedication to the prospects of developing a system of care committed to a dying process without pain, while enabling terminally diagnosed patients to maintain their sense of dignity throughout the dying process (Clark, 2002). Saunders founded St. Christopher's Hospice of London in 1967. Her model of care used a multifaceted approach, where dying patients were treated with compassion so that their final days were spent in peace rather than undergoing invasive and futile medical treatments, and where they were free to attend to the business of dying, such as saying good-bye to their loved ones.

The Connecticut Hospice, Inc. was the first hospice opened in the United States in 1974 in New Haven, Connecticut, funded by the National Cancer Institute (NCI). The hospice was created for many of the same reasons noted by Saunders—the belief that good end-of-life care was severely lacking within the U.S. hospital system, and the belief that the dying process was a meaningful one worthy of honor and respect (Stein, 2004). When the HIV/AIDS crisis first began in the 1980s, and prior to the development of antiviral treatment, hospices took on a significant role in the end-of-life care of those dying of the AIDS virus. Although there are some free-standing hospices, hospice is not a "place," but rather it is a concept of care and can be provided anywhere a patient resides (Paradis & Cummings, 1986).

The hospice movement has grown immensely in a relatively short period of time, and what began as a grassroots effort of trained volunteers supported by philanthropic agencies, such as the United Way, has become a highly regulated and profitable industry staffed by a team of professional service providers. Although the core goals and philosophy of hospice remain the same, the professionalization and governmental regulation of this field has influenced its service delivery model. For instance, although hospice care was originally developed as an alternative to hospital care, many hospices in the United States are now in some way affiliated with a hospital or other health-care organization, most are accredited, and almost all are Medicare certified (National Hospice & Palliative Care Organization, 2003; Paradis & Cummings, 1986).

The Hospice Philosophy

The hospice philosophy employed today is similar to the one envisioned by Saunders. Dying is not seen as failure, but as a natural part of life, where every human being has the right to die with dignity. Hospice care involves a team approach to the care and support of the terminally ill and their family members. A core value of the hospice philosophy is that each person has the right to die without pain, and that the dying process should be a meaningful experience. Because Western culture often perceives accepting death as synonymous with giving up, individuals battling illness are often inadvertently encouraged to fight for their survival to the "bitter end," thus the hospice philosophy is counterintuitive to Western cultural wisdom.

Hospice treatment involves **palliative care** rather than curative care. The hospice movement is highly supportive of patients remaining in their homes, but when that is not possible, hospice service is provided in hospitals, nursing homes, and long-term care facilities and can be an adjunct to other medical services provided. The only stipulation of most hospice agencies is that the patient has stopped pursuing curative treatment, and that the patient received a terminal diagnosis of six months or less.

The Hospice Team

The hospice team is multidisciplinary by design, and although there is considerable overlap in many of the roles of the various service providers, the hospice social worker serves a unique purpose on the team emanating from the distinct values underlying the human services and social work discipline (MacDonald, 1991).

The hospice team typically consists of a *hospice physician* who makes periodic visits and monitors each case through weekly reports from other team members, a *nurse* who visits patients wherever they reside at least three times per week, a *social worker* who provides case management services, counseling to the patient and family including helping the patient say good-bye to friends and family, help resolve any past conflict, and assistance with end-of-life issues such as preparation of legal documents such as wills, and advance directives (which will be explored in the next section), a *chaplain* who provides spiritual support, a *home health aid* who provides daily care such as personal hygiene, a *trained volunteer* who provides companionship including reading to patients or taking them for strolls in a wheelchair, and a *bereavement counselor* who provides counseling and support to surviving family members after the death of the patient. Although care is provided where the patient resides, the common desired goal is for patients to be able to remain in their homes and die surrounded by loved ones, rather than dying in a sterile hospital setting. The hospice team often makes this possible.

 A hospice social worker visits with a terminally ill patient to provide counsel and comfort.

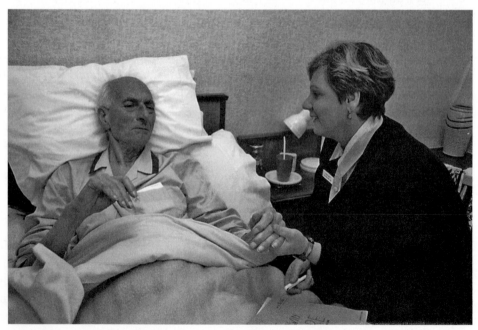

The Role of the Hospice Human Services Worker

The hospice social worker provides numerous services to hospice patients and their families including providing *advocacy* for patients, particularly in regard to obtaining services and financial assistance; *crisis intervention* when emergencies arise; *case management* and *coordination of services* for the comprehensive care of patients and their family members; *case consultation* services among hospice and other health-care staff; assisting the patient and family in *planning* for the patient's eventual death; and *bereavement counseling* to assist patients in accepting their terminal illness and in saying goodbye to loved ones, as well as counseling surviving family members after the patient's death.

The Psychosocial Assessment

Prior to providing these services a hospice social worker must complete a thorough psychosocial assessment evaluating the strengths and deficits of the patient and family members. How are the client and family accepting the reality of the terminal illness? Can the family realistically provide for current and future needs of the patient? Family members who are still reeling from the news that their loved one is dying are often unrealistic in their expectations of the rigors involved with caring for a terminally ill person and will need help to recognize their limitations and need for outside assistance.

Conducting a thorough psychosocial assessment is the first step in making these clinical determinations and ascertaining what services are needed. Chapter 4 outlines the basic criteria of a psychosocial assessment, but the information sought and the focus of the assessment changes depending on the issues at hand. Thus, a psychosocial assessment of a hospice patient will focus on many of the following issues:

1. Basic demographic information, including
   a. The patient's age, marital status, current residence, and financial status including health insurance coverage
2. Assessment of the current crisis including
   a. Nature of terminal illness or condition, including past course and expected future course
   b. Level of acceptance of the terminal illness or condition
   c. Level of debilitation and expected course of decline
   d. Nature of physical and support system
3. Assessment of physical surroundings, including
   a. Appropriateness of home environment (if the patient is not in residential care)—is the bed appropriate? Is the bed upstairs or downstairs? Is there easy access to the bathroom?

    b. Assessment and development of a safety plan: are there open staircases or other dangers that could pose a threat to the declining patient? Is someone going to be home all day in the event of an emergency or does a home health agency need to be hired?

4. Assessment of patient's current mental state, including
   a. Current and past history of depression and anxiety (which would likely affect the patient's ability to accept and manage a terminal diagnosis)
   b. Mental health history—particularly any history of depression, anxiety, or other disorders that might have an exacerbating effect on the personal management of the terminal illness
   c. Any broken or cutoff relationships in need of reconciliation before death
   d. Any unhealthy coping mechanisms such as extensive use of denial, substance abuse, or defensiveness in an attempt to manage conflict and crises
   e. History of loss, such as other deaths

5. Assessment of family relationships, including
   a. Nature of relationships such as past or current conflicts
   b. Communication patterns (does the family have an open style where feelings are openly expressed or a closed style where feelings are masked or denied?)
   c. History of loss with the patient and family system (how a family has handled past losses will often be a good indication of how they will handle this loss— do they distance themselves emotionally? Create conflict in order to avoid feeling pain? Do they deny losses they cannot control? Do they pull together or pull apart?)

6. Assessment of the patient's social support system, including
   a. The supportive nature of the patient's immediate and extended family (some patients will have a large support network and others will have little, thus will likely need volunteer support)
   b. If the patient is still residing in the home, the realistic nature of remaining in the home (based in part on the home environment assessment outlined previously).

Intervention Strategies

Once a thorough psychosocial assessment has been conducted, the social worker can determine the nature and level of *intervention* necessary to meet the needs of the patient and family members. In fact, the psychosocial assessment in many respects acts as the blueprint for the social worker, determining the course of case management and counseling intervention strategies for the patient and family.

    For instance, if the psychosocial assessment reveals that the patient is elderly and has an elderly spouse and no adult children in the immediate area, plans might need to be made for the patient's eventual placement into a facility for full-time care once the illness has progressed to a point beyond the spouse's caregiving ability. Thus, even though the patient's spouse might currently be managing the daily rigors of caring for the patient, plans will need to be made for the patient's care once the illness progresses and care requirements become more complex. This can occur either through placement in a residential facility, contracting with a home health care agency, or utilizing a day respite center (depending on the nature of the illness or condition). If the psychosocial assessment reveals that the patient has insufficient health insurance benefits, the social worker will assist the patient and family with applications for governmental assistance such as Medicare.

If the psychosocial assessment reveals a mental health history of depression or anxiety, then an intervention involving a course of antidepressant or antianxiety medication might be in order. Finally, if the psychosocial assessment reveals a history of conflict within the family then the social worker can plan an intervention strategy designed to help the family work out their issues so that they might move toward a place of resolution before the patient dies.

Case Management and Counseling Services

One of the most common roles for hospice social workers includes providing case management and counseling services to patients and their family members that address the issues noted in the psychosocial assessment. For instance, issues related to how the patient and family are dealing with the terminal illness, the loss of control because of increasing debilitation, and the impending death are all explored and counseling provided as necessary. Yet, because each family is different, the counseling will vary dramatically from patient to patient. For instance, if the patient is a five-year-old child dying of cancer, the social worker will need to assess the needs of the parents and siblings involved. Yet, if the patient is 85 years old with an ailing spouse and adult children in their 60s, the clinical issues will be different, and although it would be incorrect to automatically assume that the level of grief is lessened simply because this death is expected in the natural course of life, the needs of the different parties involved are obviously going to vary significantly. Thus, the actual nature of the illness or condition, the age of the patient, and the specific demographics and characteristics of the family members all combine to determine the nature of the counseling.

I recall working with one client who was dying of amyotrophic lateral sclerosis (ALS), also known as "Lou Gehrig's disease." She was suffering from almost complete paralysis and was unable to communicate once hospice was hired, thus I worked primarily with her husband. This couple was in their early 80s and had been married for over 50 years. The surviving spouse was heartbroken at the prospect of losing his wife who was also his best friend. Our counseling relationship lasted for months and consisted primarily of him talking about his wife, their relationship, and how agonizing it was for him to watch his once capable, articulate wife, who was a leader both in the community as well as within their family, become slowly imprisoned and paralyzed by ALS. During our initial sessions he shared some wonderful memories of their life together and of his wife's strengths and accomplishments (attending seminary after raising their children), but would then become emotionally upset when sharing the pain and powerlessness he felt as he watched her struggle to communicate, at that point by blinking. My role was not to put a "happy face" on his suffering, nor was it to reframe this tragedy in some positive light, as might be appropriate in another type of counseling in another practice setting. Rather, my role was to remain comfortable when in the presence of his emotional expressions of grief and sadness, which in some sense gave him permission to have these necessary feelings. I did my best to provide comfort and a forum for his sadness, but I never gave him the impression that his feelings were in any way wrong.

Well-meaning but misguided counselors are often uncomfortable when confronted with a client's intense emotions of sadness and anger, and in an attempt to alleviate this pain and their own discomfort attempt to make the client feel better by pointing out the positive side of a crisis or by encouraging the client to not dwell on feelings of sadness and anger. This approach often leaves the grieving client feeling as though their intense feelings are somehow unacceptable, or at the least burdensome, which in turn results not in them feeling any better, but as they shut off communication, they ultimately risk suffering in isolation.

Hence, one of the greatest challenges facing hospice workers lies in their ability to increase their comfort level for intense and unpleasant emotions. Those who are grieving can intuitively sense when those around them are comfortable with their emotions, and many hospice clients report that the hospice social workers are the only people with whom they feel safe and comfortable sharing their deepest and most painful feelings of loss, sadness, anger, and mourning.

Resisting the Reality of the Death

Another challenge hospice social workers face is resistance on the part of the patient and/or family members in directly dealing with the realities associated with a terminal diagnosis. As mentioned earlier, embracing death often feels all too much like letting go of life, and North American culture is far more comfortable embracing life. Many people are fearful that if they accept the reality of the terminal diagnosis they are essentially letting go of their loved one, which not only sends the wrong message, but also feels far too much like giving up. This attitude has helped to create a sort of taboo surrounding death where many people are resistant to even think about their own deaths, let alone the impending death of a loved one.

In some families, to accept the reality of the terminal diagnosis is synonymous with losing hope, thus resisting the acceptance of a terminal diagnosis can feel like fighting for life. A social worker might be seen as someone who will attempt to rob the patient and family of their hope, thus many times families make the decision to either reject social work services when first signing up for hospice care or to prohibit the social worker from talking about the terminal diagnosis in front of the patient. Yet, because many of the issues addressed by hospice social workers are designed to also deal with problems that will confront the family at some point in the future—perhaps even years after their loved one has died when social work services are not available to assist them, it is important that the social worker be able to confront the family's denial and assist them in understanding that to accept the impending death of their loved one is not synonymous with hastening the death or with losing hope.

Counseling can be particularly challenging when the patient is asking for information and the family does not want the information about the terminal diagnosis to be shared. In this situation, the social worker must be sensitive, but clear that the patient is the identified client, and what is in the best interest of the patient will also eventually be in the best interest of the family, even if they do not initially recognize it as such. A hospice social worker must delicately assist the family with the task of accepting the terminal illness, facing this approaching loss, and addressing each emotional complication that arises.

Hospice social workers then must be comfortable confronting the realities of death within themselves before they can ever hope to be comfortable dealing with this taboo with patients and families. Knowing how to respond effectively and compassionately when a family accepts social work services, but prohibits any discussion of the terminal illness, requires clinical skills based not only on good training and education, but also on the social worker's self-awareness and comfort level in dealing with these difficult issues.

Planning for the Death

The hospice social worker also assists the patient and family with the practical aspects of planning for increased disability and eventual death. Such practical planning may include something as specific as assisting the patient and family prepare *advanced directives,* or as broad as helping the patient and family sort through their feelings of sadness and even anger in response to the reality of the impending death. Generally, advanced directives include the spelling out of one's end-of-life wishes. Legal documents such as Do-Not-Resuscitate orders (DNR), living wills, and medical power of attorneys are designed to clearly define a patient's wishes regarding the nature of their medical care if and when they reach a point where they are no longer able to make decisions for themselves. Preparing advanced directives is an emotional process, though. Imagine sitting with a patient who recently learned he was terminally ill and will likely die in less than six months and discussing whether or not he and his family want extraordinary measures taken to save his life when he reaches a point in his disease process where he is unresponsive and stops breathing. Making a decision that essentially will mean allowing a family member to die without intervention, either through the removal of a feeding tube or not using CPR to revive their loved one, often generates feelings of immense guilt at the prospect of abandoning their family member. Such emotional turmoil has the potential to create significant conflict and rifts within a family system that is already buckling under the emotional strain of their impending loss. A social worker's role then is not simply to assist the patient and family with the practical matters involved with preparing advanced directives, but involves helping the family navigate this emotionally rocky path as well.

Another role of the social worker is to assist the patient with the preparation of *funeral arrangements.* The thought of planning one's own funeral might seem rather morbid to some, but it can actually be rather therapeutic for someone who is facing a terminal illness or other life-limiting condition. Consider experiencing a life event that stripped you of all control—you can no longer plan for your future because you have only six months to live, you can no longer bound out of the door for a morning jog or even to run errands whenever the mood strikes. A terminal illness robs its victims of their hopes for the future, but it also robs them of their control in all respects, particularly in their everyday lives, and patients—even elderly patients—often struggle with the reality of their increasing dependence on others. Planning their funeral, such as selecting scriptures, music to be played, whether it will be a celebration of life, or a more traditional and formal funeral, a graveside service, or a memorial service with no coffin, gives patients a sense of control in the midst of their increasing powerlessness.

The hospice social worker can utilize what might initially appear to be a practical matter (making funeral arrangements) to facilitate discussions and illicit feelings about the patient's increasing debilitation and resultant confinement and dependence. I recall working with a hospice patient who at the age of 93 years shared heartfelt grief at the thought that he could no longer take his dog for a walk or run to catch up with a friend. In his confinement to a bed, he recalled how he had taken his physical freedom for granted and felt powerless and hopeless in response to the realization that his body could no longer cooperate with what his mind wanted to do. Planning his funeral was the one thing he felt he still had control over in the midst of the powerless he felt in every other aspect of his life.

The Spiritual Component of Dying

Hospice care has its roots in the caring of the dying by religious orders, because religious leaders recognized the spiritual component of facing one's mortality and eventual death. Even though religious issues and spiritual concerns may technically fall under the purview of the hospice chaplain, every professional on the hospice team will likely be asked by a patient or family member to pray with them, and social workers and bereavement counselors must be comfortable in doing so, even if they do not happen to share the same faith as the patient. Facing one's mortality can be a frightening experience for many, and relying on or reconnecting to the faith of one's youth is a common experience for those dying of a terminal illness.

Counseling commonly takes on a spiritual tone as hospice patients attempt to make sense out of their terminal diagnosis. Patients might experience anger, confusion, and a loss of hope and may seek answers from God, yet pose these questions to the social worker. Although no one expects a hospice social worker to be an expert in theology, it is important that the social worker feel comfortable enough to help the patient sort through these questions and even if questions cannot be answered, the social worker can then direct a pastor or other religious leader to the patient.

I recall working with one patient who, in an attempt to find meaning in her life and her life choices, began a process of life examination that included an admission that she felt let down by God. She had been raised within a traditional denomination of the Christian church and had been taught to believe that if she kept the Ten Commandments, she would have a good life. She believed she had kept her end of the bargain, but it did not feel to her as though God kept his, as she reflected on a life filled with chaos, domestic violence, and adult children who were all alcoholics. These feelings, although authentic and understandable, created immense guilt for her, and she became panicked at the thought that by admitting her disappointment in God that this would somehow result in her not going to heaven. Although I did not have any formal training in theology and had not been raised within the same denomination, I felt comfortable sharing some commonly held perspectives on grace, forgiveness, and the importance of being free to express feelings in any relationship, including one's relationship with God. After addressing her initial concerns, I asked if she would like to talk in more detail with the hospice chaplain, and she agreed. She admitted that she had initially rejected chaplaincy services because she was so angry with God, but she now felt ready to come to terms with her feelings and felt more confident that she could make things right with God before her death.

I have also worked with patients who were Jewish, Muslim, and spiritual but not religious and have found that a common thread among all individuals with faith is a need to feel loved and accepted by a creator and the ability to transfer hope from this world to the next. These commonalities among various faiths can act as a launching point for the social worker and bereavement counselor, allowing the practitioner to provide comfort and a sense of peace as patients search for meaning in both their lives as well as their deaths. Again, it is not the social worker's personal religious affiliation that is important, but rather the social worker's willingness to be flexible and comfortable in responding to patients of various faiths who need to ask questions, consider possibilities, find meaning, and connect to their faith by having someone pray with them, listen to them, or even read their favorite scriptures to them.

Death and Dying: Effective Bereavement Counseling

Several research surveys have noted that whereas about 60 percent of human services and social work programs at both a bachelor's and master's level offered courses related to death and dying, these courses were primarily offered as electives, and only about 25 percent of students actually took them. Related studies found the over 60 percent of new social workers felt as though their social work program did not adequately prepare them for counseling clients dealing with end-of-life issues (for a complete discussion of these surveys, see Kramer, Hovland-Scafe, & Pacourek, 2003). This is unfortunate because many human service professionals work directly or indirectly with death and dying issues, including loss and bereavement. In light of this, it is essential that those in the human services field obtain the necessary education and training so that they feel competent in providing services to clients dealing with death and dying.

The Journey Through Grief: A Task-Centered Approach

Several theoretical models are available for dealing with bereavement related to death and dying. Traditional grief models, including Elizabeth Kubler-Ross's (1969) model of grief, depicts grieving in terms of distinct, but overlapping stages, where a mourner meets a loss with a sense of *denial* and disbelief, then moves on to the *anger* stage, where the mourner often feels a sense of injustice and rage in response to the loss. The object of the anger varies depending on the circumstances surrounding the loss, but might include being angry with God, the loved one who died, or everyone in general. The next stage is marked by the mourner *bargaining* to avoid the loss. Individuals whose loss is due to a death will often bargain with God—perhaps promising a sinless life if their loved one can be returned to them. The stage of *depression* follows the bargaining stage. During this stage mourners experience deep melancholy, often citing a sense of hopelessness and despair. The final stage of grieving involves the mourner's *acceptance* of the loss. Although Kubler-Ross's stage theory has dominated the field of grief and loss for many years, there has been a recent turn away from perceiving the mourning process as one where the bereaved progress through distinct emotional stages.

Many contemporary theorists have recently focused more on task theories, which suggest that mourners are confronted with tasks or challenges they need to conquer as they make their way on their grief journey. Alan Wolfelt, a *thanatologist* (an expert on death and grieving), has developed a task-based theory of grief and loss. Wolfelt (1996) cites seven reconciliation needs that both adults and children need to face and tackle to find healing. It is interesting to note that Wolfelt does not discuss healing in terms of acceptance, which he believes may put too much pressure on the bereaved, particularly those mourning a significant loss, such as the death of a child.

Wolfelt's seven reconciliation needs include

1. Acknowledging the reality of the death—Although denial can help the bereaved slowly accept the reality of the death of someone they loved, Wolfelt believes that to move forward in the grief process, one must accept that the loved one who has died will never physically return.

2. Embracing the pain of the loss—Many people naturally try to move away from pain, and the North American culture supports this desire by encouraging states of happiness and well-being over the denial of pain. Yet Wolfelt believes that mourners must allow themselves to be immersed in the pain of their loss, which at times will feel like they are getting knocked down by waves of grief, in order to truly heal from this loss.

3. Remembering the person who died—Wolfelt believes that once someone dies, the relationship can continue in the form of memories, thus it is essential for mourners to create ways in which they can remember special moments, good times, and in general the very aspects of the relationship that made it so special. Mourners can do this in many ways, but one suggestion of Wolfelt is to create a memory box where the mourner can place special mementoes such as photographs or other items that will help them remember their loved one.

4. Developing a new self-identity—Wolfelt points out that our identity is based on the nature of the relationships we have with others, and if someone close to us dies, we will likely struggle in determining who we are now that our loved one has died. For instance who is the surviving wife when her husband dies? Is she no longer a wife? What about the mother who loses her only daughter to cancer? Is she no longer a mother? Is her husband no longer a dad? Many mourners struggle to restructure their self-identity and even their purpose when they lose important self-identifying roles when someone close to them dies. You might feel good about yourself because you are such a good friend, but what if your best friend dies? Who are you then? Conquering this task is necessary to truly mourn the loss of someone close, who helped define one's identity and purpose in life.

5. Searching for meaning in the loss—Wolfelt believes that to make sense out of the death of a loved one, many mourners must make sure that the death was not in vain. This is particularly true for unexpected and traumatic deaths. In an attempt to find meaning in the death of Ryan White, the Indiana teenager who contracted the AIDS virus from medical treatment related to hemophilia, family and friends turned tragedy into a campaign to increase public awareness, reduce irrational fear and the stigma commonly associated with this disease,

and increase funding for various programs, including addressing the unmet medical needs of those suffering from the AIDS virus. Finding meaning in a loss does not mean that the mourners are happy that the death occurred, but many mourners find some comfort in allowing the death of a loved one to serve some higher purpose or cause.

6. Receiving ongoing support from others—mourners need love, understanding, and support from others. Unfortunately, many people, particularly within the North American culture with our "pick yourself up by the bootstraps" mentality, do not have a good understanding of the mourning process and inadvertently send the wrong message to the mourner, including encouraging them to move *away* from the pain rather than toward it. Suggestions such as telling mourners they are doing well because they are not crying sends the message that to cry for a loved one is wrong. Encouraging a mourner to just think of something else when confronted with sadness sends the message that to think about the loss and miss the person who has died is unhealthy. Mourners need permission to feel what they are really feeling, and the greatest gift of support friends and family can provide is the gift of comfort in the face of a grieving mourner.

7. Reconciling the grief—Wolfelt does not believe that people ever get completely over their losses. Rather, he believes that they incorporate these losses into their reality, which enables them to move on with their lives in some meaningful way without the physical presence of the person who has died. Thus, although thoughts and discussions of their departed loved one might always prompt feelings of sadness, the waves of grief lessen over time, and mourners who have reconciled themselves to the death can move forward in life, perhaps as even better people as they grow stronger from having survived such a difficult life trial.

Bereavement counseling can be facilitated by a licensed social worker, therapist, human services generalist, or even hospice volunteers. In fact, it is typically a volunteer who follows up with family members after the death of the patient to explore how the surviving family members are faring, as well as to determine the need for ongoing bereavement counseling. Human service professionals who conduct bereavement counseling may do so on an individual basis, but will commonly facilitate support groups focusing on a particular loss. Groups for children surviving the loss of a parent or groups for widows or widowers are examples of grief-specific bereavement support groups. Most hospices offer free bereavement counseling for up to one year after the death of the patient as a part of the full continuum of care. Knowing that their loved ones will be cared for after their death often provides a sense of comfort for dying hospice patients, thus bereavement counseling is an important aspect of hospice care.

Multicultural Issues

In general, individuals from cultures other than European American tend to under-utilize hospice care. The reasons for this underrepresentation appears to relate to numerous factors, including lack of awareness of hospice care, Medicare regulations, which create barriers for immigrant, low-income, and minority groups; a lack of diversity within the hospice staff leading to a general mistrust and discomfort with hospice services; and a lack of knowledge of hospice care on the part of many physicians who serve minority populations. Many ethnic groups maintain values that are inconsistent with hospice values and perceive acceptance of death negatively, and although this attitude is not significantly different from Western values in general, many within the majority culture have slowly adopted new cultural values that espouse acceptance of death as an important part of life.

A 1999 study that examined barriers to hospice service for African Americans found that many African Americans held religious beliefs that conflicted with the hospice philosophy. Subjects stated that they did not feel it was appropriate to either talk about, plan for, or accept their death. In addition, a majority of the subjects interviewed stated that they felt more comfortable turning to those within their own community, particularly their church, for support during times of crises, rather than to strangers within the health-care system (Reese, Ahern, Nair, O'Faire, & Warren, 1999).

The researchers of this study acknowledge the importance of not pushing a service on the African-American culture if it is truly unwanted and perhaps even unneeded, but they cite leaders within the African-American community who argue that members of the community would in fact benefit from hospice care, stating that a chief reason why hospice care is often rejected lies more in the lack of knowledge about the services provided. Thus rather than accepting these differences in philosophy, the principle investigators suggest that hospice agencies adapt their services to meet the needs of the African-American community (Greiner, Perera, & Ahluwalia, 2003; Reese et al., 1999). Examples of this might include finding common ground and incorporating this into an education awareness outreach program or utilizing community resources such as churches, and then coordinating services so that issues of mistrust are reduced.

No research has been conducted to date on usage patterns or barriers to service for Asian Americans, Latinos, or Native Americans, but similar issues are likely to emerge within these communities as well. It is imperative that hospice agencies remain flexible enough to meet the needs of all cultural groups, and that policies that either directly or inadvertently discriminate against ethnic minority groups, such as various admittance requirements, be challenged and if possible changed so that all individuals who desire hospice care can benefit from this service.

Ethical Dilemmas in Hospice Care

Although there is a decent body of research relating to ethical issues in health-care settings, little of this research relates directly to hospice care. Of the research that has been conducted, certain ethical issues have been noted that appear to be relatively universal among hospice care agencies. Common ethical dilemmas include issues related to (1) Family denial of terminal illness leading to the denial of patient self-determination or autonomy; (2) denial of services or full services to those unable to pay; (3) counseling patients regarding euthanasia, particularly in states where this practice is illegal; (4) poor pain management; and (5) discharge of terminal patients whose health improves (Csikai, 2004).

In situations involving family denial, patients might be coerced to leave hospice against their will to seek experimental treatment or might be involuntarily admitted to a hospital when their wish was to die at home. In the event that advanced directives have not yet been prepared, families may override patient wishes and insist that a feeding tube be inserted or that the patient be kept alive artificially, even if medical treatment is ultimately futile. It falls on each member of the hospice team to ensure that patient rights of self-determination are respected and honored, but the social worker is in the unique position of assisting the family to face the inevitable reality of their loved one's death.

Patients who apply for hospice care but have no ability to pay and are not eligible for Medicare create an ethical dilemma, particularly for smaller hospices or hospices that serve lower-income communities because any helping organization without endless funding must be careful about admitting too many nonpaying clients. A related issue involves hospices that serve communities with high immigrant populations. Such hospice agencies face considerable financial risk when a significant portion of their applicants are immigrants, both legally and illegally residing in the United States, who are not eligible for any government assistance.

Although it is understandable that hospice administrators would be motivated to protect the agency's financial resources, one of the foundational values of the hospice philosophy is that hospice care will be available to every dying individual. Thus, an ethical dilemma is created when hospices are put in the position of having to deny admittance of lower-income patients to protect their bottom line. If steps are not taken to ensure that all patients can be served, then the hospice field risks becoming elitist in the sense that patients without financial means will be denied hospice service, particularly in low-income or immigrant communities.

Certainly hospice administrators are responsible for developing admittance policies that do not directly or inadvertently discriminate against low-income patients while protecting the financial status of the hospice. But social workers who are professionally committed to advocating for low-income and underserved populations are in the unique position of securing financial assistance in the form of private and government assistance through effective case management.

Another ethical dilemma faced by hospice staff involves the issue of **euthanasia,** or physician-assisted suicide. Dr. Jack Kevorkian made national headlines in the 1990s for assisting numerous terminally ill patients in the ending of their lives and is now serving a prison sentence. Because euthanasia is illegal in all states except Oregon, patient requests for physician-assisted suicide create an ethical dilemma complicated by the illegal nature of such an act. Requests for physician-assisted suicide present a particularly challenging ethical dilemma for conservative faith-based hospice agencies that believe that issues related to death and dying fall under the sole dominion of God (Burdette, Hill, & Moulton, 2005).

Those who believe that euthanasia should be legalized typically cite an argument based on the inalienable human right to choose death when pain and suffering robs them of a meaningful life. Although a counterargument could be based on the meaningful nature of suffering, a better argument might be based on the hospice philosophy that dying persons have a right to die without physical, emotional, and spiritual pain. In fact, several studies examining similarities among terminally ill patients expressing a desire to hasten their deaths found that the chief reasons cited included (1) depression and a sense of hopelessness, (2) poor symptom management, (3) poor social support, (4) fear of becoming a burden on family members, and (5) a poor physician–patient relationship (Kelly et al., 2002; Leman, 2005). Thus, the question is: If these issues could be addressed effectively, would these same patients still seek physician-assisted suicide?

Although the hospice philosophy advocates for neither hastening nor postponing death, hospice agencies have more in common with supporters of physician-assisted suicide than one might initially think. In fact, the leading reasons among terminally ill patients for requesting a quicker end to their lives listed previously include the very issues hospice care is designed to manage. Hospice workers can respond to this ethical dilemma by advocating for the meaningful nature of the dying process from a spiritual, psychological, and social perspective, made possible when patients are helped to confront feelings of sadness and hopelessness, when symptoms are well managed, when social support is bolstered, families are assisted with the care of the patient, and the hospice physician maintains a close relationship with patients based on a palliative care model. In fact, one hospice social worker put it this way:

> I believe it is wrong to cut yourself off from any opportunity to become a greater realized human being. So [. . .] if one preempts the dying process, then we don't know what else could have happened during the rest of that time for that person, for family members; and there are so many things that I see happen in the last days, hours of a person's life that give that whole life, that whole dying, its meaning. (Messler & Miller, 2000, p. 146)

Concluding Thoughts on Human Services in Hospice Settings

Human service professionals perform a valuable service to hospice patients and their family members and serve an important function on the hospice team. Although other members of the hospice team may perform case management and counseling services as a function of their role as hospice team members, neither the nurses or chaplains have the same approach to service provision as do professionals in the human services field. Unfortunately with the increasing reliance of hospices on Medicare benefits, the psychosocial component of hospice care has eroded. This is primarily due to Medicare's (and managed care in general) cost-containment efforts, and because each service provider is billed separately in many hospice agencies, social work services have come to be seen as an "optional" service unless otherwise prescribed by law (Reese & Raymer, 2004).

Some hospice experts are concerned that this attitude has led to a "turf war," particularly among some nurses who are in the position of determining the family's needs. Reese and Raymer (2004) caution that although nurses often provide some psychosocial care, they are not trained to perform services in the same manner and with the same focus as human service professionals. In fact, Reese and Raymer's research study was borne out of this concern among social work leaders. The authors' recommendations include that hospices work toward the goals of social worker involvement in all intake interviews and that social work involvement not be solely on a crisis or as-needed basis, because ongoing social work intervention will likely prevent many of these crises in the first place.

Finally, the authors challenge the common notion that social service involvement increases and strains budgets, suggesting that although budgets might increase initially with social work involvement, consistent social work intervention from case inception reduces financial outgo in the long run as expensive and time-consuming crises are avoided. This contention is based on the well-researched connection between many psychosocial and physical crises, where many medical emergencies requiring costly intervention have their origin at least in part in the psychosocial realm, such as patient depression and anxiety (Reese & Raymer, 2004).

Another challenge facing hospice agencies is the well-established pattern of patients being referred for hospice far too late for any of the meaningful work to be effectively accomplished. Despite the immense growth of the hospice movement and the general assumption that hospice care is a wonderful concept, only 22 percent of dying individuals are actually referred for hospice services, and of these about three-quarters are referred within three weeks of their death (Stein, 2004). Lorenz, Asch, Rosenfeld, Lui, and Ettner (2004) cited numerous barriers to hospice admission including patients being rejected for hospice admittance because they were still seeking curative medical treatment such as chemotherapy. Lorenz et al. recommended that hospices reexamine their enrollment policies that might inadvertently exclude appropriate patients from receiving services. They suggested that there might be a link between the general knowledge that the majority of hospices deny enrollment to patients still undergoing curative treatment and the fact that the majority of dying patients are either not referred at all to hospice or are referred so late in their disease process.

It seems clear that hospices must take responsibility for developing educational programs focusing on the nature of hospice care and the importance of early referral. As experts in the psychosocial dynamics commonly at play in end-of-life care, those within the human services field can lead these educational efforts both with the hospice administrators who determine enrollment policies, as well as within the medical community and general public. A family's willingness to forgo curative treatment immediately on learning of the terminal diagnosis (necessary for hospice referral) is likely an unrealistic expectation on the part of hospice administrators. Deciding to pull a feeding tube or stop chemotherapy are psychosocial issues that evoke considerable emotional turmoil within families and could be considered a psychosocial goal of hospice counseling. Thus, although continuing to actively seek a cure is clearly contrary to the hospice philosophy, perhaps the transition from curative to palliative care could be one that occurs as a part of hospice care, not a condition of it.

Human service professionals are an integral part of the hospice team and must remain so for hospice care to remain true to its original goals and philosophy. But human service professionals must also be on the front lines of effecting change within the hospice field, which will ensure that hospice care is flexible in meeting the needs of a changing society.

r e f e r e n c e s

Burdette, A. M., Hill, T. D., & Moulton, D. E. (2005). Religion and attitudes toward physician-assisted suicide and terminal palliative care. *Journal for the Scientific Study of Religion, 44(1),* 79–93.

Centers for Disease Control. (1988). Quarterly report to the domestic policy council on the prevalence and rate of spread of HIV and AIDS—United States. *Morbidity and Mortality Weekly Report, 37* (36), 551–554.

Centers of Disease Control. (2004). HIV/AIDS Surveillance Report, cases of HIV/AIDS, by area of residence diagnosed in 2004—33 states with confidential name-based HIV infection reporting, 16, 1–46.

Clark, D. (2002). *Cicely Saunder. Founder of the hospice movement: Selected letters 1959–1999.* Oxford: Oxford University Press.

Csikai, E. (2004). Social workers' participation in the resolution of ethical dilemmas in hospice care. *Health and Social Work, 29(1),* 67–76.

Galambos, C. M. (2004). The changing face of AIDS. *Health and Social Work 29(2),* 83–85.

Glynn M., & Rhodes P. (2005). *Estimated HIV prevalence in the U.S. at the end of 2003.* Presented at the National HIV Prevention Conference, Atlanta, GA, June 2005.

Gottlieb, M. S., Schroff, R., Schanker, H. M., Weisman, J. D., Fan, P. T., Wolf, R. A., & Saxon, A. (1981). Pneumocystis carnii pneumonia and mucosal candidiasis in previously homosexual men: evidence of a new aquired cellular immunodeficiency. *New England Journal of Medicine, 305*(24), 1425–1431.

Greiner, K. A., Perera, S., & Ahluwalia, J. S. (2003). Hospice usage by minorities in the last year of life: Results from the National Mortality Followback Survey. *Journal of the American Geriatrics Society, 51*, 970–978.

Kaplan, L. E., Tomaszewski, E. S., & Gorin, S. (2004). Current trends and the future of HIV/AIDS services: A social work perspectives. *Health & Social Work, 29*(2), 153–159.

Kelly, B., Burnett, P., Pelusi, D., Badger, S. Varghese, F., & Robertson, M. (2002). Terminally ill cancer patients' wish to hasten death. *Palliative Medicine, 16*, 335–339.

Kramer, B. J., Hovland-Scafe, C., & Pacourek, L. (2003). Analysis of end-of-life content in social work textbooks. *Journal of Social Work Education, 39(2)*, 299–320.

Kubler-Ross, E. (1969). *Living with death and dying.* New York: Macmillan Publishing Co.

Kulys, R., & Davis, M. A. (1986). An analysis of social services in hospices. *Social Work, 31*(6), 448–446.

Leman, R. (2005). *Seventh annual report on Oregon's death and dying.* State of Oregon, Department of Human Services, Office of Disease Prevention and Epidemiology. Retrieved online March 2, 2004, from http://oregon.gov/DHS/ph/pas/docs/year7.pdf

Lorenz, K. A., Asch, S. M., Rosenfeld, K. E., Lui, H., & Ettner, S. L. (2004). Hospice admission practices: Where does hospice fit in the continuum of care? *Journal of Geriatrics Society, 52*, 725–730.

MacDonald, D. (1991). Hospice social work: A search for identity. *Health & Social Work, 16(4)*, 274–280.

Maslow, A. (1954). *Motivation and personality.* New York: Harper.

Mesler, M. A., & Miller, P. J. (2000). Hospice and assisted suicide: The structure and process of an inherent dilemma. *Death Studies, 24*, 135–155.

National Association of Social Workers. (1990). *Clinical indicators for social work and psychosocial services in the acute care medical hospital.* Washington, DC: Author.

National Hospice and Palliative Care Organization. (2003). *Hospice facts and figures.* Retrieved October 12, 2004, from http://www.nhpco.org/files/public/Hospice_Facts_110104.pdf

Paradis, L., & Cummings, S. (1986). The evolution of hospice in America toward organizational homogeneity. *Journal of Health and Social Behavior, 27(4)*, 370–386.

Reese, D. J., Ahern, R. E., Nair, S., O'Faire, J. D., & Warren, C. (1999). Hospice access and use by African Americans: Addressing cultural and institutional barriers through participatory action research. *Social Work, 44(6)*, 449–559.

Reese, D., & Raymer, M. (2004). Relationships between social work involvement and hospice outcomes: Results of the National Hospice Social Work Survey. *Social Work, 49(3)*, 415–422.

Saunders, C. (1958). Dying of cancer. *St Thomas's Hospital Gazette, 56(2)*, 37–47.

Silverman, E. (1986). The social worker's role in shock-trauma units. *Social Work, 31(4)*, 311–313.

Stein, G. (2004). Improving our care at life's end: Making a difference. *Health and Social Work, 29(1)*, 77–79.

Weaver, H. N. (1999). Through Indigenous Eyes: Native Americans and the HIV epidemic. *Health & Social, 24(1)*, 27–34.

Wolfelt, A. (1996). *Healing the bereaved child: Grief gardening, growth through grief, and other touchstones for caregivers.* Fort Collins, CO: Companion Press.

World Health Organization. (n.d.). *WHO definition of palliative care.* Retrieved online March 12, 2004, from http://www.who.int/cancer/palliative/definition/en/print.html

suggested reading

Byock, I. (1997). *Dying well.* New York: Riverhead Books.

Callanan, M., & Kelley, P. (1997). *Final gifts: Understanding the special awareness, needs, and communications of the dying.* New York: Bantam Books.

Klaas, D., Silverman, P. R., & Nickman, S. L. (1996). *Continuing bonds: New understandings of grief.* Washington, DC: Taylor & Francis.

Lord, J. H. (1992). *Beyond sympathy: What to say and do for someone suffering and injury, illness or loss.* Ventura, CA: Pathfinder Publishing.

McCracken, A., & Semel, M. (1998). *Broken heart still beats after your child dies.* Center City, MI: Hazelden.

internet web sites related to medical human services and hospice

Hospice Foundation: **http://www.hospicefoundation.org/**

Hospice.net: **http://www.hospicenet.org/**

The National Hospice and Palliative Care Society: **http://www.nhpco.org/templates/1/ homepage.cfm**

chapter 10

Substance Abuse and Treatment

Claudia Degelman

Over 20 million people in the United States suffer from either a substance abuse or substance dependence problem (SAMHSA, 2004). Every day, human service professionals are intricately involved in prevention efforts and in providing treatment services for individuals and families in over 11,000 substance abuse treatment programs in the United States (SAMHSA, 2005).

Despite the widespread nature of the substance abuse problem in the United States, specialized treatment is often viewed as a part of human service practice set apart from the mainstream, seen as operating completely independently from all other services. Many human service professionals express an aversion to working with substance abusing clients, and some believe that one must be a recovering addict to effectively counsel others with this problem. Until fairly recently, most human services and mental health providers did not receive specific training in substance abuse issues as a part of their normal course of studies.

In practice, however, all human service professionals are affected by the issue of substance abuse. Although only a small percentage may work directly in specialized substance abuse treatment programs, all will find that the issue of substance abuse frequently touches the lives of the clients with whom they work. All human service professionals need to be familiar enough with the dynamics of **substance use, substance abuse, substance dependence,** and **addiction** to be able to recognize when it may be a primary or secondary problem for their clients. Human services professionals also need to be aware of their own feelings and attitudes that may help or hinder their ability to work effectively both with clients who have substance abuse problems and those whose lives have been affected by the substance abuse of others.

Those who do choose to work directly in substance abuse treatment will encounter a diverse field with many practice settings. Human service professionals may focus on prevention, voluntary treatment with chemically dependent clients and their families, or even with mandated clients within the criminal justice system. In this chapter, we will examine the history and evolution of substance abuse treatment in the United States. We will then explore the many meaningful roles that human service professionals fulfill in this challenging area of practice.

History of the Practice Setting

Throughout recorded history, people have used psychoactive substances to change the way that they feel. Evidence from the earliest prehistoric and ancient civilizations indicate the use of fermented grains and honey to produce alcoholic beverages and the use of plants containing psychoactive substances in medicinal and religious rituals. The particular substance of choice has varied with time and from one society to another, but the use and abuse of substances has been so prevalent as to be routinely regarded as part of the human condition.

Most societies sanction some use of psychoactive substances. In the United States, it is legal for adults to consume alcohol, nicotine, and caffeine, which are all drugs that affect the central nervous system. The use of other psychoactive drugs in the United States is either prohibited or regulated. Many uses, such as the medical use of marijuana or the use of the peyote cactus in religious ceremonies by some Native Americans, remain controversial and the subject of ongoing legal and public policy debates at the state and federal level (Inaba & Cohen, 2004).

Societies have also developed ways of responding to individuals whose use of substances "cross the line" of what is considered acceptable by creating problems for the individual and the society as a whole. How a society has responded to this problematic use has varied according to that society's beliefs about the nature of the problem. For example, societies that view substance abuse as the result of personal misconduct or moral failure tend to focus on a call to repentance and/or punishment for the offender. Societies that regard substance abuse as an illness are more likely to focus on providing treatment.

History of Use and Early Treatment Efforts within the United States

Attitudes and practices regarding substance use and abuse in the United States have undergone significant changes over time and continue to evolve. William White (1998) traced the history of addiction treatment and **recovery** in the United States, focusing on the development of the professional field that has emerged in response to the problem of substance abuse. This historic review provides perspective on the prevalence of the substance problem from the very beginning of the country. In exploring social attitudes, White noted that

> Alcohol use and occasional drunkenness were pervasive in colonial America, but it wasn't until per capita alcohol consumption began to rise dramatically between the Revolutionary War and 1830 that Americans began to look at excessive drinking in a new way and with a new language. (p. xiii)

The term *alcoholism* was first introduced by physician Magnus Huss in 1849, but it took another 100 years, and the birth of Alcoholics Anonymous, for the term to become fully accepted (White, 1998).

Early efforts to provide treatment for substance abuse began in the United States in the mid-1800s, prompted by public concern over the problems resulting from increased levels of public drunkenness. White (1998) traced the roots of this increase back to colonial America, describing the variety of attitudes and practices regarding drug and alcohol use held by the diverse cultural groups that immigrated to colonial America. Many immigrant groups had previously used drugs or alcohol only in moderation and often in the context of social, religious, or medical practices. Wine may have been used to celebrate a wedding, partake in a communion service, or deaden the pain of an injury, but excessive use of alcohol was often condemned.

Coming to colonial America, immigrants were affected by what White described as "the utter pervasiveness of alcohol," which was consumed throughout the day by virtually everyone: man, woman, and child. Alcohol was commonly integrated into everyday social and political life, often in the form of more concentrated distilled liquor such as whiskey and rum. Native Americans, who previously used only weak forms of alcohol ceremonially, were also affected by the introduction of distilled liquor.

A number of laws were passed in an effort to combat public drunkenness and vagrancy, but drinking itself was not yet perceived as a problem. Other psychoactive substances in common use included laudanum, opium-laced alcohol, used for many medical problems, and tobacco, a major crop for both domestic use and export (Inaba & Cohen, 2004).

By the end of the colonial period there was a shift in societal attitudes about the use of alcohol in the United States. Instead of being seen as a blessing of God, it was increasingly seen as a curse. This shift in thinking birthed the temperance movement, which initially focused on encouraging moderate use of alcohol (thus the term, temperance), but eventually came to advocate total abstinence from alcohol when it became clear that problem drinkers were frequently unable to maintain moderate drinking. This shift in thinking coincided with the rise of medicine as a profession. Dr. Benjamin Rush suggested that chronic drunkenness represented a "progressive medical condition" rather than a moral failure, thus introducing the disease concept of alcoholism (White, 1998).

The Prohibition Movement

Attempts to eliminate drug and alcohol problems through legal prohibition lead to the passage of several pieces of federal legislation. In 1906, the Pure Food and Drug Act established the Food and Drug Administration (FDA) and gave it authority to approve all drugs meant for human consumption, to establish that certain drugs required a prescription, and to mandate warning labels on drugs that were potentially habit forming. (Prior to this time, drugs such as opium and cocaine were freely available and not regulated.) In 1914 the Harrison Act was passed, which regulated the *medical* use of certain drugs such as opium, morphine, cocaine, and their derivatives and, at the same time, criminalized the *nonmedical* use of these same drugs (Whitebread, 1995).

The temperance movement was successful in establishing alcohol prohibition laws in many states, and eventually the ratification of the 18th Amendment in 1919 made alcohol manufacture, transportation, and sale illegal in the United States. Musto (1999) noted that the 18th Amendment, like earlier state prohibition laws, enjoyed wide public support and reflected societal fear that even small amounts of alcohol posed a danger both to the individual and society as a whole.

Prohibition, described by President Hoover as a "noble experiment," proved to be short lived. The 21st Amendment repealed the 18th Amendment in 1933, ending Prohibition and thereby legalizing the manufacture and sale of alcohol once again in the United States. Several factors provided the impetus for this change, including the widespread disregard for the law and the rise of organized crime in the production and distribution of **"bootleg" liquor.** Inaba and Cohen (2004) concluded, however, that the widespread belief that Prohibition was a failure is incorrect. "An examination of medical records concerning diseases caused by excess alcohol consumption as well as criminal justice records shows that Prohibition did reduce health problems, domestic violence, crime, and consumption" (p. 323).

The perceived failure of Prohibition to rid society of drug and alcohol problems, the closing of specialty addiction treatment programs, and the financial hardships of the Great Depression combined to create an atmosphere in the 1930s that offered little help or hope for those with drug and alcohol problems (White, 1998). This combination of factors made the climate right for the birth of the mutual aid society of Alcoholics Anonymous (AA), "a fellowship of men and women who share their experience, strength and hope with each other that they may solve their common problem and help others to recover from alcoholism" (AA, n.d.). The growth of AA from two men (known simply as Dr. Bob and Bill W.) meeting in Akron, Ohio, in 1935 to a worldwide organization with over 50,000 meetings (Abadinsky, 2004) is indeed remarkable and represents a major component in the development of the current treatment of addictions.

The Rise of Modern Addiction Treatment in the United States

Several factors shaped the course of addiction treatment in the United States during the second half of the twentieth century up until the present time. The growth of Alcoholics Anonymous played a major role in the broad (but by no means universal) acceptance of the *medical model* of addiction treatment. The establishment of private health insurance provided increased access to treatment for a greater percentage of the population; this in turn led to a significant increase in the number of substance abuse treatment programs. After initially operating as separate entities, alcohol treatment and drug treatment services combined at both the public and private level in favor of substance abuse treatment that serviced both populations. With this change came further professionalization of the field.

Finally, the development of *managed care* as a means of controlling rising health care costs led to a shift from inpatient hospital treatment to outpatient services as the treatment setting most frequently authorized and approved by insurance carriers. Each of these factors has a significant impact on how human service professionals provide substance abuse treatment today (White, 1998). Before examining the various treatment settings available today, it is important to understand the scope of the problem, the professional vocabulary used to define the problem, and the ongoing effect that societal attitudes and perceptions have on the availability and utilization of services.

Demographics, Prevalence, and Usage Patterns

Over the years that I have worked in addiction treatment, I have spoken to many community groups. I often begin by asking them to describe to me their picture of an alcoholic or a person addicted to drugs. There is always a wide range of responses. As we begin, someone will usually mention the man on skid row, drinking out of a bottle concealed in a brown paper bag. Others think of the image of a "drug bust" on a television crime show, police breaking down the door as the people inside scramble to flush drugs down the toilet. As the discussion progresses, some brave soul will bring the examples closer to home. They may say "I remember my father, drunk and passed out on the couch every night," or "My favorite aunt is in detox right now . . . I've lost count of how many times she's been there." The next person may add, "My brother is in jail right now for drug possession," or "I've been in AA for 5 years now." Invariably, what begins as a discussion that focuses on someone else's problems "out there" in society becomes personal to the group. When I have this same discussion with students, they are often surprised to realize how many of their classmates' lives are affected by substance abuse.

Although it is certainly true that substance abuse is a problem that exists within all levels of society, it is usually this type of facilitated discussion that brings home this very point. As you continue to read this chapter, I encourage you to consider how substance abuse affects your life at both the personal and professional level. Because of the prevalence of the problem, and because each person with a substance abuse problem affects the lives of the people around them, most can identify a direct link to this issue.

SAMHSA, a division within the Department of Health and Human Services (DHHS), conducts an annual survey on the prevalence of substance use in the United States and the problems associated with that use. In 2003, an estimated 119 million North Americans (12 years of age or older) were current drinkers of alcohol. This represents approximately one-half of the population. About 54 million (22.6 percent of the population) had engaged in **binge drinking.** Of these, 16.1 million (6.8 percent of the population) also met the criteria for **heavy drinking.** During the same period, an estimated 19.5 million Americans (8.2 percent of the population over age 12) were current users of illicit drugs. Marijuana was the most commonly used illicit drug, followed by psychotherapeutics (nonmedical use of prescription drugs), cocaine, hallucinogens, and inhalants (SAMHSA, 2004).

The 2003 *National Survey on Drug Use and Health* estimated that 9.1 percent of Americans aged 12 and older (21.6 million persons) met the criteria for either substance abuse or dependence. The largest group (14.8 million) either abused or was dependent on alcohol but not illicit drugs. The remainder either abused or was dependent on illicit drugs alone or in combination with alcohol. During that same year, an estimated 3.3 million people received some type of treatment for the problems they experienced as a result of their drug and/or alcohol use (SAMHSA, 2004).

What do these numbers mean to the human service professional? At a minimum, they alert us to the reality that a significant number of the clients with whom we work in any practice setting already have a **primary substance abuse problem** with illicit drugs or alcohol and that many others are using alcohol in a way that may complicate their current problems and affect their ability to utilize or benefit from any services we may offer to them. These statistics also reinforce the need for all human service professionals to have a working knowledge of addictions so that they can accurately assess the needs of their clients.

The consequences of drug and alcohol abuse in the United States are enormously costly. Although the costs can be evaluated in dollars, they are more readily understood in human terms: family discord, neglect of children, personal misery, financial straits, medical problems, fetal alcohol syndrome, HIV infection, lower work productivity, and job loss—and the list goes on. Combating and reducing the source of these problems have proven to be difficult indeed, but one of the most straightforward and least controversial ways is to provide effective treatment to drug abusers (Boren, Onken, & Carroll, 2000, p. 1).

Defining Terms and Concepts

Thus far, we have used the terms *substance use, substance abuse,* and *alcoholism* in a general way, without providing detailed definitions. It is important to understand how these terms are understood in the professional community. As noted earlier, during much of the twentieth century, treatment for alcohol problems was conducted separately from treatment for problems with other drugs (White, 1998). The term *alcoholism* came into common use with the acceptance of the medical model and the understanding of alcoholism as a disease. The National Council on Alcoholism and Drug Dependence (1990) provides this definition:

> Alcoholism is a primary, chronic disease with genetic, psychosocial, and environmental factors influencing its development and manifestations. The disease is often progressive and fatal. It is characterized by continuous or periodic impaired control over drinking, preoccupation with the drug alcohol, use of alcohol despite adverse consequences, and distortions in thinking, most notably denial. (p. 1)

Note that this definition provides a list of symptoms that characterize the disease and potential outcome if left untreated.

Gradually, during the second half of the twentieth century, the treatment community focused less on the differences between alcohol abuse and that of other drugs and more on the similarities that existed between them. Most treatment programs are now designed to meet the needs of clients with alcohol and/or other drug problems. Currently, treatment professionals use the broad term of *substance abuse disorders,* with many subtypes of the disorder depending on the substance being used. In keeping with the medical model, these disorders are defined in the Diagnostic and Statistical Manual (DSM-IV-TR) of the American Psychiatric Association.

In general terms, individuals are described as abusing a substance when they continue to use the substance despite experiencing negative consequences from their use. These negative consequences can include health problems; difficulties in their family, work, and social life; and financial and legal problems. They are said to be *dependent* on the substance when, in addition to these negative consequences, they build **tolerance** and experience **withdrawal** if they stop using the drug. Tolerance occurs when a person's body has become accustomed to the drug and thus needs to use more in an attempt either to regain the pleasurable effects of the drug or merely to feel normal. Withdrawal symptoms occur when a person has become physically dependent, meaning that if they stop using the drug, their body will experience uncomfortable symptoms.

These symptoms vary depending on the nature of the drug use. If a person has been using a central nervous system depressant, such as alcohol or tranquilizers, they will experience symptoms associated with their central nervous system speeding up when they stop their use. These symptoms typically include anxiety and agitation, but may be severe enough to cause grand mal seizures. Conversely, if a person has been using a central nervous system stimulant such as cocaine or amphetamines, they will likely experience a "crash" of exhaustion and depression when drugs are withdrawn. In severe cases this can include suicidal thoughts and behaviors. The range of severity of withdrawal symptoms varies with the individual and with the amount of use. It is important to note that the withdrawal experienced from some drugs can be life threatening and therefore require medical supervision (Inaba & Cohen, 2004). For these reasons, addiction treatment programs must include appropriate medical professionals, either on their direct staff or available for consultation.

Theoretical Models of Use and Abuse

Although it might be ideal to present a single theoretical model that explains the nature of addictions and how they should be treated, no such model currently exists. In fact, there continues to be significant controversy over the best way to understand and to treat addictions. There are also significant advances in the knowledge of how the brain works and responds to drugs that inform and modify current treatment models.

Throughout history, there have been many theoretical models for understanding the nature and cause of substance abuse and addiction. For thousands of years, addiction was primarily seen as the result of an individual's moral failure. More recently, theories have been developed that incorporate new knowledge from psychology, biology, and medicine. Inaba and Cohen (2004) identified three prevalent models of understanding addiction: the Addictive Disease Model (also known as the medical model), which focuses on the influence of heredity; the Behavioral/Environmental Model, which focuses on the influences of environment and behavior; and the Academic Model, which focuses on the physiological effects of psychoactive drugs.

- ▶ *Addictive Disease Model:* We have already introduced the medical model and the related "disease concept" of addiction. Disease is defined as impairment of health or a condition of abnormal functioning. This model stresses that addiction, like other diseases, has identifiable symptoms, a predictable course, and a likely outcome if left untreated; it further understands that genetic influences may result in a predisposition, making the development of the disease more likely. "The "medical model" maintains that the disease of addiction is a chronic, progressive, relapsing, incurable, and potentially fatal condition that is mostly a consequence of genetic irregularities in brain chemistry and anatomy that may be activated by the particular drugs that are abused" (Inaba & Cohen, 2004, p. 67).

- ▶ *Behavioral/Environmental Model:* This developmental model describes the possible progression of substance use through six stages:

- Abstinence, meaning no use of alcohol or drugs
- Experimentation, marked by curiosity that leads to limited use
- Social/recreational use, marked by seeking out drugs/alcohol in these settings
- Habituation, meaning repeated use without negative consequences
- Abuse, defined as continued use despite negative consequences
- Addiction, meaning abuse plus the presence of tolerance and withdrawal

This model examines how factors in a person's environment, such as peer pressure or easy access to drugs, can foster the progression from one level to the next. Although abstinence is the only stage that can be seen as "risk free," note that it is not until one reaches the stages of abuse and addiction that the hallmark behaviors of continuing to use despite negative consequences, obsession with drug taking, and loss of control are seen (Inaba & Cohen, 2004).

▶ *Academic Model:* This model understands addiction from the standpoint of the changes that occur in a person's body over time as they use drugs. These changes occur at the cellular level and result in the development of *tolerance,* meaning that as the person becomes resistant to the drug's effects, they will need increasing amounts of the drug to achieve the desired effects. *Tissue dependence* occurs when the body has become so accustomed to the drug that it needs the drug "to feel normal." Even where tissue dependence does not occur, the memory of the pleasurable effects of the drug and the ongoing desire for that feeling may result in *psychological dependence.* If use is interrupted, the person may experience uncomfortable physical and psychological symptoms known as *withdrawal;* the fear and dread of withdrawal symptoms plays a major role in the addict continuing to use (Inaba & Cohen, 2004).

Inaba & Cohen (2004) propose that it is actually an integration of these models that best explains the predisposition and process by which addiction develops over the course of one's life. Each provides a type of lens through which an individual's substance abuse problem can be understood and solutions explored; they do not need to be seen as mutually exclusive.

Consider the adjacent case example about Jack in Case Study 10.1.

case study 10.1

Case Example of an Alcoholic

Jack is a 45-year-old married man with two teenage daughters. Jack is the manager of a busy restaurant located in a shopping mall. Over many years, Jack has developed a pattern of eating his lunch in the restaurant's bar in the quieter time between the busy lunch and dinner hours. He initially drank a beer with lunch, but that has increased to three or four beers over the years. He finds that he looks for opportunities to offer a drink to a regular customer and has another drink along with them. After the dinner rush, he will sit at the bar and have several more drinks as his employees do the cleaning before he locks up for the night. Jack is aware that many of his food servers use speed (amphetamines) to get through a busy shift, and he finds that he is doing this more and more himself. When he uses speed, he finds he needs to have a few extra drinks so that he can fall asleep at night. Because he still sleeps poorly, he increasingly needs the speed to get going the next day. The employees, who used to be happy to give him speed once in a while, now want him to pay for those pills, creating some financial problems. Jack is starting to feel uncomfortable that his employees know about his use and worries that it undermines his authority with them. Because Jack is drinking more, he is getting home later and is less involved with his family. Initially this caused arguments, but his wife and daughters have grown accustomed to his being either at work or passed out on the couch. They have learned to plan their life without much involvement from Jack. ■

Given the progressive nature of his use, Jack is now likely to experience some of the many predictable problems that could bring him into contact with a human service professional. Jack is a likely candidate for getting fired when the owner learns about his drug and alcohol use at work, for a drunk driving arrest, for escalating family problems, or for a major health problem such as a heart attack. Any of these events could create a crisis for Jack and his family that could lead to their entering substance abuse treatment.

Jack's problem would be understood somewhat differently depending on the theoretical model held by the treatment professional assessing it. Those working from the addictive disease model would identify factors that predispose Jack for substance abuse, such as a family history of alcoholism and a work environment with easy access to drugs. They would see his increasing sleep problems, financial problems, and family tension as symptoms of an escalating disease. Those working from the behavioral/environmental model would trace how Jack's use has progressed from habitual use to abuse and likely addiction. The academic model would explain how Jack's body has developed tolerance for alcohol, needing more drinks to achieve the same results, and how Jack has begun to attempt to counteract the negative depressant effects of alcohol with stimulants. No matter which model seems most helpful to the human service professional in understanding his use, it is clear that each model provides some relevant information in conceptualizing Jack's problem. Conceptual models such as these also assist in treatment planning. If, instead of considering Jack, we examined the history of a 15-year-old cheerleader who is using speed to lose weight and is partying on the weekends or a 30-year-old homeless veteran addicted to heroin since returning from the war, we would find both similarities and differences in their substance abuse that would inform the type of treatment they need.

Types of Substances Abused

Many categories of drugs are subject to abuse because they create effects that are desirable, at least to some users. Because the psychoactive qualities of drugs differ, different people find different drugs attractive. It is extremely important that human service professionals understand the effects of these drugs, so that they are able to recognize the signs of substance use in their clients as well as to understand how they may affect how their clients perceive and utilize services. Inaba and Cohen (2004) defined a psychoactive drug as "any substance that directly alters the normal functioning of the central nervous system" (p. 32) and divided psychoactive drugs into these three broad categories.

Uppers are central nervous stimulants, increasing chemical and electrical activity. Drugs in this category include cocaine, amphetamines (such as methamphetamine), caffeine, and nicotine. Note that this category includes both legal and illicit drugs. Some of the reasons people are drawn to the use of stimulants are to increase attention and energy, to suppress appetite, and to feel more confident. These effects are the result of the forced release of the brain's "energy chemicals": norepinephrine and epinephrine, two neurotransmitters. Because tolerance builds rapidly with stimulant drugs, abuse and addiction can develop quickly.

Many physical and psychological problems are associated with the abuse of central nervous system stimulants. The depletion and imbalance of neurotransmitters can lead to depression, paranoia, and psychosis. The ongoing speeding up of the central nervous system (without time to recover) may result in insomnia and the problems associated with lack of sleep, cardiovascular problems, and weight loss. In fact, with the use of stronger stimulants, the brain "does not signal the need for food, drink, or sexual stimulation, resulting in malnutrition, dehydration, or a reduced sex drive" (Inaba & Cohen, 2004, p. 131). The increasing prevalence of methamphetamine use has brought public attention to the additional dangers posed to children when their "meth"-abusing parents neglect their needs or place them at risk by creating in-home meth labs; responding to these forms of child endangerment create challenges for human service agencies.

Downers are central nervous system depressants, slowing down its overall functioning. Depressant drugs include pain killers (such as morphine, Darvon, Demerol, Vicodin, OxyContin), sedative-hypnotics (such as Valium, Xanax, seconal), and alcohol (beer, wine, hard liquor). Depressants slow heart rate and respiration, relax muscles, dull the senses, diminish pain, and induce sleep. Because they depress or lower inhibitions, the initial effect of these drugs may seem like a stimulant; someone who is drinking alcohol may feel increasingly social or sexually disinhibited, however the long-term effect is that of a depressant. As with the stimulants, tolerance builds with repeated use. As a person needs more of the drug to feel high, they experience more of the negative side effects of the drug: loss of coordination, impaired judgment, memory problems, and the development of physical dependence.

All-Arounders is the term used by Inaba and Cohen to describe psychedelics. This category includes marijuana, LSD, PCP, MDMA (Ecstasy), and mescaline. Hallucinogens distort sensory perceptions and can create altered or intensified sense of sight, touch, and hearing. Users may experience auditory and visual hallucinations or distorted thinking (delusions). Side effects from hallucinogens vary, but include increased appetite and respiratory damage (with marijuana); "bad trips" and flashbacks (with LSD); and increased blood pressure, amnesia, and combativeness (with PCP). Because these drugs are generally manufactured and processed illegally, users run the risk of taking stronger doses than anticipated or even getting a different drug than anticipated. These drugs may present even greater risks for individuals with preexisting mental disorders (Inaba & Cohen, 2004).

Other drugs commonly abused include inhalants (such as glue, metallic paints, and nitrous oxide) and anabolic steroids and other "performance-enhancing" drugs. All these drugs are associated with serious heath consequences that can be life threatening. Table 10.1 includes a breakdown of types of illicit drugs used over a lifetime, indicating that marijuana is the most commonly abused illicit drug.

Abuse of Prescription Drugs

A growing area of concern in the United States is the abuse of prescription drugs. Much media attention has been given to the problem of "street sales" of such drugs as the painkiller OxyContin, drugs used to treat anxiety such as Valium and Xanax, and those used to treat ADHD, such as Ritalin. Drug addicts have long attempted to deceive and manipulate physicians into giving them prescriptions for pain medication and tranquillizers by creating or exaggerating symptoms or by altering the number of pills authorized on the prescription form. The National Center on Addiction and Substance Abuse at Columbia University (CASA, 2005) conducted a three-year study of the abuse and diversion of prescription medications including opiods, central nervous system stimulants and depressants, and steroids. The study found that from 1992 to 2003, the number of Americans who abuse controlled prescription drugs had nearly doubled from 7.8 million to 15.1 million. Nearly one-half of physicians surveyed reported that patients commonly try to pressure them into prescribing controlled drugs. CASA places these figures in the context of the widespread acceptance of the use of prescription medication in the United States in general and the growing acceptance of the use of psychotropic medications.

Problems with prescription drugs include those who intentionally abuse and those who inadvertently become addicted to legally prescribed medication. The CASA study suggests that this is a problem that has not been adequately addressed. In assessing for substance abuse problems, human service professionals are therefore encouraged to explore use of prescription drugs with their clients in addition to their use of any "street drugs."

■ Table 10.1 Types of Illicit Drug Use in Lifetime, Past Year, and Past Month among Persons Aged 12 or Older: Numbers in Thousands, 2003 and 2004

Drug	Time Period					
	Lifetime		Past Year		Past Month	
	2003	2004	2003	2004	2003	2004
ILLICIT DRUG[c]	110,205	110,057	34,993	34,807	19,470	19,071
Marijuana and Hashish	96,611	96,772	25,231	25,451	14,638	14,576[b]
Cocaine	34,891	34,153	5,908	5,658	2,281	2,021
Crack	7,949	7,840	1,406	1,304	604	467
Heroin	3,744[a]	3,145	314	398	119	166
Hallucinogens	34,363	34,333	3,936	3,878	1,042	929
LSD	24,424	23,398	558	592	133	141
PCP	7,107	6,762	219	210	56	49
Ecstasy	10,904	11,130	2,119	1,915	470	450
Inhalants	22,995	22,798	2,075	2,255	570	638
Nonmedical Use of Psychotherapeutics[d]	47,882	48,013	14,986	14,643	6,336	6,007
Pain Relievers	31,207	31,768	11,671	11,256	4,693	4,404
OxyContin®	2,832	3,072	—	1,213	—	325
Tranquilizers	20,220	19,852	5,051	5,068	1,830	1,616
Stimulants	20,798	19,982	2,751	2,918	1,191	1,189
Methamphetamine	12,303	11,726	1,315	1,440	607	583
Sedatives	9,510	9,891	831	737	294	265
ILLICIT DRUG OTHER THAN MARIJUANA[*]	71,128	70,657	20,305	19,658	8,849	8,247

[*]Low precision; no estimate reported.

—Not available.

[a]Difference between estimate and 2004 estimate is statistically significant at the 0.05 level.

[b]Difference between estimate and 2004 estimate is statistically significant at the 0.01 level.

[c]Illicit Drugs include marijuana/hashish, cocaine (including crack), heroin, hallucinogens, inhalants, or prescription-type psychotherapeutics used nonmedically. Illicit Drugs Other Than Marijuana include cocaine (including crack), heroin, hallucinogens, inhalants, or prescription-type psychotherapeutics used nonmedically.

[d]Nonmedical use of prescription-type pain relievers, tranquilizers, stimulants, or sedatives; does not include over-the-counter drugs.

Source: SAMHSA, Office of Applied Studies, National Survey on Drug Use and Health, 2003 and 2004. (http://oas.samhsa.gov/nsduh/2k4nsduh/2k4tabs/Sect1peTabs1to66.htm#tab1.1a)

Common Clinical Issues and the Role of the Human Service Professional

The Presence of Substance Abuse Across All Practice Settings

Although some human service professionals might assert that they have no interest in working with individuals who have substance abuse problems, it is important to note that, because alcohol and drug abuse are so prevalent in the United States, it is virtually impossible to entirely avoid working with this issue.

Many human service professionals do not begin their careers with the intention of specializing in substance abuse, but quickly encounter the issue in the lives of their clients. I began my career over 30 years ago in a county public assistance office. I soon realized that many of the clients applying for General Relief were alcoholics whose long-term use of alcohol had led to loss of employment, family, and health. When I worked in hospital settings, I again found that many of the patients needing treatment were suffering from conditions that resulted from or were complicated by their use of alcohol or other drugs. I later chose to work directly in substance abuse treatment programs, eventually providing treatment in outpatient, residential, inpatient, and partial hospitalization settings with substance abusing clients and their families.

Acceptance of Problem

One of the most common clinical issues human service professionals must address with substance abusing clients is helping the client acknowledge that the substance abuse is in fact a problem. It can be perplexing for a professional to listen to clients describe various incidents occurring in their lives that clearly seem to be negative consequences of their substance abuse yet know that the client is either unable or unwilling to make that connection. Such clients may forcefully maintain that their problems have nothing to do with the substance use. Clients may describe, for example, a recurrent pattern of getting drunk (or high), followed by getting into fights with their spouse. They may even acknowledge that the fights only happen when they are using drugs, yet they still maintain that there is no connection between the two. Clients who have lost relationships, jobs, and money because of their use may still defend their alcohol or drug consumption, asserting that "with all the problems I have right now, it is the only thing that is keeping me going . . . the only friend I have left."

This *denial* of the problem is more than a psychological defense mechanism. It reflects the learned experience of most substance abusers that, at the outset of their use, the substance was giving them positive effects. A common phrase in treatment programs is *what starts out as the solution becomes the problem.* In other words, the drinking that initially provided a mild relaxation of inhibitions to feel more relaxed and

sociable at a party now with increased use results in inappropriate and aggressive behavior at the party. Hence, the solution has now become the problem, but the person
using the substance is often the last to recognize this reality; they have learned to believe
that it is the solution to their problems and are resistant to changing this belief. An additional consideration is that the psychoactive nature of the substance being used alters
the user's thoughts and perceptions in ways that may hinder their recognition of the
problem. Human service professionals who understand this dynamic are less likely to become frustrated with their client's statements and thus are more likely to be effective in
their attempts to help the client accept their problem. Figure 10.1 provides a comparison of those who perceived that they had the need for substance abuse treatment versus those who actually entered a treatment program. This graphic clearly indicates the
tendency of those suffering from substance abuse problems to avoid seeking treatment.

Hitting Bottom

Traditionally, addiction treatment professionals have thought it necessary for those addicted to drugs or alcohol to "hit bottom" before they recognize their problem and the
need for treatment. Although some individuals were described as having a "high bottom"

■ **Figure 10.1** Perceived Need and Effort Made to Receive Substance
Abuse Treatment

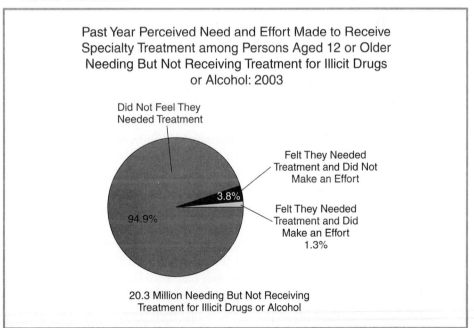

Source: Young, K. (2005). National Center on Substance Abuse and Child Welfare (www.ncsaw.samsha.gov).

because they reached this point of recognition with relatively minor consequences such as spilling a drink on an expensive rug or one relatively minor verbal outburst, the common wisdom was that substance abusers could not be helped until they were ready to help themselves. Hitting bottom was seen as the starting point, much to the dismay of concerned family members, friends, and employers who were tired of waiting for this recognition to occur because from their perspective, their loved one "hit bottom" long ago.

Clinical Interventions

There have, however, been many approaches utilized to help the substance abuser "hit bottom" more quickly. Those expressing concern for the substance abuser have been advised by treatment professionals to "stop enabling" and to instead allow the individual to suffer the natural consequences of their use. They are advised not to "call in sick" for the person when they are hungover, not to put them to bed when they pass out, and not to bail them out of jail. Friends and family members are advised that although these "enabling behaviors" are well intended, they actually help the substance abuser to continue to deny or minimize their problem. If, instead of waking up in bed, the drinker wakes up on the front lawn in full view of the neighbors, they experience the negative consequences of their drinking rather than having to trust the description provided by their spouse the next morning. They are less likely to believe that their spouse is "just exaggerating" or lying about events that they may be unable to remember.

This, of course, creates true dilemmas for family members. Allowing a loved one to wake up on the front lawn, lose a job, or remain in jail may lead to serious consequences for the individual as well as the family as a whole. Human service professionals can help concerned family members and friends to identify their options and to think through the implications of the actions they take. Clinicians who are able to listen nonjudgmentally and communicate their understanding of the difficulty of the decisions to be made are more likely to be truly effective in this helper role.

Among the options available to families seeking help are *interventions*. Formal interventions were first described by Dr. Vernon Johnson, a pioneer in alcohol treatment, in his 1973 book *I'll Quit Tomorrow*. Although many variations have been developed in addition to the original Johnson model, interventions typically bring together all the concerned individuals in a substance abuser's life to confront them with the negative consequences of their use. They meet as a group, joined by an intervention specialist, and share ways that their own lives have been negatively affected by the substance abuser's use and rehearse ways to present this information to the substance abuser in the hopes of breaking down their denial. They then meet with the substance abuser to share their concerns and encourage the person to enter treatment, often immediately after the meeting. The goal is to precipitate a crisis that will result in change. Styles for conducting interventions vary from collaborative to highly confrontational. Interventions have sometimes been subject to criticisms of conflict of interest when the intervention specialist is part of the staff at a treatment facility where the person is being encouraged to enter treatment.

Motivational Interviewing

Another common way to help the substance abuser recognize their need for treatment is through the use of motivational interviewing. This approach differs from methods that use confrontation or coercion to attempt to engage a substance abuser in treatment. As defined by Rollnick and Miller (1995), "Motivational interviewing is a directive, client-centered counseling style for eliciting behavior change by helping clients to explore and resolve ambivalence." Read (1999) explained that, in creating a safe atmosphere, motivational interviewing allows an individual to examine both the positive and negative aspects of changing their current behaviors. This approach acknowledges that it is normal for a person to have "mixed feelings" about change and invites them to explore all sides of their ambivalence. In recognizing the cost that they pay for maintaining their substance use, individuals may become more likely to willingly choose to make a change.

Motivational interviewing (and the related motivational enhancement therapy) stresses that people vary in how ready they are to make changes. Drawing on the work of Prochaska, DiClemente, and Norcross, an individual's willingness to change is understood as occurring in stages: *precontemplation, contemplation, determination,* and *action* (Miller, 2000). Although not limited to use in substance abuse, it is seen as a helpful model that allows the human service professional to build an alliance with the client toward change. *Precontemplation,* as the name implies, is the stage a person is in before they ever give any thought to the need to change their behavior (although it may be clear to others that a problem exists). If a family member or clinician tries to convince a person at this stage that they should take *action,* such as stopping their substance use or entering a treatment program, it is not likely that the suggestion will be positively received or even make sense to the person. Instead, the human service professional would focus their efforts on assisting the person to become more ready to change by exploring with them the impact of their use. As the person explores what they see as both the positive and negative aspects of their use, they may begin to *contemplate* a need for change. The clinician may help the client look at various ways to solve the problems associated with their use, increasing their *determination* to make a change. Persons who have reached these higher levels of readiness to change are more likely to respond positively to treatment suggestions made by the human service professional.

In discussing the relative popularity of these different approaches to dealing with the client's denial among treatment professionals, White (1998) described "four overlapping stages in its view of the role of addict motivation in addiction recovery"

(p. 291). He sees an evolution over the second half of the twentieth century from a "baseline position" that one must first hit bottom before they are willing to change, to a focus on teaching those in the substance abuser's life to stop "rescuing" and allow them to experience the consequences of their behavior (so that they can hit bottom), to a focus on "raising the bottom" through formal intervention. These three stages share an emphasis on increasing pain as a motivation to enter treatment. White believes that the treatment community is currently more accepting of the idea that for some substance abusers it is not an absence of pain, but rather a lack of hope that change is possible that keeps them from entering treatment. This has lead to more treatment programs providing "pretreatment" services that assist clients in becoming more ready for change, as described earlier. Here human service professionals may utilize their clinical skills to assist the client in this stage of the process.

Cultural Sensitivity

As with all areas of human services, gender and culture play a significant role in an individual's perception of a problem and their attitude about receiving help. It has long been recognized that different cultures have different patterns of alcohol and drug use. For example, among Western cultures, those that socialize children to drink responsibly by establishing patterns of when and where to drink, while at the same time discouraging drunkenness, tend to have lower rates of alcohol abuse than those that forbid their drinking altogether (Vaillant, 1995).

Yet, current research stresses the difficulty of describing any cultural group as fitting a stereotyped pattern of use. Caetano, Clark, and Tam (1998) found that ethnic minorities are underrepresented in alcohol research in the United States and that existing studies often fail to take into consideration the differences that exist between subgroups within a given cultural group. It is therefore wise to assess cultural attitudes with each client and avoid assuming that stereotypes apply. Because clients may well feel loyal to their culture, clinicians need to listen nonjudgmentally to the information shared by their clients. Cultural sensitivity also involves the practitioner being aware of how their own attitudes and beliefs have been influenced by their cultural background (Corey, 2005).

Human service professionals are routinely encouraged to consider those things that might present obstacles to their clients receiving help. It is important to keep in mind that even the concept of seeking professional help outside one's family reflects a Western worldview that is open to the idea that outsiders are appropriate sources of assistance. Many cultures reject the focus on the individual or the belief that it is helpful to share one's feelings, a theme that is central to professional counseling. Given the prevalence of group forms of therapy, this may be particularly difficult in substance abuse treatment and calls for sensitivity and understanding on the part of the treatment staff. Clients who have difficulty sharing feelings with members of the opposite sex, looking directly at another group member when they speak to them, or confronting an older group member may be reflecting their cultural norms rather than resistance (Corey & Corey, 2006).

Defining Treatment Goals

Abstinence

In most treatment programs utilizing the medical model, abstinence is seen as the necessary first step in treatment. This means that the person commits to completely eliminating the use of alcohol and all illicit drugs; in some programs this includes eliminating even medically prescribed psychoactive drugs and pain medication. Abstinence is seen as the necessary beginning point before other problems can be accurately assessed and addressed. It is not, however, generally seen as the only goal of treatment.

Harm Reduction

Although abstinence is the goal in most treatment programs, some argue that harm reduction may also be an appropriate goal (Inaba & Cohen, 2004). Harm reduction can include a variety of goals designed to limit the negative consequences (for both the individual and society) of substance use for those unwilling or unable to achieve abstinence. Those who favor harm reduction may see abstinence as the eventual goal, but believe that it may be appropriate to first focus on smaller/intermediate goals such as using less-dangerous drugs, decreasing the frequency or quantity of drug use, or limiting the health risks associated with drug use. For example, those who argue for needle exchange programs (for intravenous drug users) to reduce the transmission of AIDS base their position on the concept of harm reduction. As both a public policy issue and a treatment philosophy, harm reduction continues to be very controversial.

This approach is more likely to be advocated by programs working with clients dealing with other problems in addition to their substance abuse disorder such as homelessness or mental illness. Advocates for harm reduction argue that clients must overcome many obstacles to enter treatment, and that if a person is required to be abstinent prior to entering a treatment program, they may never do so. They draw the parallel that doctors do not ask patients with other illnesses to eliminate their symptoms before they can be treated, but that treatment programs often require some period of abstinence before a person can enter their program. Like motivational interviewing, harm reduction approaches favor "meeting people where they are," not where we would like them to be.

Mode of Service Delivery

Availability of Treatment

SAMSHA (2005) lists over 11,000 addiction treatment programs on its online re-source directory, including outpatient, residential, hospital inpatient, and partial hos-pitalization/day treatment programs. The services provided by these programs include rehabilitation, counseling, behavioral therapy, medication, and case management (NIDA, 1999). In order to be included in the directory, programs must be approved by the substance abuse agency for the state in which they are located. Also included are those programs administered by Department of Veterans Affairs, the Indian Health Service, and the Department of Defense. From the earliest days of treatment in the United States, addiction treatment has been funded by both public (government) and private sources (payment by private insurers, out-of-pocket payment by the person re-ceiving treatment, or by charitable sources).

Public Programs

Federal and state governments currently provide the majority of funding for sub-stance abuse programs. Although this is a source of ongoing public policy debate, there has been a general consensus that money invested in providing substance abuse treatment is well spent. One study found that for every dollar spent on substance abuse treatment, seven dollars are saved in reduced health care, crime, lost productivity, and the like. Studies have also established that it is significantly less expensive to pro-vide treatment to a substance abuser than to incarcerate them. However in an era where all levels of government face increasing budget deficits, providing treatment funds despite the benefits continues to be controversial (Scanlon, 2002).

Private Programs

Even those individuals who have health insurance that provides coverage for sub-stance abuse treatment are likely to find that their insurance plans provide strict guide-lines that limit how they can utilize their benefits. Beginning in the late 1980s, in an effort to control rising health-care costs, employers increasingly opted for offering managed behavioral health (mental health and substance abuse) care as a part of their group health insurance plans.

The American Society of Addiction Medicine (1999) issued a report on the im-pact of *managed care* on addiction treatment in the United States. Their study, con-ducted by the Hay Group, found that from 1988 to 1998, the value of insurance coverage for addiction treatment had declined by 75 percent for employees who par-ticipated in group health plans offered by mid- to large-size companies. During the same time period, the report found a much smaller decrease (11.5 percent) in the value of overall health insurance coverage. A major factor in the decrease of the value of addiction benefits comes from a reduction in the authorization of inpatient hospital treatment in favor of less-expensive outpatient treatment options.

For those working specifically in addiction treatment, it has often meant the loss of a job when their inpatient unit closed. In working with clients, it has meant becoming well versed in the criteria used by managed care companies. Human service professionals are often called on to provide referrals for their clients; clinicians who are able to provide direction to their clients in navigating the managed care system can be of great assistance to those needing to arrange for treatment. Many people still associate substance abuse treatment with the 30-day inpatient programs common in the 1980s. Because this is no longer a realistic option for most people, human service professionals need to be aware of other treatment options and should be familiar with the types of programs, both public and private, available locally to meet their client's needs.

Continuum of Care

The currently accepted goal is that communities provide a *continuum of care* so that individuals, groups, and families can receive the form of substance abuse treatment most appropriate for their needs. This concept acknowledges both that different people have different treatment needs, and that an individual person's needs vary over their course of treatment.

Prevention services are generally targeted to populations known to be at higher risk for substance abuse. Although it is possible for anyone to develop a substance abuse problem, the Center for Substance Abuse Prevention (2004) identifies six risk factors that may lead to substance abuse or addiction:

▶ Substance use by parents of other family members

▶ Substance use by peers and the perception that "everyone is doing it"

▶ Preadolescent use of alcohol, tobacco, or other drugs

▶ Being a victim of physical or sexual abuse

▶ Abusive or violent environment at home or in school

▶ Economic deprivation

Many well known prevention programs focus on providing youth with information about the risks associated with using drugs and alcohol and the skills to "just say no."

In addition to their role in providing services that help prevent substance abuse, human service professionals are often in a position to recognize warning signs of drug use in their clients. For example, school social workers should be alert to the possibility that a student's attendance problems, declining grades, poor physical appearance, or change of peer group may be an indication of substance use. Other behaviors that may be signs of substance use with clients in any practice setting include declining work performance, financial problems, dramatic mood changes, attempts to cover the smell of alcohol, always wearing sunglasses to hide dilated or constricted pupils, wearing long sleeves to hide needle marks, or stealing from family and friends (Hepworth, Rooney, & Larsen, 2002). Although any of these behaviors may be due to issues other than substance abuse, human service professionals should be alert to the possibility. It is often the recognition of these changes in behavior that lead concerned family members and friends to seek out assistance, initiating a request for assessment of the problem.

The skills needed to assess a substance abuse problem vary according to the clinical setting. For the human service professional in a practice setting outside substance abuse treatment, screening may be a part of the normal intake procedure. The agency's intake form may prompt the clinician to ask about current and past drug and alcohol use, family history of substance abuse, and any negative consequences associated with substance use. In some settings, this may be all that is indicated to screen for problems that may require additional referrals or may affect the client's ability to utilize services.

In agencies where the prevalence of substance abuse is more likely to be high, more extensive screening may be needed. For example, human service professionals in settings dealing with domestic violence, the homeless, or families at risk for child abuse may determine that even alcohol use that does not meet the DSM-IV-TR criteria for abuse might interfere with treatment efforts. Agencies may reasonably set policies that require clients to refrain from drinking alcohol prior to attending parenting classes, anger management sessions, or any other agency service. The intake clinician at a shelter for the homeless may need to have more sophisticated screening skills to determine if a client presenting for services can be safely housed in their program or instead needs a referral for detoxification.

Likewise, clinicians who deal directly with substance abusers need to be able to assess if a client is in need of medically supervised detoxification and, if so, whether it can be provided on an outpatient basis or requires hospitalization. Clinicians involved in this level of assessment would normally be part of a treatment team including immediate access to medical services. Here assessment would require not just the recognition of a problem, but the ability to refer to the appropriate level of treatment. Those skills needed to screen for a possible problem and initiate a referral for further assessment, and possible treatment would appropriately be considered part of *generalist* human services practice. The ability to assess or treat specific substance abuse problems would generally be considered a *specialist* skill requiring specific training.

Many assessment tools have been developed to assist clinicians and health-care providers in the assessment of substance abuse problems. The brief (four-item) CAGE Questionnaire and 25-question Michigan Alcoholism Screening Test are designed to identify the presence of negative consequences of alcohol use that may indicate a need for intervention. The more comprehensive Addiction Severity Index is more likely to be used in substance abuse specialty programs where it may be used as a part of treatment planning, outcome evaluation, or in conducting research. As previously described, diagnosis of substance abuse or dependence to the range of psychoactive drugs of abuse is performed according to criteria set forth in the DSM IV (Inaba & Cohen, 2004).

Treatment Modalities

Once an assessment is completed indicating that a problem exists, treatment options can be explored. Treatment of a substance abuse problem is a complex process that occurs in stages over a period of time. Recovery from substance abuse is often described as being *a process, not an event.* Depending on the treatment setting, staff may be drawn from a variety of disciplines with different levels of training. The multidisciplinary team may include psychiatrists and other medical doctors, nurses, psychologists, social workers, addiction counselors, family therapists, recreation therapists, occupational therapists, and chaplains. All members of the treatment team may assess the client and participate, along with the client, in developing treatment goals and plans.

The Role of the Human Services Professional

Human service professionals generally referred to as counselors working in substance abuse programs come from a wide range of experiences and training backgrounds. During the period of rapid growth of alcohol and drug treatment programs from the 1960s to the 1980s, few professionally trained counselors had specialty training in addiction treatment. In most programs, "frontline" counselors, who conducted much of the individual and group counseling, came to the field by way of personal experience in recovery; such counselors were often described as *paraprofessionals.* In some longer term residential settings, it was common for individuals to successfully graduate or "phase out" of treatment and return almost immediately as a member of the treatment team. This had the advantage of providing staff that knew the program, were dedicated to its mission, and were often willing to work for low wages.

Common problems arose if the counselors relapsed, had difficulty separating their own treatment experience from that of their clients, or became overwhelmed by the demands of attending to their own recovery while providing emotionally intense counseling for their clients. Making the transition from being a resident (or patient) in a program to being a counselor was generally not easy. There was considerable controversy as to whether personal recovery experience was a help or hindrance to working in the field (White, 1998). Over time, most programs developed policies to address the common problems that arose. For example, programs might require a graduate of their program to have a minimum of one to two years of sobriety after completing the program before they could be hired as an employee.

Many steps have been taken to advance the training of substance abuse counselors. Certificate programs were added to the curriculum of many community and four-year colleges that gave recovering individuals an opportunity to build on their life experience with academic and professional training. Specialty programs can prepare counselors who are themselves in recovery to deal with ethical issues that are unique to the field, such as how to manage interaction with one of their clients if they attend the same AA meeting (Bissell & Royce, 1994).

Other advances in the professionalization of the field are the development of standards for professional certification and the growth of professional organizations at the state and national level. At the same time, college programs (for human service professionals, marriage and family therapists, social workers, and psychologists) have added substance abuse training to their normal course of studies, as evidenced by the inclusion to this text of the chapter you are reading.

 ## Stages of Recovery

Many models have been developed that describe the process of recovery in terms of the stages one must complete to arrive at health. These incorporate basic understandings that problems that develop over a long period of time will take time to heal (in other words, "You didn't get sick in a day, you're not going to get well in a day either"). Here it is helpful to distinguish between the concepts of *abstinence* and *sobriety* as used in recovery. Terence Gorski (1989), a pioneer and leader in the area of relapse prevention, regards abstinence from mood-altering chemicals as "a necessary first step in learning what to do to get and stay healthy in all areas of life" (p. 4). Sobriety, as described by Gorski, involves more: "abstinence plus a return to full physical, psychological, social, and spiritual health" (p. 4). Recall that when an individual first begins to use a psychoactive substance, it is for them "a solution." Whether it provides the "liquid courage" to ask someone to dance, the energy to stay up all night to complete a paper or clean the house, or a means to feel accepted by one's peers, the substance used has provided some positive reinforcement for continued use.

When a person stops using the substance, at a minimum, they must determine what functions their use provided for them and how they will go about meeting these needs in healthier ways in the future. Often this journey will involve painful psychological work dealing with issues of past trauma or abuse. If, for example, a veteran has used painkillers as a way of numbing their memories of war, recovery will involve dealing with the emergence of these memories. For most clients, their substance use has led to multiple losses: often family, friends, jobs, and health. Grieving these losses is another significant treatment issue.

Most clients also become increasingly aware of the ways that their use has harmed others and must deal with the associated feelings of guilt and shame; this is often particularly painful work for parents who realize they have abused or neglected their children. The timing of this work requires sophisticated skill on the part of the counselor to decrease the likelihood of precipitating a relapse.

Relapse Prevention

Throughout the stages of treatment and recovery, counselors increasingly introduce the concept of *relapse prevention*. Although not limited to substance abuse treatment, relapse prevention draws on cognitive-behavioral strategies to help clients build skills to maintain abstinence and to address relapse should it occur (NIDA, 1999). Individuals are taught to recognize potential triggers for relapse such as being in neighborhoods where they once used, sights or smells associated with use, or experiencing difficult emotions. Counselors may help clients develop a list of coping strategies such as calling a friend, attending a support meeting, or "thinking through" the consequences if they should use. Clients may carry a list of such possible strategies with them in their wallet so that they will have to see the list if they try to buy a drink or drugs. Counselors also encourage clients to plan their response should they relapse. Rather than telling themselves that "I've blown it now, I'll never be able to stop," they are encouraged to tell themselves, "Get back to treatment." Clients are educated to understand that addiction is a disease prone to relapse, and they are encouraged to be active in their efforts to prevent relapse.

Common Treatment Settings

As previously noted, since the 1980s, there has been a shift away from inpatient treatment programs as the standard for care of substance abuse in favor of outpatient programs. In part, this has been the result of managed care efforts to control rising health-care costs. Others, however, argue for outpatient treatment on philosophical grounds. The choice of a treatment program is best made based on determining the individual needs of a specific client. However, it is important for human service professionals to familiarize themselves with all the types of programs generally available and with the specific resources available in their community. As you read about the various types of treatment programs, keep in mind that human service professionals are employed in each of these settings, generally providing the core treatment services of counseling and case management.

All treatment programs will begin by assessing the needs of the individual (or family) requesting treatment to determine if they are appropriate candidates for that program. In the event that the program is unable to provide the indicated treatment, or the client rejects the services offered, it is the ethical responsibility of the human service professional to provide the person seeking help with appropriate referrals. Most agencies keep up-to-date resource directories to aid in this process. SAMSHA maintains an online national directory of substance abuse programs; state and local directories are also available for most communities.

Detoxification Programs

As previously noted, clients who have become physically addicted to drugs or alcohol need detoxification for the medical management of their withdrawal. Although many substance abusers have withdrawn "cold turkey," this can be both uncomfortable and dangerous, depending on the drugs involved. Recall that addicts using "downer" drugs (such as alcohol, barbiturates, and tranquillizers) that depress the central nervous system will experience a speeding up of their nervous system when in withdrawal. This can result in life-threatening seizures and therefore requires medical supervision. Although "medically necessary detoxification" has been a common criterion for inpatient treatment, in most cases, this can be accomplished on an outpatient basis, a practice that is becoming more common.

Although detox is generally regarded as necessary before treatment can begin, some clients will seek detox as an end in itself, either as a way to find housing or to reduce their tolerance so that they can reduce the cost of their drug intake (Doweiko, 2006). In this setting, human service professionals play a key role in encouraging clients to remain in treatment despite the discomforts of withdrawal and the urges to leave and resume their substance abuse.

Inpatient Treatment Programs

Traditionally, the term *inpatient* was used to refer both to programs located in hospitals or free-standing programs (such as the Betty Ford Center) that were staffed to provide medical services, including detoxification. Inpatient units existed in both general hospitals and psychiatric hospitals. Although once common, the 30-day inpatient programs often associated with substance abuse treatment are now relatively rare. The treatment focus of these programs, however, continues to shape much of outpatient treatment that has become more common.

Most inpatient programs utilized what is known as the Minnesota Model of treatment, which has its roots in the 1940s and 1950s in three treatment programs in that state: Pioneer House, Hazelden, and Willmar State Hospital. Developing over time, a defining concept of the Minnesota Model was an understanding of addiction as a primary, progressive disease (rather than a symptom of other problems) that would be the focus of treatment, with lifetime abstinence as the goal. Seeing addiction as affecting all areas of a person's life, treatment was provided by a multidisciplinary team including doctors, nurses, psychologists, social workers, and clergy.

Recovered alcoholics were also part of the counseling staff. Each discipline completed an assessment of the patient, giving input into an overall treatment plan. The principles of Alcoholics Anonymous were incorporated into the treatment, and patients attended meetings as a part of their treatment program. Other treatment activities included educational lectures, group and individual counseling, family treatment, reading and written assignments, and informal discussions with other patients, which combined to make a highly structured program (White, 1998). Some programs offered specialized units for adolescents, "impaired professionals" (doctors and nurses), dually diagnosed patients who suffered from an additional mental illness, or for patients that wanted their treatment integrated with their faith (most commonly Christian). Although all these treatment activities and areas of specialization continue to be available, they are now more likely to be provided in an outpatient setting.

Partial Hospitalization Programs

Partial hospitalization allows patients to attend all the day activities provided at an inpatient program, while returning to their home to sleep. For patients who have a relatively stable home environment, this can allow them to integrate what they are learning in treatment into their family and home life. If problems arise at home, they can deal with it in treatment the next day. Because the costs are reduced, insurance companies may authorize more treatment days for partial hospitalization than for inpatient care.

Residential Treatment Programs

Although inpatient programs may also be referred to as residential, the distinction made here is that residential treatment is more likely to occur in a homelike setting, over a longer period of time, providing less medical care. Like hospital-based programs, residential programs provide 24-hour supervision so that the residents can focus on their treatment, free of the stresses and responsibilities of their outside life, and (at least theoretically) free of opportunities to use chemicals. Historically, residential programs (known as therapeutic communities) worked with drug addicts who had generally exhausted all resources. Many utilized a more confrontational approach designed to "tear down" the street image and "build up" a new, healthy identity. The resident's day was highly structured with active involvement in the needs of the house, such as cleaning and cooking, in addition to group and individual counseling. Over time, residents gave up their addict identity in favor of being a member of the program community, often referred to as family (NIDA, 1999, 2002). Human service professionals serve in all treatment roles in residential programs using titles such as case manager, counselor, clinical director, or program manager.

Some residential programs provide a "step-down" or transition from inpatient treatment or detox. In these programs, such as halfway houses or sober living facilities, residents experience living in a supportive community free of drugs and alcohol, but may continue their employment during the day. Residents are generally required to attend a set number of mutual aid meetings each week in addition to house meetings. The inclusion of additional on-site counseling, provided by human service professionals, varies from program to program.

Outpatient Treatment

Intensive outpatient treatment (IOT) provides community-based treatment for substance abuse. Programs vary in intensity, but include psychoeducational and therapeutic efforts such as lecture, group, and individual counseling and activities designed to enhance life skills. Programs vary in format, but generally involve the client in a minimum of 10 hours per week of treatment activities. To accomplish this, IOT uses many of the same principles as described for inpatient treatment including a multi-disciplinary treatment team and individualized treatment planning.

IOT has grown in popularity as inpatient treatment has become less common. In many ways, it bridges a gap between the 28-day medically managed programs once prevalent and the traditional outpatient counseling where the client was seen only once a week. In most programs, the number of hours a patient is involved in treatment decreases as their length of sobriety increases. Stepped-down aftercare services may be available for a year or longer. At this point, the client may be attending treatment services only once a week, in addition to their 12-step participation. Staffing for IOT increasingly includes licensed therapists along with other human service professionals.

Traditional outpatient counseling, where a client sees a counselor once a week, is likely to be inadequate for the client with a serious substance abuse problem. In the past, mental health counselors frequently attempted to provide such counseling, often treating the substance abuse as a symptom of underlying problems. It was the failure of this approach that birthed current addiction treatment. Today, educational programs that train human service professionals such as counselors, social workers, and psychologists should include training on recognizing substance abuse problems. At a minimum, clinicians should be aware that a client's substance abuse will severely affect their ability to participate in counseling and thus should consider referring their clients to appropriate substance abuse treatment.

Pharmacological Treatments

The use of medication to treat substance abuse and substance abusers has been a source of ongoing debate. Much of substance abuse treatment has been provided in "drug-free" programs, stressing the need for abstinence from all psychoactive substances, including medication prescribed for the treatment of psychiatric disorders such as antipsychotics and antidepressants. This meant that substance abusers with psychiatric disorders were often told that they were not appropriate candidates for substance abuse treatment programs.

Hospital-based inpatient programs were more likely to include psychiatric medications as part of treatment, but there was controversy even in those settings. Some argued that a substance abuser must be drug free for some period of time before being accurately diagnosed with a mental illness. Others maintained that providing medication for mental illness would serve to enhance the success of the substance abuse treatment. "Recent epidemiologic studies have shown that between 30 percent and 60 percent of drug abusers have concurrent mental health diagnoses including personality disorders, major depression, schizophrenia, and bipolar disorder" (Leshner, 1999, p. 1). Because the cooccurrence rate of substance abuse and mental disorders is high, there has been a growing emphasis on the importance of clinicians in both substance abuse and mental health treatment being aware of the special needs of *dual-diagnosis* patients who suffer from both disorders. Generally there has been increased acceptance of the need for psychiatric medication for these patients, although "drug-free" programs may still decide that they do not have the medical services available to accept such patients into their program.

Self-Help

Earlier in this chapter, we discussed the birth of Alcoholics Anonymous from the perspective of the history of addiction treatment. Now we will look further at AA and other 12-step programs (such as Narcotics Anonymous and Cocaine Anonymous) from the perspective of treatment. Twelve-step programs play a significant role in the treatment of addiction, both as a primary source of support and as an adjunct to professional treatment. Because they are free, well known, and widely available, self-help groups represent a major resource to human service professionals and their clients.

Twelve-step groups provide a setting in which members can share their "experience, strength, and hope" with other members. Although commonly referred to as self-help programs, the term *mutual aid society* may more accurately reflect the belief that one who suffers from addiction, but has received help, is in the best position to help a fellow sufferer. Providing this help to newcomers helps the older member to stay sober.

Family Involvement

Many substance abuse programs include a component for family participation such as a multifamily group, "family night," or separate groups for family members. These groups play a particularly important role in programs for adolescent substance abusers, where the need for family work is immediate. Support groups such as Alanon, Alateen, and Co-Dependents Anonymous also provide ongoing support for family members and friends. These groups help individuals to identify the ways in which their own life has become negatively affected by the substance abuse of another, and how to make healthy changes.

Commonly, family members come to understand that in focusing too much on the substance abuser, they have neglected taking care of themselves. Some behaviors that were intended to help the substance abuser, such as covering for them or taking over their responsibilities, may in fact have enabled the substance abuser to continue their use. Support groups for family members help them to determine clearer boundaries between "what my responsibility is and what it is not" and to make necessary changes in their own behavior. Typically family members come to realize that all attempts to control the substance abuser have been futile; that they only have the power to control their own actions. Family members can, therefore, benefit from treatment even if their chemically addicted member never participates in treatment.

Concluding Thoughts on Substance Abuse

The use and abuse of psychoactive substances has been present from the earliest known societies and continues to be a major health problem in the United States today. Efforts to address this problem in the United States have included legislation to regulate or prohibit the manufacture and sale of drugs and alcohol, prevention programs designed to decrease **risk factors** and increase **protective factors,** and treatment for those with substance abuse problems. These efforts have evolved over time, influenced by societal attitudes about substance abuse and, more recently, by scientific research.

Human service professionals play a major role in the provision of prevention and treatment services. Because substance abuse affects all areas of an individual's life, human service professionals will encounter this issue in every practice setting. Research has established that prevention and treatment are effective and is increasingly utilized in guiding program development and provision of treatment. In a variety of roles and settings, human service professionals can assist substance abusing clients in recognizing the negative affects of their use, in obtaining necessary treatment, as well as in working with them throughout the entire treatment process. Skilled human service professionals routinely find this practice setting both challenging and rewarding.

references

Abadinsky, H. (2004). *Drugs: An introduction* (5th ed.). Belmont, CA: Wadsworth.

Alcoholics Anonymous. (n.d.). *About A.A.* Retrieved September 28, 2005, from http://www .alcoholics-anonymous.org/default/en_about.cfm

American Psychiatric Association. (2000). *Diagnostic and statistical manual of mental disorders* (4th ed., Text Revision) (DSM-IV-TR). Washington, DC: American Psychiatric Association.

American Society of Addiction Medicine. (1999). *Employer health care dollars spent on addiction treatment.* Retrieved September 28, 2005, from http://www.asam.org/pressrel/hay.htm

Bissel, L., & Royce, J. E. (1994). *Ethics for addiction professionals* (2nd ed.). Center City, MN: Hazelden Foundation.

Boren, J. J., Onken, L. S., & Carroll, K. M. (Eds.). (2000). *Approaches to drug abuse counseling* (NIH Publication No. 00-4151). Bethesda, MD: National Institutes of Health.

Caetano, M. D., Clark, C. L., & Tam, T. (1998). Alcohol consumption among racial/ethnic minorities: Theory and research [Electronic version]. *Alcohol Health and Research World, 22(4),* 233–241.

Center for Substance Abuse Prevention. (2004). Risk factors for substance abuse. In *It won't happen to me: Substance abuse-related violence against women for anyone concerned about the issues (module 2).* Retrieved from http://pathwayscourses.samhsa.gov/vawc/vawc_2_pg6.htm

Center for Substance Abuse Treatment. (2004). *Substance abuse treatment and family therapy: A treatment improvement protocol* (DHHS Publication No. SMA 04-3957). Rockville, MD: Author.

Coffey, R. M., Mark, T., King, E., Harwood, H., McKusick, D., & Genuardi, J. (2000). *National estimates of expenditures for mental health and substance abuse treatment, 1997* (SAMHSA Publication No. SMA-00-3499). Rockville, MD: SAMHSA.

Corey, G. (2005). *Theory and practice of counseling and psychotherapy* (7th ed.). Pacific Grove, CA: Brooks/Cole Publishers.

Corey, M. S., & Corey, G. (2006). *Groups: Process and practice.* (7th ed). Thompson Brooks/Cole Publishing: Belmont, CA.

Doweiko, H. E. (2006). *Concepts of chemical dependency.* (6th ed.). Belmont, CA: Thompson Brooks/Cole.

Gorski, T. T. (1989). *Passages through recovery: An action plan for preventing relapse.* New York: Harper & Row.

Hepworth, D. H., Rooney, R. H., & Larsen, J. A. (2002). *Direct social work practice: Theory and skills* (6th ed.). Pacific Grove, CA: Brooks/Cole.

Inaba, D. S., & Cohen, W. E. (2004). *Uppers, downers, all arounders: Physical and mental effects of psychoactive drugs* (5th ed.). Ashland, OR: CNS Publications.

Johnson, V. E. (1980). *I'll quit tomorrow: A practical guide to alcoholism treatment* (Rev. ed.). New York: Harper & Row.

Leshner, A. I. (November, 1999). Drug abuse and mental disorders: Comorbidity is reality. In *National Institute on Drug Abuse, A collection of NIDA notes articles that address drug abuse treatment* (NIH Publication No. NN0026). Bethesda, MD: National Institutes of Health.

Miller, W. R. (2000). Motivational enhancement therapy: Description of counseling approach. In J. J. Boren, L. S. Onken, & K. M. Carroll (Eds.), *Approaches to drug abuse counseling* (NIH Publication No. 00-4151). Bethesda, MD: National Institutes of Health.

Musto, D. F. (1999). The impact of public attitudes on drug abuse research in the twentieth century. In M. D. Glantz & C. R. Hartel (Eds.), *Drug abuse: Origins and interventions* (pp. 63–78). Washington, DC: American Psychological Association.

National Center on Addiction and Substance Abuse at Columbia University. (1998, January 8). *CASA releases report: Behind bars.* Retrieved July 11, 2005 from http://66.135.34.236/absolutenm/templates/PressReleases.asp?articleid=167&zonid=49

National Center on Addiction and Substance Abuse at Columbia University. (2005). Abuse of prescription drugs: America's long history. In *Under the counter: The diversion and abuse of controlled prescription drugs in the U.S.* (chap. 2). Retrieved from http://www.casacolumbia.org/Absolutenm/articlefiles/380-final_report.pdf

National Council on Alcoholism and Drug Dependence. (1990). *Facts and information: Definition of alcoholism.* Retrieved June 27, 2005 from http://www.ncadd.org/facts/defalc.html

National Institute on Drug Abuse. (1999). *Principles of drug addiction treatment: A research-based guide* (NIH Publication No. 00-4180). Bethesda, MD: National Institutes of Health.

National Institute on Drug Abuse. (2002). *Research report series: Therapeutic community* (NIH Publication No. 02-4877). Bethesda, MD: National Institutes of Health.

National Institute on Drug Abuse. (2005). Prevention principles. In *Preventing drug abuse among children and adolescents.* Retrieved September 17, 2005 from http://www.nida.nih.gov/Prevention/principles.html

Office of National Drug Control Policy. (2004). *The economic costs of drug abuse in the U.S., 1992–2002.* Retrieved June 27, 2005, from http://www.whitehousedrugpolicy.gov/publications/economic_costs/economic_costs.pdf

Office of National Drug Control Policy. (2005). *The President's national drug control strategy.* Retrieved September 28, 2005, from http://www.whitehousedrugpolicy.gov/publications/policy/ndcs05/

Read, J. (1999). *Motivational interviewing.* Retrieved November, 13. 2004 from University of Rhode Island Office of Student Life Substance Abuse Prevention Services Web site: http://www.uri.edu/substance_abuse/motiv_interview.html

Ringwald, C. D. (2002). *The soul of recovery: Uncovering the spiritual dimension in the treatment of addictions.* New York: Oxford University Press.

Rollnick, S., & Miller, W. R. (1995). What is motivational interviewing? [Electronic version]. *Behavioral and Cognitive Psychotherapy, 23,* 325–334. Retrieved November 13, 2004 from http://motivationalinterview.org/clinical/whatismi.html

Scanlon, A. (2002). *State spending on substance abuse treatment.* Retrieved November 27, 2004 from National Conference of State Legislatures Web site: http://www.ncsl.org/programs/health/forum/pmsas.htm

Substance Abuse and Mental Heath Services Administration. (1994). Placement criteria and expected treatment outcomes. In *Intensive outpatient treatment for alcohol and other drug abuse treatment improvement protocol: TIP series 8* (chap. 2). Retrieved September 28, 2005, from http://www.health.org/govpubs/bkd139/8d.aspx

Substance Abuse and Mental Heath Services Administration. (2005). *Substance abuse treatment facility locator.* Retrieved September 28, 2005, from http://findtreatment.samhsa.gov/

Substance Abuse and Mental Heath Services Administration Office of Applied Studies. (2004). *Overview of findings from the 2003 national survey on drug use and health* (DHHS Publication No. SMA 04-3963). Rockville, MD: SAMHSA.

Treadway, D. C. (1989). *Before it's too late: Working with substance abuse in the family.* New York: W.W. Norton.

Vaillant, G. E. (1995). *The natural history of alcoholism revisited.* Cambridge, MA: Harvard University Press.

White, W. L. (1998). *Slaying the dragon: The history of addiction treatment and recovery in America.* Bloomington, IL: Chestnut Health Systems/ Lighthouse Institute.

Whitebread, C. (1995). *The history of the non-medical use of drugs in the U.S.* Retrieved December 2, 2004 from the Schaffer Library of Drug Policy Web site: http://www.druglibrary.org/schaffer/History/whiteb1.htm

Yalom, I. D. (1985). *The theory and practice of group psychotherapy* (3rd ed.). New York: Basic Books.

suggested reading

Abbott, A. A. (2000). *Alcohol, tobacco, and other drugs: Challenging myths, assessing theories, individualizing interventions.* Washington, D.C.: NASW Press.

Beattie, M. (1987). *Codependent no more: How to stop controlling others and start caring for yourself.* New York: Harper & Row.

Black, C. (1981). *It will never happen to me.* New York: Ballantine.

Johnson, V. (1980). *I'll quit tomorrow.* New York: Harper & Row.

Miller, W. R., & Munoz, R. (1982). *How to control your drinking: A practical guide to responsible drinking.* Albuquerque: University of New Mexico Press.

Philleo, J., Brisbane, F. L., & Epstein, L. G. (1997). *Cultural competence in substance abuse prevention.* Washington, D.C.: NASW Press.

Vogler, R. E., & Bartz, W. R. (1982). *The better way to drink: Moderation and control of problem drinking.* Oakland, CA: New Harbinger.

Woititz, J. G. (1983). *Adult children of alcoholics.* Deerfield Beach, FL: Health Communications.

internet web sites related to substance abuse

Adult Child of Alcoholics (ACOA): **http://www.adultchildren.org/**

Alanon/Alateen: **http://www.al-anon.alateen.org/**

Alcoholics Anonymous: **http://www.alcoholics-anonymous.org/**

Narcotics Anonymous: **http://www.na.org/**

National Center on Addiction and Substance Abuse at Columbia University: **http://www.casacolumbia.org/absolutenm/templates/article.asp?articleid=287&zoneid=32**

National Institute on Drug Abuse: **http://www.nida.nih.gov/**

SAMSHA Alcohol and Drug Information: **http://www.health.org/**

chapter 11

Human Services in the Schools

Where there are children, there will be counseling, and the U.S. public school system is no exception. The field of human services has had a strong presence in the U.S. public school system for over 100 years, and this presence continues to grow, particularly in urban areas, where crime and poverty continue to flourish.

Counseling on public school campuses is primarily conducted by three types of professionals: school social workers, who are typically MSW-trained professionals; school counselors, who have an MA in school counseling and have a background in teaching; and school psychologists, who have a master's degree or doctorate in school psychology and, in addition to instruction in educational counseling, are trained to conduct specialized educational and psychological testing of students. Together, these human service professionals comprise what is often called "student services" or "pupil support services."

Although each of these providers conducts counseling in some respect, they use somewhat different approaches to counseling and student support, have different standards of practice, and even have different service and treatment goals. And although there are significant differences in practice guidelines between various states, regions (urban, rural, etc.), and districts, school social workers tend to focus more on the psychosocial aspects of students' lives, providing counseling and case management that focus on traditional social work concerns such as the student's overall mental health, violence both on campus as well as at home, the risk of suicide among the student population, and the need for advocacy on behalf of vulnerable students, including the homeless student, students of color, and students who are at risk. School counselors tend to focus more on academic counseling, career guidance, and emotional or psychological issues that directly pertain to student achievement. School psychologists focus on testing, particularly in response to numerous federal and state mandates that require the academic testing of students to place them in the proper educational setting, but may also provide counseling for students who are experiencing emotional difficulties affecting their academic achievement.

Regardless of a counselor's designated role, when one works with human beings experiencing strife, one immediately becomes a generalist having to deal with a broad range of issues and serving in several different roles. Thus, although a school counselor might initiate a counseling session with a student regarding academic performance, study skills, or career planning, the session can take a quick detour focusing on the student's recent breakup, a bullying incident, a friend's suicide, or a parent's alcohol abuse. A school psychologist charged with the responsibility of facilitating all the school district's educational testing might easily find her- or himself spending extra time with a student who breaks down during testing because she or he is living in a homeless shelter, and no one at school knows. In a similar vein, school social workers whose goal it is to focus on students' psychological and emotional issues that are creating a barrier to learning might find themselves conducting a study skills workshop or helping students explore where they want to attend college or what they want to do for a career. Despite the overlap in the functions of these three school-based careers, each of these fields has unique professional standards and roles that, in many respects, delineates them from one other.

School Social Work

School social work has its roots in the settlement house movement discussed in chapter 2. Settlement house workers in the late 1800s and early 1900s, all of whom were women at the time, recognized the poor job urban schools were doing keeping in touch with and connecting to the parents of many of their students. Because settlement houses were designed to provide services and relief primarily to low-income immigrant populations in large urban areas, most of the children who were the original focus on these early efforts to connect school with home were from families who had recently emigrated from non-English-speaking countries. Settlement house communities frequently suffered from overcrowding, both within neighborhoods as well as within the classroom, where some schools had as many as 50 students per class (McCullagh, 1993, 1998). Thus these early school social workers served an important support function enabling teachers to focus on the task of teaching academics.

Mass urbanization was also occurring during this time with scores of families moving from agricultural lifestyles to the city in search of factory jobs. With them came children, many of whom were not adjusting well to city life, particularly when it involved living in cramped quarters with parents who worked long hours. Of chief concern among school districts that were the first to use school social workers were child "maladjustment," child "handicaps," and erratic school attendance, and it was the school social worker's primary goal to address these concerns by ensuring that children's adjustment needs were met, children with handicaps received necessary services, and children attended school regularly (McCullagh, 1993).

These school social work pioneers had many different titles: Visiting Teachers, Home Visitors, Special Visitors, and Visiting Social Counselors (McCullagh, 1998), and they often lived in the settlement houses acting as a liaison between the school, child, and home. This early work, often referred to as the *Visiting Teacher's Movement,* tended to focus on school-related matters such as irregular attendance issues, various health problems, searching the city for children who were not attending schools (such as deaf children and orphans living on the streets), and various other home-centered matters affecting students. The guiding philosophy of home and school visiting committees was that the child was to be viewed from a holistic perspective—not solely as a student causing problems for the district.

Through the development of numerous committees, and the creation of a governing and organizing association called the Public Education Association (PEA), these visiting teachers or counselors gained in popularity and quickly became an integral part of many school districts throughout New York, Boston, and Philadelphia over the next several decades (McCullagh, 1993).

By the early part of the twentieth century teachers in low-income, high-need urban neighborhoods had begun to look to these home visitors for advice and assistance on several issues related to their students, including those concerning inappropriate behaviors, potential problems at home, lack of attendance and general issues related to school functioning. This reliance and general appreciation of the services provided by these early school social workers reflected the teachers' and school administrators' increasing respect for this support service. In fact, by about 1910 many larger school districts were lobbying to have school social workers become paid members of the school district and board of education, rather than being contracted volunteers of the settlement houses supported by philanthropic organizations (McCullagh, 1993).

Schools were also seen as the chief means for "Americanizing" foreign children (and, it was hoped, their families), thus government interest remained high in social work efforts to connect schools with families because it was believed that through such connections more effective assimilation of the immigrant families would occur. This focus on expanding the purpose of schools to include both the education *and* social needs of the child is still widely reflected in today's public school systems that rarely offer solely academic education and services, but also offer counseling, case management, food programs, and on-campus health services. But even if the goal of government was social control, the focus of the school social worker remained on the individual child; the commonly cited goal of these early social workers involved making certain that the individuality of each child did not get lost in the chaos of the overcrowded classroom (McCullagh, 1993).

School social work continued to expand and professionalize over the next 40 years, along with social work in general, and although originally more aligned with teachers and the field of education, by the 1940s visiting teachers and counselors were wholly aligned with the social work profession, and the PEA officially changed its name to the American Association of School Social Workers; later in the decade the name was changed again to the National Association of School Social Workers (NASSW) (McCullagh, 1998). By 1955 several different social work-related committees merged to create the NASW, and although the NASSW still exists, it is now under the auspices of the NASW. The role of the school social worker continued to grow and expand through the 1960s fueled by the social turbulence that marked this era. This awareness led to many universities developing school social work degree programs.

Finally, in 1975 Congress passed the Individuals with Disabilities Education Act (Public Law 94–142) requiring that public schools provide "free and appropriate" public education to all school-aged children between the ages of 3 and 21, regardless of their disability. This law has required school districts to provide increased funding for social work services for students with special needs, when deemed appropriate.

Currently school social work remains a growing field that offers excellent practice opportunities for those wanting to work with school-aged children. Issues such as international academic competition, concerns about increasing violence in the schools, and continued reliance on social work services for the regular as well as special education student has continued to propel school social work forward into the twenty-first century and helped to offset periodic reductions in education budgets due to cyclical economic downturns.

The School Social Work Model

The traditional model of school social work involves the social worker providing school-based social work services as an employee of the school district and as a part of a multidisciplinary team. Although some districts utilize school-based social workers employed by outside agencies (primarily as a cost-saving measure), most school districts in the United States still employ the traditional model. Regardless of the school social worker's actual employer, the roles and functions of the social worker are typically generalist in nature, but have become increasingly specialized as managed care has forced many school districts to seek government reimbursement for services (such as Medicaid or Medicare), which in turn has prompted an increase in specialized credentials beyond licensing (Lewis, 1998).

Most states require that school social workers have an MSW with a specialization in school social work, have accrued several hundred hours in an internship at a public school, and have passed a state content-area test. Some states still only require a bachelor's degree from an accredited social work program, but there is a national push toward master's level education.

School Social Work Roles, Functions, and Core Competencies

School social workers perform a variety of tasks, serve numerous functions, and operate within several different roles depending on the demographics of the school population, the type of children served, and the capacity in which the social worker is functioning. In general, school social workers exist to assist children in managing any psychosocial issues that are creating a barrier to learning. These could include physical barriers in the form of a disability, cognitive barriers such as intellectual or learning disabilities, or behavioral barriers such as students who are depressed, anxious, or acting out. School social workers also work to develop, enhance, or maintain a close working relationship between student families and the school, advocating for the family in a variety of situations.

According to the NASW school social workers should be competent in providing individual, group, and family counseling; should be well versed in theories of human behavior and development; and should have knowledge of and be sensitive to the demographic makeup of the school population with which they work, including relevant issues related to socioeconomic level (SES), gender, race, sexual orientation, and any community stressors that might affect a student's ability to perform (such as a high crime rate or gang infiltration). School social workers must also have competencies in the areas of assessment, must be familiar with local referring agencies, and must be committed to the values and ethics of the social work profession, including those relating to social justice, equity, and diversity (NASW, 2003).

School social workers may work with the general school population or may be hired to work within the special education department with either physically or mentally handicapped children or with students who are **behavior disordered.** Direct practice will often include individual counseling and group counseling, as well as some family counseling, if necessary. In most school settings, for a child to receive social work services it either must be designated as a required service per the **Individualized Education Plan** (IEP), which serves as a sort of contract between the school and family for students identified for special education services, or the student's emotional or psychological problems must in some way be interfering with academic performance. Thus, if a student was experiencing depression, but his academic performance was not affected, this student might not be an appropriate candidate for social work services and would likely be referred out for mental health services.

Individual counseling might include psychological counseling for a high school student, or it might involve play therapy, including drawing, therapeutic games, or doll play, for an elementary school-aged student. Likewise, *group counseling* might involve getting six or eight students together whose parents recently divorced, or who recently moved from another school, and providing them with an opportunity to talk about their struggles and feelings. Yet group counseling might also have a structured and specific curriculum focusing on such issues as anger management or social skills training. School social workers also conduct home visits to obtain vital information about the student's life outside school as well as to ensure a strong link between home and school.

Case management is also provided and can include the organization and coordination of numerous services received by a student. For instance, a student's case might involve an outside therapist who is providing psychological counseling, a psychiatrist who supervises **psychotropic medication** such as antidepressants, a truancy officer, the police department, a child welfare agency, the family, all the student's teachers, and the school principal. Thus, depending on the actual issues of the student receiving services, the social worker will likely be involved in the coordination of services and the appropriate dissemination of information of a number of involved parties. For instance, if a student is suffering from clinical depression and has recently started a new medication (or had her or his medication changed), this would be important information that the entire team would need to know.

Crisis intervention is also an important role of a school social worker. Whether the crisis involves a natural tragedy, such as a tornado or earthquake, the crisis surrounding a student suicide, or the crisis of on-campus violence such as student-on-student assaults, school social workers provide crisis counseling to the entire student population, families, and even the school staff. Crisis counseling might include helping students face the initial shock of some tragedy, but also often involves implementing a safety plan. For instance, the suicide of a student often elicits emotional distress in other students and can lead to an increased chance of other students committing suicide. A school social worker will be involved in creating awareness (through classroom presentations or staff meetings), maintaining a visible presence on campus, and conducting outreach services to vulnerable students.

School social workers may also facilitate *conflict resolution* and *violence prevention* programs. For instance, a school social worker might conduct a structured violence prevention workshop or presentation in a classroom or manage a peer-led conflict resolution program, training students to conduct resolution counseling sessions with students who are engaged in some conflict.

Most social workers are assigned to more than one school, thus they might spend only a few days per week at any one school site. They typically have a caseload of students they must see on a weekly or biweekly basis either on an individual basis or in a group, and perform these various other tasks on an as-needed basis. Because the range of student population types is so wide, it is difficult to describe precisely what a school social worker does on a daily basis, but as with most human services positions, school social workers must be generalists to effectively manage the variety of issues with which they are confronted. Case Study 11.1 provides a wonderful example of some of the issues a school social worker might encounter, but again the specific nature of the work depends in great part on the demographics of the student population, the age of the students, and the capacity in which the social worker was hired.

c a s e   s t u d y   11.1

Case Example—A Day in the Life of a School Social Worker

Mary is nine years old and has been living in foster care for four years. She was diagnosed with clinical depression and oppositional defiance disorder, a disorder characterized by behavior marked by a significant negative attitude, tremendous hostility, and markedly defiant behavior (DSM-IV-TR), and often has dangerous tantrums at school in which she has injured her classmates and even her teacher. Up until four years ago

Mary lived with her mother and father and three younger siblings. When Mary was five her mother became very ill. She recalls not being allowed to spend much time with her mother, and her father was upset and cried a lot. Her parents never told her or her siblings what her mother was sick with, but one evening she recalls trying to awaken her mother, but being unable to do so. She also recalls her mother feeling very cold. After telling her father she was unable to rouse her mother, Mary recalls being whisked away to a neighbor's house for the night, without her siblings.

Mary learned later that each sibling was taken to a different place, which was part of a prearranged plan. She remained at the neighbor's house and after repeatedly asking for her mother, the neighbor finally told her that she was dead. Two months later, the neighbor decided to move and left Mary with another neighbor. Mary recalls this neighbor being abusive to her, both physically and emotionally, particularly when she cried for her family. It was Mary's repeated absences from school that alerted authorities to her unstable and illegal custody arrangement, and once child protective services was notified by the school, she was taken into custody. By this time, an entire year had gone by, during which she had not seen anyone in her family. Once she was in foster care, her caseworker made contact with extended family members and learned that Mary's mother had died of AIDS. Her siblings were placed with various relatives, but prior to her death, her mother had made arrangements to allow Mary to stay with a good friend and neighbor, apparently never suspecting that the neighbor would abandon Mary when another opportunity arose.

I began working with her as her school social worker in the latter part of her fifth-grade year. When I learned all that she had endured, I realized that much of her anger was related to unresolved grief. She had had only one picture of her mother, and that had been taken by her foster mother in her therapeutic foster care group home as punishment for a tantrum and was never returned. She rarely saw her siblings and her father, and extended family members appeared to have little interest in her. After doing some preliminary research I was able to learn where Mary had lived when her mother had died. I then began calling cemeteries with the hope that I could find where Mary's mother was buried. I struck gold on only the third try! After receiving all the necessary releases, Mary and I set out to visit her mother's graveside and to hopefully set into motion a process of mourning that would aid in her healing. We stopped at the cemetery gift shop, bought some flowers and two helium balloons. I then helped Mary write her feelings down on paper, expressing some things that she wanted to say to her mom—in other words, Mary needed to be able to say goodbye, something that had been robbed from her two years earlier. We finally made our way back to the "pauper's" graves and found her mother's gravesite. There was no headstone to mark the spot—only the number, and other headstones to guide us. Once we found her mother's grave, Mary read her poem. Mary then said a brief prayer, letting go of both balloons—one to represent her mother's love for her and the other to represent her love for her mother, both now set free. In chapter 9 the importance of using rituals to help in the grieving process was discussed. Creating a ceremony around saying goodbye enabled Mary to mark the beginning of her recovery. I was

transferred to another school later that year, but I'll never forget the ride back from the cemetery. Mary was quiet, but after a few moments told me that she experienced softness in her heart that she hadn't known for two years. When I followed up with her caseworker, I shared our experience and also shared my concerns about her current group home placement. Her caseworker shared that Mary had been difficult to place because of her temper and oppositional behavior as well as her age, but with the new turn of events, she was willing to take a chance and place Mary in a more traditional foster home. The last time I checked Mary was doing well, and although she continued to experience inappropriate anger from time to time, she was far more motivated to work on her issues, and continued to gain insight into her emotional problems. Although she had been in counseling for several years, it was a school social worker who recognized that unresolved grief was at the core of many of her psychological issues and had the means to address this grief in a meaningful way. ■

School Counseling

Historical Roots of School Counseling

The professional school counselor often has an overlapping role with the school social worker, but typically focuses more on academic concerns and career guidance. School counseling also has a history reaching back to the late 1880s and early 1900s, with roots in the vocational guidance counseling movement (Schmidt & Ciechalski, 2001). In fact, early school counselors focused primarily on matching male high school graduates with an appropriate vocational or job placement.

In the 1920s theories of intelligence and cognitive development became popular, influencing the work of school guidance counselors who, with the advent of intelligence and aptitude testing, now had new tools with which to do their jobs. The 1930s saw advancements in the areas of personality development and motivation, which directly influenced the field of school counseling, enabling counselors to further assist students in identifying areas of aptitude, as well as developing motivational techniques. Social trends and political movements were chief among various influences that led to a gradual shift from a primary focus on the vocational needs of students to a more comprehensive focus where school counselors proactively meet various developmental needs of students (Schmidt & Ciechalski, 2001). Many school counselors working in a secondary school setting continue to provide general guidance and academic counseling, but continue to strive to meet the needs of the whole student.

As with school social work, The Educational Act for All Handicapped Children of 1975 (PL 94–142)—which required, among other things, that children with special needs receive all support services necessary to their academic success—led to school counselors becoming involved in special education departments. In addition, governmental committee reports such as *A Nation at Risk* (1983) and federal legislation, such as the No Child Left Behind Act (U.S. Department of Education, 2001), have meant an increase in funding in many school districts' budgets for school counseling, because concern for academic achievement (or, in some districts, concerns about academic decline) have countered budgetary concerns.

School Counselors: Professional Identity

Although school counseling programs have continued to grow within most school districts, one challenge consistently plaguing the field is role definition. A review of the literature relating to the school counseling field clearly reveals a long-standing struggle to define the role and function of school counselors. This is perhaps due to the overlap—and even some professional territorial struggles—with school social workers and school psychologists, all of whom are concerned with psychosocial counseling and intervention with students.

School districts that have made budgetary decisions to hire only one mental health provider may employ a school counselor to provide all counseling to students, including guidance, career, and mental health. In this instance, the role of the school counselor is similar to that of a school social worker. Yet in many schools that employ both school social workers and school counselors, the latter commonly will provide more academically related counseling and even be responsible for many administrative functions, including maintaining school records and monitoring attendance. For instance, Lambie and Williamson (2004) complained that in many school districts school counselors are working as assistant principals. Lambie and Williamson cite this practice as an example of role confusion within the school counseling field, suggesting that the American School Counselor Association (ASCA), the professional organization for school counselors, continue its quest to outline and define the professional identity of school counselors.

The Urban Problem

The plight of urban schools has received considerable attention in the past several years, both from educators and the federal government. In response to these concerns ASCA and the Education Trust (a not-for-profit agency committed to working for high academic achievement among all children) have made numerous recommendations regarding school counseling programs, including developing systematic programs designed to address many of the issues currently confronting urban schools, such as gang activity, poverty, child abuse, violence on and off campus, increasing rates of clinical depression, unplanned pregnancy, and low academic performance (Holcomb-McCoy, 2005; Lee, 2005).

In addition, urban schools face what is referred to as an "achievement gap" when compared to suburban youth. Urban youth are far more likely to drop out of high school and are less likely to meet the minimum standard on national standardized tests. Urban schools have far greater difficulty retaining quality teachers, must contend

■ Urban schools are often overcrowded and located in high-crime neighborhoods.

with political issues often not confronting suburban schools, and are often located in high crime areas of concentrated poverty (Olson & Jerald, 1998).

Other issues facing urban schools and school counselors working in these settings include dealing with high student absenteeism, unstable family systems, including a high percentage of students living in foster care, and high student transience, where students often transfer in and out of school frequently (Lee, 2005). Each of these issues is far more complex than one might think initially. For instance, consider the issue of high student mobility: One might think that this issue would not necessarily affect the school the student is leaving, yet students who leave schools suddenly due to family instability often fail to return their textbooks, which can lead to significant financial losses for schools, many of which are already suffering serious budgetary shortfalls. California is one state that has a significantly higher incidence of student mobility than many other states, due in part to the immigrant population. In a 1999 study of the impact of student transience on school districts, school researchers made several suggestions including utilizing school counselors to reach out to departing and incoming students to coordinate transfers and minimize disruptions (Rumberger, Larson, Ream & Palardy, 1999).

Common Roles and Functions of School Counselors

School counseling programs generally focus on three basic areas: *academic counseling, career development,* and *personal-social development* (Dahir, 2001). What form this counseling takes depends in large part on whether the counselor is working at an elementary school, middle school, or high school. Other issues influencing the nature of the counseling include the size of the student population, whether the school is in an urban or rural area, and the nature of surrounding community. A school counselor who works at a high-crime, overcrowded high school in inner-city Chicago will certainly have a different role and perform different functions than a school counselor working in a high-income suburban elementary school.

In general, school counselors provide classroom guidance, such as helping students develop good study skills, do some preliminary career planning, develop effective coping strategies, and foster good peer relationships through the development of prosocial skills, such as exhibiting empathy, showing kindness to others, and managing anger appropriately. School counselors also develop and facilitate programs on substance abuse awareness and multicultural awareness. School counselors assist students with goal setting, academic planning, and planning for college. They facilitate crisis intervention with individual students, the student body, families, and the school as a whole. They collaborate with parents, teachers, and school administrators and provide community referrals as necessary. They may also facilitate programs focusing on making the transition to the next level in school or to work. School counselors identify and work with at-risk students, managing behavioral and mental health issues such as substance abuse, suicide threats, classroom disruptions, student–teacher conflicts, and other issues as they arise.

Among school counseling competencies, Lee (2005) lists *cultural competence,* the ability to advocate for students in an attempt to remove barriers to academic success, a willingness to be leaders in educational reform, and the ability to effectively communicate with and collaborate with other educational professionals.

Although it may be true that the school counseling profession is still struggling to assert a strong professional identity, establish the roles and functions of school counselors, and maintain a presence among other student services professionals, as educational reform movements continue to grow, schools will benefit most from a multidisciplinary team that addresses the comprehensive needs of all students. Although school social workers and school counselors often have overlapping roles and missions, a school with a student body of about 3,000, that employs two school social workers and four school counselors will certainly have enough student issues to keep all student services personnel busy!

School Psychologists

The National Association of School Psychologists (NASP) includes the following statement on its Web site: "School psychologists help children and youth succeed academically, socially, and emotionally. They collaborate with educators, parents, and other professionals to create safe, healthy, and supportive learning environments for all students that strengthen connections between home and school" (NASP, n.d.).

If you think this explanation is similar to the description of school social workers and school counselors, you are correct! As with the other two student services positions discussed in this chapter, school psychologists have a broad range of responsibilities and functions that depend on the actual school environment. But one significant difference between a school psychologist and a school social worker and/or school counselor is that a school psychologist conducts academic testing on students to evaluate and assess their academic ability and deficits and often are the only student services professional who is trained in evaluating intervention programs.

Most school psychologists have a master's degree in educational psychology, have completed a lengthy internship at a school, and have a special credential designating them as a school psychologist. Those with master's degrees in social work and counseling who want to become a school psychologist can earn an Ed.S. (Educational Specialist degree), which will enable them to obtain a school psychologist credential.

Common Clinical Issues and Effective Responses by Human Services Personnel

Due to the overlap that exists in the roles and functions of school social workers, school counselors, and school psychologists, any of these professionals will encounter similar clinical issues while working in a public school. Thus, although some of the information contained in this section might appear to be oriented more toward one discipline or the other, it is important to remember that all human service professionals working in a school setting could conceivably confront these same issues, depending on their role within their assigned school.

I mentioned earlier that the nature of work performed by school social workers, school counselors, and school psychologists can vary significantly, depending on a wide range of variables and circumstances, yet certain issues will arise on virtually every public school campus, and human service professionals working on school campuses must be trained to both recognize and respond to them when they occur.

Depression and Other Mental Health Concerns

The National Institutes of Mental Health (1999) state that approximately 3 percent of children and 8 percent of adolescents suffer from some form of depression. These statistics underscore the importance of human service professionals having the tools necessary to both recognize and respond to depression in the school environment.

Symptoms of depression in children and adolescents are similar to that of adults, except that oftentimes children exhibit symptoms of irritability rather than melancholy. Another important consideration is that it is often the quiet child, sitting in the back of the classroom bothering no one, suffering silently, who is the most in need of help, yet is the likeliest to be overlooked by school personnel because they are not acting out in any visible way.

Abrams, Theberge, and Karan (2005) recommended that school counselors (and other mental health providers) use an ecological model (discussed in chapter 1) as a lens through which a depressed student is assessed. Students who are identified as suffering from depression are evaluated from a perspective that considers a student's "contextual map" to truly grasp the reciprocal nature in the relationships between the depressed students and their environment, including their families, close friends, neighborhoods, and school (microsystem); the relationship between depressed students and their broader community (mesosystem); and finally this model allows the counselor to evaluate the impact of the broadest aspects of the student's world, including the effect of cultural mores, various social reforms, political policies, and the impact of natural tragedies (exosystem).

For instance, in assessing and evaluating a potentially depressed student, the clinician would evaluate the relationship the student has with peers, family members, and even teachers. Is the student experiencing conflict with one or both parents? Has the student recently experienced fights with peers? The counselor will then evaluate the relationship the student has with the broader community. Is the student involved with the legal system? Does the student have involvement with a truancy officer? Finally, the clinician will evaluate how anything in the broader society might be affecting the student.

For instance, the terrorist attacks of September 11, 2001, had a devastating impact on virtually everyone. The evaluation of any student for depression in the months subsequent to September 11 was likely assessed in the context of these devastating events. Did the student have any friends or family members who were directly affected by these attacks? Does the student have a parent or close family member who was deployed to Iraq or Afghanistan in response to these attacks? Similarly, any significant changes in governmental social policy have the potential to affect students, particularly those who are living in government-subsidized housing and who have parents who are subsidized by public assistance. Do these changes in policy affect the student's family in a way that consequently puts pressure on the student because of increased stress within the household?

In general, the human service professional evaluates anything that might be a contributing factor to the student's current mental health status, but also evaluates strengths and support within the student's world (Abrams et al., 2005). Does the student belong to a church body or faith community that offers or has the potential of offering support? Does the student have any extended family members who might come forward and offer to support the student during a difficult time? A student who is experiencing depression because his father was deployed to Afghanistan might have an untapped support system in a support group for children sponsored by the U.S. Army.

The value of this model is that it is complementary with the overall model of human service professionals who are trained to consider the entire context within which the student is operating. This approach also enables the social worker and counselor to provide more effective case management once contributing factors and support systems are identified. This model also encourages the involvement of the student's family system. In fact, research so strongly supports the positive impact of parental involvement in the student's mental health on academic achievement that Vanderbleek (2004) suggested that school social workers and school counselors identify and address any barriers to families becoming involved in the counseling process. These barriers might be cultural or racial, such as a less than welcoming environment toward non-English-speaking parents, or parents who do not feel well treated by school personnel. Barriers can also be more concrete, such as a parent's lack of transportation or a work schedule that makes meeting with school personnel impossible. Flexibility on the part of support services personnel, including a willingness to conduct home visits—after school hours, if necessary—will help to reduce the majority of these barriers.

Auger (2005) wrote in favor of a multifaceted approach to depression intervention within the school system and suggested that school counselors collaborate with school personnel, families, and other mental health practitioners, challenge the student to address any pessimistic or negative thinking, encourage the development of greater insight into feelings and their connection with behavior, help the student develop better social skills, and create opportunities for the student to succeed. Auger even advocated encouraging the student to increase physical activity because there appears to be a relationship between physical activity and positive mental health.

There is, of course, a limit to the amount of mental health services a school can provide to its students. Student support personnel must learn to recognize when a student's mental health problems have evolved past the purview of the school social worker's or counselor's area of expertise. Many students experience a level of depression that can successfully be addressed within the school, but human service professionals' training may not extend to the level necessary to deal with a student who is profoundly depressed and/or whose family system is so desperately impaired, that outside referral—and possibly hospitalization—is the only viable option.

Diversity and Race

In virtually every school, some students fit into the mainstream and others do not. It is often the student who does not fit in who is most likely to be vulnerable to scapegoating, bullying, and violence. Students who do not feel safe in school, who are subject to bullying, and who are made to feel as outcasts because of race, sexual orientation, or any reason that seems to set them apart from other students will be at risk for academic failure or at least academic difficulty.

Although the responsibility for keeping students safe lies with all adults associated with the student—teachers, all school personnel, and even parents—human service professionals are in a unique position to identify potential problems related to diversity and intervene by advocating for diverse students.

Racial diversity can be a wonderful asset to any school environment leading to a richness in experiences for students and teachers alike. But in some school environments racial prejudice and discrimination can lead to violence and conflict among many within the student population. Students who comprise a part of a racial minority either within the school or within the broader society are at risk for academic failure for many reasons including social, economic, and political conditions such as poverty, racial intolerance, and higher rates of violence often associated with the urban school environment discussed earlier in this chapter. A school environment that is hostile to racial minorities contributes to an environment where students feel unwelcome and possibly where school policies either directly or indirectly discriminate against students of color. The target of racial discrimination is not limited to people of color though, particularly on a school campus where any student who is a racial minority can be a ready target for bullying and violence.

Human service professionals can assist teachers and school administrators in recognizing and addressing discrimination and prejudice on campus. They can also assist in the development of cultural diversity training focusing on racial sensitivity and respect for diversity. Equally important is the cultural competence of the counselors themselves. It is vital that human service professionals undergo training focusing on the nature of counseling from a multicultural perspective.

An examination of traditional counseling theories and interventions reveals a bias against racial minorities, particularly African Americans. Fusick and Charkow (2004) discussed the tendency of traditional Euro-American theories to pathologize racial minorities rather than recognizing the social oppression that contributes to violence, gang activity, and juvenile delinquency. For those who disregard the power of long-standing racism and its resultant oppression, one must ask whether they believe that certain racial groups are simply more violent than others. If not, then credence must be given to the possibility that dysfunctional behavior is not solely a result of individual pathology, but can be the result of social causes as well.

Because of a history of abuse by child welfare agencies (as discussed in chapter 5) and a court system that has often not recognized the long-standing effect of generations of racial discrimination, certain minority groups may be mistrustful of counseling and mental health treatment (Horejsi, Craig, & Pablo, 1992; Surbeck, 2003). Thus, counselors should not assess a student's or family's wariness of mental health personnel as paranoia or as a sign of deception, but should recognize and understand the roots of such mistrust—one that can often be overcome through the development of an authentic helping relationship and student-centered advocacy.

Fusick and Charkow (2004) also discussed the effect of biased assessment tools that were created for assessment and evaluation of the majority culture, with Caucasian middle-class values and mores. African-American students in particular are far likelier to be referred for counseling and social work services for behavioral problems, further exacerbating the hostility often felt toward mental health professionals. Fusik and Charkow recommend that social workers and counselors be neither too directive nor too appeasing in counseling sessions, but instead focus on developing a truly authentic relationship.

I worked as a school social worker in an urban school that was primarily African-American. Not only was I one of the only Caucasians on campus, but my caseload consisted primarily of boys, and as a woman there was a natural discomfort with me on the part of my students. A fellow social worker suggested that I try to speak to the students using some of the slang used by many of the African-American or Latino youth. Knowing that I could never get away with this I decided to just be myself and express my desire to get to know each of them. I spent time getting to know them and their interests, and I quickly learned that many of the boys loved athletics. I purchased packs of sports cards as encouragement and rewards. In time, the majority of my students recognized my sincere desire to understand and help them. And although I never judged them or their feelings, I was never afraid to jump in and make suggestions for either perceiving or handling situations in a different way.

Gay, Lesbian, and Transgendered Youth

Students who are in the sexual minority, such as gay, lesbian, transgendered, and students who are questioning their sexuality, are often the victims of violence, both verbal and physical. Many of these children spend a considerable amount of time feeling different and isolated, often believing that no one will understand their feelings and accept them unconditionally. Such individuals have an alarmingly high rate of suicide attempts, with over 30 percent admitting to having attempted suicide at some point in their lives. Approximately 75 percent of gay and lesbian students admit to having been verbally abused at school, and over 15 percent have been physically abused (Pope, 2003).

Most of the youth in Pope's study reported that the violence they experienced was a direct result of their sexual orientation, with boys being abused more often than girls. Pope discussed this type of abuse in terms of the pressure on most high school students to conform to the norms of their peer group. When faced with the overwhelming demands to be just like everyone else, students who stand out, either because they look different or, as is the case with gay and lesbian students, when their sexual orientation is different, they can quickly become outcasts.

It is vital that school personnel address the harassment that most gay and lesbian students experience and develop a plan for combating this response to students in the sexual minority. The first step is to establish a *zero-tolerance policy,* where teachers, school administrators, and student services professionals make it clear to the student population through policy and action that harassment will not be tolerated in any respect. Developing a plan for making school safe for all vulnerable students begins with the education of school personnel.

School social workers, counselors, and psychologists are the ideal candidates to educate both school staff and students on the importance of tolerating diversity. Such a program must begin with the school staff, particularly the teachers, who are most likely to be present when the abuse of gay and lesbian students occurs. Teachers do not need to be convinced that homosexuality is acceptable behavior. In fact, regardless of how strongly the student support professionals feel about wanting to create a consensus of acceptance, it is probably unrealistic to assume that everyone on the campus is going to perceive alternate sexual orientations as a positive, albeit alternative, lifestyle choice. What needs to be emphasized is that regardless of one's personal beliefs about the issue of sexual orientation, no human being should be subjected to verbal and physical harassment and abuse. Nor should one ever be defined by his or her sexual orientation or any other singular aspect of their personhood. School personnel should be taught that personal feelings should be set aside and the focus should be placed instead on teaching students to respect human dignity and everyone's basic right to self-determination.

A particularly effective program facilitated by school social workers, counselors, and psychologists across the nation is called the Making Schools Safe project (Otto, Middleton & Freker, 2002). This program was developed by the American Civil Liberties Union (ACLU) and was designed to combat antigay harassment on school campuses. The ACLU recommends that all teachers and administrators use this curriculum, which focuses on the vital importance of creating a safe learning environment for all children.

The Terrorism Threat and the Impact of Living During Wartime

On September 11, 2001, members of a terrorist organization called Al-Qaeda hijacked four commercial airliners and crashed two of them into the World Trade Center towers in New York City and one into the Pentagon in Arlington, VA. The fourth airplane, allegedly intended for the White House, crashed in Somerset County, Pennsylvania, after passengers temporarily overpowered the hijackers. This series of terrorist attacks was followed by a months-long bioterrorism attack with letters sent through the post office laced with anthrax (Baggerly & Rank, 2005). The media was filled with reports of feared future attacks.

Students of all ages were filled with fears. My six-year-old son would sit for hours drawing pictures of the towers with planes sticking out of them. As a parent, I wanted to limit the information I gave him, but I also knew that he was hearing information at school, and I was not certain that he would tell me what he had heard. I, like many other parents, was in the difficult position of having to choose between giving him too much information or limiting the information I gave him—yet risking that he was hearing things at school and worrying about things without telling me.

Many school districts scrambled to develop programs to address students' feelings and concerns in the wake of the September 11 attacks. The most common psychological response was posttraumatic stress disorder (PTSD), a disorder that often occurs in the wake of a traumatic event. Individuals with PTSD continue to experience fear, hopelessness, and horror long after the event (American Psychological Association [APA], 2000). **Vicarious victimization** was also prevalent on many school campuses. The events of September 11 were difficult for adults, but were particularly hard on children who lack the ability to think abstractly and who often lack the ability to communicate their feelings.

A 2004 study found that 65 percent of respondents reported that students experienced moderate to high levels of distress in the weeks following the attacks (Auger, Seymour, Roberts, & Waiter, 2004). The most frequently reported symptoms included fear, worry, anxiety, sadness, anger, and aggression. Students who were personally affected by these terrorist attacks or who already suffered from some mental health issues, such as depression, were the most at risk for developing PTSD symptoms.

Auger, Seymour, Roberts, and Waiter (2004) also noted that although most schools surveyed took appropriate action in responding to the attacks, 12 percent took no responsive action. The majority of the schools surveyed took no action to assist school personnel in dealing with their own feelings. Over one-third of school counselors stated that they did not feel prepared to respond to a serious trauma, suggesting that ongoing training of all school personnel is essential.

Since the September 11 attacks, the U.S. government has released numerous warnings of possible terrorist attacks, adding to the sense that something bad could happen again at any time. The 2005 attacks in the London subway (the "tube") added to concerns that no one is safe and that terrorists can strike at any time. Human service professionals should be trained to respond in the event of another attack and need to be sensitive and deal with the ongoing effect on students of living in an age of terrorist threat.

Substance Abuse

Substance abuse both on and off campus continues to be a growing problem across the United States, primarily in high schools, but also in some middle schools. School social workers, counselors, and psychologists must be able to identify the signs of substance abuse as well as being prepared for the various ways of intervening when substance abuse is suspected. (See chapter 11 for more on the issue of the lack of training in the area of substance abuse.) Although many graduate programs in the mental health–related fields are addressing this issue by including more courses on substance abuse, the majority of programs still only offer substance abuse courses as electives. Many mental health professionals in student services are unprepared to deal with substance abuse issues or the complexity of adolescent substance abuse, particularly with regard to complicated family systems (Lambie & Rokutani, 2002). The reality is that 74 percent of high school seniors in suburban high schools have reported using alcohol, and 40 percent of high school seniors in suburban high schools have reported using illegal drugs (Greene & Forster, 2004), making substance abuse one of the most significant issues confronting school personnel.

School counselors need to be able to identify adolescent substance abuse and respond with an intervention strategy. That strategy must include a response from the school as well as outside referral sources that will involve the entire family system.

The model most often used to describe the nature of adolescent substance abuse is similar to an adult model and does not take into consideration factors related to adolescent development. Adolescents tend to be egocentric, often acting and feeling in ways that tend to be self-focused. They also tend to display behavior that is impulsive, appearing to lack any real sense of consequences. This seeming sense of omnipotence, coupled with developmental egocentrism, often complicates traditional models of substance abuse.

Lambie and Rokutani (2002) suggested using a systems perspective in evaluating substance abuse in the adolescent population. Rather than viewing substance abuse in the adolescent as an individual problem, a systems perspective views the substance abuse as a sign of something amiss within the family system. The substance-abusing adolescent often serves some purpose within the family system, such as enabling the parents to focus on the adolescent's dysfunctional behavior rather than on problems in the marriage. The substance-abusing adolescent sometimes serves as an apparent symptom of deeper problems within the family system that are purposely hidden from view. For instance, the family who works hard to appear "normal" and healthy will be compelled to deal with underlying dysfunction when one or more of the children begin acting out in ways that require outside attention and intervention, such as abusing drugs and alcohol.

Another issue to consider when using a systems perspective is whether the adolescent's substance abuse is mirroring a parent's substance abuse. A parent's abuse of alcohol or drugs has been shown to influence an adolescent's decision to begin drinking (Lambie & Sias, 2005; Piercy, Volk, Trepper, Sprenkle, & Lewis, 1991). In general, families that have system problems such as parental substance abuse and other forms of maladaptive behavior tend to be rigid closed-family systems and lack the ability or capacity to handle the increased stressors associated with children entering the adolescent years. Adolescents demanding changes to long-standing rules, pushing for more privileges, developing a far wider circle of peers, and questioning family rules can often leave a family that is wary of outsiders and rigidly adheres to rules and discipline with few effective coping skills to adapt to these changes. In addition, problems that have their roots in early childhood most often manifest during adolescents. In fact, I have worked with adolescents for years and cannot think of a single adolescent who did not act out in response to an issue or condition with roots in her or his childhood.

A school social worker, counselor, or psychologist working with substance-abusing adolescents must first be able to identify the common signs of abuse, including erratic behavior, mood swings, red eyes, and slurred speech. They must then be able to provide support to both the student and family, acting as a liaison between student, family, school, and community-based treatment programs.

On a broader level, student services personnel can institute prevention programs in the school, such as the DARE program that involves police and other community agencies coming into the schools and creatively (through plays, dance, and songs), and, in an age-appropriate manner, enlighten students about the dangers of drug abuse and encourage students to avoid substance use and abuse.

Child Abuse and Neglect

School social workers, counselors, and psychologists are often in the position of having to report child abuse to their local child welfare agency. (See chapter 5 for a discussion of child protective services' involvement in child abuse cases.) School social workers, counselors, and psychologists are often in the precarious position of having to decide what should constitute a "hotline" call. For instance, a child showing up to school with bruises, who discloses she has been physically abused by her mother, clearly mandates a call to child protective services, but frequently a counselor might not have such a clear indication of abuse and must make a determination based on suspicion. It is important for student services personnel to understand that they do not need to be certain of abuse; if there are indicators of any type of abuse it is their legal obligation to file a report and allow child protective services to conduct an investigation.

It is important that the school social worker, counselor, or psychologist remain composed when a student discloses abuse, but express compassion, support, and encouragement. It is equally important that promises are not made that cannot be kept. For instance, the counselor should not promise not to tell anyone, because the student will feel betrayed when report of child abuse is made (Lambie, 2005). There might also be reticence on the part of the counselors to make a report of child abuse if they know the parents and are suspicious of the student's disclosure, but the counselor must adhere to the law, which requires that any abuse disclosure be reported as required.

Teenage Pregnancy

A newspaper article in 2005 reported that 13 percent of the female students at an Ohio high school were pregnant, causing serious concern about why this high school's pregnancy rate was nearly double the national average (Garvey, 2005). Although teenage pregnancy has been on the decline in recent years (Karraker, 2004), it remains a serious concern, with over 60 percent of high school seniors reporting they were sexually active (Greene & Forster, 2004). Various research studies have pointed to many factors that might influence pregnancy. Beyond sexual activity in the adolescent population, other factors include early alcohol use (Stueve & O'Donnell, 2005) and poverty (Young, Turner, Denny, & Young, 2004).

Research on prevention points to religiosity (Rostosky, Regnerus & Comer Wright, 2003), peer influence, appropriate parental supervision, good and direct parental communication, SES, race (Corcoran, Franklin, & Bennett, 2000), and involvement in sports that is correlated with remaining abstinent in high school, or at least becoming sexually active later in adolescence.

Sex and pregnancy prevention programs have been included in school curriculums for several decades with mixed reviews. *Abstinence-only* programs, although somewhat controversial, have shown to be surprisingly successful (Toups & Holmes, 2002). In fact, Toups and Holmes reviewed several studies that revealed marked reductions in teenage pregnancy after experiencing a school-based abstinence-only program. In fact, one cited study evaluated all 5,000 teenagers who participated in an abstinence program in one year. Not only did few of these teenagers become sexually active, but also over 50 percent of the students who had been sexually active stopped having sex. Proponents of abstinence-only sex education cite the decrease in adolescent sexual activity as evidence that these programs work. Yet others have questioned whether these programs are as successful as some of these studies indicate, citing poor study designs and a wide range of abstinence programs with some defining abstinence as postponing sex until early adulthood and some more religiously based programs sending the message that premarital sex should always be avoided. Without a clear definition of "abstinence," critics claim that it's impossible to determine the success of these programs (Kirby, 2002).

Some educators are concerned, though, that abstinence-only programs will not work for all teenagers, particularly those who have any of the complicating factors mentioned earlier. Teenagers living in poverty, who have poor communication with their parents, and who are not supervised well by their parents may not respond positively to abstinence-only programs because of the other forces pushing them in the direction of sexual activity. Based on the belief that some adolescents will have sex no matter who tells them not to, education programs focus on safe sex practices, such as using condoms during sexual intercourse. Many of these programs focus among other things on HIV/AIDS education, which is often later cited as a chief reason among adolescents for using condoms. Although there has been some concern that educating teenagers to use contraception and even making contraception available is sending a mixed message (i.e., "You should not have sex during adolescence, but just in case you do, use a condom!"), which in essence promotes sexual activity during adolescence, a review of 28 studies examining this issue clearly shows that such programs do not increase sexual activity among teenage participants, nor do they lead to sexual activity at an earlier age. In fact, many studies indicated that safe sex programs increase the usage of contraception (Kirby, 2002).

One of the most popular programs currently used in high schools across the nation is called the Baby Think It Over (BTIO) program, which uses a computerized doll programmed to cry and fuss intermittently throughout the day and night to educate teenagers on the realities of having a baby. This program has been successful in educating teenagers about the hardship and burden of having a child at such an early age (Somers, Johnson, & Sawilowsky, 2002).

Another issue commonly noted by school social workers, counselors, and psychologists who work with female high school students is a pervasive tendency for girls who are sexually active to report that they had not considered the possibility that they could have said no to a boyfriend's sexual advances. Developing "empowerment" support groups where girls can have a safe place to talk about their feelings about sex, support each other in their right to say no, and consider the positive consequences of doing so can be a successful tool in encouraging better boundary setting, which is likely to result in a reduction of sexual activity.

ADD and ADHD

In the past 20 years diagnoses of attention deficit disorder (ADD) and attention deficit hyperactivity disorder (ADHD) have literally skyrocketed, with school personnel being on the leading edge of those referring children for evaluation and assessment. According to the DSM-IV-TR (APA, 1997) individuals with ADD suffer from inattention, have difficulty following directions, have difficulty maintaining a sense of organization, and are reluctant to engage in activities that require sustained mental effort (American Psychiatric Association, 2000). The additional symptoms that might warrant a diagnosis of ADHD include hyperactivity, impulsivity, and poor self-control (Kos, Richdale, & Jackson, 2004).

Children diagnosed with ADD/ADHD often present significant challenges in the classroom due to a difficulty in paying attention to the teacher and sitting still for extended periods of time. Classroom management with such children can often be difficult because many children with ADD/ADHD symptoms have difficulty with social skills as well, making peer relations a problem.

The most common treatment for ADD/ADHD involves the use of medication, most commonly Ritalin, which is a stimulant that has a calming affect on the child. But many schools have instituted behavioral plans that include token rewards for children who are able to remain focused for increasing amounts of time and who display prosocial behaviors. School social workers, counselors, and psychologists are often called on to work with children exhibiting ADD/ADHD symptoms, both in the classroom and outside the classroom. Many schools utilize a therapeutic group model bringing several such students together to work on issues such as impulse control, social skills, and maintaining attention. Many therapeutic board games on the market are designed to encourage these skills by engaging the students in play while teaching them how to delay gratification and control their impulses as a winning strategy.

Despite the prevalence in the diagnosing of these disorders, many are concerned that too many referrals for ADHD are coming from educational circles. With most disorders, such as depression or anxiety, referrals for evaluation and counseling might come from one's employer, spouse, or friend. Yet schools tend to be by far the largest source of referrals for ADD/ADHD, presumably because children with these symptoms can cause serious disruption in the classroom, and with class sizes increasing, it can be taxing on a teacher to contend with students who are not paying attention and are acting on their every impulse.

Another concern is that the DSM-IV-TR criteria are too broad and in many respects self-fulfilling. For instance, criteria number 1-d states: "Often does not follow through on instructions and fails to finish schoolwork, chores, or duties in the workplace (not due to oppositional behavior or failure to understand instructions)." This criterion is extremely broad and in many respects could be used to describe just about any child at one point or another during their academic career! Certainly most clinicians would not diagnose a child with ADD simply due to one or two incidences of procrastination, but rather they would look for a pattern of behavior. But, a recent study that compared a group of school-aged children assessed using DSM-IV-TR criteria and a group of school-aged children using neuropsychological criteria found that the DSM-IV-TR group had an 18 percent prevalence rate and the neuropsychological group had a prevalence rate of only 3.5 percent (Guardiola, Fuchs, & Rotta, 2000). This seems to support the criticism that the DSM-IV-TR criteria may be too broad.

Another criticism of what some claim is the overdiagnosing of ADD/ADHD includes a concern that boys are disproportionately referred for and diagnosed with ADHD for what many consider to be typical "boy" behavior, including being more naturally active than girls (Sciutto, Nolfi, & Bluhm, 2004). In addition, several recent studies have found several other factors might account for ADHD-like behavior including lack of sleep (Brown & Modestino, 2000) and even gifted intelligence with high creativity, leading to a concern that many children are being misdiagnosed with ADHD when other issues might better account for the child's inability to focus, such as fatigue or in the case with the intellectually gifted child, a need for increased mental stimulation (Hartnett, 2004).

One of the most significant concerns of all, though, involves concern among medical personnel, therapists, and parents about the wisdom of giving children a stimulant with cocaine-like properties throughout their developmental years. Historically the medical community did not believe that Ritalin caused any permanent brain changes, yet many recent studies seem to contradict this belief. A 2001 study on rats found that Ritalin use did cause permanent neurological brain changes (Andersen, Arvanitogiannis, Pliakas, LeBlanc, & Carlezon, 2002), and although rats are certainly not humans, they are amazingly similar to humans in the sense that they often respond chemically in ways similar to humans. The results of this study were surprising to researchers because the initial goal of the study was to evaluate whether long-term Ritalin use made subjects *more* vulnerable to drug abuse later in life. What they found, though, was that the rats who were on Ritalin, desired cocaine *less*. Further research discovered that this was due to Ritalin causing an increase in a certain protein that affects the pleasure centers of the brain. So although this result might be good with regard to decreasing one's desire for drugs, it is not so good if it makes other activities less rewarding, such as eating and sexual activity.

Another 2001 study also indicates that Ritalin, commonly thought to have a short-term life in the body, has long-term effects, many of which are permanent and most of which remain unknown. This study found that Ritalin may affect gene expression, which may lead to enduring changes in brain cell structure and function (Brandon & Steiner, 2003). Basically what this means is that the Ritalin may actually be turning a certain gene on that then turns other genes on, a reaction also found in the brains of those who abuse cocaine. Because these studies are still in the animal model phase, it is impossible to conclude anything other than the implication of the results, which at this point seems to clearly indicate that long-term use of Ritalin in developing children will likely have a permanent effect on their brains. Even at this preliminary stage it seems clear that Ritalin should only be used in cases of serious hyperactivity and perhaps only with neurological testing to determine if the Ritalin is medically necessary.

Despite these criticisms and concerns, children who exhibit behaviors that are not conducive to the classroom environment need assistance to learn to adapt to a structured world. School social workers, counselors, and psychologists can work with the students in a manner that both respects different learning and personality styles and at the same time encourages children to work effectively in a structured environment.

Concluding Thoughts on Schools

Human service professionals are an integral part of the public school system providing emotional guidance and academic counseling to thousands of students every year. School counselors, school social workers, and school psychologists work within their respective specialties as a part of a multidisciplinary team meeting student needs and increasing student success.

The role of all of these human service professionals is expected to continue to expand in the future in response to a projected increase in many of the social trends experienced today, including an increase in poverty, homelessness, and single-parent families. Teams of human service professionals work together to remove barriers to learning paving the way for teachers to do what they do best—teach students in their designated academic discipline.

r e f e r e n c e s

Abrams, K., Theberge, S. K., Karan, O. C. (2005). Children and adolescents who are depressed: An ecological approach. *Professional School Counseling, 8(3),* 1096–2409.

Acheson, A. W., Thompson, A. C., Kristal, M. B. & Baizer, J. S. (2001) Methylphenidate induces c-fos expression in juvenile rats. *Society of Neuroscience Abstracts, 27,* 223–4.

American Psychiatric Association. (2000). *Diagnostic and statistical manual of mental disorders* (4th ed., Text Revision) (DSM-IV-TR). Washington, DC: American Psychiatric Association.

Andersen, S. L., Arvanitogiannis, A., Pliakas, A. M., LeBlanc, C. & Carlezon, W. A. (2002). Altered responsiveness to cocaine in rats exposed to methylphenidate during development. *Nature Neuroscience, 5(1),* 13–14.

Andreasen, S. A., Froyen, G., McCullagh, C., & Harrington, D. (2004). Iowa Journal of School Social Work, 1993–1995. *Iowa School Social Workers' Association,* Cedar Falls. (ERIC Document Reproduction No. ED 461 055).

Auger, R. W. (2005). School-based interventions for students with depressive disorders. *Professional School Counseling, 8(4),* 1096–2409.

Auger, R. W., Seymour, J. W., & Roberts, W. B. & Waiter, B. (2004). Responding to terror: The impact of September 11 on K-12 schools and schools' responses. *Professional School Counseling, 7(4),* 1096–2409.

Baggerly, J. N., & Rank, M. G. (2005). Bioterrorism Preparedness: What school counselors need to know. *Professional School Counseling, 8*(5), 458–465.

Baggerly, J., & Borkowski, T. (2004). Applying the ASCA national model to elementary school students who are homeless: A case study. *Professional School Counseling, 8(2),* 116–124.

Brandon, C. L., & Steiner, H. (2003). Repeated methylphenidate treatment in adolescent rats alters gene regulation in the striatum. *European Journal of Neuroscience, 18(6),* 1584–1592.

Brown, T. E., & Modestino, E. J. (2000). Attention-deficit disorders with sleep/arousal disturbances. In T. E. Brown (Ed.), *Attention-deficit disorders and comorbidities in children, adolescents, and adults* (pp. 341–362). Washington, DC: American Psychiatric Publishing.

Corcoran, J., Franklin, C., & Bennett, P. (2000). Ecological factors associated with adolescent pregnancy and parenting. *Social Work Research, 24(1),* 29–39.

Dahir, C. A. (2001). The national standards for school counseling programs: Development and implementation. *Professional School Counseling, 4(5),* 320–327.

Fusick, L., & Charkow B. (2004). Counseling at-risk Afro-American youth: An examination of contemporary issues and effective school-based strategies. *Professional School Counseling, 8(2),* 102–116.

Garvey, M. (2005, September). Preggo high school; kids are readin', writin' & reproducin'. *New York Post,* p. 19.

Green, A. G., Conley, J. A., & Barnett, K. (2005). Urban school counseling: Implications for practice and training. *Professional School Counseling, 8(3),* 1096–2409.

Greene, J. P., & Forster, G. (2004). *Sex, drugs, and delinquency in urban and suburban public schools* (Education Working Paper 4). New York: Center for Civic Innovation. Manhattan Institute, (ERIC Document Reproduction No. ED 483335)

Guardiola, A., Fuchs, F. D., & Rotta, N. T. (2000). Prevalence of attention-deficit hyperactivity disorders in students: Comparison between diagnostic and statistical manual of mental disorders-IV (DSM-IV-TR) and neuropsychological criteria. *Arquivos de Neuro-Psiquiatria, 58(2b),* 401–407

Hartnett, D. N., Nelson, J. M., & Rinn, A. N. (2000). Gifted or ADHD? The possibilities of misdiagnosis. *Roeper Review, 26(2),* 73–76.

Holcomb-McCoy, C. C. (2004). Assessing the multicultural competence of school counselors: A checklist. *Professional School Counseling, 7(3),* 178–186.

Holcomb-McCoy, C. C. (2005). Investigating school counselors' perceived multicultural competence. *Professional School Counseling, 8(5),* 414–423.

Horejsi, C., Craig, B. H., & Pablo, J. (1992). Reactions by Native American parents to child protection agencies: Cultural and community factors. *Child Welfare, 71(4),* 329–343.

Karraker, M. W. (2004). Adolescent pregnancy: Policy and prevention services. *Family Relations: Interdisciplinary Journal of Applied Family Studies, 53(1),* 115.

Kirby, D. (2002). Effective approaches to reducing adolescent unprotected sex, pregnancy and childbearing. *Journal of Sex Research, 39(1),* 51–57.

Kos, J. M., Richdale, A. L., & Jackson, M. S. (2004). Knowledge about attention-deficit/hyperactivity disorder: A comparison of in-service and preservice teachers. *Psychology in the Schools, 41(5),* 517–526.

Lambie, G. W. (2005). Child abuse and neglect: A practical guide for professional school counselors. *Professional School Counseling, 8(3),* 249–258.

Lambie, G. W., & Rokutani, L. J. (2002). A systems approach to substance abuse identification and intervention for school counselors. *Professional School Counseling, 5(5),* 353–359.

Lambie, G. W., & Sias, S. (2005). Children of alcoholics: Implications for professional school counseling. *Professional School Counseling, 8(3),* 1096–2409.

Lambie, G. W., & Williamson, L. L. (2004). The challenge to change from guidance counseling to professional school counseling: A historical proposition. *Professional School Counseling, 8(2),* 1096–2409.

Lee, C. C. (2005). Urban school counseling: Context, characteristics, and competencies. *Professional School Counseling, 8(3),* 184–188.

Lewis, M. R. (1998). The many faces of school social work practice: Results from a research partnership. *Social Work in Education, 20(3),* 177–190.

McCullagh, J. G. (1993). The roots of school social work in New York City. *Iowa Journal of School Social Work, 6,* 49–74.

McCullagh, J. G. (1998). Early school social work leaders: Women forgotten by the profession. *Social Work in Education, 20(1),* 55–64.

McCullagh, J. G. (2001). NASW and school social work: Selected events, developments and publications, 1947–2001. *Journal of School Social Work, 12(1–2),* 5–35. (ERIC Document Reproduction Service No. ED 467 859)

National Association of School Psychologists. (n.d.). *What is a school psychologist?* Retrieved on January 5, 2005, from http://www.nasponline.org/about_nasp/whatisa.html

National Association of Social Workers. (2003). *NASW standards for school social work services.* Washington, DC: Author.

The National Institutes of Mental Health. (1999). Depression research at the National Institute of Mental Health. (NIH Publication No. 00-4501). Bethesda, MD: National Institute of Health.

Olson, L., & Jerald, C. D. (1998). *Quality counts '98: The urban picture.* Retrieved June 18, 2004, from http://www.edweek.org/reports/qc98/challenges.htm

Otto, N., Middleton, J., & Freker, J. (2002). *Making schools safe: An anti-harassment program from the Lesbian & Gay Rights project of the American Civil Liberties Union.* New York. (ERIC Document Reproduction Service No. ED 475 274)

Piercy, F. P., Volk, R. J., Trepper, T., Sprenkle, D. H., & Lewis, R. (1991). The relationship of family factors to patterns of adolescent substance abuse. *Family Dynamics of Addiction Quarterly, 1(1),* 41–54.

Pope, M. (2003). *Sexual minority youth in the schools: Issues and desirable counselor responses.* Information Analysis. (ERIC Document Reproduction No. ED 480 481)

Rostosky, S. S., Regnerus, M. D., & Comer Wright, M. L. (2003). Coital debut: The role of religiosity and sex attitudes in the add health survey. *The Journal of Sex Research, 40(4),* 358–367.

Rumberger, R. W., Larson, K. A., Ream, R. K., & Palardy, G. J. (1999). *The educational consequences of mobility for California students and schools.* Berkeley, CA: Policy Analysis for California Education. (ERIC Document Reproduction No. ED 441 040)

Schmidt, J. J., & Ciechalski, J. C. (2001). School counseling standards: A summary and comparison with other student services' standards. *Professional School Counseling, 4(5),* 1096–2409.

Sciutto, M. J., Nolfi, C. J., & Bluhm, C. (2004). Effects of child gender and symptom type on referrals for ADHD by elementary school teachers. *Journal of Emotional and Behavioral Disorders, 12(4),* 247–253.

Somers, C. L., Johnson, S. A., & Sawilowsky, S. S. (2002). A measure for evaluating the effectiveness of teen pregnancy prevention programs. *Psychology in the Schools, 39(3),* 337–342.

Stueve, A., & O'Donnell, L. N. (2005). Early alcohol initiation and subsequent sexual and alcohol risk behaviors among urban youths. *American Journal of Public Health, 95(5),* 887–893.

Surbeck, B. C. (2003). An investigation of racial partiality in child welfare assessments of attachment. *American Journal of Orthopsychiatry, 73(1),* 13–23.

Toups, M. L., & Holmes, W. R. (2002). Effectiveness of abstinence-based sex education curricula: A review. *Counseling and Values, 46(3),* 237–240.

U.S. Department of Education. (2001). No Child Left Behind Act of 2001 (H.R.1). Washington, DC: Author.

Vanderbleek, L. M. (2004). Engaging families in school-based mental health treatment. *Journal of Mental Health Counseling, 26(3)*, 211–224.

Young, T., Turner, J., Denny, G., & Young, M. (2004). Examining external and internal poverty as antecedents of teen pregnancy. *American Journal of Behavior, 28(4)*, 361–373.

suggested reading

Brock, S. E., Lazarus, P. J., & Jimerson, S. R. (2002). *Best practices in school crisis prevention and intervention.* Washington, DC: NASP.

Huxtable, M., & Blyth, E. (2002). *School social work worldwide.* Washington, DC: NASW Press.

Sprick, R. S., & Howard, L. (1995) *The teacher's encyclopedia of behavior management.* Longmont, CO: Sopris West.

Torrey, E. F. (2001). *Surviving schizophrenia: A manual for families, consumers, and providers* (4th ed.). New York: Collins.

Tourse, R. W. C., & Mooney, J. F. (Eds.). (1999). *Collaborative practice: School and human service partnerships.* Westport, CT: Praeger Publishers.

internet web sites related to human services in the schools

American School Counselor Association: **http://www.schoolcounselor.org/**

International Network for School Social Work: **http://internationalnetwork-schoolsocialwork.htmlplanet.com/index.htm**

National Association of School Psychologists: **http://www.nasponline.org/**

School Social Work Association of America: **http://www.sswaa.org/**

chapter 12

Faith-Based Agencies

Historically the mental health and medical communities in Western society have had a tendency to divide human beings into biological, intellectual, social, emotional, and spiritual parts, with minimal recognition of how each of these dimensions interacts with the other. But in recent years there has been a growing interest both within professional circles as well as within the general public in moving away from such a dichotomous view and toward regarding humans from a *holistic* perspective, where a person is considered as a whole with each aspect of the person being inextricably linked with the other.

Essentially, a holistic approach to mental health involves the process of acknowledging, addressing, and evaluating the mind, the body, and the spirit (or soul) when considering any potential issue affecting one's psychological health. In other words, rather than attempting to determine whether depression is a biological disorder with psychological manifestations or a psychological disorder with biological implications, depression would be seen as a disorder or condition having a reciprocal impact on the whole person: mind, body, and soul.

Although mental health providers in the past have had a tendency to shy away from integrating spirituality within the counseling relationship, recent studies have revealed the dramatic ways in which one's religion or personal spirituality affect their physical and mental health. In fact, several recent research studies have focused on the mind-body-soul connection in an attempt to understand the reciprocal relationship of each, with a specific focus on how spirituality affects an individual's physical and mental health (Idler & Kasl, 1992; Koenig, George, et al. 1998; Koenig, Larson, & Weaver, 1998; McLaughlin, 2004; Powell, Shahabi, & Thoresen, 2003).

For instance, many of these studies have shown that personal religiousness and spirituality have been linked to a decrease in depression, an increase in greater social support, an increase in cognitive functioning (Koenig, George, & Titus, 2004), an improvement in the ability to cope with crises (McLaughlin, 2004), and better ability to cope with substance abuse problems (Fallot & Heckman, 2005). Although there is some confusion about the difference between "*religiousness*" and "*spirituality*," religiousness is commonly defined as a social experience grounded in traditional religion, whereas spirituality is often defined as having an independent relationship with God (Miller & Thoresen, 2003). Of course, people can be religious *and* spiritual (having a personal relationship with a deity that is grounded in a particular religious faith), religious without being particularly spiritual (a cultural or **secular** involvement in a religious faith), or spiritual without being grounded in a particular religious tradition. Thus it is important for practitioners to explore what religiousness and spirituality mean to their individual clients.

The issue of faith is one of importance to all clinical practitioners, particularly mental health practitioners and those within the human services field. Several recent studies have revealed that the majority of U.S. Americans (between 80 and 90 percent) identify themselves as being either religious or spiritual, stating that their faith is an important aspect of their lives (Gallup & Lindsey, 1999; Grossman, 2002). In fact, several of these research studies suggest that clinicians should both acknowledge and address the spiritual dimension of mental and emotional disorders within the counseling relationship, particularly if clients identify themselves as being "spiritually grounded" (Fallot, 2001; Kliewer, 2004; Miller, Korinek, & Ivey, 2004).

Yet human service professionals (or any service provider) must realize that as much as incorporating spirituality into the counseling relationship may be helpful for some clients, there is also the potential for harm, particularly when the religion of a provider is pushed onto a client in a directive or aggressive manner.

Incorporating spirituality into a counseling relationship requires cultural competent counseling skills because many religious traditions are rooted in cultural tradition. Thus, religious abuse is similar in many ways to culture abuse where a provider of a dominant culture is inappropriately directive in forcing the values of the dominant culture onto a client of a different culture. For instance, prior to the recent surge of interest in holistic health, practitioners in the West were often dismissive of Eastern philosophy, which acknowledged the mind-body-soul connection for centuries (Tseng, 2004), rendering many in the human services profession ill-equipped to provide effective services to Asian clients from Buddhist or Hindu traditions (Hodge, 2004).

Religious abuse can be avoided through the sensitivity of the human service professional who although recognizing the value of addressing matters of faith, also recognizes that the issue of spirituality is only helpful if this exploration is client driven and client centered (Hall, Dixon, & Mauzey, 2004).

 ## Faith-Based versus Secular Organizations

Human service professionals can incorporate matters of spirituality in virtually any practice setting in response to their clients' disclosure that faith is an integral part of their lives or something they wish to explore. Thus it is important that providers receive training on the nature of various religious traditions, particularly those they might have an opportunity to encounter in their clinical practice. But there are also numerous human services agencies that operate within a particular religious faith reaching out to those within the tradition as well as those from without.

Such faith-based agencies are often ignored in discussions of human services practice settings, but any review of helping agencies should include an exploration of faith-based agencies because of the long history of religious traditions offering help to those in need, and the fact that matters of spirituality are now recognized as being integral to many people's lives.

What is a faith-based organization? And what makes it different—in nature and service delivery—from a secular agency? It's easy to identify a faith-based organization when it's a synagogue, church, or mosque filled with religious symbols and a mission statement that identifies serving God as a primary function and purpose of the organization. But what about agencies that might be considered **parachurch organizations** that do not function as churches but more as a human services agencies? Or human services agencies that have their roots in a particular religious tradition but don't integrate religion or faith into practice? Would those agencies be considered "faith-based"?

These are more challenging questions than they might appear. Even the courts are not particularly clear on what makes an organization religious in nature (Ebaugh, Pipes, Chafetz, & Daniels, 2003). The difficulty lies in the fact that many secular agencies provide almost identical services as faith-based agencies and there is often no distinguishable difference between the two. Ebaugh et al. (2003) discussed the various ways in which policy makers, social scientists, and historians have defined faith-based organizations, with most criteria relating to an organization's *dependency* on religious entities or denominations for support, whether the *mission statement* identifies agency goals that reflect *core values* that are religious in nature, and whether the employees of the organization are religious and adhere to a *statement of faith*.

However "faith-based" is defined, it is important to remember that "faith-based" does not necessarily mean *Christian*. Despite this country's Christian roots, a number of religiously oriented organizations provide faith-based human services grounded in faiths other than Christianity. Thus although it is true that the majority of faith-based organizations are Christian in nature, many are not. Faith-based agencies may be Jewish, Muslim, Mormon, and Buddhist, each serving communities either broadly or choosing to serve individuals of that particular faith.

Faith-based human services can be facilitated as a ministry of a house of worship, or they can be facilitated as a program within a religious organization that functions as a human services agency, such as the Salvation Army. Such organizations might have the goal of converting clients to that particular faith, believing that conversion is the first step toward wholeness, or they might deliver human services in a manner similar to secular agencies, but operating in a manner consistent with the values of its religious roots. It's important to be aware of the church's or agency's mission because it will have a significant impact on how human services are delivered.

Faith-Based Community Initiatives Act

Historically it has been difficult, if not impossible, for a faith-based agency to receive government monies in support of services. The Fourth Amendment to the U.S. Constitution, which guaranteed freedom of worship, had been interpreted by the courts to require separation between religions and the government. Thus, unless the agency operated as a secular organization and did not incorporate faith into practice, it could not receive government funding. The government remains sensitive to those members of society who do not share the same faith as the majority culture and, as such, attempts to protect these individuals by passing laws that ensure that they will not be placed in positions where they are either directly or indirectly coerced into praying to a God in which they do not believe.

But in 2001 President George W. Bush passed the Faith-Based Community Initiatives Act, also known as Charitable Choice, which made it legal for faith-based organizations to receive federal funding as long as these organizations were not involved in religious worship, instruction, or proselytization, at least within the aspect of the organization seeking federal funding. Many see this is a positive step toward reengaging religious organizations in the care of those in need. Their belief is that it was unfair to exclude faith-based organizations from government funding, as well as a belief that churches and other faith-based organizations can often provide human services more proficiently than government agencies. Yet others express concern that faith-based organizations may enforce arbitrary conditions on service delivery based on religion-based morality that either directly or indirectly discriminates against certain groups, such as gays and lesbians, single parents, the poor, or individuals who embrace different values (National Association of Social Workers [NASW], 2002).

This area of disagreement will not soon disappear and amounts to concerns over whether individuals can be better assisted within some sort of moral framework or whether a moral framework results in an infringement on a client's right to self-determination. Is a homeless single mother who abuses alcohol and has three children, each from a different father, helped more by government assistance that cannot make assistance contingent on behavioral change? Or would she be helped more by a human services agency that offers financial assistance that might include a housing subsidy, but offers these services contingent on the mother entering into a drug and alcohol treatment program, not having male overnight guests, and agreeing to avoid future pregnancies until she reaches a point of self-sufficiency? Many would argue that the latter agency would have a greater chance of truly helping this woman authentically change her life.

But does making services contingent on the performance of some behavior or act rob the client of self-determination and risk forcing cultural and moral values on those who do not share these same social mores? Take, for example, single women in the 1940s and 1950s who had children out of wedlock. It was not uncommon for these women to have services denied to them unless they agreed to place their infants for adoption—a practice based on the cultural and moral belief that premarital sex was wrong and that it would be immoral for a single mother to raise an out-of-wedlock child (Edwards & Williams, 2000). The goal of this chapter is not to determine which side of this debate has a stronger argument. Certainly each side has merit, and a meaningful debate must continue.

NASW has expressed concerns about President Bush's faith-based initiative. These concerns relate primarily to issues of forced morality, the value of self-determination, and the importance of keeping services *voluntary* for all members of society regardless of their race, gender, religion, and sexual orientation. All one needs to do is conduct a cursory review of history to recognize how easy it is to confuse faith with cultural values. For example, slavery was once considered a practice sanctioned by God, and scriptural support was even offered in support of a Christian man's right to have a slave. In fact, a host of issues once considered sinful (for example, divorce, homosexuality, women in the ministry, single parenting) are now considered appropriate within many mainstream religious denominations, indicating that the interpretation of biblical scripture—and thus God's intent—is influenced by the current moral climate of society.

Most critics of President Bush's faith-based initiative are not necessarily critical of faith-based agencies' ability to provide effective human services; rather, they feel that faith-based agencies should not become the primary human services providers in the United States. The NASW advocates for government remaining responsible for providing comprehensive human services programs to the public to guarantee equal and available access to human services that encourages utilization on a voluntary basis, human service delivery that is accountable to the public and professional community in all respects, and a guarantee that service providers have appropriate levels of education and are professionally licensed in their field (NASW, 2000).

Proponents of the faith-based initiative cite the importance of fairness and equity in government funding, arguing that they should not be excluded from funding opportunities solely because of a faith orientation. In addition, many clients prefer to receive services from an organization that shares their religious values, and government funding enables these agencies to keep fees at a reasonable rate making counseling services affordable.

Methods of Practice in Faith-Based Agencies

The counseling methods used in faith-based counseling are also sometimes debated, with some expressing concern that certain behaviors are moralized in some faith-based counseling, which can be hurtful to the client. Certainly some faith-based counseling techniques may incorporate a moralistic style, a method some will agree with and some will not. But faith-based agencies can address issues of immorality such as marital unfaithfulness or child maltreatment with grace and forgiveness *as well as* a measure of accountability. What many human service professionals in faith-based agencies may argue is that too often secular practitioners assume that clients are "hit over the head with their sin" in a faith-based practitioner's office, when many times clients who are buried in shame for past poor choices are taught to approach their past mistakes and the mistakes of others with a sense of grace, forgiveness, and mercy. Thus, faith-based counseling can be less about theology and more about grace, forgiveness, mercy, and love—concepts that are universal to nearly every religion in the world.

Such debates regarding the appropriateness of how faith-based human services are provided arise even within religious circles, with some religions or denominations focusing more on social justice, where issues related to social oppression, racism, and classism are addressed in the same manner as secular agencies, and other religions and denominations professing a belief that problems in life are solved by having a relationship with God, thus bringing someone into relationship with God is the necessary first step toward healing. Even if a consensus could be obtained on this issue, evangelism in a counseling relationship outside a ministry setting remains inappropriate in most circumstances if for no other reason than it would violate the foundational principles underlying the human services profession.

The Benefits of Faith-Based Services

The majority of U.S. Americans not only identify spirituality as being an important part of their lives, but many also identify themselves as being members of faith communities (groups of individuals who share similar religious beliefs and come together for a time of worship and fellowship). Many members of faith communities rely on their congregations when going through a difficult time. Faith communities provide individuals with a valuable support system during difficult times, providing both guidance and emotional support. One goal of human services is to connect people to a broad support system, and a faith community can easily provide this for its active members. Religious coping has also been found to provide more benefits over other coping methods such as general social support and other counseling methods (Pargament, Tarakeshwar, Ellison, & Wulff, 2001).

A recent study questioned individuals within a church congregation who had recently experienced a crisis. The subjects were asked to rank various resources that they found helpful during their crisis. Factors included family, friends, religious beliefs, praying, reading scripture, and professional services, including counseling, legal services, and psychological services. The researchers were surprised to learn that most people ranked professional services last as far as helpfulness and ranked religious beliefs and praying the highest (Stone, Cross, Purvis, & Young, 2003).

Another study conducted after the September 11 terrorist attacks on the World Trade Center and the Pentagon revealed that of 560 adults questioned in a national telephone survey, 90 percent sought positive religion often in the context of a faith community as a way of coping with this tragedy. Examples of positive religion include seeing God as a source of strength and support and perceiving God and a faith community as supportive rather than a source of judgment (Meisenhelder & Marcum, 2004). These studies confirm what many therapists would likely say: that in times of crisis, many people draw strength and support from their faith communities, which provide them with a sense of comfort and familiarity while providing a sense of being a part of a larger whole and reminding them that they are not alone.

Religious Diversity in Faith-Based Organizations

Understanding the distinction in theology and ideology between the various faith-based organizations, whether that includes interfaith differences or variations among various denominations within the same faith, is important because a religious organization's theology and underlying ideology about human nature will likely serve as a reflection of the types of interventions utilized in the delivery of human services.

Many non-Christian faith-based organizations provide many of the same services as Christian-based services. Jewish Family Services, which acts as an umbrella agency for Jewish Community Centers, offers comprehensive human services to Jewish and non-Jewish communities across the nation. Islamic human services agencies focus

■ Volunteers with the Muslims of Greater Houston prepare lunch for survivors of Hurricane Katrina at a shelter in New Orleans.

primarily on the Muslim community both within the United States as well as extending services to Muslims overseas, such as Bosnians and the Palestinians, but also support causes outside the Muslim faith as well.

In fact, a recent Associated Press article discussed the outpouring of Muslim support for victims of Hurricane Katrina, the devastating natural disaster that hit New Orleans and surrounding states in August 2005 and left thousands of people homeless and with absolutely nothing. Faith-based organizations such as the Muslim American Society, the Council on American-Islamic Relations, Islamic Relief, and the Muslim American Society all participated in the Muslim Hurricane Relief Task Force, which took turns manning relief shelters and feeding those left homeless by Katrina. This is an example of how various religious faiths and houses of worship often come together to offer assistance to the poor and destitute through donations and assistance during times of crisis and natural disaster (Associated Press, 2005).

Faith-Based Agencies: Services and Intervention Strategies

In this section we'll look at several different types of faith-based agencies offering human services and examine their success in both identifying and addressing the needs of their target population. We'll also explore the role of the human service professional working in these faith-based organizations, noting any significant differences between their role and those played in secular agencies. Most of the agencies featured in this section operate separately from any church or religious entity but are either supported by a particular faith or are operated as an arm or branch of a particular denomination. All featured agencies operate in a manner consistent with the commonly accepted definition of a faith-based agency discussed earlier in this chapter.

It is important to have a basic working understanding of the values held by these different religious faiths in the event that a human service professional has a client who practices a different faith or if a human service professional coordinates services with a faith-based agency of a different faith. Having more than a superficial understanding of different faiths will enhance the human service professional's experience by enabling them to move beyond common negative stereotypes and see the value of diversity within a service delivery context.

Jewish Human Services: Agencies and the Role of the Human Service Professional

> If one of your countrymen becomes poor and is unable to support himself among you, help him as you would an alien or a temporary resident, so he can continue to live among you. (Leviticus 25:35)

The Jewish faith is rich in admonitions and examples of charity and general provision of the poor. The *Torah*, the Jewish holy book called the *Tanakh*, is what Christians call the Old Testament. The *Talmud* is the transcribed collection of oral tradition handed down from generation to generation, guiding the interpretation of the Tanakh. Charity, as referenced in both the Tanakh and the Talmud, is defined as giving to the poor and is a requirement for the Jewish people. According to Jewish law forgiveness of sins is granted with prayer, repentance, and giving to charity.

As with the Christian faith, the Jewish faith has different denominations called movements, including Orthodox, Conservative, Hasidic, Humanist, Reform, Sephardic, Ashkenazi, and Reconstructionist. Some of these movements evolved through geographic divisions and some through philosophical divisions. Nevertheless, all Jewish movements hold that charity and benevolence (kindness and compassion) are an integral part of righteousness. Good financial stewardship is highly valued in many faith traditions, and the Jewish faith is no exception. Unlike some Christian denominations that consider giving all of one's earthly possessions to the poor a blessed act, giving 5 to 10 percent of one's income to charity is considered an obligation among all Jewish denominations. Charity is not solely related to duty, though, but also reflects the value of community and the commitment to remain connected to all Jews worldwide. This sense of community is based on shared experiences of both current and historical persecution, which binds the Jewish people together in a communal determination of self-sufficiency and survival. The Talmud specifies different levels of giving, with the lowest level involving giving begrudgingly and the highest levels including giving anonymously to a stranger and helping someone attain self-sufficiency by giving them a work (Babylonian Talmud, Chagigah 5a; Maimonides, Hilchos Matnos Aniyim 10: 7–14).

Jewish human services agencies are coordinated into a national umbrella organization that serves as a network of support for smaller human services agencies that provide direct service. Human services are directed toward Jewish and non-Jewish communities as well as targeting domestic and international causes.

United Jewish Communities: The Federations of North America

The United Jewish Communities (UJC) is an international umbrella humanitarian organization that represents over 100 Jewish Federations in North America alone. The UJC and its federations provide humanitarian relief and human services worldwide to those in need. The goals of social justice and strengthening Jewish community are a reflection of the scriptures in the Talmud that command giving to the poor, sick, widows, and orphans. The UJC exists to provide financial support and educational services to Jewish Federations and Jewish community centers; it also funds the rescue and resettlement of Jews living in high-conflict or unsafe areas worldwide.

A component of the UJC is the Human Services and Social Policy Pillar (HSSP), which is responsible for social lobbying action on local and national levels in an attempt to influence social policy. Whether it's lobbying for increased funding for elderly services, homeless resources, or refugee programs, the HSSP, or "the pillar" as it is commonly called, relies on human service professionals and volunteers to coordinate services of human services agencies within and without the Jewish community.

Association of Jewish Family Services and Children's Agencies

The Association of the Jewish Family Services and Children's Agencies (AJFSCA) acts as the umbrella organization for Jewish Family Services and Jewish Community Centers across the United States and Canada. The AJFCA also acts as an information clearinghouse for local Jewish Family Services agencies, which provide comprehensive human services to the Jewish community. AJFSCAs also provide funding for local federations of Jewish human services agencies, advocate for social justice, and provide information on education and training opportunities.

Local *Jewish Family Services* (JFS) agencies offer a number of different services including individual and family counseling, marital counseling, substance abuse counseling, AIDS counseling and awareness programs, anger management courses, employment services, parenting workshops, children's camps, teen programs, and elderly programs including Kosher Meals-on-Wheels and hospice. No one is denied services due to an inability to pay, and payment for services is typically on a sliding scale.

One program that is relatively unique to this organization includes refugee resettlement programs, which assist individuals and families who have legally entered the United States having fled from persecution. Refugees of either Jewish or non-Jewish descent come from various countries, including Russia and other former Soviet-block countries, the Middle East, and Africa. Services typically include providing short-term housing on arrival, emergency financial support, case management, medical care, assistance with school enrollment, job placement, and language courses. These agencies have excellent reputations in assisting refugees to gain financial independence rapidly, particularly in light of the often tragic circumstances the refugees have faced prior to coming to the United States.

Services focused exclusively on the Jewish community include Holocaust survivor services to Jews who lived in European countries under Nazi rule between 1933 and 1945. In addition to providing counseling services related to post-traumatic stress disorder, in-home services related to elderly care are also provided. Other Jewish-related services offered include counseling and case management services for Jewish armed services personnel, Jewish chaplaincy services, family services, and outreach focusing on assisting families reconnect with their Jewish roots by learning how to incorporate Jewish traditions and values into their family systems. Premarital and marriage services are also offered to Jewish couples and interfaith couples, focusing on marriage and parenting in a Jewish context.

Human service professionals within these agencies provide a wide range of services because JFSs typically offer comprehensive human services similar to those discussed through this entire text. In fact, many of the JFSs offer just about every type of human services one could imagine! The primary difference between the manner in which human services professionals deliver services at a JFS versus a secular agency is the focus on connecting Jewish clients to the broader Jewish community, both domestically as well as worldwide, as well as the incorporation of Jewish values throughout the various programs. Counselors and case managers are also primarily Jewish and well connected to the Jewish community, including being familiar with local synagogues and other Jewish services within the local community.

Virtually all JFS programs are eligible for federal funding as long as **proselytizing** does not occur as a function of any program receiving funding. Even synagogues offering human services programs are eligible to receive government funding as long as the programs are operated separately from any religious functions.

The Jewish human services agency network provides a network of comprehensive services designed to address human needs on all levels. They provide invaluable services to the Jewish community, as well as those outside of the Jewish faith, both within the United States and abroad.

---

case study 12.1

Case Example of a Client at a Jewish Faith-Based Agency

Raisa, a 77-year-old Jewish widow, began counseling at a local Jewish Community Center about one year ago for depression. Her initial psychosocial assessment revealed a long history of mild depression with mild anxiety that had escalated in recent years to a point where intervention was necessary. Raisa shared that her normal sadness increased dramatically when she lost her husband four years ago and did not abate even when she found herself feeling more at peace with her husband's death. Raisa and her husband were married for 45 years, both having immigrated from Europe shortly after World War II. They were unable to have children of their own and thus adopted one child, a daughter, who resides in a different state about three hours away by car. Raisa's daughter is married and has one child, also through adoption. Sarah, her counselor, presumed that Raisa may have been a Holocaust survivor, and if so that some of the earlier trauma and grief issues were likely at play in her current depressive state, but Sarah chose not to address this possibility in counseling, choosing to wait until Raisa was ready to share her experience. Despite weekly counseling sessions and several courses of antidepressant medication, Raisa's depression and anxiety continued to worsen. During one session approximately nine months into their counseling relationship, Raisa was discussing the difficult early years of her marriage when she and her husband first moved to the United States. Raisa became extremely emotional as she shared that they were both orphans because of the war and thus had no family to help or guide them, either in their transition, or in their marriage. Sarah immediately recognized the grief Raisa was reexperiencing, but also noted that once Raisa became obviously distressed, she became equally uncomfortable, apologized for her "outburst," and then she quickly changed the subject and regained her composure. Sarah did not push Raisa, understanding that Raisa's decision to share her distant but obviously still-powerful memories was just that—Raisa's decision. As the months progressed Raisa began to pensively share more stories of her early marriage, which seemed to be marked by considerable loss and struggle. She was 18 when the war ended. She met her husband, Reuben, one year later, although they had met once or twice several years before. They became inseparable almost immediately, likely out of sheer loneliness, Raisa suspected, rather than any type of love at first sight, although in retrospect Raisa wasn't sure there was a difference—both were emotions that encompassed a significant amount of passionate intensity. Raisa and Reuben spent two years searching for family members. Her husband located an aunt and uncle in the United States. Raisa learned that her brother had escaped to Israel. They never located any other surviving family members. After some thought and consideration, they decided to move to the United States in the hope of connecting with her husband's relatives. When they first arrived in New York, they experienced a long-overdue measure of relief, but this was to be short-lived when Reuben's aunt and uncle announced plans to move to California. Deciding not to follow, Raisa and Reuben were left to survive on their own in a big city that offered as much risk as it did opportunity. Although Raisa spent most of her time focusing on the physical and financial hardships of her early life, she appeared to avoid any discussion of her feelings. In fact, Sarah noted that whenever Raisa risked becoming emotionally grieved such as when Sarah asked any question that required Raisa to reflect on her childhood (even positive aspects of her youth), Raisa became emotionally and physically rigid, as if she were talking herself out of the "nonsense" of her feelings to regain composure. Sarah became increasingly concerned about Raisa's psychological stability, particularly in light of her very recent increase in anxiousness. In fact, there were two recent occasions where Raisa was so anxious she did not feel comfortable leaving her home to attend her counseling session. In light of Raisa's worsening condition and her fear that Raisa might be at risk of suicide, Sarah made the decision to have a session with Raisa where she would more assertively address Raisa's Holocaust experience, believing that to be the root of her unresolved grief and the source of complicated mourning related to many of the losses she experienced after the war. Sarah went to Raisa's house for this session so that Raisa could remain in the safety of her surroundings if the session became too difficult. Sarah also had implemented a safety plan for Raisa, including collecting a list of emergency numbers and the number of a local elderly outreach center that Raisa had been involved with intermittently for several years. Sarah began her session with Raisa by gently expressing her concern about her emotional well-being, as well as sharing her belief that Raisa may be suffering long-term affects from being a Holocaust survivor, and that unless she faced her past, her depression and anxiety might not get better and may, in fact, continue to worsen. Raisa was immediately uncomfortable, but Sarah reassured her that although she wanted to push Raisa a bit, she had made sure she could remain with Raisa for the entire afternoon, thus Raisa could take her time. Although Sarah had spent considerable time in counseling sessions with Raisa conducting "psychoeducation"—teaching Raisa about the normal stages of grief and the common psychological responses to trauma—Sarah reiterated this information now in the hope that Raisa would begin to accept that her feelings were normal. During this session Raisa shared that her early childhood was one of constant happiness. Her father was a professor at a local university in Holland. Although they were not very religious, they attended synagogue weekly and observed the Sabbath. Without realizing it at the time, Raisa's family was quite immersed in the Jewish culture, which in her family meant close ties to extended family and friends within the community who had a shared culture, customs, and life perspective. Raisa recalled the emergence of a different feeling in her neighborhood when she was about 11 years old. She is not sure if this marked the slow invasion of the Nazi party into her small town, but she does recall that it was about this time that her family could no longer protect her brother and her from the fact that their lives were about to change forever. Raisa shared that her family started closing the front door and drawing the shades more frequently, and that various neighbors suddenly began to disappear. She recalls the day, at the age of 13, when almost everyone in her neighborhood was forced to wear yellow stars on their sleeves, and she marked this as the day she realized that some of her favorite neighbors were apparently not Jewish, because they did not have to wear the yellow star. Raisa emotionally shared the night she and her brother, two years her senior, were awakened in the middle of the night by their parents and told to dress quietly in the dark. They were going on a long trip but had to remain quiet. She shared that she did not recall thinking much about what was happening. Perhaps she was too scared, or maybe she had experienced so much change and shock in the past year, she simply accepted this as one more confusing event in a long line of bewildering experiences. Months earlier Raisa's father had told her that it was important for her to obey him without asking questions because not obeying him might have serious consequences. She recalled crying when he said this to her because he was so firm, an emotion she rarely saw in her father. He responded by telling her that tears were useless now—they would not help, and that she needed to be strong. She obeyed him now as she folded one change of clothing into a small dark knapsack, confused and afraid, but resolved not to cry. The next thing Raisa remembers is that she and her family were crouching down outside in the dark and running along the hedge line. She recalled that there was no moon, and the night was so dark she was certain she would lose her brother, who was directly in front her. She kept running though, trusting that someone would come back for her eventually if she lost her way. They arrived at a stranger's house, and her father knocked on a back door that appeared to lead to a basement. A young woman opened the door and hurried Raisa and her brother through the door. Raisa had only a quick moment to look back and see her mother and father, who to her horror were not following behind her and her brother. Instead, her father and mother were crying, peering into the dark basement with a look of dread and horror on their faces. Raisa immediately recalled her mother telling her earlier that she loved her very much, yet Raisa could not recall having said it in return. This was something that would torment Raisa for years. Did she tell her mother that she loved her? She would never be sure that she had. That was the last time that Raisa and her brother saw their parents. Raisa learned after the war that their parents were forced to leave their home shortly after arranging to smuggle their children out of Holland, and after a short stay in what became known as a Jewish ghetto, they were sent to a concentration camp. Although she was never able to obtain exact information, Raisa learned that both of her parents were executed likely sometime in early 1943. Raisa and her brother remained in the dark basement with little food or water for about three days before being driven, during the middle of the night, to another home. Raisa recalled crying sometimes but her brother, like her father, told her to stop and to be strong, and she complied. This time period was particularly difficult for both Raisa and her brother, who were tempted to escape and return home to their parents. She is not sure whether it was fear or wisdom that kept them from this course, but she realizes now that had they returned home, their fate would have been the same as their parents. The next trauma for Raisa occurred when she learned that she would be separated from her brother. Although her parents had arranged for them to remain together, increased risk led her rescuers to conclude that two children suddenly showing up in a home was far riskier than one, thus in the middle of one night several weeks into their frightening journey, Raisa's brother was hurried into one car, and she into another. This, too, would remain a source of considerable pain for Raisa, as she realized that once again she was denied a proper good-bye. Her last memory of her brother was his surprised face looking out the car window as he realized that she was being escorted into a different car. Raisa fled to Italy, where she lived in a converted attic, and although enjoying some measure of freedom, she had to remain relatively hidden until the war was over. Her foster parents were nice, but stern. They were not Jewish, thus Raisa was compelled to live a lifestyle very different from the one she had enjoyed in Holland. She dressed differently, attended church rather than synagogue, and ate food very different from what she was used to. It did not occur to Raisa until she was much older that there was any possibility of not seeing her family again. Her attitude during the balance of her childhood was one of "waiting it out" until the war was over and she could go home and resume life as she had known it before the war. But of course that was a dream that would never come true. When the war ended, her host family wished her good fortune, and at 17 years of age Raisa was completely on her own and alone in the world. Although God had never played much of a role in her life before, she found herself praying to the God of her childhood that her family was safe and waiting for her at home. Raisa got a job in town so that she could earn enough money to return to Holland. She met Reuben her first day of work. He was employed at the same shop, but for different reasons. It was Reuben who told her there was nothing to return to—that his family, and likely hers, was dead, and the only choice Jews had was to immigrate somewhere safe. Raisa had been sheltered by her host family and had heard nothing of the concentration camps and the unchecked slaughter of millions of Jews. She had difficulty describing the way she felt once she learned that her entire family was likely dead. She described it as both surreal and numb. She had no idea where her brother had been taken, and she had fantasized for years about finding him walking down an Italian street or shopping in the town center, but he was all she could think of now. She had to find him. She and Reuben made the singular goal of finding whatever family they had left. At some point in their planning, they became a couple and decided to marry. Raisa learned through a charitable organization that her brother was living in Israel. She shared earlier that their decision to immigrate to New York to join Reuben's family was a practical one. She shared now Reuben's fear that if they immigrated to Israel, they might find themselves in the same situation as in Holland—in the center of a war—and he could not risk becoming involved in another war ever again. Raisa let go of her hope to return to her brother when Reuben decided it would be wiser for them to move to the United States. Raisa did reconnect with her brother again, but they never enjoyed the closeness of their childhood. When she and Reuben visited her brother in Israel many years later, it felt to Raisa as if she were visiting a complete stranger. Her brother had become quite religious, embracing the faith of their youth—a choice antithetical to Raisa's, who in response to their earlier losses chose to distance herself from her Jewish roots. Raisa shared all these stories with emotion, but no tears; she was still being strong. Although Sarah decided to hold off on approaching the subject of Raisa and Reuben's infertility resulting in the adoption of their daughter, she made a mental note that she would visit this issue in a later session. Sarah knew this too would likely be a very difficult subject for Raisa and a source of great pain—both from a generational perspective (issues related to infertility were typically not discussed in earlier generations) as well as from a loss perspective. Sarah assumed that Raisa and Reuben looked forward to having their own children not simply as a way of starting their own family as so many couples do, but as a way of *replacing* the family that had been taken from them both. Sarah would learn later that Raisa's first child was a stillbirth, that the loss was almost too much for Raisa to bear, and that this was likely when Raisa's melancholy transitioned into a clinical depression. Even when Raisa and Reuben experienced the joy of adopting their daughter, Raisa shared that a sense of sadness remained hidden within her. After this intense and very long session Sarah developed a treatment plan for Raisa—one that involved both trauma and grief counseling. Sarah suspected that in addition to depression and anxiety Raisa also suffered from PTSD, thus she incorporated aspects of treatment designed to help her deal more effectively with being a survivor of trauma. Sarah suspected that Raisa was in many ways still operating with a survivor mentality, which compelled her to obey her father's distant admonition to resist crying and remain strong. Raisa's tendency to equate crying with weakness could be addressed through cognitive behavioral therapy, where Raisa would be encouraged to recognize that such rules about emotion may have been necessary in wartime, but were no longer needed and were actually damaging. The challenge for Raisa would likely lie in a fear that to change her perspective on crying might indicate a betrayal of her father. One of Sarah's ultimate treatment goals for Raisa was to help her develop a more realistic and timely definition of authentic strength that did not dishonor her father's guidance. Another treatment goal involved helping Raisa learn to grieve all her past losses and finally to rebuild the community she lost so many years ago. Although Raisa had a daughter, she had avoided ever getting too involved in her community, perhaps out of a fear that she might lose again what she had lost as a child—a close-knit community of neighbors who shared a culture and a faith and who operated in many respects as an extended family. Although Sarah suspected that Raisa might have some objections to getting involved in the local Jewish community, Sarah planned to explore this possibility with her to reconnect her to the faith and culture of her childhood. A significant portion of Raisa's healing came from a pilgrimage of sorts that Sarah helped her plan involving returning to Holland with her daughter and her brother. During this long-overdue visit Raisa and her brother tearfully revisited their childhood home, as well as other places of nostalgia, and although things had changed significantly since their youth, Raisa and her brother found great healing in their trip "home." The final leg of their trip involved creating a memorial for Raisa and her brother's parents and all her lost family and friends. Raisa's last session with Sarah prior to her trip involved writing a poem that they would leave at the site where the Chelmno concentration camp once stood. The trip not only helped her to create meaning surrounding the death of her parents, but it also helped her to reconnect emotionally with her brother and involve her daughter in a part of her life she had previously kept hidden. In succeeding years Raisa's debilitating depression lifted, and her anxiety receded. She learned how to genuinely grieve her past losses and learned to recognize how her early trauma and loss impacted virtually every area of her life. She did ultimately become involved in her community, and in the years preceding her death at the age of 84, she even resumed attending synagogue. Sarah's relationship with Raisa involved more than counseling. It involved incorporating aspects of faith and culture into sessions, case management that involved connecting Raisa to a community from which she had been generally estranged. It also involved Sarah drawing on her own Jewish faith, which enabled her to understand much of what Raisa experienced both in her past and in her current life. ■

Christian Human Services: Agencies and the Role of the Human Service Professional

For I was hungry and you gave me something to eat, I was thirsty and you gave me something to drink, I was a stranger and you invited me in, I needed clothes and you clothed me, I was sick and you looked after me, I was in prison, and you came to visit me . . . I tell you the truth, whatever you did for one of the least of these brothers of mine, you did for me. (Matthew 25:35–36, 40)

Because a fair amount of faith-based organizations in the United States are Christian in nature, it is valuable to have an understanding of the range of theologies and ideologies within the Christian church. The historic role of the Catholic Church discussed earlier in the chapter reflects Catholicism's strong commitment to caring for the poor. This commitment is reflected in today's Catholic Church in such ministries as Catholic Charities, which facilitates numerous human services programs throughout the United States.

Mainstream Protestant denominations such as Methodist, Presbyterian, and Lutheran often embraced the "**social gospel,**" the Old Testament mandate to provide for those in society in need, but these denominations did not necessary link charity to evangelism. Rather, the predominant view among these mainstream denominations was to show the love of Christ through giving as well as through addressing social concerns for the poor and the oppressed.

Conservative Christians, such as evangelicals, fundamentalists, and Pentecostals tend to focus on evangelism as the initial priority, addressing social causes and the needs of the poor through winning souls for Christ. If one truly believes that the only path toward wholeness is by surrendering one's life to Christ, repenting of one's sins, and becoming a new creation through a personal relationship with God, then it makes sense to want this experience for anyone who is suffering. The conflict arises when such evangelism occurs in the counseling office or anywhere else where social services are being provided, without the client understanding that this is the goal of the service provider. As mentioned earlier in this chapter, professional standards of the human services field, whether social work, counseling, psychology, or psychiatry, discourages proselytizing to clients. Critics of evangelical practitioners who do attempt to evangelize clients might suggest that as worthy as this act might be perceived, it is more appropriately conducted in the vein of pastoral counseling or ministry efforts (Belcher, Fandetti, & Cole, 2004).

This ethical dilemma is worth exploring in both secular and religious circles and can be addressed in a variety of ways. For instance, there is nothing inherently unethical in talking about matters of faith and spirituality as long as it is client driven. In fact, it is the human service professional's comfort level in talking about such issues and willingness to allow the client to determine the depth and direction of the discussion that is important. For instance, consider the client who enters a counseling session utilizing negative religious coping strategies such as perceiving God as punishing, abandoning, and distant, particularly when tragedy occurs. A human service professional in a faith-based agency can comfort the client by reframing the client's punitive view of God by teaching the client to use positive religious coping methods where God is perceived in a positive manner and a source of guidance, strength, and support. Because research supports the mental health benefits of **positive religious coping,** this intervention strategy can be used with the understanding that it is truly in the best interest of clients who are being hurt by their negative views of God.

Although evangelizing clients is not appropriate in a secular setting or even in a faith-based organization receiving federal funding, it is appropriate if the human service professional works for a religious organization that makes clear its goal is to evangelize the client so that the client enters the counseling relationship with full disclosure and equal participation. For instance, many outreach ministries provide emergency services such as food pantries or homeless shelters, but do not hide the fact that the ultimate goal of the agency is to lead one down the path of greater religious commitment, which may involve a deepening relationship in a client's existing faith, or it may involve a complete conversion to a new faith.

Rural Communities and the Black Church

Rural communities, typically those with high minority populations tend to be significantly underserved with regard to mental health services. Yet research in the last 10 to 15 years has revealed that African-American churches, particularly those within rural communities, have picked up the slack by offering significantly more human services than do White churches (Blank, Mahmood, Fox, & Guterbock, 2002).

There are several potential reasons for including the long-held conflict between secular mental health providers and clergy. It has been addressed in recent years but remains a point of contention with clergy not necessarily endorsing the "medical model," or secular approaches to mental health concerns, and secular mental health providers not readily perceiving mental disorders in spiritual terms. Yet as mentioned earlier in this chapter the church has a long history of providing for the social and mental health-care needs of individuals within society, and the fact that African-American churches tend to offer far more human services programs than do White churches may be a reflection of the African Americans' general sense of distrust of the mainstream mental health community and having greater trust of African-American providers (Blank, Mahmood, Fox, & Guterbock, 2002; Thomas, Quinn, Billingsley, & Caldwell, 1994).

Regardless, one variable often neglected in research on human services in the church is that for many generations the African-American church has been the center and backbone of the African-American community, thus these clergy might be more willing to engage deeply in the lives of their parishioners and those within their community. It appears that in many respects African-American churches, particularly those in rural communities have acted in some respects as the Catholic Church in the Middle Ages, taking responsibility for the mental health concerns and basic needs of those within the community.

Catholic Charities

Catholic Charities USA is a network of Christian human services agencies that has a long tradition of caring for those in need. Services are provided to all individuals seeking assistance regardless of religious affiliation. Currently there are approximately 1,600 local Catholic Charities agencies across the United States offering a wide variety of human services designed to meet the needs within the particular community served. According to the Catholic Charities Web site (www.catholiccharitiesinfo.org) services provided at most of its agencies typically fall into one of three categories:

1. *Emergency services* focusing on meeting one's basic daily needs including disaster relief, food banks, shelters, and emergency financial assistance

2. *Individuals and family services* focusing on helping people improve their life conditions including elderly care, youth counseling, foster care, health services, and refugee resettlement

3. *Community building* focusing on supporting and organizing communities including youth camps, community centers, and affordable low-income housing

Catholic Charities USA claims to have provided services to over 9 million individuals in the year 2000 alone, making it one of the largest networks of human services agencies in the world, similar in nature to the Jewish federations. The majority of funding comes from federal and state sources, with only a small percentage coming from the Catholic Church. Catholic Charities has not had significant problems obtaining federal funding because providing services directly linked to religious ministry is not typically an aspect of services provided, thus Catholic Charities has not been particularly affected by the Faith-Based Initiative.

In many respects Catholic Charities provides similar services as secular agencies except that most local Catholic Charities agencies also provide support to archdiocesan schools and parishes. Adoption and children's services are also provided, but remain consistent with the values of the Catholic faith, thus option counseling of women experiencing an unplanned pregnancy would not include referrals to abortion services. Most agencies also provide Catholic Youth Organizations (CYO), an after-school and weekend athletic program focusing on the development of sportsmanship-like behavior and ethical values consistent with the Catholic faith.

Other services include child care, domestic and international adoption, domestic violence, employment and job training, gang intervention, health care, HIV/AIDS services, immigration and naturalization services, nutrition counseling, refugee resettlement services, senior services, homeless assistance and emergency housing, senior housing, and substance abuse counseling. Most local Catholic Charities agencies also offer community centers that focus on providing comprehensive human services for those who are homeless or at risk of becoming homeless.

Human service professionals are not required to be Catholic, but many of those in leadership positions are due to the close and supportive relationship with local Catholic parishes. Human service professionals include social workers (with MSWs) and therapists, psychologists, and caseworkers and practitioners (with BSWs). Services provided are generalist in nature, and as is the case within the Jewish Federation agencies, human services interventions and clinical issues depend on the actual services being provided. Human service professionals working at Catholic Charities have the benefit of working within a broad network of agencies that provide extensive support and educational opportunities.

Prison Fellowship Ministries

Chuck Colson reached the peak of his political career as President Richard Nixon's aide, or as many referred to him, President Nixon's "hatchet man." In 1973 Colson became a Christian, and in 1974 he pleaded guilty to obstruction of justice charges in association with the Watergate scandal. Colson served seven months of a three-year sentence and on his release founded Prison Fellowship Ministries (PFM) in 1976, based on his own dramatic religious conversion and his belief that no one is beyond hope. His ministry is now one of the largest prison ministries in the world, reaching out to prisoners, ex-prisoners, their families, and victims. PFM is also involved in criminal justice reform through a PFM affiliate, Justice Fellowship, which focuses on numerous social justice issues including prison safety and eliminating prison rape.

Such social advocacy is particularly important for groups of individuals who do not evoke sympathy in the average person, and prisoners certainly fall into this category. Yet, it is essential for people to realize that prisoners are not a uniform group of evil pedophiles and serial rapists who deserve whatever hardship the prison system can dish out. Most prisoners have had childhoods marked by poverty and abuse, many serve longer sentences because they could not afford adequate legal services, and some are innocent. PFM is committed to stop the intergenerational cycle of crime and poverty by offering prisoners hope for a second chance through the Christian faith.

Citing the difference that this ministry can make in the lives of prisoners as well as in society in general, Colson references the dramatic shift in climate experienced at Angola Prison in Louisiana, once touted as the most dangerous prison in the United States, but now considered the most peaceful under the leadership of Burl Cain, a Christian who invoked the services of local seminaries to minister to inmates. In a similar vein, PFM trains volunteers to counsel and minister to prisoners in virtually every prison across the country.

PFM facilitates a number of ministries including training volunteers to visit prisoners, many of whom receive no other visits. The ministry does not receive federal funding because PFM volunteers focus extensively on the evangelism of prisoners and their family members. The goal of PFM is to bring the gospel of Christ to every prisoner incarcerated in the United States. PFM also facilitates a "pen pal" program linking prisoners with volunteers who are willing to minister to them in writing. PFM also provides services to the family members of prisoners, particularly those with children. An example of such services includes the Angle Tree program, which collects Christmas presents for these children and also facilitates a camp and a mentoring program.

Human service professionals, who are primarily volunteers, working with PFM provide markedly different services than those working in secular agencies. Because evangelism is the primary intervention tool, volunteers facilitate Bible studies and in-prison seminars, mentor at-risk youth, counsel prisoners and crime victims, serve in youth camps, organize Angel Tree programs, visit prisoners regularly, counsel ex-prisoners and crime victims, and write letters to prisoners in the pen pal program. Human service professionals also hold paid positions with PFM, including field director positions, which manage and provide support of ministry teams, including recruiting and training volunteers and reaching out to local churches for assistance and financial support.

Teen Challenge

Teen Challenge is a faith-based Christian organization that has centers worldwide, including 170 centers in the United States. Teen Challenge was founded in 1958 in New York City based on the principle that people who suffer from life-controlling addictions need to learn how to live completely different lives. Clients do not need to be Christians, but employees of Teen Challenge are and their goal is to have every client served in Teen Challenge leave the program a practicing Christian.

Teen Challenge offers residential and nonresidential care to adolescents 13 to 17 years of age, although many centers also provide services to individuals over the age of 18. Residential programs are one year in duration and focus on emotional, physical, and spiritual wholeness and healing. Residential treatment curriculum is decidedly Christian and addresses issues such as temptation, developing a personal relationship with Christ, and learning how to live a successful life as a Christian. Residents follow a daily regimen involving strict rules and discipline including attending chapel, Bible classes, and completing various work assignments. Both residential and aftercare involve counseling, group work, family counseling, job training, and life skills training. Teens and other clients remain involved in outpatient care as they learn to reintegrate into society in a sober state. The hope of Teen Challenge is to positively affect entire communities for the better as graduates go out with new attitudes and often a new faith affecting those who they previously hurt with their addiction.

Human service professionals working for Teen Challenge are practicing Christians and work as paid professionals and volunteers. Positions range from substance abuse counselors, to intake coordinators and houseparents. All human service professionals must be equipped to provide crisis counseling, individual counseling focusing on issues related to self-image, self-esteem, and intergenerational behavioral patterns, as well as social issues such as peer pressure and social constructs encouraging substance abuse. Family counseling focuses on the healing of broken relationships caused by substance abuse and other destructive behaviors.

Because Teen Challenge approaches addictions from a holistic perspective, the human service professional must be equipped to provide comprehensive counseling and case management services and must be familiar with the nature of substance abuse. But because Teen Challenge believes that the only path toward authentic change is through a relationship with Christ, human service professionals must be comfortable in the role of ministry where evangelism is the primary goal.

Independent research studying the success rate of Teen Challenge has revealed impressive results, some boasting that 86 percent of graduates remaining alcohol and drug free up to seven years after leaving the program, as compared to 6 to 7 percent in secular programs (Bicknese & Kenney, 1999; National Institute on Drug Abuse [NIDA], 1977).

---

c a s e   s t u d y   12.2

Case Example of a Client at a Christian Faith-Based Agency

Castle Christian Counseling Center (CCCC) is a not-for-profit, ecumenical counseling center contracted by the county to provide mandated counseling services, including anger management and alcohol counseling for individuals who have been charged with an alcohol offense. Julie was required to attend anger management as a part of her probation for a domestic battery charge. Julie's initial psychosocial assessment recommended that she participate in both group and individual counseling. The group counseling consisted of a 26-week program focusing on anger management and personal accountability. Her individual counseling was designed to help Julie deal with the underlying reasons for intense anger and inappropriate behavior. Julie was 24 years old when she was charged with domestic battery against her husband of three years. When Julie began counseling she was both emotionally needy and defensive. Her counselor, Dana, suspected that beneath Julie's defensiveness lay a tremendous amount of shame, so she chose not to confront Julie until much later in their counseling relationship. During the first several months of counseling Julie expressed much anger and frustration with her husband, who she perceived as being quite passive. In response to his seeming inability to make decisions or take the lead in any aspect of their life, Julie expressed extreme disappointment and at times rage. It became clear to Dana that Julie's husband was in many respects being set up for failure by Julie. For instance, Julie often expressed to her husband that she wished he would be more proactive in their social life, but if he did forge ahead and make plans without checking with her first, she would become irate that he chose an activity he knew she would not like. Yet if he checked with her first before making plans, she would become angry that he did not have the confidence to make plans without her, and she would accuse him of ruining the surprise for her. The incident that resulted in the charge of domestic battery involved a fight that escalated over their finances. Julie had decided to quit her job to try to get pregnant, even though her husband had expressed concerns that he did not make enough money to be the sole provider. He ultimately supported her decision, and Julie quit her job, but after a few months, when money got tight, and they ultimately did not have enough money to pay bills, Julie lost her temper. During her tirade she accused her husband of not caring about their finances and of sabotaging their plans to start a family. Julie became physically abusive toward her husband when he attempted to stand up to her by telling her that he had not in fact wanted her to quit her job because he feared this very thing. Julie became hysterical, accusing her husband of hating her and of just looking for an excuse to leave her. Dana recognized Julie's tendency to change the facts to support whatever theory she was attempting to prove at the moment. She also recognized Julie's all-or-nothing thinking—people either loved her or hated her, were for her or against her. According to secular psychology Julie would have met the criteria for borderline personality disorder, but Dana recognized her behavior as indicative of a contemporary form of idol worship. Julie was expecting her husband to be God, yet there was only one God who could meet all Julie's needs. Dana knew that over the next several months she would be Julie's representative of God—showing her unconditional love as well as truth. She made a commitment to Julie that she would always be honest with her, and there would be nothing that Julie could do that would lead Dana to end their relationship. She trusted that Julie could handle the truth if it were delivered in love, not shame. It was only a few days later that Julie seemed to test Dana's commitment. Julie called Dana and left a frantic message, stating that she was very upset and needed to talk immediately. When Dana had not returned her call within the hour, Julie called again and but this time was enraged. She accused Dana of being like everyone else—making promises but then abandoning her when she was most in need. Before returning Julie's call, Dana prayed for wisdom and insight. She immediately had an image of truth as light, and for Julie, any truth at all was like a flashlight blaring into her eyes, causing Julie to have to bat the light away to avoid the pain. Dana knew immediately from then on that she would have to be gentle not only in the amount of truth she shared with Julie, but also in the way she shared her wisdom. In the face of Julie's intense and abrasive defensiveness, Dana resisted the natural tendency to force truth on her. Instead she indulged Julie a little, suspecting that Julie's initial feeling when she made a mistake was intense shame, but before she could respond to this emotion she reacted by flipping her shame outward into anger against anyone who represented the source of shame—anyone who made her feel guilty in some way, who exacted accountability, even someone who cried in response to one of her rages. Dana's intuition told her that if she could relieve some of Julie's shame—take her off the hook in some manner—this might give Julie the emotional space to explore her feelings of intense shame and guilt. When Dana did call, she suspected that Julie would already be feeling immense shame and guilt, regretting her tirade. Dana also suspected that Julie would not be able to emotionally manage these feelings, thus would have a need to rationalize her behavior by escalating Dana's "sin" to match her own reaction. Dana knew that if she admonished Julie for her tantrum, this would set this process in motion, so she did something different; she took Julie off the hook and rather than admonishing her, she praised her for her ability to communicate her feelings! Julie was so taken off guard that it actually enabled her to experience feeling a small amount of guilt. After Dana had finished complimenting Julie on her willingness to communicate, Julie admitted that she should have handled her feelings differently, that she should have been more patient, and that in some respects she believed she was expecting to be let down by Dana, thus she didn't even give her a chance to meet her needs. Success! By taking this counterintuitive approach and lifting the burden of shame, Julie was able to actually recognize her internal process without rationalizing her feelings away. During the course of their counseling Dana addressed Julie's negative feelings about God. Julie shared that she felt very insignificant whenever she thought of God. She then shared new elements of her childhood. She had already disclosed a childhood wrought with abuse and emotional humiliation at the hands of both her father and her mother, but during this particular session, Julie shared that whenever she made a mistake as a child, her father would tell her she was going to hell, that she was a disappointment to God, and that she could not hide from God—he could see her wherever she was and he knew what she was doing, and what she was doing the majority of the time was bad. Julie's father would often physically abuse her, sometimes using a Bible to beat her on the head. When Dana asked Julie to draw a picture of her relationship with God, Julie drew a picture where she was quite small, crouched down and running, and God, a large presence on the page, was looking down on her with a stern scowl on his face. Dana asked Julie if she ever turned to God when going through a difficult time. Julie looked shocked, expressing her belief that if she was in trouble, God would be the last she would consider turning toward. In fact, Julie shared that she believed that the only time God paid any attention to her was when she had messed up. She imagined God saying, "There you go again—I knew you would blow it eventually!" Dana told Julie that she would like to spend some time sharing a different type of God with her, not a punishing God, but a loving God who acted as a father to his children—guiding his children when they were walking down the wrong path, like any good father, and applauding when they did well. Dana shared about her own feelings toward her young son. She found herself chuckling even when he got himself into a bit of trouble, like the time he wrote his name in purple crayon all over his closet door, only to deny his culpability when Dana came upon his artwork. Dana was not harsh, nor punishing, but she did want to teach her son that defacing property was not the best choice. She did this in love, extending grace and forgiveness because she understood that at this age her son did not know any better. She also smirked as she admired her son's artwork, knowing that drawing on the wall with crayon was a perfectly normal thing to do. Julie could not fathom a God who was anything but condemning but she was very interested in learning about the concepts of grace and forgiveness. Once Dana was confident that Julie trusted her, she began to respond to each of Julie's rage episodes by first empathizing with Julie's emotions—her disappointment, her fear, her anger—but then followed by gently sharing truth. When Julie asked if Dana thought she was wrong to have such high expectations of her husband, Dana said yes, but that did not mean that Julie should have no expectations. Rather, Dana explained that once Julie developed a more solid emotional base within herself, including having a more solid relationship with God, her expectations of her husband would likely be more realistic. Julie's counseling also consisted of a significant amount of grief counseling, mourning her lost childhood, gaining insight and understanding of the abuse she had endured, and learning her emotional triggers and ways to avoid them. Dana taught Julie to contain her emotions, so that she wouldn't have to react the moment she experienced an intense emotion, such as the intense fears that she was going to be abandoned, which would often turn toward anger. Dana used guided imagery directing Julie to imagine Jesus holding her firmly, but lovingly. Imagery exercises of this type also helped Julie make God more real in her life. Dana also encouraged Julie to read one new scripture per week. Julie's favorite was Romans 8:28, "And we know that in all things God works for the good of those who love him who have been called according to his purpose." For Julie this meant that even the abuse she endured would be used for good—like making lemonade out of lemons. Another favorite scripture that brought great comfort to Julie was Jeremiah 29:11-13, "For I know the plans I have for you," says the Lord. "They are plans for good and not for disaster, to give you a future and a hope. In those days when you pray, I will listen. If you look for me in earnest, you will find me when you seek me. I will be found by you." Julie felt that this scripture meant that God had good intentions for her, not evil ones. He wanted the best for her, not the worst. He would not hide from her, and she did not have to hide from him. Julie continued counseling even after she met her mandated requirement. In her second year of counseling Dana shifted focus from Julie's childhood, to her current relationships, including the relationship with her husband. Julie's intense fear of abandonment often led her to be so self-focused that she was blinded to the damage she caused other people. As her fear of abandonment subsided and her shame diminished, Dana was able to coach Julie into looking through the eyes of her husband. This process would have been impossible a year ago because the shame would have paralyzed her, but with her increasing internal strength, Julie was able to accept her behavior and the pain it caused. Once she saw herself as deserving of forgiveness, she could address her own abusive behavior. Within the second year of therapy, Julie's anger receded significantly, and she was able to talk through her feelings rather than act them out. She remained in counseling intermittently for years to maintain her program of faith building, emotional containment, and extending forgiveness to self and others. ■

Islamic Human Services: Agencies and the Role of the Human Service Professional

It is not righteousness that you turn your faces towards East or West; but it is righteousness to believe in Allah and the Last Day and the Angels and the Book and the Messengers; to spend of your substance out of love for Him, for your kin, for orphans, for the needy, for the wayfarer, for those who ask; and for the ransom of slaves; to be steadfast in prayers and practice regular charity; to fulfill the contracts which you made; and to be firm and patient in pain (or suffering) and adversity and throughout all periods of panic. Such are the people of truth, the God fearing. (Qur'an 2: 177)

Islam is a religion that is often misunderstood and mischaracterized, both by the general public and by the media. This mischaracterization is due in part to the differences between more liberal Western values and the more conservative values held by many in the Islamic community. The terrorist acts of September 11 have further exacerbated the tendency to view the entire Muslim world as one that endorses violence and female oppression. In truth, every culture and every religious faction has its peaceful members and its violent ones. A domestic batterer who uses the Christian fundamentalist concept of submission to justify the oppression and abuse of his wife does not define Christianity any more than does a terrorist bent on destruction define the Muslim religion.

The word *Islam* means submission, and followers of Islam submit themselves to the monotheistic God, Allah. The Muslim holy book is called the *Qur'an*, (sometimes referred to as Koran, but because this is the Anglicized spelling, most Muslims prefer the spelling included previously because it most accurately reflects the correct pronunciation in Arabic). The Qur'an is considered by Muslims to be the recited word of God revealed to the prophet Mohammad in the seventh century. Islam recognizes and relies on the holy books of Judaism and Christianity (the Old and New Testaments), but Muslims consider the Qur'an to be God's final revelation to humankind.

There are approximately one billion followers of Islam, which makes it the second-largest religion in the world. The majority of Muslims live in Southeast Asia, Northern Africa, and the Middle East. There are two primary sects within Islam due to an early dispute over who should have been Mohammad's predecessor. The Sunnis tend to be more religiously and politically liberal (for instance, they believe that Islamic leaders should always be elected). Approximately 90 percent of all Muslims are Sunni. Shiites, on the other hand, tend to be more orthodox in their religious beliefs and political philosophies, having developed a more strictly academic application of the Qur'an. They believe that all successors to Mohammad (Imams) are infallible and sinless. They appoint their clergy and hold them in high regard.

The majority of Muslims who live in the United States are Sunnis, 75 percent of whom are foreign born. The Muslim community tends to be both college educated and middle class, thus they tend not to rely on government-sponsored human services to meet basic needs, and much of the focus of charity is directed toward Muslims in other parts of the world who are suffering, either because of war or some other form of oppression, or is focused on concerns related to marriage and family.

Because Muslims hail from many different countries there is considerable diversity within the Muslim community, particularly in the United States. Yet despite the variability of cultural beliefs and practices, the House of Islam shares five basic pillars of faith:

- ▶ *Shahada:* Faith in one God
- ▶ *Salat:* Ritual prayer five times a day while facing Mecca
- ▶ *Zakat:* Charitable giving to the poor with the understanding that all wealth belongs to God
- ▶ *Sawm:* Fasting from sunrise to sunset during the month of Ramadan
- ▶ *Hajj:* Pilgrimage to Mecca

The three foundational values within the Islamic community include community, family, and the sovereignty of God. Family is often defined as the joining of two extended families, thus what might be considered "enmeshment" in North American society is often seen as a sign of respect as extended families are drawn close and remain an active part of the immediate family's life. Men and women typically adopt traditional roles with men working outside of the home, and women caring for the home and children. Modesty is seen as an important ingredient necessary for keeping order within society, and women often wear clothing (*hijab*) that covers the greater percentage of their bodies (Hodge, 2005).

Hodge (2005) pointed out the areas of obvious conflict between Islamic values and liberal North American values. For instance, Western culture values individualism, self-expression, and self-determination, whereas Islamic culture values community, self-control, and consensus. Thus whether working with an Islamic human services agency, coordinating services with one, or directly serving the Islamic community, Hodge cautions human services workers not to view Islamic values through the eyes of Western culture.

For example, it is common for Westerners to view the Islamic tenet of modesty as primitive and oppressive to women, which for most Westerners is a "hop, skip, and a jump" away from endorsing domestic violence. Yet the Qur'an states that husbands and wives must express respect and compassion toward one another, and domestic violence is not endorsed. To truly understand the values of modesty and traditional roles embraced within the Islamic culture, one must take the time to understand what these values mean to the men and women within the Islamic culture itself.

Hence, although a human service professional might not share the traditional values held within the Islamic community, working in association with Islamic human services agencies provides human service professionals with an opportunity to display their respect for cultural diversity.

There has been a recent surge in interest in developing human services programs within mosques and Islamic centers across the United States in response to growing concerns about social issues and demonstrated needs within the Muslim community, particularly related to marriage, family, and general hostility often expressed toward this community in the post–September 11 climate. The disciplines of human services or social work are relatively new to the Islamic community, but charity is not new and has been practiced within the Islamic community for generations. Islamic human services professionals include social workers, counselors, and psychologists, but these services can also be offered by an *Imam,* a Muslim religious leader.

Islamic charities have suffered since the September 11 terrorist attacks, though, because many Muslims in the United States are afraid that monies they donate in good faith to Islamic charities may be frozen by the U.S. government and not directed to humanitarian causes as planned. Muslims are also giving less because they are afraid that they might be held in suspicion if a charity they donate money to is later investigated for the possibility that monies are being diverted to terrorist causes. Mosques and Islamic centers across the nation are reaching out to legislators in a campaign called "Charity without Fear," asking them to establish a list of Islamic charities in good standing, so that devout Muslims can give to charity without fear of being accused of supporting terrorist organizations. (Council of Islamic Organizations, 2005).

Islamic Social Services Association

Although human services agencies are not yet prolific within the Muslim community, they are increasing in numbers. The *Islamic Social Services Association* (ISSA) acts as an umbrella organization for all Muslim human services agencies in the United States and Canada. The ISSA provides training and educational services, acting as a network linking and equipping Muslim communities.

Inner-City Muslim Action Network

One group of agencies is called *Inner-City Muslim Action Network* (IMAN), which focuses on meeting the needs of those in the inner city in Chicago by operating food pantries, health clinics, and prayer services. The agency's offices, which are located in a storefront on Chicago's South Side, offers a free computer lab with free Internet service, GED courses, and computer training classes. IMAN is also involved in community activism such as lobbying against the granting of liquor licenses in high-crime areas, community development, and coordination of outreach events with other community agencies both Muslim and non-Muslim.

Muslim Family Services

There is considerable concern within the Islamic faith community that Muslim marriages are being negatively affected by the casual nature of divorce in the United States. Muslim Family Services, which are sprinkled throughout the United States, focus on divorce prevention. Muslim Family Services are a division of the Islamic Circle of North America (ICNA), an organization designed to assist Muslims live a more devout life. Muslim Family Services offers human services to families and couples, teaching them how to have a marriage according to Islamic principles.

Muslim Family Services provides education, such as workshops for married couples and training for Imams; premarriage, marriage, and parenting counseling; emergency services; foster care; and advocacy in court and with social services, particularly in relation to Muslim family values. Islamic values are stressed, including the belief that marriage is the foundation of society and the pillar on which family is built. Human service professionals working for Muslim Family Services understand that Muslim couples living in the United States are often caught between two cultures, thus many are influenced by the more liberal Western values. This has led to increased divorce rates and also many parenting challenges as adolescents in particular challenge traditional Islamic values such as modesty and male–female relationships.

Although there are not an abundant number of human services agencies such as Muslim Family Services, human services professions working within these agencies are Muslim and must be familiar with Islamic family values and the Qur'an, particularly in matters related to marriage and raising children. Many human service providers use similar counseling methods as do providers in secular agencies, but case management and generalist services are not as widely practiced because a human services network is not as well developed within this community.

Yet as the Muslim community within the United States continues to be confronted with issues related to acculturation, modernization, and the eroding of traditional values, problems within the family will no doubt continue to rise. Competing marital roles, adolescent rebellion, and at times social isolation, including the internalization of the majority culture's negative views of the Muslim faith, all contribute to the gradual breakdown of the Muslim family system. Human services agencies can assist Muslim families feel less isolated, can provide much-needed education and support, and can provide a sense of connectedness among Muslims who are feeling unsupported within their communities.

case study 12.3

Case Example of a Client at a Muslim Faith-Based Agency

Maya is a 42-year-old Muslim woman who was referred to an Islamic women's center for advocacy and counseling. She has been married to Asad, a 44-year-old physician, for 18 years. Maya is the stay-at-home mother of their three children, ages 10, 12, and 14. Both Maya and Asad are originally from Egypt, having immigrated to the United States shortly after getting married. Maya reports that she and her husband have always been devout Muslims, being very involved in their local mosque. They have had what she considers a traditional Muslim marriage, where her husband is the leader of the home and provides for the family financially, and Maya takes care of the home and the children. For the majority of their marriage Maya believes that their marriage has been a good one. She believes that her husband was always very respectful of her and relied on her wisdom and input in making decisions impacting the family, particularly with regard to the children. Because Maya was an accountant prior to getting married, Asad has relied on her to help with financial matters related to his medical practice. Maya reported that about five years ago Asad began to "bring his work home with him," which led to an increase in his general irritability and frustration. In the last two years Maya noted that he began to become more controlling of her whereabouts, getting angry with her if he could not reach her at a moment's notice. She did not reach out then because she believed Asad when he said that it was his right to control her in this manner. Although Maya's father did not behave in this manner, she began to believe that perhaps she needed to endure Asad's behavior in order to be a good Muslim wife. Maya shared that in the past few months his aggression has escalated to the point of screaming at her, both at home and in public, backing her into corners. His drinking has escalated as well. The incident that prompted Maya to finally reach out for help occurred after she refused to sleep with Asad because he was extremely intoxicated and verbally abusing her. Asad became irate and began beating her citing his right per the Qur'an (4:34-35). Maya initially went to the Imam at her mosque, who supported her completely and also explained that her husband's use of the Qur'an was a misinterpretation. He explained that Islam did not in any way condone abuse. He provided her with a considerable amount of information regarding the "cycle of violence" and services in the community for victims of domestic violence, including support groups for both adults and children. Maya contacted the Muslim women's center that day and saw a counselor later in the week. During Maya's first counseling center she expressed relief that her community was so supportive of her, but she expressed sadness as well because the information and resources she received seemed so fatalistic and hopeless. Her counselor explained that her husband was acting in a manner inconsistent with the will of Allah and if he was truly committed to following Islam and being a good Muslim husband and father, then perhaps he would be open to receiving counseling as well. Domestic violence, the counselor explained, not only destroyed everyone in the family but also affected the entire community, thus the Muslim community was as concerned about Asad as it was about Maya. During counseling Maya began to understand the underlying dynamics of her husband's behavior and gained wisdom regarding the difference between a husband who led his family with respect, as described by Mohammad, and the controlling and abusive behavior exhibited by her husband. As Maya gained confidence in herself and her decisions, she felt strongly that Allah was leading her to be strong for the sake of her family. Strength, according to her counselor, meant that she could not tolerate abuse. Asad met with the Imam for several weeks and then reluctantly agreed to attend a one-year anger management program that was led by a Imam at the community Islamic center, and Maya agreed not to make any decisions about whether to consider a divorce until after Asad had finished his program. Both the Imam and the counselor agreed that family counseling should not occur until after Asad had received enough counseling to recognize that the root of the family and marital problems lay within him. As Maya continued counseling, she began to realize the intergenerational cycle of abuse that existed in her husband's family and how important it was, particularly for the sake of her children, that she become strong enough to break the cycle. The most difficult aspect of this process for Maya was maintaining good boundaries with Asad and realizing that he had the choice not to change, which would force her hand in a sense, forcing her to leave the marriage to avoid repeating the patterns of abuse. ◼

Concluding Thoughts on Faith-Based Human Services Agencies

As the field of human services evolves and matures, the scope with which this discipline is viewed is broadened and the value of services provided by those not within the mainstream mental health community will be increasingly recognized. Whether these services are delivered informally through church-sponsored programs or through highly organized faith-based human services agencies such as those provided by the Jewish Federations or Catholic Charities, embracing a broad approach to human services delivery acknowledges the reality that different people seek help in different ways.

r e f e r e n c e s

Associated Press. (2005). *Muslim groups help Katrina victims on 9/11 anniversary.* Retrieved on August 25, 2005, from http://www.cnn.com/2005/US/09/11/katrina.muslims.ap/

Belcher, J. R., Fandetti, D., & Cole, D. (2004). Is Christian religious conservatism compatible with the liberal social welfare state? *Social Work, 49(2),* 269–276.

Bicknese, A. T., & Kenney, A. C. (1999). *Teen Challenge's proven answer to the drug problem: A summary of a dissertation, "The Teen Challenge drug treatment program in comparative perspective."* Unpublished manuscript, Northwestern University, Evanston, IL.

Blank, M. B., Mahmood, M., Fox, J. C., & Guterbock, T. (2002). Alternative mental health services: The role of the Black church in the South. *American Journal of Public Health, 92(10),* 1668–1672.

Counsel of Islamic Organizations. Charity without Fear. (2005). Retrieved on August 24, 2005, from: http://www.ciogc.org/pages/Menu/campaign/charities/pageDetailPB2.html

Ebaugh, H. R., Pipes, P. F., Chafetz, J. S., & Daniels, M. (2003). Where's the religion? Distinguishing faith-based from secular social service agencies. *Journal for the Scientific Study of Religion, 42(3),* 411–426.

Edwards, C. E., & Williams, C. L. (2000). Adopting change: Birth mothers in maternity homes today. *Gender and Society, 14(1),* 160–183.

Fallot, R. D. (2001). Spirituality and religion in psychiatric rehabilitation and recovery from mental illness. *International Review of Psychiatry, 13,* 110–116.

Fallot, R. D., & Heckman, J. D. (2005). Religious/spiritual coping among women trauma survivors with mental health and substance use disorders. *Journal of Behavioral Health Services and Research, 32(2),* 215–226.

Gallup, G., & Lindsey, D. M. (1999). *Surveying the religious landscape: Trends in U.S. beliefs.* Harrisburg, PA: Morehouse.

Grossman, C. L. (2002, March 7). Charting the unchurched in America. *USA Today,* p. D01.

Hall, C. R., Dixon, W. A., & Mauzey, E. D. (2004). Spirituality and religion: Implications for counseling. *Journal of Counseling & Development, 82,* 504–507.

Hodge, D. R. (2004). Working with Hindu clients in a spiritually sensitive manner. *Social Work, 29(1),* 27–38.

Hodge, D. R. (2005). Social work in the house of Islam: Orienting practitioners to the beliefs and values of Muslims in the U.S. *Social Work, 50(2),* 162–173.

Idler, E. L., & Kasl, S. (1992). Religion, disability, depression and the timing of death. *American Journal of Sociology, 97,* 1052–1079.

Kliewer, S. (2004). Allowing spirituality into the healing process. *The Journal of Family Practice, 53(8),* 616–624.

Koenig, H. G., George, L. K., Hays, J. C., Larson, D. B., Cohen, H. J., & Blazer, D. G. (1998). The relationships between religious activities and blood pressure in older adults. *International Journal of Psychiatry Medicine, 28,* 189–213.

Koenig, H. G., George, L. K., & Titus, P. (2004). Religion, spirituality, and health in medically ill hospitalized elderly patients. *Journal of American Geriatrics Society, 52(4),* 554–562.

Koenig, H. G., Larson, D. B., & Weaver, A. J. (1998). Research on religion and serious mental illness. *New Directions in Mental Health Surveys, 80,* 81–95.

McLaughlin, D. (2004). Incorporating individual spiritual beliefs in treatment of in-patient mental health consumers. *Perspectives in Psychiatric Care, 40(3),* 114–119.

Meisenhelder, J. B., & Marcum, J. P. (2004). Responses of clergy to 9/11: Post-traumatic stress, coping and religious stress. *Journal for the Scientific Study of Religion, 43(4),* 547–554.

Miller, M. M., Korinek, A., & Ivey, D. C. (2004). Spirituality in MFT training: Development of the spiritual issues in supervision scale. *Contemporary Family Therapy 26(1),* 71–81.

Miller, W. R., & Thoresen, C. E. (2003). Spirituality, religion, and health: An emerging research field. *American Psychologist, 58,* 24–35.

National Association of Social Workers (NASW). (2002, January). *NASW Priorities on faith-based human services initiatives.* Retrieved September 13, 2005, from http://www.naswdc.org/advocacy/positions/faith.asp

National Institute on Drug Abuse (NIDA). (1977). *An evaluation of the Teen Challenge treatment program.* Rockville, MD: Author. (DHEW publication no. ADM. 77-425)

Pargament, K. I., Tarakeshwar, N., Ellison, C. G., & Wulff, K. M. (2001). The relationships between religious coping and well-being in a national sample of Presbyterian clergy, elders, and members. *Journal for the Scientific Study of Religion, 40(3),* 497–513.

Powell, L., Shahabi, L. & Thoresen, C. E. (2003). Religion and spirituality: Linkage to physical health. *American Psychologist, 58,* 36–52.

Stone, H. W., Cross, D. R., Purvis, K. B., & Young, M. J. (2003). A study of the benefit of social and religious support on church members during times of crisis. *Pastoral Psychology, 51(4),* 327–340.

Teen Challenge. (n.d.). *Teen Challenge: About us.* Retrieved July 3, 2005 from http://www.teenchallenge.com/socal/index.cfm?infoID=1&centerID=1024

Thomas, S. B., Quinn, S. C., Billingsley, A., & Caldwell, C. (1994). The characteristics of Northern Black churches with community health outreach program. *American Journal of Public Health, 84(4),* 575–579.

Tseng, W. S. (2004). Culture and psychotherapy: Asian perspectives. *Journal of Mental Health, 13(2),* 151–161.

White House Office of Faith-Based and Community Initiatives. (n.d.). *President Bush's faith-based and community initiatives: Overview.* Retrieved July 11, 2005 from http://www.whitehouse.gov/government/fbci/mission.html

suggested reading

Allender, D. B., & Longman, T. (1993). *Bold love.* Colorado Springs, CO: Navpress Publishing Group.

Bloom, J. H. (Ed.). (2006). *Jewish relational care A-Z: We are our other's keeper.* Binghamton, NY: Haworth Judaica Practice Press.

Cloud, H., & J. Townsend (1994). *Boundaries.* Grand Rapids, MI: Zondervan.

Cnaan, R. A., Wineburg, R. J., & Boddie, S. C. (1999). *The newer deal: Social work and religion in partnership.* New York: Columbia University Press.

Derezotes, D. *Spirituality social work practice.* Boston: Allyn & Bacon.

Donaldson, D., & Carlson-Thies, S. W. (2003). *A revolution of compassion: Faith-based groups as full partners in fighting America's social problems.* New York: Baker Books.

Ellor, J. W., Netting, F. E., & Thibault, J. M. (1999). *Religious and spiritual aspects of human service practice.* Columbia, SC: University of South Carolina Press.

Martin, E. P., & Martin, J. M. (2003). *Spirituality and the black helping tradition in social work.* Washington, DC: NASW Press.

Yarhouse, M. A., Butman, R. E., & McRay, B. W. (2005). *Modern psychopathologies: A comprehensive Christian appraisal.* Downers Grove, IL: Inter-Varsity Press.

internet web sites related to faith-based agencies

Islamic Social Welfare Association: **http://www.radio786.co.za/community/org/ISWA/**
United Jewish Communities: **http://www.ujc.org/**

chapter 13

Violence, Victim Advocacy, and Corrections

The field of forensic human services includes areas in which the human services discipline intersects with the legal system. Thus, human service professionals who work in practice settings dealing with domestic violence, sexual assault, gang activity, and criminal justice agencies such as police departments, probation, state, and county prosecutors, and within correctional facilities such as jails and prisons are considered forensic human service providers. The role and function of these practitioners will vary dramatically depending on the legal or criminal issues at play, but most forensic areas require specialized training in areas such as crime victimization and crisis counseling, as well as developing a thorough understanding of the legal and criminal justice system.

Violence has always been a part of human history. In fact, violence exists in all segments of life among living creatures. A lion's survival is dependent on its killing of a wildebeest or zebra, which involves an act of violence. Yet although biologists would likely argue that violence is a natural aspect of survival in the animal kingdom, controversy abounds when this theory is applied to humankind. Does a review of history reveal that war is necessary? Certainly war has always existed, but is our existence dependent on competition for resources won through violent means? At what point does the act of war become the act of **genocide?** How can ordinary people live side by side peaceably for years and suddenly commit heinous acts, such as was the case during the Holocaust or the more recent genocide in Rwanda, and somehow justify their actions? Perhaps having the ability to respond in intense anger that manifests in violence is necessary when one is defending oneself, but doesn't the unjust use of violence make this defensive response necessary in the first place?

Determining the answer to these questions lies at the heart of violence research within the domain of social scientists such as sociologists, social psychologists, anthropologists, and criminologists, as well as those who work in the "applied" fields such as human services and those working within the criminal justice system. In this chapter the various types of violence will be explored, such as domestic violence, sexual assault, battery, and murder. Ways in which society and those within the human services fields most often intervene to reduce violence that not only affects its victims but also society as a whole will be explored.

Domestic Violence

Domestic violence, also referred to as family violence and intimate partner violence, involves the physical and emotional abuse acted out between intimates. This may include violence between husbands and wives, boyfriends and girlfriends, violence within gay and lesbian relationships, and violence between siblings. Domestic violence can include hitting, punching, slapping, pinching, shoving, and throwing objects at or near the victim. It is also typically associated with verbal and emotional abuse including name-calling, harassment, taunting, put-downs, and ridiculing. Emotional and verbal abuse can occur without physical abuse, but rarely does physical abuse occur without emotional or verbal abuse.

Statistics on the incidence of domestic violence are alarming. In 2003 alone (the most recent year available) approximately 5.3 million women were the victims of intimate partner violence in the United States, resulting in over 2 million injuries per year and about 1,300 deaths (Centers for Disease Control, 2003). Nearly 325,000 women are victims of domestic violence while pregnant, and research suggests that pregnancy can actually make women more vulnerable to abuse. Once considered a personal family matter, the public realized in recent generations that domestic violence affects entire communities, both fiscally as well as socially. Women with a history of domestic violence report having significantly higher rates of physical health problems. Physical problems from assaults, partner rape, and the stress of living in a violent environment can lead to chronic pain, gynecological problems, HIV/AIDS, and other sexually transmitted diseases, gastrointestinal problems, unwanted pregnancy, miscarriage, and premature births. The estimated health costs related to domestic violence is close to $6 million per year and $1.8 billion in lost productivity including lost time from work, unemployment, and increased dependence on public aid. (Gazmararian et al., 2000)

Domestic violence does not just affect the abused spouse. The children living in the home are victims as well, even if the violence is not aimed directly toward them. Children who are raised in homes where domestic violence is practiced are 60 percent more likely to get involved in juvenile delinquency and 30 percent more likely to become a perpetrator of abuse when adults (Maxfield & Widom, 1996). Clearly, then, domestic violence is not a private family matter. The cost to society, both in injured members and lost revenue, is far too high to ever allow this issue to be ignored again.

The Nature of Domestic Violence: The Cycle of Violence

Lenore Walker (1979) was the first to coin the phrase the *cycle of violence* to describe the pattern of interpersonal violence in intimate relationships. Most abusive relationships often begin in a *honeymoon-like state* with the abusers often telling their new partners that they are the only people in the world they can trust—the only ones who understand them. New partners are usually swept off their feet with compliments and many promises for a wonderful future. Once the abuser feels comfortable in the relationship, a dual process occurs. The abuser begins to feel vulnerable by recognizing their partner's power to hurt them deeply, and as familiarity in the relationship increases, the abuser often increases his sense of entitlement to have all his needs met.

Plagued with fears that they will be abandoned, taken advantage of, and humiliated (as many were in their childhoods), jealousy, possessiveness, and accusations begin. Emotional immaturity often prevents abusers from being able to separate their internal feelings from possible causes (i.e., Are their feelings of jealousy caused by their own insecurities, or caused by their partner's unfaithfulness?), thus a common assumption among batterers is that if they feel badly, their partners must be doing something to cause it.

In response to these threatening feelings of vulnerability and entitlement, and poised to be hurt once again, innocent partners often become the focus of the batterer's mistrust, fear, and ultimate rage. Abusers often misinterpret the intentions of their partners, mentally ticking off injustice after injustice. These types of negative misperceptions and misassumptions are prevalent and are rarely checked against fact.

Most partners of batterers will sense the increasing *tension* brought about by the abusers' underlying anger that is bubbling to the surface. Batterers might ask more questions, make sarcastic comments, ask why two cups are out rather than one, or question why the phone wasn't answered more quickly when they called. They will typically have a shorter fuse, becoming easily frustrated often without provocation. In response, most victims do their best to *walk on eggshells* to avoid an explosion. But no amount of running interference or offered reassurances will help because the process is an internal one, occurring within the mind of the abuser. In fact, most abusers have an actual *need* to be proven correct in their fear of being hurt and humiliated again because to a batterer, being too trusting is often synonymous with being an unsuspecting fool.

Eventually the *explosion* occurs despite all peacemaking efforts. Abusive rages can take on several forms including frightening bouts of screaming and yelling; intimidation; and physical abuse such as hitting, kicking, scratching, grabbing, slapping, and shoving. Attacks might also include throwing objects at or near the victim, punching walls, and making threats to harm either the person or personal property of the victim.

Once batterers have experienced a violent rage, they are often temporarily relieved of their internal feelings of rage and in many respects take on the persona of a remorseful child seeking reassurance and approval. Batterers often *honeymoon* their partners and other family members who were victims of the abuse, promising never to repeat the abusive behavior. There is commonly a manipulative aspect to the batterer's professions of regret and apologies, with the extent of authentic remorse being somewhat questionable. One reason for this is that the batterer's apologies are often riddled with a series of "buts": "I'm sorry I hit you, *but* you know how I hate to be awakened early in the morning." "I'm sorry I shoved you, *but* you know I don't like you talking to other men." "I'm sorry I slapped you, *but* you know how stressed I get when work is so busy."

Rarely is the batterer's focus authentically placed on the pain and trauma caused to the partner or other family members. Rather, the honeymoon phase involves more of a panicked pleading, begging the victim not to leave, to forgive and forget, to move on quickly by minimizing the extent of the abuse. Statements intended to reframe the abuse, such as "I can't believe you think I shoved you! I clearly remember me reaching out to you and you jerking away and tripping . . ." are common.

This can be an immensely confusing time for the victim, who usually knows instinctively that the batterer needs help, but any attempt to point out a pattern of abuse or to hold the batterer accountable (particularly after the batterer gets comfortable once again and stops apologizing) will hasten the tension-building phase, something the victim desperately wants to avoid. Attempts to demand authentic change in the abuser often result in the batterer accusing the victim of holding a grudge, being unforgiving, and punishing. Comments such as, "How dare you rub my face in this when I've already apologized . . . What do you want me to do? I've already said I'm sorry 100 times. Let's move on!" are common.

With the hope that the honeymoon phase might just last forever, victims often comply with the dangerous demands of the batterer to relinquish their own sense of reality and accept the reality of the batterer that the abuse was not that bad, that it will never happen again, and that it was a one-time event. Living in the here and now allows both the batterer and victim to avoid seeing the pattern of abuse, which in some respects allows them both to avoid their fear of facing the truth and seriousness of the situation. But no matter how many promises the abusive partner makes or how desperately the victim wants to believe the abuse will never occur again, without intervention the cycle is destined to repeat itself.

Counseling Victims of Domestic Violence

Whose Fault Is It Anyway? Attributing Causality of Abuse in the Relationship

Counseling victims of domestic violence requires specialized training that focuses on the unique dynamics commonly at play in abusive relationships. Many of these dynamics relate to the cycle of violence discussed earlier, but many relate solely to the victim, including understanding common personality traits encountered in those who have a pattern of getting romantically involved with abusive partners, as well as traits commonly seen in individuals who will not leave, or who continue to return to their abusive partners.

One significant element of counseling victims of domestic violence is assisting them in making decisions about their future that will not compromise their safety. Thus although a human service professional may not actually tell a client to leave an abusive relationship, they will often lead abused clients down this path, particularly if it is the only way to secure their safety and if the batterer has refused to enter into a structured treatment program.

Many victims of domestic violence have a **locus of control** that is far too internal. This means that they have a tendency to see themselves as responsible for more than they actually are, and they do not necessarily recognize when their personal responsibility ends and when someone else's begins. In an unhealthy respect, this makes them a good "match" for a partner with an *external locus of control*. Someone with an external locus of control has a tendency to see outside factors as responsible for the events in their lives. Batterers commonly have an external locus of control and blame their partners (as well as a host of other people and things) for their mistakes and failures. Those with a healthy locus of control will be able to recognize when something lies without their domain of responsibility and when outside forces are to blame. A healthy locus of control indicates that someone has good personal boundaries and will likely refuse to accept responsibility for something she knew was not her fault. But many victims of domestic violence do not have healthy personal boundaries and readily except responsibility for virtually everything that is wrong in their relationship or with their partners. So, the batterer externalizes blame, and the victim internalizes blame.

A theory attempting to explain this core issue in domestic violence relationships focuses on *attribution theory,* specifically exploring how the victim attributes the partner's abusive behavior. If victims hold their partners at fault for the abusive behavior, attributing the abuse to personality factors such as an inability to manage anger, a refusal to take responsibility for their behavior, or a lack of empathy, then they will be more likely to leave the abusive relationship (Pape & Arias, 2000; Truman-Schram, Cann, Calhoun, & Vanwallendael, 2000). But victims who tend to attribute their partners' abusive behavior to situational or outside sources such as work stressors, family problems, or even alcoholism will have a greater likelihood of forgiving the batterer quickly and returning to the abusive relationship (Gordon, Burton, & Porter, 2004).

The human service professional can assist the victim in learning how to attribute causality of the abusive behavior to the batterer, incorporating an "even if" attitude: even if work is stressful, your mother is ill, you've had too much to drink, you've lost your job, money is tight, the kids are acting up, or you injured your knee, it's never okay to behave in an abusive manner. Victims of domestic violence also commonly need to develop more healthy personal boundaries so that they can understand what they are and are not responsible for in their relationships and with their abusive partners. For instance, the client might be responsible for responding to her husband's question in an irritable tone, but she is not responsible for her husband's choice to hit her in response; that was his choice, and it was unwarranted and an unreasonable response, one for which he was completely responsible.

A common clinical issue in helping someone develop new boundaries is the experience of unreasonable guilt. Many victims of domestic violence feel toxic guilt in response to setting limits with others, often believing that saying no to someone or upsetting another person is equivalent to being unkind. An emotionally healthy individual with good personal boundaries might feel badly when saying no to a request, or when firmly telling a partner that she is not responsible for his behavior, but she will not allow these bad feelings to influence what she knows to be true. In other words, she knows that despite feeling some guilt, she must honor her personal boundaries because to neglect them will negatively affect her self-esteem and self-respect. Yet victims of domestic violence will often allow their irrational guilt to determine their actions. If an action makes them feel guilty, they commonly assume that this action must be wrong.

Human service professionals can help clients see the irrationality of this way of thinking. **Cognitive Behavioral Therapy (CBT)** is a counseling technique commonly used to help victims of domestic violence recognize and change unhealthy relationship styles. Helping victims of domestic violence realize that feelings are not always the best indicators of appropriate action will assist them in setting better boundaries in their relationships and more efficiently recognizing the signs that a partner or potential partner is merely looking for a life scapegoat, rather than a life partner.

Does She Stay or Does She Go?

One of the most frustrating aspects of counseling victims of domestic violence is the pattern of the victim returning to the abusive relationship despite intervention efforts and the risk of continued abuse. One theory that attempts to explain this dynamic is called the *social-exchange theory*. This theory posits that victims of domestic violence enter into a kind of cost-benefit analysis when attempting to make a decision about whether to stay or leave the abusive relationship. Is the cost more if the victims stay in the abusive relationship where they will be forced to endure more abuse? Or will the cost be higher if they leave, possibly facing economic insecurity, navigating the court system if a divorce is imminent, and managing work and family responsibilities alone? The *investment model of decision-making* can be used when attempting to realistically weigh these pros and cons. This model involves the victim evaluating such things as her resources with and without the batterer, her ability to manage risk, and the risk involved in leaving, as well as estimating, what will be gained or lost if she leaves the relationship (Rusbult & Martz, 1995).

For the objective observer the cost of staying means enduring abuse of increasing escalation, and the cost of leaving may mean enduring financial hardship and other struggles relating to managing work and family alone, but the first option promises worsening conditions, whereas the latter option typically promises to improve with time. But victims of abuse often have a somewhat skewed perception of the risks of staying or leaving, using a positive bias when evaluating the cost-benefit analysis of staying—idealistically assuming that their partner will really change "this time," that the abuse was "really not that bad," and overestimating their ability to rescue and compel change in their abusive partner. They may consider the difficulties they are bound to face the first few months on their own and assume that this transitional stage will last forever. They may use negative thinking, assuming that they will never get a job, will never be able to balance work and family, partly based on years of emotional abuse and partly based on the fear and low self-esteem that may have even been the prime motivators for getting into the unhealthy relationship in the first place.

Human service professionals can help victims of domestic violence more effectively process the pros and cons of leaving by helping them evaluate realistic risk factors and accurate scenarios. Counseling can also assist victims in learning how to manage risk more effectively without lapsing into negative thinking. In addition, practitioners can help the client "think outside of the box": exploring all alternatives and avoiding all-or-nothing thinking (I will either be financially secure or living on the streets, I will either be a part of an intact family, or I'll be constantly lonely and a social outcast). Encouraging the client to consider possibilities not previously acknowledged can help the client realize that she has far more control over her destiny than she might have previously thought. For instance, obtaining *factual* information about her financial situation, including learning laws related to an equitable division of property and the likely levels of child support and spousal maintenance, will assist victims of domestic violence in making good decisions that are based on fact, not fear.

Despite the specialized nature of working with victims of domestic violence, a generalist approach is most effective, often involving case management, court advocacy, individual counseling, group support, counseling children and adolescents, providing housing assistance, job coaching, and assistance with life skills. The human service professional working with victims of domestic violence must be familiar with contemporary theories of abuse, effective intervention strategies, common clinical disorders associated with being a survivor of domestic violence, such as PTSD, domestic violence laws, the criminal justice process, and resources designed to meet the needs of victims and their children.

Domestic Violence Practice Settings

One of the most common practice settings where human service professionals work with victims of domestic violence is a *battered women's shelter*. Such shelters typically offer numerous services, including

▶ A 24-hour hotline for immediate access to information and services
▶ Immediate safety shelters for domestic violence victims and their children

▶ Individual counseling for all victims

▶ Survivor support groups

▶ Court advocacy

▶ Children's programs

▶ Teen programs

▶ Information referral

▶ Medical advocates who provide on-site support at hospitals

▶ Immigrant programs (depending on the ethnic makeup of the community)

Although battered women's shelters often have a physical site where counseling and case management occur, their actual shelters are usually sprinkled throughout the community in confidential locations to ensure the safety of the victims utilizing shelter services. Shelters may include houses converted into shelters or even rented apartments located throughout a community. Victims of domestic violence and their children usually remain in a shelter for a time determined by their primary counselor, but the goal of shelter services focus on self-sufficiency, thus job placement, child care assistance, and transportation needs are also addressed.

Most shelters involve communal living, where residents share their living space with other victims. Residents are required to participate in group counseling sessions with other residents as well as assisting with the general function and maintenance of the shelter. Human service professionals are assigned to each shelter living space and facilitate in-house programs to maintain smooth functioning within the home, as well as among the residents. Most shelters institute rules such as a no alcohol or drugs policy and mandated maintenance of the confidentiality of the location of the shelter. Residents who release this information to their abusive partners will be asked to leave the program. Residents are also required to work on the meeting of program goals, and serious noncompliance may also be a reason to terminate services.

The Prosecution of Domestic Violence

In 1993 the federal government passed the Violence Against Women Act (updated in 2000), which was an amendment to the Violent Crime Control Act of 1994 (Pub. L. No. 103-322). The Violence Against Women Act established policies and mandates for how states were to handle domestic violence cases, such as encouraging mandatory arrests, interstate enforcement of domestic violence laws, and maintaining state databases on incidences of domestic violence. This act also provides for numerous grants for educational purposes (for example, the education of police officers and judges), a domestic violent hotline, battered women's shelters, and grants to improve the safety of public areas such as public transportations and parks.

This legislation spurred several states to pass similar legislation, which continues to change the nature of domestic violence prosecutions. It is important to note that unlike a civil case, where a plaintiff brings an action and thus has the right to subsequently drop the case, in criminal cases the plaintiff is the state, and the victims are witnesses. But in the past prosecutors have allowed victims to drop a case (typically at the urgings of the batterer). Domestic violence legislation has for the most part put a stop to this practice. Instead, domestic violence is typically treated as any other crime where the victim is called as a witness and must appear at the trial to testify on behalf of the state.

This can create emotional tension for victims, who may initially want court involvement immediately after experiencing violence, but then wants to resist any intervention when the honeymoon phase begins and renewed hope for authentic change seems possible. Counseling for the victim of abuse often focuses on the ways in which the victim can respond (often in **counterintuitive** ways) that will have the greatest likelihood of moving the batterer toward real change. As long as victims relinquish their own reality of the events and yield to the batterers' demands to forgive and forget without any real accountability, no real change will occur. Any effective counseling program must address the *denial, wishful thinking, indiscriminate forgiveness* (without accountability), and a desire to *protect* the batterer, as well as the *fear* of the future that many victims of domestic violence experience, which can prevent an honest and realistic appraisal of their abusive relationship.

Batterers Programs

It might be tempting to focus treatment efforts solely on the victims of abuse, leaving the perpetrators of abuse to fend for themselves. But if those who committed abuse were treated effectively, then domestic violence would no longer be a pressing social problem. It is also important to be aware that not all "batterers" are alike. In fact, although there are many batterers who are narcissistic with antisocial tendencies (sociopathy) and abuse their intimates with no remorse, there are also those who act out in anger but are truly remorseful, some who have never committed violence before but a combination of circumstances lowered their impulse control, some who are in reciprocally abusive relationships, and some who have been falsely accused.

It is vital that human service professionals take the time to understand the dynamics involved and not assume that if an accusation were made, it must be true. I have worked in domestic violence for years and worked with many authentic victims who had extremely abusive partners. Yet I will never forget the case involving a woman who presented with plausible stories of abuse at the hands of her husband, who was recently arrested for domestic violence. I was sold before having even met her husband, because my client's stories were convincing. Yet the criminal trial revealed that *she* had been emotionally abusive for years, and when he sought a divorce she threatened to seek revenge. She did so by causing self-injury and going upstairs privately to call the police. The tape of the 9-1-1 call was chilling as she screamed and cried while reporting the alleged abuse. If it had not been for the friend she told, who bravely testified at trial on behalf of the defense, her husband might have been convicted of a crime he did not commit, and she might have unfairly gained custody of their children because everyone, including me, was so quick to believe her simply because of her gender.

In the past the criminal justice system sought traditional forms of justice for those convicted of domestic violence, but this approach was often unsuccessful because judges were sometimes reluctant to break apart families, and more often victims of domestic violence were reluctant to testify against their partners or spouses, particularly if it meant a possibility of incarceration. Thus, several years ago domestic violence courts started mandating batterers to attend treatment programs often in lieu of jail.

Most interventions for domestic violence batterers consist of group treatment focusing on cognitive-behavioral therapy and anger management training. Programs range in duration from six weeks to one year and are often mandated by the court as a part of sentencing. These programs enjoy moderate success, but one challenge faced is that many batterers do not complete the program. Batterers are taught to respect personal boundaries, learn the difference between feelings and actions, and discover the dynamics of social learning theory including modeling so they can discover how their violent behavior is likely patterned after their parents' or some other influential person in their lives. They also learn how to identify their personal triggers and how to avoid them, how to control impulses, and how to use "I" statements to avoid getting caught up in making accusations.

Most batterers' treatment programs have similar goals, including *increasing awareness of violent behavior* and *encouraging the batterer to take responsibility for violent behavior.* Common program philosophies include the following beliefs:

► Violence is an intentional act.
► Domestic violence uses physical force and intimidation as coercive methods to obtain and maintain control in the relationship.
► Using violence is a learned behavior and as such can be unlearned.

Many participants make authentic changes in group treatment not only because of the curriculum, but also because of the built-in accountability that a group setting provides. Ironically it is the other group members who have been charged with domestic battery who often challenge those who refuse to engage or who consistently blame the victim. Unfortunately, at least an equal number of participants do not authentically change while in the program. Some batterers fail to complete the program, and others are reluctant to change because they actually love the rush and power they get from feeling intense anger (Pandya & Gingerich, 2002).

Sexual Assault

Another form of personal violence is the act of rape, or sexual assault. Sexual assault involves forcing some form of sexual act on another person without his or her consent. Determining the rate of sexual assault in the United States is difficult due to dramatic variations in the way sexual assault is defined. Although both men and women can be raped, women are victims of rape far more often than men. Approximately 70 percent of sexual assault victims know their assailant, and less than one-third of rape victims report their assault to the police, making sexual assault one of the most underreported crimes in the nation (Catalano, 2004).

Approximately 300,000 women and 90,000 men report being raped within a 12-month period. One in 6 women and 1 in 33 men have been the victim of rape or attempted rape. Twenty to 25 percent of female college students report that they have been a victim of either completed or attempted rape, and about 9 percent of high school students have reported being the victim of rape (Tjaden & Thoennes, 2000). Finally, about 2 in 1,000 children have been the victim of child sexual assault, although this is likely grossly underreported because most child sexual abuse and assault incidents go unreported or cannot be substantiated due the child's age or reluctance to cooperate with child welfare investigators.

Rape can be committed by a complete stranger, an acquaintance, a date, a partner, or a spouse and is defined as any sexual act that is forced and against another person's consent. According to the CDC, sexual acts typically fall into four categories (Basile & Saltzman, 2002):

1. *Completed sexual acts* such as sexual penetration, but may also include any act of a sexual nature attempted or otherwise such as contact been a sexual organ and another part of the body.
2. *Attempted sexual assault*
3. *Abusive sexual contact* such as intentional touching even through clothing
4. *Noncontact sexual abuse* such as intentional exposure and exhibitionism ("flashing") and voyeurism ("peeping Tom")

Why People Commit Rape

Human service professionals who work with victims of sexual assault must understand the psychological dynamics of rape. One of the more common myths of why rape occurs includes blaming the victim by asserting that the victim wanted it, liked it, or in some way deserved the sexual assault because she provoked the assailant (by dressing or acting provocatively, etc.). Myths about rapists include assertions that only truly evil or insane men rape, and that men just cannot control their sexual desires, thus are not responsible for sexually assaulting women (Burt, 1991). The damage done by the proliferation of these rape myths is plentiful because they blame the victim while exonerating the perpetrator, which undermines societal prohibition against sexual violence.

In fact, a 1998 study at University of Mannheim in Germany (Bohner et al., 1998) found that such myths actually encourage sexual assault by giving rapists a way of rationalizing their antisocial behavior. In other words although Western social customs may claim to abhor rape, popular rape myths provide rapists a way around such social mores by convincing themselves that the woman in some way *asked for it,* and that men simply *cannot control themselves,* thus they really haven't done anything wrong, or at least nothing that many other men don't do.

The Psychological Impact of Sexual Assault

The physical and psychological impact of sexual assault is serious and long-lasting and may include PTSD, depression, increased anxiety, fear of risk-taking, development of trust issues, increased physical problems including exposure to sexually transmitted diseases, including HIV/AIDS, chronic pelvic pain, gastrointestinal disorders, and unwanted pregnancy (Centers for Disease Control, 2005).

In 1975 Lynda Holmstrom and Ann Burgess coined the term *rape trauma syndrome* (RTS), a collection of emotions similar to PTSD, commonly experienced in response to being a survivor of a forced violent sexual assault. RTS includes an immediate phase where the survivor experiences both psychological and physical symptoms such as feeling extreme fear, consistent crying and sleep disturbances, and other reactions to the actual assault as well as the common fear of being killed during the assault. Survivors in subsequent phases of recovery include avoidance of social interaction, experiencing a loss of self-esteem, inappropriate guilt, and clinical depression. Many survivors deny the effects of the sexual assault because they do not want to be subject to the negative stigma associated with being a rape victim. In fact, one of the primary reasons most rape crisis advocates refer to clients as *survivors* rather than as *victims* is to reduce this stigma by focusing on the strength it takes to survive a sexual assault.

Male-on-Male Sexual Assault

Men are also victims of sexual assault, both in the form of child sexual abuse, same-sex date rape, and male-on-male stranger rape. Research on male-on-male sexual assault is sparse with the exception of some early efforts to identify the nature and dynamics of male rape. The reason for the lack of studies in this area may be related to the belief that male rape is rare, at least outside prison walls. In fact, in many states, the legal definition of rape does not even account for males being victims.

Due to the stigma associated with being a victim of male-on-male sexual assault, most incidences of rape go unreported, thus it is impossible to know just how common this crime is. Even rapes that occur in prisons are often unreported both because of fear of retaliation but also due to the shame men feel in response to being victimized in this manner.

Treating men who have been sexually assaulted is similar in some respects to serving the female survivor population except that the shame men feel, although equal in intensity, tends to be more focused on their gender identity as males. Heterosexual men who were victims of rape reported questioning their sexual orientation because they were unable to fight off their attackers. Men also have a greater tendency to turn toward alcohol and drugs in response to the rape. Men also experience sexual dysfunction, problems getting close to people, particularly in intimate relationships, and as is the case with female victims, some male victims become sexually promiscuous (Mezey & King, 1989).

More studies need to be conducted on both female and male rape, particularly on the differing dynamics of sexual assault in minority populations. What research there is on ethnic minority populations seems to indicate that victims of sexual assault who are Caucasian and have higher levels of academic education tend to seek mental health counseling more often than victims of color or those with less education (Ullman & Brecklin, 2002; Vearnals & Campbell, 2001). This certainly has practice implications for human service professionals who through assessment or advocacy have the opportunity to reach out to victims or potential victims of sexual assault.

Common Practice Settings: Rape Crisis Centers

Human service professionals working in any practice setting will likely encounter a victim of sexual assault at some point in their careers. This might involve a recent victim seeking support services on the heels of an assault, but it is far more likely that rape victims will present for counseling at some point long after an assault, perhaps even years later, and might not even connect that the problems they are currently experiencing are with a past sexual assault.

Human service professionals who work directly with victims of sexual assault usually do so at a rape crisis center or sexual assault advocacy organization. Many states require that each county have at least one rape crisis center that offers a wide range of services including a 24-hour hotline, around-the-clock on-site advocacy during medical examinations and investigative interviews, and crisis counseling, as well as long-term individual and group counseling.

Many human service professionals who work with sexual assault victims receive between 40 to 50 hours of specialized training focusing on the history of the rape crisis movement, the nature of crisis counseling, the dynamics of RTS, rape myths, and the dangers of gender oppression. Training also includes information on normal child and adult developmental stages and how these stages are affected by sexual violence and trauma.

■ Hundreds of people take part in a candlelight march to call attention to violence against women and children during "Take Back the Night" event.

Victims of Violent Crime

Domestic violence and sexual assault are two types of violent crime that receive considerable attention within the human services field as well as within the public arena. There are other types of victimization that do not garner as much attention, but are also important. Every year millions of people in the United States become victims of a crime, many of which are violent crimes. In 2004, 24 million crimes were committed, 5.2 million of which were violent in nature (National Crime Victimization Survey, 2004). Although violent crime has been declining in recent years, the issue of victimization and the recognition and enforcement of victims' rights remains a relevant issue for human service professionals.

The victims' rights movement is a relatively new phenomenon having gained momentum in the 1980s when victims of crime came together along with advocates in the human services field to secure both a voice within the criminal justice community and some basic rights in the criminal justice system. Historically victims of crime had virtually no rights in criminal proceedings because the U.S. criminal justice system is based on the presumption of innocence. Because defendants charged with a criminal offense are innocent until proven guilty, legally there can be no victims. If there are no victims prior to a defendant being convicted, then there are no rights to enforce. In addition, in criminal proceedings the case is considered an action committed against the state, thus other than being a witness, historically, victims of crime have had no special status. This logic, which is consistent with the U.S. criminal justice system, is completely backward for most victims and victim advocates.

The Victims' Bill of Rights

The victims' movement is not based on a desire to lessen the rights of criminal defendants, but rather on the desire to increase the rights of victims including being notified of court hearings, to appear at all legal proceedings, to make a statement at sentencing, and to be kept apprised of the incarceration status of the perpetrator.

Most victims and victim advocates state that a primary goal of the victims' movement is to ensure that crime victims have a voice within the community, specifically within the criminal justice system (Mika, Achilles, Halbert, Amstutz, & Zehr, 2004). How that voice gets heard is certainly up for debate. Whether through direct face-to-face meetings with criminal justice officials or through an active involvement in victim-sensitive training of police personnel, prosecutors, and judges, victims advocacy groups continue to work toward a system that sees victims as a central aspect of the criminal justice process (Quinn, 1998).

In response to victims' movements and subsequent federal legislation [42 U.S.C. § 10606(b)], all states now have a Victims' Bill of Rights ensuring certain basic rights as well as protection. Although there is some variation from state to state, most states ensure that victims of violent crime be afforded the following rights:

▶ The right to be treated with dignity and fairness and with respect for the victim's dignity and privacy

▶ The right to be reasonably protected from the accused offender

▶ The right to be notified of court proceedings

▶ The right to be present at all public court proceedings related to the offense, unless the court determines that testimony by the victim would be materially affected if the victim heard other testimony at trial

▶ The right to confer with the attorney for the government in the case

▶ The right to restitution

▶ The right to information about the conviction, sentencing, imprisonment, and release of the offender

Victim-Witness Assistance

In response to federal legislation and victims' rights bills state prosecution units within prosecutors offices (state's attorney, district attorney, and attorney general offices) developed specialized units called Victim-Witness Assistance, designed to enforce victims' rights. Human service professionals work within these departments offering the following services:

- ▶ Crisis intervention counseling
- ▶ Referrals to coordinating human services agencies, such as rape crisis centers, battered women's shelters, and crime victim support groups
- ▶ Referrals to advocacy organizations such as Mothers Against Drunk Drivers (MADD), who have a presence in court to ensure enforcement of victims' rights
- ▶ Advocacy and accompaniment in court proceedings
- ▶ Special services or units for victims of domestic violence, child victims, the elderly, and handicapped victims
- ▶ Case status updates including notification of all public court proceedings
- ▶ Foreign language translation
- ▶ Assistance with obtaining compensation such as reimbursement for counseling and medical costs
- ▶ Assistance in preparation and writing of victim impact statements to be read by the victim at the sentencing hearing

Victim-witness advocates may have a master's degree in any of the applied social science disciplines (social work, psychology, general human services), but often work at the bachelor's level with some specialized training in the dynamics involved in violent crime victimization. Advocates must also be familiar with the inner workings of the criminal justice system because victims of violent crime often feel revictimized when they must endure the often confusing labyrinth of the prosecution system. The average person may not be familiar with the differing duties of a local police department and a state prosecuting office, nor may the average person know how a criminal case proceeds toward prosecution. Those individuals who have become victims of a crime must be quick studies so that they can be prepared for what is going to happen next. Victim-witness advocates can help crime victims understand the process of a criminal trial and the importance and value of each step within the prosecution process.

If a case goes to trial the victim-witness advocate will work closely with the victims to help prepare them for testifying. The clinical issues involved depend on the nature of the crime and victimization. For instance, if the defendant is the victim's spouse who is charged with domestic battery the clinical issues will likely involve fear of retaliation and guilt in response to testifying against a spouse, particularly if there is a possibility that the defendant might have to serve time in jail or prison. If the defendant was charged with sexual assault, the victim will likely experience feelings of shame, embarrassment, and fear. A victim of home invasion might experience intense fear of retaliation once the defendant becomes aware of the victim's cooperation and testimony. In each instance the victim-witness advocate will work with community human services agencies and advocates to provide support and assistance to the victim in preparation for trial.

Once a defendant is found guilty, either through trial or a plea arrangement, a sentencing hearing is scheduled. In a sentencing hearing both sides have an opportunity to advocate for a sentence they believe is appropriate. It is the responsibility of the victim-witness advocate to assist victims in writing their Victim-Impact Statement, which will be read in open court before the judge, jury, and defendant. Although the statements are written in the words of the victim, they have a dual purpose—giving victims a voice in court and assisting the prosecutor obtain the desired sentence—thus it is important that victims receive guidance in the preparation for writing their statement. This also serves as another opportunity for victims to express and work through their pain, thus it is often an effective clinical tool.

Surviving Victims of Homicide

Some of the most emotionally intense and difficult cases for victim-witness advocates are homicide cases, particularly when the primary victim is a child. The victim-assistance advocate must develop a high threshold for dealing with another's emotional pain because the pain of losing a loved one through violence is often unlike any other loss. Revictimization through the criminal justice process is almost a certainty as surviving victims of homicide are forced to balance their desire to represent their loved one in court by being present at all hearings with the trauma inherently involved in having to witness the gruesome details of the crime.

Research strongly suggests the importance of providing supportive counseling services and advocacy in the weeks immediately following the homicide. Surviving victims of intrafamilial homicides, where one family member kills another, are particularly prone to psychologically complex reactions involving both internal and external stressors. Most experts suggest the use of crisis counseling immediately following the crime that focuses on the concrete needs of the surviving victims. This approach is important in light of research, which suggests that surviving victims of homicide are mostly likely to utilize advocacy services during the initial crisis phase (Horne, 2003).

The needs of surviving victims of homicide are complex, particularly in the weeks and months after the murder. Surviving victims of homicide must cooperate with various law enforcement agencies, and attend court proceedings at the same time that they must plan a funeral and contend with the effects and belongings of the murdered victim (which may include pets or even children in addition to physical belongings). This can be significantly overwhelming during a time when they are dealing with the paralyzing shock of losing a loved one in a sudden and violent manner.

Common Clinical Issues When Working with Victims of All Violent Crime

Regardless of the nature of the crime committed, victims of violent crime all have basic needs that need to be addressed by the human service professionals working with them in treatment (Courtois, 2004). These issues or treatment goals include

1. Building formal and informal social support systems
2. Reinforcing ways to regain a sense of safety
3. Teaching victims how to manage their emotions, such as anger, sadness, and fear
4. Achieving physical and psychological stability
5. Building skills that will help victims regain a sense of personal power and control over their lives
6. Educating the client on the nature of the crime victimization so they know what to expect
7. Reconditioning victims to minimize negative triggering of the traumatic incident
8. Helping victims through the mourning process
9. Seeking resolution and closure, which leads to personal growth and allows the victim to regain the confidence and strength to trust people once again

By focusing on these core issues, as well as addressing the factors and needs specific to each type of crime victimization, the human service professional will be instrumental in fostering healing and growth in victims of crime so they can begin the process of seeing themselves no longer as victims but as true survivors.

Perpetrators of Crime

Forensic human service professionals working in the criminal justice arena often work with victims, but they may also work with offenders or perpetrators of crime as well. Direct practice with offenders might occur in an agency setting that offers mandated programs, such as batterers programs discussed earlier in this chapter, programs for alcoholics with drunk driving convictions, or group therapy for pedophiles. Many work within the criminal justice system in probation departments or juvenile justice programs, and many work in programs that facilitate outreach efforts focusing on gang members, recently released prisoners, or individuals who are at risk for continued criminal activity.

Gang Activity

Gangs consist of groups of individuals who actively participate in criminal activities on an organized or coordinated basis. Gang activity has become an increasingly severe problem in recent years, not only with regard to the number of gangs in operation within the United States (estimated to be somewhere between 700,000 and 800,000 nationwide), but also with regard to the type of violent activities in which many gang members participate. Gang activity remains primarily a big-city phenomenon, with some of the larger cities having more than 30 gangs operating at one time (National Youth Gang Center, 2005). Smaller towns and rural communities also experience gang problems but these tend to be relatively sporadic with gangs that are loosely organized.

Gang members not only commit crimes such as theft and drug trafficking to support gang activity, but some of the most serious crimes committed by gang members involve turf wars where one gang is in conflict with another, leading to gang fights that often include both assaults and homicides. In some inner-city communities drive-by shootings are a way of life, and parents respond by keeping their young children off the streets and away from windows.

Most gang members are between the ages of 13 and 25, but some studies found gangs that have members as young as 10. Most gang members come from backgrounds of poverty and racial oppression, live in high-crime urban communities, and live in neighborhoods with high gang activity (Vigil, 2003). Although there has been a recent increase in female gang activity (Chesney-Lind, 1999), most gangs are still primarily comprised of males.

Risk Factors of Gang Involvement

There are several theories regarding why adolescents join gangs. Most sociological and anthropological theories focus on the sense of solidarity and feelings of belonging that gangs can provide disenfranchised youth. Identifying risk factors is important so that effective intervention strategies can be developed and put into action.

A comprehensive study facilitated by the U.S. Department of Justice evaluated the gang membership and backgrounds of over 800 gang members from 1985 to 2001 in an attempt to identify some of the reasons why adolescents join gangs. This study, referred to as the Seattle Social Development Project, confirmed that the majority of gang members are males (90 percent) and that gang members came from diverse ethnic backgrounds including Caucasian (European American), Asian, Latino, and Native American, and African Americans, with African Americans having the highest rates of gang membership. Interestingly, the study found that the majority of gang members joined for only a short time, with 70 percent of youths belonging to a gang for less than a year (Hawkins et al., 2003).

The study identified multiple risk factors for gang membership including living in high-crime neighborhoods, coming from a single-parent household, poverty, parents who approved of violence, poor academic performance, learning disabilities, little or no commitment to school, early drug and alcohol abuse, and associating with friends who commit delinquent acts. The study's authors recommended early prevention efforts that target youth with multiple risk factors. Programs need to focus on all aspects of the adolescent's life including family dynamics, school involvement, peer group, and behavioral issues such as drug and alcohol abuse as well as any antisocial and delinquent behaviors.

What this study seems to underscore is that for youth with multiple risk factors gang membership may be less an option and more a way of life. Adolescents who are fortunate enough to have cohesive families where high-functioning parents work hard to maintain structure, provide accountability, and keep teens engaged in positive activities can often help adolescents avoid the temptation to join a gang. This is particularly true for black youth living in large urban areas (Walker-Barnes & Mason, 2001).

Adolescents without the benefit of such positive influences, including those who have neglectful and uninvolved parents, often face a reciprocal pull into gang life where they are targeted by existing gang members who recognize the existence of these risk factors, and the adolescents themselves are drawn to gang life because of the benefits gangs appear to provide such as a sense of belonging, a life of excitement, and the feeling of empowerment.

Human Services Practice Settings Focusing on Gang Involvement

Human service professionals who work with gang populations may do so on school campuses, in agencies that target at-risk youth, in faith-based outreach agencies, at police departments, or within the juvenile justice system. Most outreach programs target adolescents who live in large urban communities where gang activity is prolific and violent behavior a fact of life, especially those who come from single-parent homes, have poor academic histories, and have shown early signs of delinquent behaviors. Human service professionals also target social conditions on a macro level such as poverty, racism, and the lack of opportunities in urban communities, because these factors contribute to the development of gang activity.

Many human service programs that target at-risk adolescents operate after-school programs or evening community programs that give adolescents a place to go to socialize other than the streets. This is particularly important for youth who are in search of a sense of cohesion, security, and social belongingness, elements that might be missing from their home life. In light of the research indicating that most gang members have relatively loose, short-term affiliation with gangs, these types of programs have the potential of being successful in steering even active gang members away from gang life.

Finally, human service programs committed to reducing the gang problem must be willing to engage in active and aggressive outreach efforts, maintain a highly visible presence in the community, coordinate services with other gang intervention programs, and be willing to engage at-risk adolescents and their family on multiple levels.

Human Services in Prison Settings

The human services profession has a long history of association with the criminal justice system, most notably working in jails, prisons, government probation departments, police departments, and agencies offering services to recently released offenders. Human service professionals working within the criminal justice system may be employed as prison or correctional psychologists who conduct psychological evaluations on recently charged defendants or who provide assessment or counseling to offenders within the prison system. They may be licensed social workers who provide counseling and facilitate support groups focusing on various treatment issues designed to reduce *recidivism* (the process of relapsing into criminal behavior). They may be probation officers charged with the responsibility of coordinating treatment and supervising the offender's compliance with the conditions of probation (for example, entering a drug treatment program, obtaining counseling, attending an anger management program, or completing community service), or they may be bachelor's level correctional treatment specialists or case managers who provide general counseling to the prison population assisting them prepare for release and reentry into society.

Human service professionals may also work on a community level advocating for prison reform such as the development of mental health courts, substance abuse treatment programs in prisons, or increased mental health services for mentally ill prisoners. Thus although this field of service is broad, the clinical issues are specialized requiring training focusing on the common issues facing offenders both within prison and on release.

The U.S. prison system is plagued with violence including sexual assaults, drug problems, and mental illness. Human service professionals working within the area of corrections will likely encounter a wide range of issues that vary with the level of incarceration security, the gender and race of the prisoners, and the culture and climate of the specific prison. One of the chief problems affecting prisons across the country relates to the problem of overcrowding, with most state and federal prisons operating at either full or over capacity (Harrison & Beck, 2003). In an environment already wrought with tension, overcrowding can be the ingredient that leads to increased violence against both inmates and correctional staff.

The War on Drugs

Many people might be surprised to learn that violent crime in the United States has steadily declined since the early 1990s. Homicides, rapes, assaults, robberies, firearms-related crimes, and even violent juvenile crimes have all plummeted in recent years, yet the population in prisons and jails across the country has skyrocketed. In fact, the United States has the highest prison population of any country in the world (Walmsley, 2003). So what is to account for this seeming contradiction? Why, when virtually all forms of violent crime are on a downhill slide for many years, is the nation's prison system experiencing such a dramatic increase in population? Many social scientists agree that the primary reason for prison overcrowding relates to the U.S. war on drugs.

In fact, approximately 55 percent of all federal prisoners are incarcerated for drug-related offenses (Harrison & Beck, 2003), and 80 percent of the increase in prisoners in the federal prison system between 1985 and 1995 is related to increased convictions of drug-related offenses (Bureau of Justice Statistics, 2003).

The U.S. war on drugs might seem like a good policy on the surface. Certainly no one would argue that the using and selling of illicit drugs is good for the American public. But many argue that the federal government's aggressive policies related to the prosecution and punishment of drug offenders unfairly targets poor, young ethnic minorities, many of whom are serving extremely long prison sentences due to minimum federal sentencing guidelines (sometimes 20 years to life), despite not committing any violent crime (Human Rights Watch, 2000a).

Human service professionals should be concerned about any governmental policy that either directly or indirectly targets a certain segment of the population. The war on drugs appears to do just this, evidenced by the significant overrepresentation of ethnic minorities, particularly African-American males, within the federal and state prison system (Human Rights Watch, 2000b). Whether by design or not, one must ask why the U.S. government has not waged a "War on Domestic Violence," or a "War on Child Sexual Abuse," two social ills that have seriously negative consequences for U.S. society and that would target offenders across all socioeconomic levels and racial groups.

Human service professionals working within the U.S. criminal justice system must be aware of potentially unfair political policies to develop a truly objective perspective of social conditions leading to the overrepresentation of minorities in correctional facilities, the reasoning behind sentencing guidelines for various criminal offenses, even identifying social influences that tend to hold one behavior in a particular era as socially acceptable, only to criminalize it several decades later.

For instance, determining what drugs are socially acceptable and which ones are not is influenced by constantly shifting social mores. During the Prohibition era the use and sale of alcohol was considered criminal, yet today it is considered perfectly socially acceptable. Thus there is a temporal aspect to the criminalization of certain behaviors, and it is vital that human service professionals recognize this dynamic.

Clinical Issues in the Prison Population: The Role of the Human Service Professional

The issues confronting human service professionals working within the criminal justice system, particularly within a correctional facility, will vary depending on the gender, race, and type of crime committed by the defendant. A key goal of the criminal justice system is to reduce recidivism, thus "success" in terms of treatment is often focused on whether a prisoner once released reoffends and returns to prison.

Mental Health Programs in Correctional Facilities

Behavioral programs within prisons can focus on many clinical issues, some related to criminal behavior and some related to other issues the inmates might be experiencing. Programs related to criminal behavior typically focus on issues such as drug abuse, sexual violence, domestic violence, anger management, and the development of social skills (for prisoners with antisocial tendencies). Programs designed to address psychosocial issues not directly related to criminal behavior typically focus on grief and separation issues, sexual abuse victimization (particularly for female inmates because a large proportion of the female inmates population has been the victim of sexual violence at some point in their lives), self-esteem, and issues related to the impact of being incarcerated.

Prison and Pregnancy

Female inmates are often incarcerated for offenses related to drug addictions (writing bad checks, petty theft, prostitution, etc.), and those who are pregnant or parenting often have to rely on the county foster care system for the care of their children during their incarceration (Siefert & Pimlott, 2001). Human service professionals working in a correctional facility will likely encounter women (particularly women of color) who are grieving over the loss of their children or are anticipating their loss once they give birth. One of the roles of human service professionals is to work with outside agencies that can arrange to transport children to see their incarcerated mothers to maintain the mother–child bond. Parenting issues are often explored as well, as is the impact of drug abuse during pregnancy, with the goal of maintaining close family ties and reducing the incidence of prenatal damage and infant mortality related to drug use during pregnancy.

Some prisons have grant-funded programs that provide intensive prenatal care, nutrition counseling, substance abuse treatment, and individual and group counseling. One such program is called the Women and Infants at Risk program (WAIR), which helps mothers break intergenerational cycles of abuse, giving infants the best start in life possible. This is particularly important in light of how the "cards" are already stacked against infants who are born behind prison walls (Siefert & Pimlott, 2001).

STDs and AIDS

Another significant issue often confronting both inmates and human service professionals involves the high rate of infectious diseases that exists within the prison population, made worse by the ongoing problem of sexual assaults. Diseases such as Hepatitis B and C are prevalent in some prisons, and HIV/AID remains a serious concern among prisoners and correctional staff alike. A 2002 report by the National Commission on Correctional Health Care (NCCHC) indicated that the incidence of AIDS in the U.S. prison population is five times that of the general population, and the primary method of transmission is sexual assault (Robertson, 2003).

The fear of being raped is the number one fear among men serving time in prison, and although no one is certain of the exact number of male-on-male sexual assaults within the prison system, it is estimated that between 7 percent and 12 percent of the male prison population has been a victim of sexual assault while incarcerated, although the actual number is presumed to be much higher (Human Rights Watch, 2001), with many prisoners suffering multiple rapes throughout their incarceration. This issue is of such significant concern that in 2003 President George W. Bush signed an act appropriating $13 million to fund rape prevention programs within the prison system (Robertson, 2003).

Barriers to Treatment

One complaint among mental health providers in correctional settings is the underfunding and understaffing of mental health programs often experienced in many jails and prisons across the country. Developing effective and comprehensive mental health services within correctional facilities is an important aspect of efforts to reduce recidivism rates among the prison population, but the U.S. criminal justice system is punitive in nature and not based on a rehabilitation model thus mental health programs are often not a priority within the criminal justice system, evidenced by a consistent lack of funding, understaffing, and limited outreach.

Yet even in prisons that have sufficient mental health services, barriers still exist that often prevent prisoners from accessing these services. A 2004 study surveying prisoner attitudes about mental health services identified several perceived barriers to service, including being uncertain how or when to access counseling, a belief that mental health services are for "crazy" people, the lack of confidentiality involved in the counseling relationship with a fear that the information shared would later be used against them, a fear that other prisoners would believe they were a snitch, a belief that people should deal with their own problems, a preference for talking with friends and family rather than a professional counselor, and having had a past bad experience with counseling (Morgan, Rozcyki, & Wilson, 2004).

Human service professionals need to be aware of these common perceptions held by prisoners so that strategies can be designed to overcome both real and perceptual barriers to seeking mental health counseling. Although many of these negative perceptions held are common among the general population as well, many are related to being in custodial care where prisoners' personal rights are extremely limited by necessity.

Concluding Thoughts on Forensic Human Services

Working within the criminal justice system offers rich opportunities for human service professionals at all education levels. The opportunity to interact with several other advocacy organizations and coordinating services with agencies offering complimentary services provides the human services professional with a broad range of professional experiences. Human service professionals provide counseling, case management, and advocacy to both victims and offenders, thus making a difference in the lives of the members of society most in need.

Victims of violent crime such as domestic violence, sexual assault, and other violent crimes need advocacy and counseling to turn tragedy into triumph and powerlessness into empowerment. Human service professionals are on the front lines of bringing issues formerly kept in the dark out into the open, removing stigmas, and creating change that makes survivors out of victims.

Criminal activity and subsequent incarceration leaves long-lasting scars on the families of offenders, often plunging them into a cycle of poverty and social isolation. This process significantly increases the likelihood of creating an intergenerational pattern of incarceration, thus some of the most important work that forensic human service professionals do involves working with the family members of prisoners, particularly children who not only feel abandoned by their incarcerated parents but are often forced to enter the foster care system if no family members are available to care for them.

Rehabilitation offers the most hope of lowering recidivism rates among the prison population, yet a correctional philosophy that incorporates rehabilitation is controversial because in the eyes of many in the general public counseling and other mental health programs feel too much like a luxury, not deserved by those who have committed crimes. Yet not only are prisoners not a homogeneous group (i.e., many prisoners have been incarcerated for relatively minor offenses), those who have committed the most serious offenses are in many cases those who need mental health services the most. Unfortunately, mental health programs are often the first to be cut from state and federal budgets because on the whole the prisoner population does not garner much sympathy within the general public. For this reason it is imperative that human service professionals advocate for the basic rights and needs of prisoners, as they do with all vulnerable populations.

r e f e r e n c e s

Basile, K. C., & Saltzman, L. E. (2002). *Sexual violence surveillance: Uniform definitions and recommended data elements version 1.0.* Atlanta GA: Centers for Disease Control and Prevention, National Center for Injury Prevention and Control. Retrieved on September 14, 2005, from http://www.cdc.gov/ncipc/pub-res/sv_surveillance/sv.htm

Bohner, G., Reinhard, M., Rutz, S., Sturm, S., Kerschbaum, B., & Effler, B. (1998). Rape myths as neutralizing cognitions: Evidence for a causal impact of anti-victim attitudes on men's self-reported likelihood of raping. *European Journal Social Psychology, 28,* 257–268.

Bureau of Justice Statistics. (2004). *Crime in the United States, annual, uniform crime reports.* U.S. Department of Justice, Office of Justice Programs. Retrieved on November 4, 2005, from http://www.ojp.usdoj.gov/bjs/glance/tables/drugtab.htm

Burt, M. R. (1991). *Rape myths and acquaintance rape.* In A. Parrot & L. Bechhofer (Eds.), *Acquaintance rape: The hidden crime* (pp. 26–40). New York: Wiley.

Catalano, S. M. (2004). *National crime victimization survey, crime victimization, 2003.* Bureau of Justice Statistics. U.S. Department of Justice, Office of Justice Programs. September 2004, NCJ 205455.

Centers for Disease Control. (2003). Intimate partner violence: Fact sheet. Atlanta, GA: *National Center for Injury Prevention and Control.* Retrieved on September 14, 2005, from http://www.edc.gov/ncipc/factsheets/pvfacts.htm

Centers for Disease Control. (2005). Sexual violence: Fact sheet. Atlanta, GA: *National Center for Injury Prevention and Control.* Retrieved on September 15, 2006, from http://www.edc.gov/ncipc/factsheets/svfacts.htm

Chesney-Lind, M. (1999). Challenging girls' invisibility in juvenile court. *Annals of the American Academy of Political and Social Science, 564,* 185–202.

Courtois, C. (2004). Complex trauma, complex reactions: Assessment and treatment. *Psychotherapy: Theory, Research, Practice, Training, 41(4),* 412–445.

Ehrensaft, M. K., Cohen, P., Brown, J., Smailes, E., Chen, H., & Johnson, J. (2003). Intergenerational transmission of partner violence: A 20 year prospective study. *Journal of Consulting and Clinical Psychology, 71(4),* 741–753.

Gazmararian J. A., Petersen R., Spitz A. M., Goodwin, M. M., Saltzman, L. E., & Marks, J. S. (2000). Violence and reproductive health: Current knowledge and future research directions. *Maternal and Child Health Journal, 4(2),* 79–84.

Gordon, K. C., Burton, S., & Porter, L. (2004). Predicting the intentions of women in domestic violence shelters to return to partners: Does forgiveness play a role? *Journal of Family Psychology. 18(2),* 331–338.

Groth, N. A., & Burgess, A. W. (1980). Male rape: Offenders and victims. *American Journal of Psychiatry, 137,* 806–810.

Harrison, P. M., & Beck, A. J. (2003). *U.S. Department of Justice, Bureau of Justice Statistics, Prisoners in 2002.* Washington, DC: U.S. Department of Justice.

Hawkins, J. D., Smith, B. H., Hill, K. G., Kosterman R., Catalano, R. F., & Abbott, R. D. (2003). Understanding and preventing crime and violence: Findings from the Seattle Social Development Project. In T. P. Thornberry & M. D. Krohn (Eds.), *Taking stock of delinquency: An overview of findings from contemporary longitudinal studies* (pp. 255–312). New York: Plenum.

Henning, K., & Feder, L. (2004). A comparison of men and women arrested for domestic violence: Who presents the greater threat? *Journal of Family Violence, 19(2),* 69–80.

Hodge, S., & Canter, D. (1998). Victims and perpetrators of male sexual assault. *Journal of International Violence, 13,* 222–239.

Holmstrom, L. L., & Burgess, A. W. (1975). Assessing trauma in the rape victim. *American Journal of Nursing, 75(8),* 1288–1291.

Horne, C. (2003). Families of homicide victims: Service utilization patterns of extra- and intrafamilial homicide survivors. *Journal of Family Violence, 18(2),* 75–81.

Human Rights Watch. (2000a). *Key recommendations from punishment and prejudice: Racial disparities in the war on drugs.* Retrieved on November 4, 2005, from http://www.hrw.org/campaigns/drugs/war/key-reco.htm

Human Rights Watch. (2000b). *Punishment and prejudice: Racial disparities in the war on drugs,* 12(2). Retrieved on November 4, 2005, from http://hrw.org/reports/2000/usa/index.htm#TopOfPage

Human Rights Watch. (2001). *No escape: Male rape in U.S. prisons.* Retrieved on September 27, 2005, from www.hrw.org/reports/2001/prison/report.html

King, M., Coxell, A., & Mezey, G. (2000). The prevalence and characteristics of male sexual assault. In G. Mezey & M. King (Eds.), *Male victims of sexual assault.* Oxford: Oxford University Press.

Maxfield, M. G., & Widom, C. S. (1996). The cycle of violence: Revisited six years later. *Archives of Pediatrics and Adolescent Medicine 150,* 390–395.

Mezey, G., & King, M. (1989). The effects of sexual assault on men: A survey of 22 victims. *Psychological Medicine, 19,* 205–209.

Mika, H., Achilles, M., Halbert, E., Amstutz, L., & Zehr, H. (2004). Listening to victims—a critique of restorative justice policy and practice in the united States. *Federal Probation, 68(1),* 32–39.

Morgan, R. D., Rozycki, A. T., & Wilson, S. (2004). Inmate perceptions of mental health services. *Professional Psychology: Research and Practice, 35(4),* 389–396.

National Youth Gang Center. (2005). *Highlights of the 2002–2003 national youth gang surveys.* Washington, DC: U.S. Department of Justice, Office of Justice Programs, Office of Juvenile Justice and Delinquency Prevention. Washington, DC: U.S. Department of Justice.

Nelson H. D., Nygren P., McInerney, Y., & Klein, J. (2004). Screening women and elderly adults for family and intimate partner violence: A review of the evidence for the U.S. Preventive Services Task Force. *Annals of Internal Medicine, 140(5),* 387–396.

Office of National Drug Control Policy. (2002, February). *National drug control strategy: FY 2003 budget summary,* Table 3. Washington, DC: Office of the President.

Pandya, V., & Gingerich, W. J. (2002). Group therapy intervention for male batterers: A microethnographic study. *Health & Social Work, 27(1),* 47–55.

Pape, K. T., & Arias, I. (2000). The role of attributions in battered women's intentions to permanently end their violent relationships. *Cognitive Therapy and Research, 24,* 201–214.

Quinn, T. (1998). An interview with former visiting fellow of NIJ, Thomas Quinn. *The National Institute of Justice Journal.* Washington, DC: Office of Justice Programs, U.S. Department of Justice.

Robertson, J. E. (2003). Rape among incarcerated men: Sex, coercion and STDs. *AIDS Patient Care and STDs, 17(8),* 423–430.

Rusbult, C. E., & Martz, J. M. (1995). Remaining in an abusive relationship: An investment model analysis of nonvoluntary dependence. *Personality and Social Psychology Bulletin, 21,* 558–571.

Siefert, K., & Pimlott, S. (2001). Involving pregnancy outcome during imprisonment: A model residential care program. *Social Work, 42(2),* 125–134.

Tjaden P., & Thoennes, N. (2000). *Full report of the prevalence, incidence, and consequences of violence against women: Findings from the national violence against women survey.* Washington: National Institute of Justice. Report NCJ 183781.

Truman-Schram, D. M., Cann, A., Calhoun, L., & Vanwallendael, L. (2000). Leaving an abusive dating relationship: An investment model comparison of women who stay versus women who leave. *Journal of Social and Clinical Psychology, 19,* 161–183.

Ullman, S. E. & Brecklin, L. R. (2002). Sexual assault history, PTSD, and mental health service seeking in a national sample of women. *Journal of Community Psychology, 30(3),* 261–279.

U.S. Department of Justice. (2004). *National crime victimization survey.* Office of Justice Programs, Bureau of Justice Statistics. Retrieved on November 3, 2005, from http://www.ojp.usdoj.gov/bjs/cvictgen.htm

U.S. Department of Justice, Bureau of Justice Statistics. (2001, November). *Federal criminal case processing, 2000, with trends 1982–2000,* Table 6. Washington, DC: U.S. Department of Justice.

U.S. Department of Justice, Office for Victims of Crime. (1998.) *New directions from the field: Victims' rights and services for the 21st century.* Washington, DC: U.S. Department of Justice.

Vearnals, S., & Campbell, T. (2001). Male victims of male sexual assault: A review of psychological consequences and treatment. *Sexual and Relationship Therapy, 16(3),* 279–286.

Victim's Rights Act of 1998, 42 U.S.C. § 10606(b) (West, 1993).

Vigil, J. M. (2003). Urban violence and street gangs. *Annual Review Anthropology, 32,* 225–42

Violence Against Women Act of 1993 (Report 103-138). Committee on the Judiciary United States Senate, 103d Cong., 1st Sess. (1993).

Violent Crime Control and Law Enforcement Act of 1994, Pub. L. No. 103-322, Title IV, § 40001 et. sequ., 108 Stat. 1902 (1994).

Walker, L. (1979). *The battered woman.* New York: Harper and Row.

Walker-Barnes, C. J., & Mason, C. A. (2001). Ethnic differences in the effect of parenting on gang involvement and gang delinquency: A longitudinal, hierarchical linear modeling perspective. *Child Development, 72(6),* 1814–1831.

Walmsley, R. (2003). *World prison population list* (5th ed.). U.S. Census Bureau, Population Division. London, England, UK: Home Office Research, Development and Statistics Directorate.

s u g g e s t e d   r e a d i n g

Lord, J. H. (1990). *No time for goodbyes: Coping with sorrow, anger and injustice after a tragic death.* Ventura, CA: Pathfinder Publishing.

i n t e r n e t   w e b   s i t e s   r e l a t e d
t o   v i o l e n c e   a n d   f o r e n s i c   h u m a n   s e r v i c e s

American Civil Liberties Union: **http://www.nicoa.org/**

Family Violence Prevention Fund: **http://endabuse.org/**

Legal Services for Prisoners for Victims: **http://prisonerswithchildren.org/index.htm**

National Center for Victims of Crime: **http://www.ncvc.org/ncvc/Main.aspx**

National Coalition Against Domestic Violence: **http://www.ncadv.org/**

National Organization for Victim Assistance: **http://www.trynova.org/**

Office for Victims of Crime: **http://www.ojp.usdoj.gov/ovc/**

Prisoner Policy Initiative: **http://www.prisonpolicy.org/index.shtml**

Rape, Abuse and Incest National Network (RAIIN): **http://www.rainn.org/**

YWCA: **http://www.ywca.org**

part three

Macro Practice, Ethics, and Future Considerations

chapter 14

Macro Practice and International Social Justice

> Know that many personal troubles cannot be solved merely as troubles, but must be understood in terms of public issues—and in terms of the problems of history making. Know that the human meaning of public issues must be revealed by relating them to personal troubles—and to the problems of the individual life. (C. Wright Mills, 1959, p. 226)

When students consider entering the field of human services, they often do so because they want to help people meet their basic needs by counseling them, helping them obtain much-needed services, and teaching them to learn new ways of meeting their needs in the future. In other words, most students think of direct clinical practice with individuals and families when considering a career in the human services profession. But many times the "personal troubles" a client is encountering are being caused by some external source—an injustice that is structural or systemic such as the school system that offers no bus service and therefore inadvertently contributes to low-income students' truancy rates, or a government social welfare policy that inadvertently punishes single mothers who work part-time by cutting their benefits, or a "three-strikes" law that sends a young man to jail for 25 years for a third, yet relatively minor, offense. How does the human service professional combat harmful policies that punish when they should reward or unfair legislation that hurts certain segments of the population?

The human services profession is grounded in the notion that people are a part of larger systems and to truly understand the individual one must understand the broader system this individual is operating within. The discussion of Bowen's Family Systems Theory in chapter 3 is a good place to start in understanding how systems work, noting that there is a reciprocal dynamic involving both the individual and the system, where each has an impact on the other. Hence, an individual can receive years of counseling but until structural deficiencies are addressed, they will continue to experience difficulty in some manner.

It is important, then, for human service professionals to recognize that people can be helped by approaching problems on various levels. By way of comparison, if as a human service professional you were committed to eradicating violence within society you might choose to work with victims of domestic violence in the hope that counseling them might help your clients recognize the signs of abuse and avoid engaging in abusive relationships in the future. This approach would involve *micro practice*—practice with individuals. You might also decide to facilitate treatment groups for batterers believing that the greatest likelihood of change can be accomplished by addressing the perpetrators of violence in a group setting where each group member can learn from the other. This approach would involve *mezzo practice*—practice with groups.

But, if you decided to address the problem of violence by working with an entire community, either locally, nationally, or perhaps even globally by creating a new program in your agency, by conducting a public awareness campaign to educate the population about the prevalence of violence, or by lobbying for the passage of antiviolence legislation, then you would be conducting *macro practice*—practice with communities and organizations.

Macro practice involves addressing and confronting social issues that can act as a barrier to getting one's basic needs met on an organizational level by creating structural change through **social action.** The most basic themes involved in macro practice include advocating for *social and economic justice* and *human rights* for all members of society to end human oppression and exploitation (Weil, 1996). There are several ways *social change* is accomplished through macro practice, including *program development, community development* through *community organizing, policy practice*, and *international* or *global advocacy.*

Thus, although direct clinical practice is important, working with entire systems to promote positive structural change on all fronts is equally important. Some human service professionals work solely in macro practice in administrative positions or policy practice conducting no direct practice whatsoever, but a great many human service professionals who are involved in micro practice are also involved in macro practice on at least some level. For instance, when I worked as a victim advocate for a local state's attorney's office, I counseled victims of violent crime. But I also served on a domestic violence advisory coalition that evaluated community concerns and interagency coordination.

Why Macro Practice?

Human service professionals might ask themselves why they should be concerned about what is happening to people in an entire community, in a different part of the country, or in a completely different part of the world. But a foundational value of the human services profession is a commitment to social justice and human rights achieved through social action and social change. This is particularly relevant to human service professionals living in the United States in light of the fact that many clients in need of human services assistance have immigrated from countries where they were victims of oppression and human rights violations. This requires an understanding on the part of the human service professional of the wide range of global abuses related to **social injustice** and human rights abuses, as well as recognizing how these abuses have implications on direct practice with individual clients.

Human service professionals must also be aware of the history of social injustices and human rights abuses that have occurred within U.S. borders as well as including developing an awareness of what groups are most likely to be targets of discrimination and oppression. For instance, Calkin (2000) discussed the abuse and oppression of minorities and the poor within the U.S. criminal justice system and the importance of human service professionals accepting a call to social action:

> Moment by moment in the practice process, there are opportunities to recognize and support, or to ignore, the power that people bring or could bring to their lives and communities. There are opportunities to act respectfully toward someone for whom that is so uncommon, or not to—and to acknowledge when we really can't understand, to acknowledge the errors of sensitivity we make so often. Human services organizations and professionals can easily be seduced into colluding with violations of human rights, ranging from disrespect toward people already struggling with mental illness or substance abuse to acceptance or resignation in the face of deprivations of basic human rights. (p. 2)

This foundational commitment to social justice is so integral to the human services profession that the professional obligation to social action is reflected in the ethical principles of the discipline. For instance, the NOHS (1996) ethical standards reference the human service professionals' responsibility to society, which includes remaining aware of social issues that impact communities, and initiating social action when necessary by advocating for social change. The NASW (1999) ethical standards go one step further by expanding the social worker's responsibility to the international level stating that "[s]ocial workers should promote the general welfare of society, from local to global levels, and the development of people, their communities, and their environments" (p. 26).

Unfortunately, the human services profession has gradually moved away from its original call to community action, turning instead to a model of individualized care (Mizrahi, 2001). This is likely due to an increased focus on the increasing popularity of individual psychotherapies within all the mental health professions in the twentieth century. This doesn't mean that macro practice or social advocacy has ceased. Rather, as those in the human services fields have pulled away from community work, other disciplines have moved in to fill the vacuum, such as urban and public planners and those in the political sciences. This pattern has resulted in the human services profession often being out of the loop of community building and organizing efforts (Johnson, 2004). Concerns have also been expressed regarding the trend of neglecting the subject of macro and community practice in human services and social work educational programs, thus compounding the tendency for human service professionals to avoid macro practice because many recent graduates feel ill equipped to enter into social advocacy or policy practice on an organizational level (Polack, 2004).

This movement away from macro practice is apparently an international trend as well because studies generated outside the United States have made some similar observations. For instance, Weiss (2003) cited examples of how many human service professionals in Israel do not feel competent addressing social issues on a community or global level because the majority of their training focused on practice with individual clients. Weiss encourages those in the human services professions both in Israel and abroad to reengage in policy-related activities and social advocacy on a macro level.

The reality is that social issues such as poverty and human exploitation must be addressed through advocacy efforts for social change on a macro level as well as a micro level to create much needed structural changes. Influencing changes in social policy that affects public aid (such as welfare reform legislation), mental health care (such as mental health parity laws), and even domestic violence issues (such as policies that mandate cooperation between criminal justice agencies and battered women's shelters) are an integral aspect of human services that directly affect clients' daily lives.

Vulnerable and Oppressed Populations

Before beginning any discussion on social advocacy efforts it is important to identify populations that are often the target of social injustice, oppression, and human rights violations. It is challenging to comprise a comprehensive list of vulnerable populations because there is some shifting in oppressed people from era to era. For instance, chapter 4 discussed how children although still quite vulnerable are no longer considered an oppressed group in the same way that they were around the turn of the century when poverty and harsh economic conditions led to thousands of children flooding the streets of New York, leading to a significant reduction in sympathy toward orphaned children. Yet children, although still vulnerable, are no longer commonly considered an oppressed group in the United States.

One revealing way to identify vulnerable populations is to evaluate the history of commonly used human subjects in medical research because the most vulnerable members of society are often targeted as subjects for medical research experiments reflecting a sentiment that certain members of society are "disposable." Even a review of relatively recent research experiments reveals the tendency to exploit vulnerable members of society who are either so poor that they will often compromise their mental or physical health for a meal or a small amount of money, or because they are in situations where they are unable to decline participation.

Table 14.1 includes a partial list of human subjects used in U. S. research studies reflecting a pattern of exploitation of vulnerable populations. Review this table and identify those who appear to be the "disposable" members of society. What made these subjects vulnerable? Clearly, those who were considered unable to make valuable contributions to society, those who may have been considered "less than human," and those who may be perceived as deserving harsh treatment were often targeted for risky experiments because their loss to society would not have been considered particularly damaging to the community. Yet additional hallmarks of a vulnerable population include those who were unable to defend themselves including subjects who were incapacitated in some manner, either through limitations in intellect, language, or poverty, rendering them unable to give **informed consent,** indicating that they understood and readily agreed to the risks of participating in the experiment.

■ Table 14.1   Human Experiments: A Chronology of Human Research

1845–1849: J. Marion Sims, "the father of gynecology" performed multiple experimental surgeries on enslaved African women without the benefit of anesthesia. After suffering unimaginable pain, many lost their lives to infection. One woman was made to endure 34 experimental operations for a prolapsed uterus.

1900: Walter Reed injects 22 Spanish immigrant workers in Cuba with the agent for yellow fever paying them $100 if they survive and $200 if they contract the disease.

1913: Pennsylvania House of Representatives recorded that 146 children had been inoculated with syphilis, "through the courtesy of the various hospitals" and that 15 children in St. Vincent's House in Philadelphia had had their eyes tested with tuberculin. Several of these children became permanently blind. The experimenters were not punished.

1919–1922: Testicular transplant experiments on five hundred prisoners at San Quentin.

1927: Carrie Buck of Charlottesville is legally sterilized against her will at the Virginia Colony Home for the Mentally Infirm. Carrie Buck was the mentally normal daughter of a mentally retarded mother, but under the Virginia law, she was declared potentially capable of having a "less than normal child." By the 1930s, 17 states in the U.S. had laws permitting forced sterilization.

The settlement of *Poe v. Lynchburg Training School and Hospital* (same institution, different name) in 1981 brought to an end the Virginia law. It is estimated that as many as 10,000 perfectly normal women were forcibly sterilized for "legal" reasons including alcoholism, prostitution, and criminal behavior in general.

1939: Third Reich orders births of all twins be registered with Public Health Offices for purpose of genetic research.

(continues)

■ **Table 14.1** (*continued*)

1939: Twenty-two children living at the Iowa Soldiers' Orphans' Home in Davenport were the subjects of the "monster" experiment that used psychological pressure to induce children who spoke normally to stutter. It was designed by one of the nation's most prominent speech pathologists, Dr. Wendell Johnson, to test his theory on the cause of stuttering.

1940s: In a crash program to develop new drugs to fight malaria during World War II, doctors in the Chicago area infected nearly 400 prisoners with the disease. Although the Chicago inmates were given general information that they were helping with the war effort, they were not informed about the nature of the experiment. Nazi doctors on trial at Nuremberg cited the Chicago studies as precedents to defend their own research aimed at aiding the German war effort.

1942: Harvard biochemist Edward Cohn injects 64 Massachusetts prisoners with beef blood in U.S. Navy-sponsored experiment.

1943: Refrigeration experiment conducted on 16 mentally disabled patients who were placed in refrigerated cabinets at 30 degrees Farenheit, for 120 hours, at University of Cincinnati Hospital "to study the effect of frigid temperature on mental disorders."

1944–1946: University of Chicago Medical School professor Dr. Alf Alving conducts malaria experiments on more than 400 Illinois prisoners.

1945: Malaria experiment on 800 prisoners in Atlanta.

1947: Nuremberg Code is established.

1950: Dr. Joseph Stokes of the University of Pennsylvania infects 200 women prisoners with viral hepatitis.

1951–1960: University of Pennsylvania under contract with U.S. Army conducts psychopharmacological experiments on hundreds of Pennsylvania prisoners.

1952–1974: University of Pennsylvania dermatologist Dr. Albert Kligman conducts skin product experiments by the hundreds at Holmesburg Prison; "All I saw before me," he has said about his first visit to the prison, "were acres of skin."

1950s–1972: Mentally disabled children at Willowbrook School (NY) were deliberately infected with hepatitis in an attempt to find a vaccine. Participation in the study was a condition for admission to institution.

1956: Dr. Albert Sabin tests experimental polio vaccine on 133 prisoners in Ohio.

1962 to 1966: A total of 33 pharmaceutical companies tested 153 experimental drugs at Holmesburg Prison (PA) alone.

1962–1980: Pharmaceutical companies conduct phase I safety testing of drugs almost exclusively on prisoners for small cash payments.

1965–1966: University of Pennsylvania under contract with Dow Chemical conducts dioxin experiments on prisoners at Holmesburg.

■ **Table 14.1** (*continued*)

1969: San Antonio Contraceptive Study conducted on 70 poor Mexican-American women. Half received oral contraceptives, the other half placebo. No informed consent.

1980: The FDA promulgates 21 CFR 50.44 prohibiting use of prisoners as subjects in clinical trials shifting phase I testing by pharmaceutical companies to nonprison population.

1987: "L-dopa challenge and relapse" experiment conducted on 28 U.S. veterans who were subjected to psychotic relapse for study purposes at the Bronx VA.

1991: World Health Organization announces CIOMS Guidelines, which set forth four ethical principles: respect for persons, beneficence, nonmaleficence, and justice.

1996: Yale University researchers publish findings of experiment that subjected 18 stable schizophrenia patients to psychotic relapse in an amphetamine provocation experiment at West Haven, VA.

1997: Researchers at the University of Cincinnati publish findings of experiment attempting to create a "psychosis model" on human beings at the Cincinnati VA. Sixteen patients, experiencing a first episode schizophrenia, were subjected to repeated provocation with amphetamine. The stated purpose was to produce "behavioral sensitization. This process serves as a model for the development of psychosis, but has been little studied in humans. Symptoms, such as severity of psychosis and eye-blink rates, were measured hourly for 5 hours."

1997: U.S. government sponsored placebo-controlled experiment withholds treatment from HIV infected, pregnant African women. NY Times, Sept. 18.

2001: A biotech company in Pennsylvania asks the FDA for permission to conduct placebo trials on infants in Latin America born with serious lung disease, though such tests would be illegal in U.S.

Source: Sharay, V. H., Alliance for Human Research Protection (http://www.ahrp.org/history/chronology.php)

In essence, vulnerable populations can include any group of individuals who are vulnerable to exploitation due to lifestyle, lack of political power, lack of financial resources, and lack of societal advocacy and support. Currently vulnerable populations, those groups who may be at increased risk of social oppression and injustice in need of advocacy, include ethnic minorities, immigrants (particularly those who do not speak English), indigenous people, the elderly, women, children in foster care, prisoners, the poor, the homeless, single parents, lesbians, gays, bisexual and transgendered individuals, members of a religious minority, and the physically and intellectually disabled. In addition, in many regions of the world certain groups of individuals are selected and oppressed due to their ethnic background, religious heritage, and caste (their level of status within society, which in many regions of the world is a level one is born into), and although these individuals may not be in the minority as far as numbers, they typically have little to no political power and are subject to mistreatment and exploitation.

Mobilizing for Change: Shared Goals of Effective Macro Practice Techniques

Macro practice is a multidisciplinary field shared by those in the human services, social sciences, political sciences, and urban planning disciplines. Within the general field of macro practice, models have been developed to frame the various ways of approaching social concerns on a broad level. Although there is a very broad range of theories and models of macro or community practice, most models have at their core the basic goal of societally based social transformation where a community on any level (local, national, or global) incorporates values that reflect human dignity and worth of *all* its members.

Within most macro practice models empowerment strategies are used that focus on social and economic development, creating liaisons between community members and community organizations, political and social action, which will likely involve advocating for policy changes that address injustices and inequalities within society (Netting, Kettner, & McMurtry, 2004). Various aspects of macro practice will vary depending on the area of concern and the vulnerable population being targeted, but virtually all models of macro practice include a focus on community development, which can refer to the development of a geographic community, such as a neighborhood or city, or a community of individuals, such as women, immigrants, or children.

Common Aspects of Macro Practice

Community Development

Community development dates back to the settlement house movement when Jane Addams and her colleagues worked with politicians, various community organizations, political activists, and community members to create a better community for all members. Addams was personally concerned with child labor, compulsory education, rights of immigrants, and voting rights for woman (women's suffrage). By engaging residents, community leaders, local politicians, and other community organizations Addams was able to develop a sense of community cohesion, which resulted in several laws being passed that benefited the members of her community, including those who resided in the settlement houses.

Community development in Addams's day is similar in many respects to today, where effective community building depends on the participation of community organizations and community members working together to address issues that are of concern to the entire community (Austin, 2005). The actual issues involved could be anything from addressing crime in the community, to educational concerns such as low state test scores, developing an after-school program to combat juvenile delinquency, bringing new businesses to the community to create jobs for community members, or rallying community leaders to develop more open spaces, including parks in densely population neighborhoods.

A community development approach is empowering because the mutual collaboration of several agencies and area organizations provides support for community members in ways not possible through human service agencies alone. Another empowering aspect of community development is that the collaboration process can create a sense of collective self-sufficiency that often leads to civic pride for community members. In fact, effective community development is based on the conviction that any community is capable of mobilizing ". . . economic, social, and political resources to support families" (Austin, 2005, p. 109).

There are several necessary components of successful community development including diversity among group members, a sense of shared values among members, positive and collaborative teamwork, good communication, equal participation of all team members, and a good network of connections outside the community (Gardener, 1994). Good community development also depends on the ability to secure enough funding to support group members' activities and efforts. Good networking skills are also essential as are good technology skills because so much of networking in contemporary society is accomplished through e-mail and other technological means (Austin, 2005; Weil, 1996).

Community Organizing

Community development depends on the efforts of community organizing efforts, which in turn depends on the efforts of community organizers. The first step in community organizing is to create a consensus on what the community needs, in particular what negative issues the community is facing or areas of needed improvement. Once community members agree on the problems to be addressed, community organizers set about to recruit members to join in the effort to create change. It is important to once again note that the term *community* does not necessarily refer to a geographic community, but might also refer to a community of people, such as women, victims of domestic violence, prisoners, or foster care children.

Community organizers can be professional policy makers or licensed social workers, or they can be individual people with a particular passion and calling for social action. A schoolteacher who gets a group of his students together to remove graffiti from public buildings is a community organizer. The single mother of three, who organizes a voluntary after-school tutoring program for the kids in her neighborhood, is a community organizer. The father of a child victim of sexual abuse who organizes a campaign to increase prison time for sexual offenders is a community organizer. The licensed social worker whose agency is hired to canvas a neighborhood in an antidrug educational campaign is a community organizer.

Community organizing efforts usually begin around a problem or concern of many people in a community. Once a problem has been identified, community organizers must conduct research to define the issues, understanding how the problem or issue developed and what if any forces exist to keep the problem in place. For instance, the community activist who is organizing efforts to increase the labor rights of undocumented immigrants will likely encounter opposition by factory owners who rely on the paying untaxed low wages to **undocumented workers.** Thoroughly researching this issue will enable community organizers to identify constituents in the community who will support their cause as well as those who will oppose it. Research will also enable community organizers to identify additional harm done by unfair labor practices not initially identified that might increase the strength of any collating forces.

Once the problem has been identified and research has been conducted, a plan of action must be determined based on the research conducted. Community organizers might decide to picket factories who they perceive abuse undocumented workers; they might decide to distribute press releases and have a press conference to gain media involvement, organize a work walkout, or conduct a letter-writing campaign to local political leaders. Successful community organizers also organize fund-raising efforts to support their social activism. Sources of fund-raising can include a number of strategies including a direct request for donations, auctions, fund-raising dinners, membership fees, or government grants.

Policy Practice

Policy practice is a more narrow form of community practice where the human service professional works within the political system to influence government policy and legislation on a local, state, federal, or even global level. The form that policy practice takes depends in large part on the issues at hand, but certain activities in policy practice are consistent despite the issue. This is a relatively new field within human services, with few researchers focusing on policy practice prior to the 1980s. It remains an often neglected area of practice, both within human services and social work education as well as within human services practice setting. One reason for this may be that effective policy practice relies on a broad range of skills that reaches far beyond the clinical realm (Rocha & Johnson, 1997).

Policy activities center on either reforming current social policy or initiating the development of new policy that addresses the needs of the underserved and marginalized members of society with the primary goal of social justice through social action and advocacy. Policy practice is based on the belief that many problems in society, such as poverty, are structural in nature and can be addressed through making structural changes within society (Weiss, 2003).

Although various approaches to policy practice have been defined within academic literature, Iatridis (1995) has defined several skills necessary for effectively integrating social policy practice into direct service or micro practice. The first skill involves the human service professional's ability to understand the nature of social policy including what it is, how it is developed, its influences and effect on society as well as how social welfare policies are most often implemented. The second skill involves the ability and willingness to view direct practice from a systems perspective, where individual practice is seen as a part of a greater whole. In other words, human service professionals engaged in policy practice must be able to link issues confronted in direct service to structural problems in society (i.e., institutionalized racism, laws that oppress certain groups) by using a P-I-E paradigm (Person-In-Environment), a concept addressed throughout this text relating to the importance of viewing social issues such as poverty on a societal as well as an individual level. Another equally important skill involves the human service professional's commitment to improving social justice within society by working toward a more equitable distribution of the community's resources.

Those who engage in policy analysis research various social issues in an attempt to determine the short- and long-term effect of new policies and legislation. Policy activists and analysts might focus their attention broadly on social injustices in general, or they may focus on more narrow issues such as the quality of mental health delivery systems, or the focus may be extremely narrow such as the social injustices confronted by those seeking mental health care. Human service professionals engaging in policy practice must be able to identify key trends and issues, as well as becoming familiar with legislation or pending legislation that will affect the area of concern. Let's assume you are involved in policy practice working for an agency concerned with the elderly population. The federal administration's policies regarding Social Security funding would be a matter of great concern to you. Yet if you were involved with policy practice advocating for the rights of the children of undocumented immigrants, you'd be very concerned about possible legislation that would prohibit these children from attending public school. Regardless of the area of concern, policy analysts must be able to identify the "ripple effect" of new policies and legislation to identify their potential harm or benefit to their target population as well as the entire community.

The Global Community: International Human Services

The world is getting smaller, not in terms of population, of course, but in terms of globalization—the increase in international connectedness among all countries and, consequently, all people. No longer are countries completely isolated either in their financial economy or their political climate. In the world's new globalization each country is connected to every other country through increased ease in communication, the development of a global economy (international financial interdependence, mutual trade, and financial influence), and increased international migration combining to create a situation where the political state of one country influences the economic and political climate of another (Ahmadi, 2003).

Although many consider the term *globalization* to refer solely to matters of economics where businesses can sell goods and trade services as if there were no geographic borders, globalization also reflects the increased awareness, communication, and cooperation among social advocates. In fact, social reform on a global level is more possible now than ever before. Consider the impact the Internet has had on the exchange of information between relatively remote communities or on regions wrought with oppression. Although limits can be placed on information exchange, the Internet has made global awareness of social issues as easy as pressing a few buttons. Of course that is a somewhat simplistic statement, but the importance of the Internet cannot be underscored both in regard to direct communication as well as with regard to global awareness of social issues through Web site publication. For instance, Amnesty International (www.amnesty.org) includes a comprehensive list of human rights abuses and concerns occurring throughout the world. Within this Web site, individuals can obtain detailed information on the types of abuses currently occurring throughout the world, as well as instructions on how to take steps to assist in the global campaign to stop such oppression and abuse.

This increased ease in global communication has meant that human service professionals in one part of the world can quickly communicate with human service professionals in another part of the world sharing valuable information and coordinating efforts and services. In fact, there are several international organizations that exist for this very purpose. The International Federation of Social Workers ([IFSW] www.IFSW.org) is an international organization founded in 1956 that works with other international human services and human rights organizations to encourage international cooperation and communication among human service professionals around the globe. The IFSW has members from 80 different countries throughout the world including countries in Africa, Asia, Europe, Latin America, and North America.

The International Association of Schools of Social Work ([IASSW] www .iassw-aiets.org) is a support organization and information clearinghouse that works to ". . . develop and promote excellence in social work education, research and scholarship globally in order to enhance human well being" (www.iassw-aiets.org). The IASSW also supports an exchange of information and expertise between social work educational programs.

The International Counsel on Social Welfare (www.icsw.org) is an independent organization founded in 1928 in Paris, which is committed to social development and works with the United Nations (UN) on matters related to social development, social welfare, and social justice throughout the world. The work of the ICSW is an excellent example of community development at work using networking and international liaisons with other organizations to achieve its goals. According to its Web site,

> [T]o achieve its mission, ICSW advocates policies and programmes which strike an appropriate balance between social and economic goals and which respect cultural diversity. It seeks implementation of these proposals by governments, international organisations, non-governmental agencies and others. It does so in cooperation with its network of members and with a wide range of other organisations at local, national and international levels. ICSW's main ways of pursuing its aims include gathering and disseminating information, undertaking research and analysis, convening seminars and conferences, drawing on grass-roots experiences, strengthening non-governmental organisations, developing policy proposals, engaging in public advocacy and working with policy-makers and administrators in government and elsewhere.

The ICSW mission captures the way in which macro practice occurs through a comprehensive network of agencies and organizations on all levels of society to achieve the global mission of eliminating social injustice.

Even professional counselors whose training has traditionally leaned more in the direction of clinical practice have recently been encouraged to venture into global matter by advocating for social justice. Chi-Ying Chung (2005) made several recommendations to professional counselors to get involved in international human rights work, suggesting that they apply their training in multicultural counseling and competencies to the international arena to combat human rights abuses.

Although the human services profession exists worldwide, and concerns about specific social issues such as violence and children's rights are shared among all countries, the nature of the social issues and the function and role of the human service professional will vary depending on the political and economic conditions unique to each country. Human service professionals around the globe have many shared values but have differences in values as well. For instance, in the United States, self-determination is very highly valued in all the human services, particularly the social work profession, but not only is self-determination not considered a core value of the profession in other countries, in Asia, Africa, and even Denmark the concept of self-determination is considered either unimportant or dangerous as it detracts from the value of community and cooperation (Weiss, 2005).

Overall, though, human service professionals in virtually every country place a high value on the protection of human rights, social justice, and the end to human oppression in whatever form it might be taking within that particular region. For instance, a primary concern of the human service professionals in South Africa relates to issues of race emanating from its former system of apartheid. School social workers are commonly used to teach positive race relations among the students in South African public schools. Race issues take on a different form in the United States related to our history of slavery and mass immigration.

HIV/AIDS Pandemic

Another chief concern of human service professionals particularly in the sub-Saharan regions of Africa is the crisis brought on by the HIV/AID pandemic. In 2003 the number of individuals living with AIDS worldwide reached an estimated 38 million, and 25 million, or two-thirds of these individuals, live in sub-Saharan Africa, killing one or both parents of an estimated 12 million children, 1.1 million of whom live in South Africa. Women bear the primary burden of this disease both with regard to stigma as well as bearing the brunt of caregiving, despite the fact that they are being infected at far higher rates than men (Joint United Nations Programme on HIV/AIDS, 2004).

Human service professionals in South Africa as well as other countries in sub-Saharan Africa must contend with the devastating impact of the AIDS virus, including the very complicated and far-reaching implications of so many children being orphaned as a result of deaths due to AIDS. This situation is further complicated by the fact that many of the child welfare agencies are ill equipped to handle the vast number of orphans, many of whom are not being well cared for and may be infected with the HIV virus as well.

Several human services agencies exist solely to care for these orphaned children. Other agencies focus their efforts on education and testing. This public health crisis has far-reaching implications that must be addressed internationally if there is going to be any real remedy that will positively affect the lives of those infected and those at risk of infection.

Crimes Against Women and Children

Crimes against women and children are of concern to countries throughout the world, and human service professionals, including social workers, psychologists, and professional counselors as well as human rights workers, are involved in advocacy, counseling, and political activism on all levels to create international awareness and social action to put a stop to such atrocities as government sanctioned **honor killings,** punitive sexual assaults, exploitation and harassment, and discrimination that strips women and children of their basic human rights.

Female Genital Mutilation

Another issue often confronting human service professionals in all of Africa involves female genital mutilation (FGM), or "female circumcision," where historical tradition and tribal culture prescribes that a girl's external genitalia, typically including her labia and clitoris, be cut away in a rite of passage ceremony celebrating her entry into her womanhood. It is estimated that nearly 100 to 130 million girls have undergone FGM, which can cause serious health risks including lifelong pain, infertility, and death (WHO, 1998). FGM is rarely performed by a physician, but is frequently conducted by a village leader with no pain medication. Girls are often tied down and subjected to this surgery, which is intended to ensure chastity and purity. There has been a re-

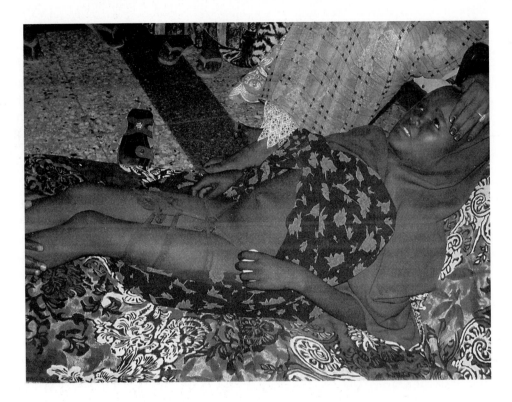

cent backlash among women in some African countries who are discouraging FGM in their communities, although this practice is still quite prevalent in many rural regions. Human service professionals are conducting educational campaigns to influence local leaders who have the power to discourage this practice, as well as influencing many Western countries to add those escaping FGM to qualify for refugee status.

Human Sex Trafficking

Human service professionals in many Asian countries must contend with numerous human rights violations, the most prevalent and disturbing of which includes the human trafficking of women and children for the purposes of slavery, forced marriage, and the sex trade. For instance, according to the Human Rights Watch (HRW), approximately 10,000 women and girls are "recruited" from Burma to Thailand brothels each year (Human Rights Watch, 2002). The most recent U.S. State Department Traffic in Persons report (2005) states that government corruption and the involvement of public officials in the human trafficking trade makes matters even more challenging for human rights workers who are attempting to achieve social justice for these women and children.

The U.S. government estimates that there are approximately 800,000 individuals who are victims of human trafficking worldwide, the majority of whom are females under the age of 18. In fact, young girls are the most sought after targets of large criminal organizations that are in the business of trafficking human beings. Although people can be sold for various reasons, including forced servitude and child labor, the majority of human trafficking involves forced sexual slavery, where young women and girls are forced to become prostitutes. Girls are either sold into sex slavery by family members in need of money, are kidnapped, or are lured into the sex trade with promises of modeling contracts or domestic work in other countries. Many of these girls are kept in inhumane environments where they are forced to have sex with up to 10 men a day. Many contract the HIV/AIDS virus and are cast out onto the street once they become too sick to be useful (U.S. State Department, 2005).

Much of the effort of human service professionals in countries with high rates of human trafficking, including India, Burma, Thailand, and Sri Lanka, is focused on rescuing these women and children and ensuring that they are delivered to safe communities where they will not be exploited again. Complicating intervention strategies is the fact that many government officials in these Asian countries either look the other way when confronted with the illegal sex trade or openly contribute to it by protecting criminal organizations responsible for human trafficking. Human rights organizations have reported that many police officers, members of the military, and other government officials in Thailand often arrest victims who attempt to escape, putting them in prison on charges of prostitution, a clear act of retaliation, rather than helping them to escape (Human Rights Watch, 2004).

Street Children

Human service professionals in Central and South American as well as Eastern European countries must contend with the significant problem of thousands of homeless street children roaming the streets in search of food and shelter. The problem of street children is growing around the globe leading several human rights organizations to call human service professionals to action. Street children are sometimes orphans, but are often children who have parents but who have left home due to poverty or lack of supervision. In many Eastern European countries, including Romania, the problem of street children is a direct result of political policies resulting from families having a large number of children with the promise of government provisions, only to be left in terribly vulnerable positions when these governments failed, leaving families with no means for providing for their exceptionally large families. Street children are at risk of abuses by older children as well as police and government officials who often physically abuse children as young as five (Human Rights Watch, 2002). Children have even been murdered by the police with no official response. Drug abuse is also rampant within the street children population, who often sniff glue to keep warm and abate hunger pains.

Human service professionals have organized agencies that reach out to these children by finding homes for them, either with religious organizations or through international adoption. International human services agencies work with local agencies to bolster aid efforts, including lobbying government officials to address this issue by funding child welfare efforts.

Child Labor and Economic Injustice

Child labor is a social justice issue across the globe, but is a particular concern in Asian, African, and Latin American countries, where children as young as four are required to work up to 12-hour days in jobs that put them in both physical and psychological danger. Child labor abuses include children in India who plunge their hands into boiling water while making silk thread, and children as young as four years old in Asia who are tied to rug looms for many hours a day and forced to make rugs.

Of the 120 million children forced into full-time labor, 61 percent reside in Asia, 32 percent in Africa, and 7 percent in Latin America (Human Rights Watch, 2004). International human rights organizations such as Human Rights Watch, Amnesty International, and UNICEF work diligently to protect children's rights, including lobbying of international policies and legislation that protect children as well as funding human rights efforts in specific countries allowing for intervention at the local level. But the problem of child labor, particularly in sweatshops in the Global South (Central and South America, Southeast Asia, India, and the Southern region of Africa) remain a serious problem impacting the entire world both socially and economically.

For instance, Polack (2004) discussed the impact of hundreds of billions of dollars in loans made to countries in the Global South by countries in the North (England, Spain, France, U.S., etc.). Polack argued that the cumulative impact of these loans to some of the poorest countries in the world has been devastating to the poorest members of these countries because these loans either (1) financed large-scale projects, such as hydroelectric plants, that either benefited the North or displaced literally millions of people pushing them even further into poverty, (2) financed military armaments for government regimes that oppressed the countries' most vulnerable and poorest residents, or (3) lined the pockets of corrupt leaders of many countries in the Global South, resulting in increased oppression of the country's least-privileged members.

Very little if any of this loan money has benefited the majority of the citizens of these countries; rather, it has harmed them and in fact continues to harm them by increasing the poverty within these already devastatingly poor regions. In an attempt to repay this debt many countries of the Global South exploit their own workers to make loan payments. For example, countries in South America have sold sections of rain forest formerly farmed by local residents to Northern timber companies, and other countries have been forced to privatize and then sell utility services formerly provided by the government, resulting in dramatic increases in the cost of utilities. These developments have resulted in many Northern companies making millions of dollars literally at the expense of the poorest residents of these debt-ridden countries.

One of the most devastating impacts of what has now evolved into trillions of dollars of debt for these southern countries is the evolution of the sweatshop industry, large-scale factories that develop goods exported to the North. Some of the poorest people in the world, including children, work in sweatshops throughout Asia, India, and southern Africa, where horrific abuses abound. This occurs legally in many of these countries because in a desperate attempt to attract export contracts, many countries in Asia as well as India created "free-trade" agreements or Free Trade Zones for Western corporations allowing them to circumvent local trade regulations such as minimum wage, working hour limits, and child labor laws, if they would open factories in their impoverished countries.

Polack (2004) suggests that literally every major retail supplier in the United States benefits from these sweatshop conditions such as extremely low wages, extremely poor working conditions, physical and sexual exploitation without retribution, excessively long working hours (sometimes in excess of 12 hours per day with no days off for weeks at a time), and severe retribution such as immediate termination for complaints or requests for better working conditions. Child labor is the norm in these sweatshops with most sweatshop owners preferring adolescent girls as employees because they tend to be more compliant and are more easily exploited.

Although local and international human rights advocates work diligently to change these working conditions, at the root of the problem of child exploitation is economic injustice rooted in generations of intercountry exploitation. Thus, there is significant complexity not easily confronted without government involvement, which is often slow in coming when large corporations are making millions of dollars with the system as it currently operates. For instance, as labor unions have become the norm in the United States, many companies such as Nike and Wal-Mart moved their factories to Asia and Central and South America, where millions of dollars can be saved in wages and benefits cuts (National Labor Committee, n.d.). Addressing the issue of child labor and economic injustice will take the lobbying efforts of many international human rights organizations working with the media to create public awareness where buying power is often the only tool powerful enough to influence sweatshop owners and large retail establishments.

case study 14.1

Testimony of Mahamuda Akter MNC Garment Factory, September 2002

My name is Mahamuda Akter. I am 18 years old. I've only had the chance to go through fifth grade. I was 13 when I began working in the garment factories. For the last two years I have been working at the MNC factory in the Chittagong Export Processing Zone, where we sew clothing for Wal-Mart. I am a sewing operator.

Until September 5, we were working on Ozark Trail shirts. Before that—for six or seven months—we worked constantly on Sportrax athletic clothing. Now we are sewing Faded Glory shorts. Depending upon the type of garment we are working on, my job is to join the collar, or to sew either the pocket or the hem of the sleeves. Attaching the collars is very complicated since you must match the patterns of the fabric. The supervisors scream at us to do 40 pieces an hour. But it's impossible. Working as fast as we can, I can only finish 30 collars in an hour.

The supervisors tell us we have to meet Wal-Mart's target. There is constant pressure on us to work faster. They beat us. They slap our faces or slap us on the back of the head. They grab us by the hair and jerk our heads. They push and shove us.

I was beaten several times in August and September. My supervisor, who is a man, slapped my face and cursed at me that I was a son of a bitch and that my parents were whores. They use vulgar and filthy words, they made me cry. Many of us girls cry, but they make you keep working.

I work on Line "D." In July, the supervisors kicked one of the girls on our line, yelling that she had made a mistake. They threw her against the wall and her mouth was bleeding. They took her to the office and fired her that afternoon.

Another thing they do as punishment is to make a girl stand on a bench in front of all the other workers, forcing her to hold her ears and pull them down. It's a shameful insult. They do this especially to the young girls and it makes them feel terrible.

There are 4,000 workers in our factory. Eighty-five percent of us are women. We have lots of helpers who are 10 to 12 years old.

Our regular work schedule is from 7:30 AM to 10:00 PM. But they often force us to work until 3:00 AM. In August, I had to work 13 nights till 3:00 AM. In other sections it was even worse, and they had to work 20 to 25 nights to 3:00 in the morning. We work seven days a week. In August we had just one day off. For the year, I think I got a total of 15 days off.

When we work through to 3:00 AM, we get three breaks, a half hour for lunch from 1:00 to 1:30 PM; ten minutes from 7:00 to 7:10 PM, and an hour off for supper from 11:00 to midnight. After the 3:00 AM shift, we sleep in the factory. It is so crowded that we sleep sitting on our benches slumped over our sewing machines. There is no place to even lie down on the floor. At 5:00 AM they ring a loud bell to wake everyone up, so we can get ready to start work again. We wash our faces, use the bathroom, eat something and go back to work. Sometimes we are forced to do these 19½-hour shifts three days in a row.

We are exhausted. Many times the workers faint. The supervisors throw water on their faces and they have to get back to work. They also play loud music to keep us awake.

I earn 2,100 taka a month, which is $35.60. I'm told this comes to 17 cents an hour.

We are not allowed to talk at work, and if we are caught we are punished. You need permission to use the bathroom. When we work until 3:00 in the morning for example, we can use the bathroom just three times in the entire shift.

We have a daycare center at the factory, but it is a joke. It is just for show to the buyers. It is never really used.

We are not allowed sick days, or national holidays, or any vacation.

They also cheat us on our overtime wages. They keep two sets of time cards. The phony one is for Wal-Mart. It says that we work just from 7:30 AM to 6:30 PM, in other words, that we work two hours of overtime a day. It also says that we receive every Friday off. That's a lie.

None of us have ever heard of the Wal-Mart Code of Conduct. Before the Wal-Mart buyers come to the factory, the factory is always cleaned. The supervisors tell us to lie if the buyers ever question us—we are supposed to say that we work just to 6:30 and that we have one day off a week. The buyers always walk around with the manager. Everyone is so frightened, no one dares complain. Sometimes the buyers ask us to smile and they take a picture. They usually come around 1:00 or 2:00 in the afternoon. They never come at 10 PM or 3:00 AM.

I live in one room with three other girls who are co-workers. We must pay 1,150 taka rent each month. We cannot even afford a fan or a TV. We share one water pump, an outhouse, and one gas stove with 20 other people.

Every day we eat rice, rice with lentils or with mashed potatoes. Sometimes we have an egg at night. I'm always hungry. I weigh 79 pounds. Maybe once in a month we can eat beef.

We work so hard, but it is not right that they mistreat us so and pay us so very little.

I am afraid of getting old. Living and working like this, by the time you are 20 you are already old, and your health is failing. When you reach 30, they fire you. It is not just. I have no savings. I have nothing.

I would like a better life for myself and the other girls. ■

Source: National Labor Committee

Indigenous People

Protecting the rights of indigenous people is a common concern of human service professionals practicing in countries such as the United States, Australia, and many Central and South American countries. The human rights issues pertaining to indigenous peoples of Australia, primarily comprised of Aborigines, are similar in nature to those in the United States, where the historic immigration of Europeans displaced the indigenous tribal communities. In addition, both countries engaged in an official campaign of discrimination and cultural annihilation as indigenous tribes were forced off their lands and onto restricted areas, where they were unable to practice traditional methods of self-support. Both Native Americans in the United States and Aborigines in Australia were subject to the mass forced removal of children, who were mandated to attend schools where they were forced to abandon their cultural heritage and native language.

In response to the intergenerational trauma that has resulted from generations of cultural genocide, many indigenous people have developed problems with depression and alcoholism. Human service professionals work with indigenous people in reconciliation efforts to restore them to a level of self-sufficiency and cultural pride. Several movements are underway within indigenous tribal communities intended to move them toward wholeness and a life without substance abuse, depression, and the brokenness in families that has so often been the result of social ills.

One program within a Native American community was developed by a tribal member who suffered from alcoholism for years and who received inspiration and input from tribal elders who shared wisdom regarding traditional cultural laws for authentic change. The four laws of change became known as the *Healing Forest Model*, which is based on the philosophy of the Medicine Wheel, a Native American concept that addresses the interconnectedness of everything in life. According to the teachings of the Medicine Wheel, the pain of one person creates pain for the entire community thus there are no individual issues or concerns. This community concept of healing is very consistent with a model of macro practice, which posits that there are no such things as individual problems but instead people make up communities and therefore all individual problems become community problems. This philosophy may be counterintuitive to North Americans, who as a society place an exceedingly high value on individuality, oftentimes at the cost of community. Yet many believe that the key to reclaiming physical and mental health in indigenous culture is through such a community practice approach (Coyhis & Simonelli, 2005).

Torture and Abuse

Countries in Eastern Europe as well as countries in Northern and Western Africa are overwhelmed with the repercussions of war and genocide where human service professionals and human rights workers deal with numerous human atrocities such as torture, war crimes, and the crisis of thousands of refugees. But the problem of abuse and torture is truly worldwide, and as much as members of industrialized countries would like to believe that human torture is a problem known only to lesser developed countries, the physical and sexual torture of the Iraqi detainees at Abu Ghraib prison is a clear reminder that human torture occurs on all soils at the hands of people from the most "civilized" of countries.

Countries in the midst of war are particularly vulnerable to human rights abuses involving torture because war seems to have an ameliorating effect on human compassion and empathy. Human torture and abuse can include anything from random physical abuse, to the systematic abuse and even murder of groups of people common in genocide, prisoner of war camps, and refugee camps. Many of the abuses documented in the Taliban-ruled Afghanistan included sexual assault, government-sanctioned gang rapes of women who brought disgrace on their countrymen, and physical torture such as the cutting off of limbs for minor infractions (U.S. State Department, 2000).

Most if not all victims of wartime atrocities such as rape and torture, many of whom are being revictimized in refugee camps, suffer from PTSD and other psychiatric conditions related to grief and loss. Human service professionals work with victims of torture on all fronts—some within refugee camps, and some in other countries who have accepted victims on refugee status. The psychological issues involved are vast and in addition to the disorders mentioned earlier include depression, anxiety, and adjustment disorders. Most human service professionals in developing countries and former Soviet block countries are employed by the government and deliver broad-ranging services on a community level focusing on the manifestation of a history of war, as well as the ramifications of transitioning from a communist society to a democracy. For instance, a relatively significant portion of human services in Croatia is focused on postwar issues as well as the care of Bosnian refugees and other war victims, focusing on trauma recovery and helping victims to manage the comprehensive impact of war on the individual and families (Knežević & Butler, 2003).

Lesbian, Gay, Bisexual, and Transgendered Rights

Individuals who have nontraditional sexual orientations, including lesbian women, gay men, bisexual men and women, and transgendered individuals (those who have undergone surgery to physically become the opposite gender) have long been the victims of abuse, discrimination, and at the very least a tremendous amount of misunderstanding. *Homophobia* is defined as irrational fear of homosexuals or of homosexual behavior. Lesbian, gay, bisexual, or transgendered (LGBT) individuals are subjected to homophobic sentiments and outright discrimination and violence in all parts of the world. Until recently the majority opinion of those in Western culture was that LGBT individuals were either morally perverse or mentally ill. In fact, it wasn't until 1987 that all references to homosexuality were completely removed from the DSM.

Acts of harassment and violence against LGBT individuals based on their sexual orientation are prevalent all over the world causing significant distress, depression, and even suicidal ideation (Huebner, Rebchook, & Kegeles, 2004). LGBT youth are at risk of discrimination in school and community settings in both the United States and the U.K., although many school districts now use policies designed to protect adolescents whose sexual orientation are known to others in the school or community (Ryan & Rivers, 2003). LGBT individuals are commonly the victims of direct or subtle discriminatory practices, verbally abused and harassed, and the victims of violence, sometimes even murder, solely because of their sexual orientation.

Although abuse and discrimination against LGBT individuals is assumed to be far worse in developing countries, this is not always the case. In many regions of the world the line between heterosexuality and homosexuality is quite thin, particularly compared to Western cultural norms. This contention is based on the practice of male-on-male sexual activity commonly practiced in many parts of the world when one or both men are married. For instance, in Bangladesh married men often frequent male prostitutes but do not necessarily consider themselves homosexual. They are rarely victims of harassment or abuse because they do not violate gender stereotypes, which essentially means that men continue to act like men and women continue to act like women (Dowsett, 2003). The relevance of this is that in many parts of the world violence against LGBT is based more on behavior that is contrary to traditional gender stereotypes than it is on their sexual activities.

Yet in many regions of the world homosexual behavior is considered a criminal act punishable by anything from a prison sentence to death. Homosexuality is considered illegal in South Africa, and LGBT individuals are often the victims of human rights abuses, including punitive rapes. In addition, they are often unjustly blamed for the HIV/AIDS crisis currently occurring in Africa (Graziano, 2004). LGBT individuals in Saudi Arabia are subject to public floggings and imprisonment for even suspected homosexual behavior. In Egypt vice officers travel through towns in vans arresting in excess of 100 men at a time for suspected homosexuality. Many of these men were arrested because they knew what the word *gay* meant, a North American word assumed to be known only by homosexual men. Men arrested on suspected homosexuality are then subject to severe beatings until they agree to sign arrest papers admitting to their homosexuality. Signing these papers means a lifetime of certain harassment and refusing to sign them means certain death. In Jamaica LGBT individuals are often the target of horrible human rights abuse, oftentimes fueled by the police who often invite bystanders to attack men suspected of homosexual behavior. One incident reported to a human rights organization involved a man suspected of being gay who was attacked by police and ultimately beaten and stabbed to death in the middle of the street by bystanders who joined in on the beating. Police in Jamaica also commonly stop individuals suspected of being LGBT on the streets searching them looking for any sign of homosexual activity such as condoms or lubricants. If these items are found, the men are often beaten and arrested (Human Rights Watch, 2004).

Human service professionals and human rights workers around the globe are working tirelessly to reduce crimes against LGBT individuals through the passage of policies and legislation designed not only to protect individuals whose sexual orientation is not traditional, but also to decriminalize homosexual behavior in all countries. After years of attempting to pass legislation in the United States protecting individuals who are victims of crimes based on their sexual orientation, gay rights advocates won a significant victory in September of 2005 when the Local Law Enforcement Hate Crimes Prevention Act of 2005 was passed adding sexual orientation to hate crimes legislation.

This was a controversial bill because some conservative religious organizations fear that such legislation would criminalize "thoughts" and control free speech. Many

Christian organizations, such as the Family Research Council and Focus on the Family, argue that making homosexuals a protected group might put preachers at risk of criminal prosecution on conspiracy charges if they preach a message against homosexual behavior that inadvertently incites someone listening to go out and kill a homosexual (Family Research Council, 2005; Trobee, 2005).

Yet others argue that the First Amendment of the U.S. Constitution guarantees free speech. In addition, to commit a conspiracy two people must conspire together to commit an unlawful act (Religious Tolerance, 2004). Proponents of the legislation argue that the bill legally protects a group of people who have long been victims of harassment and violence solely because of their sexual orientation by increasing punishment for such crimes and by sending a message that the U.S. society will not tolerate hate crimes targeted against someone because of who they are.

What might be one of the most important issues to consider is that regardless of whether one considers homosexuality a lifestyle choice, a genetically predetermined orientation, a nontraditional sexual orientation no better or worse than heterosexuality, or an act of perversion and immorality, violence against someone based on their sexual orientation is never permissible under any conditions, thus even those human service professionals who because of religious faith, or cultural tradition believe that heterosexuality is the only physically and psychologically healthy lifestyle, should be called to action to ensure that *all* individuals, despite their sexual orientation, are treated with compassion and dignity.

Macro Practice in Action

Local advocacy organizations such as the YWCA lobby for governmental policies and laws that protect victims of crime, including sexual assault. Mothers Against Drunk Drivers (MADD) has been instrumental in lowering the legal alcohol limit for driving to .08 from .10, as well as establishing stiffer penalties for alcohol-related crashes. Amnesty International advocates for human rights and social justice for oppressed individuals around the world, releasing annual reports of human rights violations within each country. The passage of one domestic violence law can protect thousands of women. An antidrug educational campaign can convince thousands of adolescents to stay off drugs. One press release can lead to a boycott that can increase wages for thousands of young women in sweatshops in India. Direct practice with individuals can change the lives of a few people, but macro practice can change the lives of an entire community or a whole country. The power of macro practice should serve as an impetus for all human service professionals to consider embracing macro practice on some level, whether that means conducting voter registration drives in politically underserved areas, conducting a letter writing campaign in support of legislation designed to protect a vulnerable population, or working on behalf of an international human rights organization that works tirelessly on behalf of exploited children, abused women, or traumatized refugees. Such positions offer significant rewards to those human service professionals willing to develop multidisciplinary expertise through education and experience that when combined with the networking power of other organizations can create positive change for all members of society.

references

Ahmadi, N. (2003). Globalisation of consciousness and new challenges for international social work. *International Journal of Social Welfare, 12,* 14–23.

Austin, S. (2005). Community-building principles: Implications for professional development. *Child Welfare, 84(2),* 105–122.

Calkin, C. (2000, June). Welfare reform. *Peace and Social Justice: A Newsletter of the Committee for Peace and Social Justice, 1(1).* Retrieved September 17, 2005, from http://www.naswdc.org/practice/peace/psj0101.pdf

Chi-Yang Chang, R. (2005). Women, human rights & counseling: Crossing international borders. *Journal of Counseling and Development, 83,* 262–268.

Coyhis, D., & Simonelli, R. (2005). Rebuilding Native American communities. *Child Welfare, 84(2),* 323–336.

Dowsett, G. W. (2003). HIV/AIDS and homophobia: Subtle hatreds, severe consequences and the question of origins. *Culture, Health & Sexuality, 5(2),* 121–136.

Family Research Council. (2005). Urgent: The homosexual agenda is winning in the House. Alert. Retrieved October 16, 2005 from http://www.frc.org/get.cfm?I=AL05I13

Gardener, J. W. (1994). *Building community for leadership training programs.* Washington DC: Independent Sector.

Graziano, K. J. (2004). Oppression and resiliency in a post-apartheid South Africa: Unheard voices of black gay men and lesbians. *Cultural Diversity and Ethnic Minority Psychology, 10(3),* 302–316.

Huebner, D. M., Rebchook, M., & Kegeles, S. M. (2004). Experiences of harassment, discrimination, and physical violence among young gay and bisexual men human rights watch. *American Journal of Public Health, 94(7),* 1200–1203.

Human Rights Watch. (2002). *Burmese women and girls trafficked to Thailand.* The Human Rights Watch Report on Women's Human Rights. Retrieved September 30, 2005, from http://www.hrw.org/about/projects/womrep/General-123.htm#P1937_535306

Human Rights Watch. (2004). All Jamaicans are threatened by a culture of homophobia. Retrieved September 30, 2005, from http://hrw.org/english/docs/2004/11/23/jamaic9716.htm

Human Rights Watch. (2005). Saudi Arabia: Men "behaving like women" face flogging sentences imposed for alleged homosexual conduct violate basic rights. Retrieved September 30, 2005, from http://hrw.org/english/docs/2005/04/07/saudia10434.htm

Iatridis, D. (1995). Policy practice. In R. L. Edwards (Ed.), *Encyclopedia of social work* (19th ed., pp. 1855–1866). Washington, DC: NASW Press.

Johnson, A. (2004). Social work is standing on the legacy of Jane Addams: But are we sitting on the sidelines? *Social Work, 49(2),* 319–322.

Joint United Nations Programme on HIV/AIDS. (2004) *Report on the global AIDS epidemic.* Geneva: UNAIDS.

Knežević, M., & Butler, L. (2003). Public perceptions of social workers and social work in the Republic of Croatia. *International Journal of Social Welfare, 12,* 50–60.

Mills, C. W. (1959). *The sociological imagination.* New York: Oxford University Press.

Mizrahi T (2001). The status of community organization in 2001: Community practice context, complexities, contradictions, and contributions. *Research on Social Work Practice, 11,* 176–189.

National Association of Social Workers. (1999). *Code of ethics of the National Association of Social Workers.* Washington, DC: Author.

National Labor Committee. (n.d.). Working conditions in China. Retrieved on December 21, 2005 from http://www.nlcnet.org/campaigns/archive/report00/introduction.shtml

National Organization for Human Services. (1996). *Ethical standards of human service professionals.* Washington, DC: Author.

Netting, E., Kettner, P., & McMurtry, S. (2004). *Social work macro practice.* Boston: Pearson Education.

Polack, R. (2004). Social justice and the global economy: New challenges for social work in the 21st century. *Social Work, 49(2),* 281–290.

Religious Tolerance. (2004). U.S. Hate Crimes: Ethical and Civil rights concerns. Retrieved on December 21, 2005 from http://www.religioustolerance.org/horn_hats.htm#procon

Rocha, C., & Johnson, A. (1997). Teaching family policy through a policy framework. *Journal of Social Work Education, 33 (3),* 433–444.

Ryan, C., & Rivers, I. (2003). Lesbian, gay, bisexual and transgender youth: Victimization and its correlates in the U.S. and U.K. *Culture, Health and Sexuality, 5(2),* 103–119.

Trobee, K. (2005). Hate crimes amendment passes House. *Focus on the Family, Citizen Action Link.* Retrieved on November 7, 2005 from http://www.family.org/cforum/fnif/news/a0037944.cfm

U.S. Department of State. (2005). *Traffic in persons report.* (USDS Publication No. 11252). Washington DC: U.S. Government Printing Office wol(http://www.state.gov/g/tip).

Weil, M. O. (1996). Community building: Building community practice. *Social Work, 41(5),* 481–499.

Weiss, I. (2003). Social work students and social change: On the link between views on poverty, social work goals and policy practice. *International Journal of Social Welfare, 12,* 132–141.

Weiss, I. (2005). Is there a global common core to social work? A cross-national comparative study of BSW graduate students. *Social Work, 50(2),* 102–110.

World Health Organization. (1998). *Female genital mutilation—an overview.* Geneva, Switzerland: World Health Organization.

suggested reading

Hokenstad, M. C., & Midgley, J. (Ed.). (2004). *Lessons from abroad: Adapting international social welfare innovations.* Washington, DC: NASW Press.

Langer, L. L. (1991). *Holocaust testimonies: The ruins of memory.* New Haven, CT: Yale University Press.

Rosenfeld, L. B., Caye, J. S., Ayalon, O., & Lahad, M. (2004). *When their worlds fall apart.* Washington, DC: NASW Press.

Van Soest, D. (1997). *The global crisis violence: Common problems, universal causes, shared solutions.* Washington, DC: NASW Press.

internet web sites related to macro practice

American Indian Movement (AIM): **http://www.aimovement.org/**
American Red Cross: **http://www.redcross.org/**
AmeriCares—Humanitarian Lifeline to the World: **http://www.redcross.org/**
Amnesty International: **www.amnesty.org**
Anti-Defamation League: **http://www.adl.org/**
Anti-Slavery: **http://www.antislavery.org/**
Antiracism.net: **www.antiracismnet.org/main.html**
Cultural Survival: **http://209.200.101.189/**
Doctors on Call: **www.dogs.org**
Doctors without Borders: **www.doctorswithoutborders.com**
Human Rights Watch: **www.hrw.org**
International Federation of Social Workers: **http://internationalnetwork-schoolsocial-work.htmlplanet.com/index.htm**

chapter 15

Professional Ethics and Values in Human Services

The Merriam Webster dictionary defines "ethics" as ". . . a set of moral principles or values; principles of conduct governing an individual or a group (as in 'professional ethics'), and a guiding philosophy" (Merriam-Webster, 1993). Ethical standards then are based on a foundational value system designed to tell us what good behavior is and what bad behavior is. Or another more basic way of putting it is that ethical standards and principles tell us what we *ought* to do in any given situation.

Now you might be asking yourself—I'm a good person, so why do I need a detailed set of ethical values to tell me what to do? Don't good people behave "good" naturally? The answer may surprise you! Although it may be true that very few people wake up in the morning and say to themselves, "Hey! I think I'm going to lie, cheat, and steal today!"—it is true that many people become hysterical, enraged, are biased, selfish, naive, or ignorant—and in the process of being so very human, they may very well behave quite unethically as they make decisions based on their urges, desires, passions, personal biases, negative stereotypes, or uninformed opinions.

Ethical values and principles are a very necessary part of life, both personally as well as professionally, and although some may argue that one's personal ethical values are not necessarily tied to his or her professional ethics, a strong argument can be made that they are in fact very much a reflection of one another. Most of you probably remember former President Bill Clinton's impeachment hearings, which centered on his perjury in a sexual harassment claim filed against him, as well as his inappropriate relationship with a young White House intern. Many of his supporters argued fervently that what he did in his personal life had no bearing on his ability to be a good president. Yet others argued that poor character demonstrated in one's personal life will most definitely play out in one's professional life, and one cannot draw a line between these two domains.

Moral, But by Whose Standards?

It would be very convenient if there were one long list of rules and all situations could be perceived in the same manner by everyone. But of course that is not how life works. Most people will argue that there are universal moral principles, particularly relating to issues such as murder and robbery, and so forth. But even with these seemingly black-and-white moral issues, the gray seems to abound. Such is the case when someone kills in self-defense, or someone steals bread for a starving child. So, is morality absolute or relative? What I mean by this is, is there an absolute right and wrong in this world? Or, is the rightness and wrongness of a decision or action dependent on perspective, culture, or one's own truth? This is an age-old question and not one that I will answer definitively here. In fact, many moral theorists deal with this very issue, and although some argue for either extreme position, most will argue that both are true—there are ultimate moral principles that are universal (sexually abusing a child is always wrong), and there are many occasions when one must consider the appropriateness of a certain behavior within the context of one's culture (burping in public).

I want to address some of the issues that have the greatest potential of "muddying" the waters a bit when it comes to determining how we know whether an action is moral or immoral, which in turn will help us determine how we can ensure we're making moral decisions. We will then apply what we've learned to the professional arena, specifically the human services profession.

Ethical Values vs. Emotional Desires: "I Know It Was Wrong, But We Were in Love!"

Other than the most rigid of people, most people will find themselves caught in a tug-of-war between their ethical standards and their emotional desires, or feelings, with the latter often leading to some breaking down of moral behavior at some point in their lives. I have a counseling practice, and I often tell my clients that feelings and emotions are like the interior design of a house—moving and poignant, even beautiful at times, but only truly useful if protected by the exterior and structure of the house—the walls and roof, which are the framework, like our ethical standards, values, and principles. Thus, although human beings are certainly emotional beings, an individual with high character is one who is not driven to act solely on the basis of their desires and passions.

In fact, individuals who are motivated primarily by emotions are often emotionally unstable, not because their emotions are wrong, but because their values and principles are not well enough defined and/or developed to contain or regulate their emotions, oftentimes leading to the inability to control their impulses. For instance, an employee might become so angry with his boss that he feels like striking him, but he doesn't because he values nonviolence. A person's ethical values should then be the rudder of behavior, and although there are certainly times when people will be driven by passion, or will need to follow their hunches, emotions and desires serve people best when they aren't chief in the decision-making process.

Another reason why it is important to understand the relationship between our ethical values and our emotions is because we often use our emotions to justify our unethical behavior. Cheating on a test is wrong, unless the test is too hard and we hate our teacher; adultery is wrong, unless we're in a loveless marriage, are extremely lonely, and fall hopelessly in love with someone else; lying is wrong, unless we need the day off and will only get paid if we say we're sick, even though we're not; violence is wrong unless we're provoked; and drinking too much alcohol is wrong, unless we've gone two weeks without and just had a very bad day. Thus, one of the primary functions of ethical values is to keep us on a good moral track, particularly when we find our ethical values at odds with our emotional desires and urges. Certainly there are times when emotions should lead, and we certainly do not want to become heartless in our application of rules. When someone is driven to act solely on the basis of their values or rules, they are often deemed rigid legalists. But when someone behaves in a manner that is solely driven by his or her feelings and desires, they are often deemed immature, volatile, and impulsive.

When Our Values Collide: "I Value Honesty, But What If Lives Are at Stake?"

Ethical behavior is not just made difficult because of competing emotions and desires, but oftentimes we find ourselves in situations where our values are competing with one another. We value family dinners with our kids, but what if that conflicts with our value of their extracurricular involvement? We value our friendships, but what if they are interfering in our marriage which we also value? Many times an individual acts in a way that is later perceived to be unethical, when at the time they were committing the act they may have believed they were acting in a very ethical manner, but were forced to choose among competing values. An employee who shreds documents to protect his employer may very well believe he is acting ethically based on his ethical value of loyalty to his employer. Yet he is later charged with obstruction of justice because someone else perceived his behavior to be immoral. Perhaps in retrospect this employee will realize that his values were misguided, or he may forever feel as though he was behaving morally, and the government was not.

In 1945 when Corrie ten Boom (1974) was hiding Jews in her attic, she chose to lie to the Nazi officers who came to her door questioning her, even though she believed lying to be wrong. Corrie was put in a position where she had to choose the higher value. What did she value more? Complete honesty at all costs? Obedience to authority? Personal safety? Or interceding in matters of inhumane cruelty and injustice at all costs? In light of what we now know about Nazi Germany and the Holocaust, Corrie and her family are lauded as heroes, behaving in the highest moral fashion, refusing to stand by and do nothing as an evil government slaughtered thousands of innocent people. Yet does this mean that those who did not hide Jews acted immorally? What if you had the opportunity to interview a family who refused to hide a Jewish neighbor? What if this person told you that Nazis used the practice of dressing as Jews and going door-to-door asking for refuge, and that the punishment for harboring a Jew was imprisonment in a concentration camp, and likely death? What if this person explained that they believed they behaved morally because their first responsibility was to their own children? Would you still consider their behavior immoral? Or what about the ruling authorities' perspective? Corrie ten Boom and her family broke the law. From the authorities' perspective, then, their behavior was immoral. What makes the ten Boom's family's behavior moral now? Our belief that the Nazis were evil? So does this mean that if you or I believe that one of the laws, or even our entire government was evil, that we'd be justified in disobeying its laws? Many protective parents "kidnap" their children because they strongly believe that the family courts will not protect them from the other abusive parent. If this is true, is their behavior justified? Many African-American men believe that if they are pulled over by the police, it is because they are being racially profiled, and they may be arrested for no reason. Does this justify an attempt to flee? Would their behavior be any more or less moral than a slave who escaped prior to the Civil War?

I hope you are beginning to see that evaluating ethical behavior in retrospect, when we have the benefit of perspective and outcome, is a far easier task than determining what is truly ethical in the moment. And the lens that we use to evaluate the moral rightness of a behavior is often determined by the outcome—something that the person involved doesn't have the benefit of knowing when they're making their decisions or any control over in many circumstances, which explains why some people who are initially perceived as highly immoral are later considered heroes, and some people who authentically believe they are behaving morally, end up in prison.

The Development of Moral Reasoning

Before developing a set of ethical values, it is important to understand the nature of moral development, and there is no shortage of theorists who have attempted to do just that. Obviously what people base their values on can vary dramatically. Value systems can be based on the values of one's family of origin, on one's culture, or on one's religious beliefs. Lawrence Kohlberg (Gibbs, 2003) believed that the capacity to reason morally developed along with cognitive development. Kohlberg conducted interviews with people of all ages and discovered that children (or immature adults) cited something as being immoral because they would get into trouble, thus relying on external references of right and wrong, whereas more mature adults could understand and grasp the various shades of gray involved in a moral dilemma and cited the moral nature of a situation relying on internal references. Kohlberg theorized that the type of moral reasoning that adults use to evaluate the moral dilemmas in their lives is dependent on abstract reasoning ability, a cognitive function that children lack. And although the capacity for moral reasoning does not necessarily mean that someone will behave morally, it is important to consider someone's cognitive ability to apply moral reasoning to their behavior before judging them.

Developing a Professional Code of Ethics

It is because of the difficult nature of determining what constitutes moral behavior—including the balancing of our ethical values and emotional urges, of knowing which competing values to choose in any given situation, of having the benefit of perspective when making moral decisions—that many professions have elected to develop foundational ethical standards and professional values to safeguard from emotion, bias and misguided commitments being the primary motivators in ethical decision making. Many professions begin with some stated set of values or underlying guiding assumptions, oftentimes found reflected in their **Mission Statement,** and sometimes ethical standards are developed from some form of abuse. The ethical standard prohibiting a human service professional from dating a client was likely developed in response to a human service professional using poor judgment in dating a client, who later filed a complaint because they felt exploited and abused.

Regardless of how standards are developed, virtually all professions rely on some form of ethical standards to maintain integrity and trust within their profession. Numerous professions espouse basic ethical principles, which serve as a foundation for their business practices and standards, but in addition to such values of choice, an increasing number of professions are bound by legally enforced ethical standards, and if violated can result in quite punitive consequences, ranging from professional or financial sanctions (such as license suspension or fines), to a wide range of criminal penalties (including incarceration).

Virtually every professional group operates under a professional organization or licensing entity that enforces ethical codes in some form. Attorneys operate within certain legal ethical standards administered by the American Bar Association (ABA). Psychologists must abide by particular professional standards that are set forth by the

American Psychological Association (APA). Even a stockbroker must abide by the ethical standards and values of their company, which may include putting the client's needs first and not overcharging for services, but they must also abide by the legally binding ethical standards set forth by the Securities and Exchange Committee (SEC), which if violated can include both professional sanctions, or in extreme cases even a criminal indictment.

Resolving Ethical Dilemmas

It is very important that any professional code of ethics be considered an ever-growing and changing entity, never in final form, and always open for evaluation and debate. West (2002) discussed the importance of "ethical mindfulness," citing several real-world examples of questionable ethical practices in the counseling and human services field, including issues related to informed consent (informing a client of their rights and making sure they know all that is involved in engaging in the counseling process), the use of real clients in therapist educational videotapes, and other ethical issues appropriate for discussion and evaluation.

But even if everyone agrees that having ethical standards is a good thing, and that constant evaluation is necessary, the next challenge is to determine how to respond when an ethical breach may have occurred. Kitchener's (1984) model of ethical decision making was designed to guide professionals in navigating the sometimes-murky waters of decision making in difficult situations. Kitchener's model is based on four assumptions that he maintains need to be at the heart of any ethical evaluation and can in a sense be used as a "litmus test" when attempting to determine whether a certain act was in fact unethical. These assumptions include (1) autonomy, (2) beneficence, (3) nonmaleficence, and (4) justice.

In Kitchener's model, when a certain act is being evaluated to determine its ethical nature, the model would have the evaluators ask whether the professional acted with free will (autonomy); whether the professional's actions were intended to benefit the client (beneficence); whether the professional's actions involved evil, illegal, or harmful intentions (nonmaleficence); and whether these acts were carried out in a manner that respected the rights and dignity of all involved parties (justice).

Let us use Corrie ten Boom's actions as an example. The ruling government certainly considered her behavior unethical, and although we have the benefit of perspective and outcome in evaluating her behavior, as I mentioned before rarely does one have this luxury when in the midst of a moral dilemma. If one were to use Kitchener's model in determining the ethical nature of ten Boom's behavior, although she was acting in autonomy, the Nazi regime forced her to hide her activities, thus it could be argued that she was not acting in a manner that was based on her free will (i.e., Would she normally oppose government officials?). Her behavior was beneficence, in the sense that it involved acts of kindness toward her fellow man, she refused to do harm by standing by and allowing atrocities against her Jewish neighbors and friends, and she was motivated by her hatred for injustice. Thus ten Boom's behavior should be considered ethical regardless of the fact that history deems the Nazis an evil regime.

Cultural Influences on the Perception of Ethical Behavior

Cultural context is another very important variable to consider when evaluating the rightness or wrongness of behavior. Garcia, Cartwright, Winston, and Borzuchowska, (2003) discussed a model of ethical decision making that stresses the importance of being culturally sensitive when evaluating any ethical decision-making process. Garcia et al. challenged the notion that all cultures value autonomy equally and reminded the reader that many cultures operate on a very interdependent basis. He also cautioned that what one culture considers abnormal, another culture considers perfectly normal. But regardless of how one goes about determining what is ethical and how ethical decisions are made (or how unethical decisions were made), it is very important to remember to be sensitive to differences between: *cultures, genders,* and *ages* (across the generations).

Again, it is also very important to remember that oftentimes what appears blatantly unethical in retrospect may have seemed quite ethical, or at the very least somewhat muddy, in the midst. Thus, taking the time to truly understand the behavior from the professional's perspective, keeping issues related to enculturation in mind, is absolutely imperative and undoubtedly very challenging.

Ethical Standards in Human Services

The ethical standards that govern the human services profession depend on many variables, including the human service professional's level of education, professional license, and even the state in which they practice. A social worker who practices with a Master's of Social Work (MSW) is bound by the professional ethics of the National Association of Social Workers (NASW), which has set forth several ethical standards of conduct for social workers in practice, as well as a set of values associated with the profession in general. The NASW national Web site includes a three-section comprehensive list of core values and ethical standards (NASW, 1999). Many human service

■ **Table 15.1**   National Association of Social Worker Ethical Principles

Core Value	Ethical Principle
Service	Social workers' primary goal is to help people in need and to address social problems.
Social Justice	Social workers challenge social injustice.
Dignity and Worth of all Persons	Social workers respect the inherent dignity and worth of the person.
Importance of Human Relationships	Social workers recognize the central importance of human relationships.
Integrity	Social workers behave in a trustworthy manner.
Competence	Social workers practice within their areas of competence and develop and enhance their professional expertise.

Source: National Association of Social Workers (www.naswdc.org/pubs/code/code.asp)

agencies, insurance companies, and courts, as well as most licensing and regulatory bodies, have adopted the NASW Code of Ethics to manage and enforce the ethical behavior of social workers. If a licensed social worker violates the Code of Ethics, the complaint progresses through a peer-review process allowing the profession to discipline its own members.

With the increasing popularity of the human services discipline, The National Organization for Human Service (NOHS) was founded in 1975. The NOHS Web site states that its purpose is to ". . . unite educators, students, practitioners and clients" within the field of human services. Although it has no enforcement powers, its members agree to abide by a code of ethics that is very similar to the one put forth by the NASW, but includes a focus on the ethical standards as they apply to educators as well (NOHS, 1999).

Ethical principles are an integral part of everyday life, enabling us to conduct business, both personal and professional, in a respectful and safe manner, striving to respect the dignity of all persons, regardless of age, gender, race and socioeconomic level (SES). Without ethical guidelines to help us navigate through various situations, we're all at risk for allowing emotions to rule, leaving each person open to the influence of personal biases. Ethical principles in the human services profession are foundational to the continued development of a helping profession that strives to objectively, professionally, and compassionately meet the complex needs of the most vulnerable members of our society, and without such guidelines we are at risk of exposing clients to potential revictimization.

Closing Thoughts on Professional Ethics

I began this chapter by discussing how many professional fields have adopted ethical codes of conduct. Virtually all the helping professions have such codes mandating how practitioners must conduct themselves professionally. There are significant similarities among the various counseling licensing bodies. For instance neither counselors, family therapists, clinical psychologist, nor licensed social workers can have a romantic relationship with clients, but one significant difference that sets the human services and social work fields apart from the other helping professions is the added responsibility to advocate for social justice, whereas the American Psychological Association, for instance, refers to justice in individuals' terms as it relates to every individual's right to benefit from the contributions of psychology (APA, 2002). The NASW ethical standard on social justice takes a macro approach stating that social workers should ". . . pursue social change, particularly with and on behalf of vulnerable and oppressed individuals and groups of people. Social workers' social change efforts are focused primarily on issues of poverty, unemployment, discrimination, and other forms of social injustice." This focus on social justice in a broader context is important because it highlights the macro focus of the human services field, with the recognition that society plays a significant role in the relative mental and physical health of its members.

Human service professionals are unique among the helping professionals in that they are more likely to be working in a broader range of practice settings, with a broader range of clients. Thus, the likelihood of them confronting ethical dilemmas of greater complexity if for no other reason than the majority of clients seeking services at human services agencies will likely have more complex individual and social problems than clients seeking counseling services with the average psychologist.

references

American Psychological Association. (2002). *Ethical principles of psychologists and code of conduct.* Washington, DC: Author.

Garcia, J. G., Cartwright, B., Winston, S. M., & Borzuchowska, B. (2003). A transcultural integrative model for ethical decision making in counseling. *Journal of Counseling & Development, 81(3),* 268–277.

Gibbs, J. (2003). *Moral development and reality: Beyond the theories of Kohlberg and Hoffman.* London, England: Sage Publications Ltd,

National Association of Social Workers. (1999). *Code of ethics of the National Association of Social Workers.* Washington, DC: Author.

National Organization for Human Services. (1999). *Ethical standards of human service professionals.* Washington, DC: Author.

Merriam-Webster's collegiate dictionary. (10th ed.). (1993). Springfield, MA: Merriam-Webster.

Kitchner, K. S. (1984). Intuition, critical evaluation, and ethical principles: The foundation for ethical decisions in counseling psychology. *The Counseling Psychologist, 12,* 43–55.

Ten Boom, C., Sherrill, J., & Sherrill, S. (1974). *The hiding place.* New York: Bantam Books.

West, W. (2002). Some ethical dilemmas in counseling and counseling research. *British Journal of Guidance & Counseling, 30*(3), 261–268.

suggested reading

Dolgoff, R., Lowenberg, F. M., & Harrington, D. (2004). *Ethical decisions for social work practice.* Belmont, CA: Wadsworth Publishing.

Kenyon, P. (1998). *What would you do?: An ethical case workbook for human service professionals.* Belmont, CA: Wadsworth Publishing.

Nash, R. J. (1996). *"Real world" ethics: Frameworks for educators and human service professionals.* New York: Teacher's College Press.

Reamer, F. G. (1998). *Ethical standards in social work: A critical review of the NASW code of ethics.* Washington, DC: NASW Press.

internet web sites related
to ethical practices in human services

Josephson Institute of Ethics: **http://www.josephsoninstitute.org/**

National Association of Social Worker Code of Ethics:

   http://www.naswdc.org/pubs/code/code.asp

National Organization for Human Services Ethical Standards:

   http://www.nohse.com/ethics.html

The Future of Human Services

The human services profession exists to assist people meet their basic needs. One of its strengths is its multidisciplinary approach wherein individuals with education and training in various disciplines, including human services, social work, and counseling, work side by side addressing the barriers to self-sufficiency. Moreover, human services is attracting an increasing number of psychologists who often serve in administrative roles within human services agencies (Clements, 1992). Unlike many other mental health disciplines, human services professionals are true generalists, and their specializations are in a particular social condition, such as domestic violence or substance abuse, rather than in a particular psychotherapeutic modality or a specific population.

The passion to create meaningful change in the lives of others creates a drive in many human service professionals that compensates for the relatively low pay and often less than glamorous working conditions. It is this drive and passion that pushes so many individuals forward in a career that does not have high status, but affords the unique experience of having the power to literally save someone's life by reminding them of their worth, holding someone's hand as they are dying, reminding a grieving child that there is still hope, or standing with a victim of violence when they face their attacker in court. This is an empowering career, one that changes with every new client.

Human services is a unique career in that it can often lead to other opportunities including a career in academia, writing, public speaking, policy analysis, or international human rights work. Even a career track that leads to clinical private practice can remain exciting and varied if the human services professional remains committed to social justice and advocacy.

Avoiding Professional Burnout

As wonderful as this career is, it is also wrought with stress, crisis, and a significant potential to "burn out" quickly. There are many ways to avoid burnout, and several of these ways involve developing mental paradigms that help the professional avoid becoming overinvolved in the lives of her or his clients. One paradigm that benefits many human services professionals is to recognize that the client is on a journey—on *their own* journey—and role of the human services professional is to assist the client on small portion of this journey. Many human services professionals experience professional burnout because they take too much responsibility for the lives of their clients. Understanding that clients are on their own journey and trusting that the human service professional is one of many mentors, counselors, or guides that will come along in their clients' lives puts the clinician–client relationship into healthy perspective.

Another paradigm that can be useful in helping human service professionals to avoid burnout is to make a commitment to never work harder than your clients. Human services professionals typically enter the helping profession because they care about people and want to help them have better lives. It is easy for human service professionals to fall into the trap of overworking for client who they so much want to help. But one must ask whether doing too much for a client is actually helpful. Or could it be harmful to clients who may already feel powerless and unable to take the steps necessary to make positive changes in their lives? This does not mean that it is inappropriate for a human service professional to help an overwhelmed client make a telephone call, or that it is "enabling" for the counselor to make initial contact to a referral. But whenever I begin to feel overwhelmed working with certain clients, the first question I ask is whether I am working harder than they are. If the answer is "yes," then I need to step back and give my client the room to decide whether or not to take the necessary, albeit often difficult, steps to create positive change in her or his life. If she or he chooses not to exert the necessary energy then, as saddened as this might make me, I must accept my client's inaction as a choice to remain in whatever situation she or he is in.

Human Services and Technology

Technology has changed (and continues to change) the world; the human services profession has been slow in making use of technological changes. Reasons for this include the lack of security in e-mail communication, which has an impact on confidentiality. E-mail communication between practitioner and practitioner discussing clients or e-mail communication between practitioner and client may expose a human services agency to legal liability if privacy cannot be guaranteed. Another reason for human service agencies' general reluctance to become more technologically based relates to the costs associated with purchasing and maintaining computer systems.

Despite these concerns, the Internet can be a wonderful resource for human services professionals searching for appropriate referrals for clients. Most counties have Web sites that include comprehensive information about available services. Many human service organizations, government assistance programs, and various grant-giving agencies not only have invaluable information on their Web sites, but some also allow applicants to apply for services online, expediting the application process.

The Internet can be tremendously useful for human services professionals who want to coordinate services with other professionals or obtain information on a particular issue. Technology is also being used to facilitate various types of testing, including personality and career assessments, ADHD evaluation, and adaptive functioning evaluations. Advocacy efforts have been made easier through the Internet: legislation can be researched online, and a virtual letter-writing campaign can be conducted in minutes.

Despite the concerns about privacy and confidentially, technology can serve both the human service professionals and clients. The Internet can be empowering for clients, enabling them to be more self-sufficient in finding resources, including housing, job opportunities, and child care. In addition, there are resources for homebound individuals who might not be able to benefit from an on-site support group but can garner some of the same benefits from online support groups or bulletin boards.

Increased Need for Services

The U.S. Department of Labor predicts that the human services and social work professions will grow at an excellent rate (a rate of at least 36 percent or more) (Bureau of Labor Statistics, 2005). There are various reasons for this, including our increasingly complex society that puts increasing stress on individuals, families, and systems. As the challenges facing societies increase, human service agencies will continue to be a valuable resource providing services for a broad range of clients. Whether working in schools, hospitals, criminal justice agencies, or the government, human services professionals serve those individuals who do not have the resources to meet their most basic needs.

Those in the human services field are committed to addressing problems in society, often before those within society are prepared to admit that such problems even exist. Human service professionals are consistently on the front lines of social problems creating change in the lives of individuals, communities, and globally. Society is constantly evolving, which creates the sometimes negative by-products of conflict, complexity and challenges for many. It is for this reason that human service professionals will always be needed to recognize and confront human problems, helping society's most vulnerable members meet their basic emotional, physical, and spiritual needs.

r e f e r e n c e s

Bureau of Labor Statistics, U.S. Department of Labor. (2005). *Occupational outlook handbook, 2004–05 edition,* Social and Human Service Assistants. Retrieved on November 17, 2005, from http://www.bls.gov/oco/ocos059.htm

Clements, C. B. (1992). Training in human service for management for future practitioner-managers, professional psychology, *Research and Practice, 23*(2), 146–150.

Activities of Daily Living A term used to describe various activities related to self-care such as bathing, dressing, going to the bathroom, mobility, and eating. Those within the elderly population are assessed based on their ability to perform these tasks independently, with assistance, or whether they are completely dependent on others for self-care.

Addiction Although there is no single definition for addiction, the term implies continued use of a substance despite negative consequences driven by cravings, compulsion, and loss of control of the use so that one's life becomes organized around use of the substance.

Adoption Triad A term used to describe the relationship between the birth parents, adoptive parents and the adoptee, each of whom plays an important role in the adoption of the child. The triad paradigm recognizes this interrelatedness between each party in the adoption process.

Behavior Disordered A collection of behaviors demonstrated by children and adolescents that are markedly outside of expectations within the school or community, requiring some type of formal intervention.

Binge Drinking Drinking five or more alcoholic beverages on the same occasion.

Bootleg Liquor Alcohol sold illegally during Prohibition.

Clinical Disorder A serious mental disorder such as clinical depression, anxiety disorders, and schizophrenia that are often biochemical in nature or have a biochemical component. These disorders affect personality but are not rooted in psychological development. Child-

hood abuse may or may not be a component of a clinical disorder.

Closed Family System A family that tends to be emotionally guarded, is often suspicious of outsiders, and considers any dissent a form of betrayal. Family secrets such as sexual abuse or alcoholism often become closed systems as a by-product of attempting to keep such family secrets out of awareness and under wraps. Unhealthy family systems often develop a false sense of strength and identity by setting themselves apart from others, making acceptance and support conditional on a long list of criteria such as unconditional support, keeping family secrets, and avoiding uncomfortable subjects (such as wanting to discuss a parent's alcoholism).

Cognitive Behavioral Therapy (CBT) A common psychotherapy designed to address the distorted and irrational thinking of the client that may contribute to depression and anxiety and replacing it with more logical and rational thinking based on facts.

Cohort A group of people who are clustered based on age or some other characteristic. In demographic research, a cohort typically refers to those individuals who live within the same generation.

Counterintuitive A feeling, thought, or action that is against someone's better judgment or intuition. Because personal intuition is influenced by personal experience, past negative personal experiences can distort thinking and beliefs, leading some people's intuition to lead them astray.

Custodial Care A type of comprehensive care provided for individuals who cannot care for themselves. Care for the severely and chronically mentally ill population has historically consisted of room and board and assistance with activities of daily living.

Eclectic   Pulling elements from a variety of sources. Within the human services fields having an eclectic theoretical orientation typically indicates that the professional draws from several theories in approaching clients and client problems rather than drawing from a single theory.

Economic Injustice   The practice of barring some individuals and groups of individuals from getting their basic needs met, by blocking their access to adequate employment, food, housing making them vulnerable to exploitation, such as occurs in sweatshops and within the human trafficking industry. Many cases of economic injustice involve an unfair distribution of wealth where segments of the population are unfairly rewarded on a status basis, and not upon a system of hard work.

Emancipation   The emancipation of minors refers to the legal process of granting a minor the same rights as an adult. In many states, a pregnant or parenting teen over the age of 16 can be legally emancipated, meaning that her parents will no longer be legally responsible for her.

Emotional Regulation   The ability to control one's emotional expressions most often accomplished through the development of "rules" about when and how to express emotions in a socially acceptable manner. The development of coping strategies can assist clients in learning how to express emotions in a way that is adaptive and psychologically health. Learning the appropriate way to express anger, when it is okay to burst into tears, and when it is not are some of the most types of emotional regulation issues addressed in a counseling setting.

Empowering   To be empowered involves the capacity and tools (both personal and tangible) necessary to accomplish various tasks and achieve desired goals to operate at an optimal level of functioning. Empowering a client involves assisting them to see that they are capable of self-sufficiency by providing them with the intrinsic and extrinsic tools necessary.

Enmeshed   To be enmeshed technically means to be blended. This is typically a neutral term, but often is used to describe individuals who are too close to each other thus potentially experiencing a loss of identity and independence. A mother can be appropriately enmeshed with her infant, but such enmeshment would not be appropriate if her child was an adolescent.

Epidemic   A widespread outbreak of an infectious disease.

Euthanasia   The practice of killing a person (or animal) to end his or her suffering. Also called "mercy killings," euthanasia typically involves terminally ill patients voluntarily choosing to end their lives to end or avoid pain and in some instances to avoid being a burden on others.

Freud's Psychoanalytic Theory of Human Behavior   Sigmund Freud was a neurologist from Vienna who developed a theory of human behavior and development in the first quarter of the twentieth century. His psychoanalytic theory was the first to introduce the concept of the unconscious mind. Freud believed that much of human behavior was motivated by unconscious conflict rooted in childhood experiences.

Generalists   A term commonly used to describe the role of those within the human services fields referring to a broad range of skills used to address an even broader range of problems and issues clients encounter in their lives. Simply put, human service professionals are mental health experts who are "jacks of all trades," knowing a little bit about a lot of things.

Genocide   The systematic killing of a large number of people on the basis of their ethnicity, religious orientation, political beliefs, or social status. The Holocaust remains one of the most well-known and atrocious genocides in human history.

Gerontologists   A professional distinction reserved for those who study aging and problems related to aging.

Grassroots Efforts   A type of advocacy organized by ordinary citizens who because of their passion about an issue create change in a political system through mobilizing support, raising awareness, and advocating for some positive change that addresses a social problem within society.

Heavy Drinking   Drinking five or more alcoholic beverages on the same occasion on at least 5 of the past 30 days.

Honor Killings   The cultural practice of killing of a female by another family member when the female has in some way brought dishonor on the family, typically through suspected sexual misbehavior (sometimes including rape). Perpetrators of honor killings are rarely prosecuted, and such a practice is often considered a private family matter.

Impulse Control Problems   We all have thoughts and desires that "pop" into our heads but that does not mean we necessarily act on them. The mature individual utilizes patience and self-control to avoid acting on any impulse that might harm one's self or others such as committing violence, spending more money than one has, or engaging in unsafe sexual behavior.

Impulsivity   A tendency to behave in a quick, unplanned reaction in response to a thought that comes to mind or some external stimuli without much regard to the possible negative consequences of these behaviors, either for the individuals or others.

Individualized Education Plan   Every student identified for special education services has a written educational plan detailing designated educational support services, goals, and expected outcomes. Student IEPs are typically prepared for each academic year with intermittent updates throughout the year. The IEP

team usually includes the student's teachers, an instructional aide, the school psychologist, school counselor, and school social worker, and any other professional related to the student's educational plan (such as an occupational therapist). The student's parents are allowed to be at any IEP meetings and are instrumental in both requesting services and giving feedback on how previously instituted services are working.

Industrial Revolution   A term used to describe the evolution that occurred both in England and in the United states from an economy based on manual labor agriculture to one of factory and machine manufacturing.

Informed Consent   A legal term referring to a person's agreement to participate in some action, such as a medical procedure, a research experiment, or psychological counseling, after all aspects of the procedure or action are disclosed.

Intervention Strategies   Techniques used by those in the helping professions designed to effect emotional and psychological change to help clients achieve optimal functioning in society.

Locus of Control   The tendency of people to attribute events in their lives to either internal or external causes. Those with an internal locus of control will have a tendency to see themselves as responsible for events in their lives, whereas those with an external locus of control might attribute events in their lives to destiny or luck.

Marginalized Populations   Those members of society who are displaced due to poverty, racial disparity, or some other characteristic that reduces their status in society and makes them vulnerable to exploitation and denial of opportunities. Marginalized populations often do not have access to many of the same services enjoyed by higher status members of society, such as education, employment opportunities, and health-care services. Within the United States, commonly marginalized populations include the poor, racial minorities, women, lesbians and gays, those with HIV/AIDS, immigrants, and prisoners.

Mission Statement A statement of an organization's fundamental purpose, including its commitments and goals.

Mores Accepted, traditional customs embraced by a particular society. These can include commonly held moral values and norms practiced by the majority within that culture. Social mores tend to change from era to era and from culture to culture. For instance, in the 1950s social mores within the United States prescribed that most married women were homemakers. Social mores in contemporary society now support women remaining in the workforce after marriage. Yet many societies in the world have social mores that do not embrace women in the workforce.

Omnipotence The sense that someone is all-powerful, untouchable and godlike. This term is used in reference to human behavior when describing someone who does not believe he will be harmed or is immune to negative consequences. Adolescents often participate in risky behavior because of a sense that they are omnipotent believing that nothing bad can happen to them.

Palliative Care The World Health Organization defines palliative care as an approach to treatment that although relieving pain and discomfort associated with a terminal illness, affirms life while acknowledging death as a normal process, neither hastening death nor unnecessarily prolonging life.

Pandemic An epidemic over a wide geographic area.

Parachurch Agency Distinct agencies partner with and support the Evangelical church in matters related to social issues, mission work, and evangelism.

Parity The term *parity* means equal or equivalent. The purpose of the Mental Health Parity Act was to put mental health coverage on the same level as general medical coverage.

Personality Disorder Previously called character disorders, personality disorders involve maladaptive ways an individual relates to others and the world, often involving rigidity of thought, a defensive style of relating to others, and misperceptions of others' intentions and events.

Positive Religious Coping The tendency to see God in a positive light, as a deity that is *for* them, not against them. Examples of positive religious coping include believing that one can rely on God during difficult times and that God works as our partner, supporting us and providing us with guidance. Conversely, negative religious coping includes believing that God is punishing and critical.

Predestination John Calvin, one of the leaders of the Protestant movement often considered responsible for the new era of capitalism, believed that God selected who was destined for heaven and who was destined for hell before the world even began. Calvin believed that God selected a small number of men and women who were called "saints" based on his foreknowledge (God's divine wisdom of who was worthy to be allowed into heaven). In other words, people did not get into heaven by living a good and moral life because this decision was made before they were born. But in time, Calvinist and other followers of the Protestant Reformation began to promote the belief that one's good life (although not able to save them) was an indication or a sign that one was heaven-bound. This concept is referred to as *Predestination*.

Primary Substance Abuse Problem The use and abuse of psychoactive substances is at the root of other problems such as relationship problems, work problems, health, or legal difficulties. Substance abuse treatment emphasizes treating the primary problem first.

Proselytizing The act of converting someone to a particular faith. To proselyte traditionally meant the process of converting someone to the Jewish faith. More recently it is a term used to describe the active attempt to convert someone to the Christian faith.

Protective Factors Factors in a person's life that can reduce a person's risk of starting to use drugs and alcohol again. Common protective factors include a strong bond between parents and children, parental involvement in a child's life, and academic success.

Psychotropic Medication A class of drugs that alters brain function, including mood, behavior, and perception. Also referred to as psychoactive drugs.

Recovery The process by which a person who has abused or become dependent on a psychoactive substance stops that use and replaces it with healthy ways to meet their needs.

Reframing The process of helping an individual perceive a situation or experience from a different perspective. Reframing can be particularly valuable when individuals become polarized or rigid in how they view emotionally charged events in their lives, such as arguments with family members.

Reframing The process of helping someone see a situation from another perspective. Many individuals get locked into seeing relationships, situations, or experiences from one, often a polarized, perspective. Although some clients are resistant to reframing an experience or relationship (because they may be getting certain needs met by holding onto their polarized perspective), reframing often frees them to see productive aspects of a situation they have previously viewed in a negative light.

Respite Housing Respite means an interval of rest. Respite housing for the homeless population commonly refers to a temporary housing program offered to someone who has no place to live. Respite housing is often offered in combination with other services addressing the comprehensive needs of the homeless client.

Risk Factors Factors in a person's life that can increase the chance of a person's use of drugs and alcohol. Common risk factors include early acting-out behavior, lack of parental supervision, and the availability of drugs and alcohol.

Safe Sex A set of practices used during sexual activity that reduce the risk of transmitting and contracting sexually transmitted diseases (STDs). Common safe sex practices include using a condom, which prevents fluid exchange.

Secular A movement away from religion, or lacking in religion, with a move toward worldliness. A secular government would signify a government that is not grounded on a foundation of religious doctrine.

Self-Esteem One's overall self-appraisal, which functions on a range from low, where individuals do not think much of themselves, to high, where individuals have a positive self-regard and is often connected to achievement. Situational self-esteem is temporal, thus can fluctuate depending on what an individual is going through at the time, but general self-esteem tends to remain stable over time.

Single Residence Occupancy SROs refer to housing units of single rooms for single persons for a relatively inexpensive price. The term dates back to the 1930s in New York when the poor lived in tenements, hotel-like buildings housing the city's poorest residents for a modest weekly rent.

Skid Row Alcoholic Skid row refers to a run-down area in a city where alcoholics and drug addicts congregated. The stereotypical skid row alcoholic was a homeless vagrant who spent his days loitering in an alleyway and drinking alcohol out of a paper bag. Many people in the general public still associate those who are homeless with the skid row alcoholic.

Social Action Advocacy actions intended to address and confront social injustice.

Social Darwinism Herbert Spencer, an English philosopher, developed the theory now referred to as Social Darwinism, although Spencer's theory of social "survival of the fittest" was actually developed before Darwin's biological theory of natural selection. Spencer believed that people who could change to adapt to their environment would survive, and those who could not change and adapt to life's changing challenges would not. Spencer's theory of "survival of the fittest" did not gain widespread popularity in England but became very popular in the United States, particularly within the Protestant church. Spencer's concept of social survival of the fittest was preached throughout churches in the nineteenth century and coupled with the concept of Predestination.

Social Gospel   The process of applying Christian principles to social problems such as poverty, homelessness, and racial discrimination. Originally a part of the progressive movement intended to combat social injustice, the Social Gospel movement has been on the decline since the increasing popularity of more conservative Christian movements. Martin Luther King was one leader in the Social Gospel movement.

Social Injustice   Unfairness within society in how it rewards some members and burdens or punishes others. Examples of social injustice include racial oppression.

Squatting   The practice of people living in an abandoned space when they have no right to do so. In the United States this practice consists primarily of individuals illegally occupying an unoccupied unit in government-subsidized projects, typically high-rise projects where anonymity is almost guaranteed.

Stigma   Originally the term *stigma* came from the Roman practice of branding a slave's forehead.

Substance Abuse   Continued use of a psychoactive substance despite experiencing negative consequences from that use to one's health, relationships, employment, or legal problems.

Substance Dependence   Substance abuse in which the person's body has become so accustomed to the presence of the psychoactive substance that, if they stop or decrease their use, they will experience physical and/or psychological discomfort.

Substance Use   Use of psychoactive substances such as alcohol or drugs to change one's perceptions, emotions, or behaviors.

Suicidal Ideation   The process of thinking or fantasizing about suicide. Sometimes adolescents have thoughts of suicide but they never act them out. But sometimes these thoughts are a precursor to a suicide plan.

Systems Theory   Systems theory has its origin in the biological and environmental sciences, where one element has a demonstratable relationship on another element. Social scientists began applying systems theory to the social sciences around 1970 in recognition of how human beings operate within various systems in society, where the personality and behavior of individuals affect elements within various elements of their worlds, and various elements or events within one's world will have an affect on that individual's personality and behavior.

Tolerance   Tolerance occurs when a person's body has become accustomed to a psychoactive substance so that they need to use increasing amounts of the substance to gain the desired effect.

Transactional Exchange   A term commonly used in "systems theory" to describe an interaction between elements of two different systems. In the human services fields a transactional exchange typically refers to the reciprocal relationship and affect between an individual and various aspects of his or her environment. For instance, what a person "brings to the table" in his or her job (skills, experience, effort) will have an affect on salary and promotion within the company.

Undocumented Workers   Individuals who do not have the legal right to work in the United States.

Vagrancy   The legal definition of vagrancy typically refers to someone who has no home and no visible means of support. The term *vagrancy* became synonymous with the "wandering poor," those who often engaged in loitering, drunkenness, prostitution, and other forms of "depraved" behavior. Vagrancy laws were designed to punish these wandering poor with imprisonment (among other punishments) until the 1960s, when they were constitutionally challenged.

Vicarious Victimization   The process of feeling victimized by watching someone else being victimized.

Withdrawal   Withdrawal occurs when a person's body has become accustomed to a psychoactive substance so that they experience physical or psychological discomfort if they stop using the substance or decrease the amount of substance used.